CZECH AND SLOVAK CINEMA
Theme and Tradition

Peter Hames

EDINBURGH UNIVERSITY PRESS

© Peter Hames, 2009, 2010

Edinburgh University Press Ltd
22 George Square, Edinburgh

First published in hardback by Edinburgh University Press in 2009

www.euppublishing.com

Typeset in 10/12.5 Adobe Sabon
by Servis Filmsetting Ltd, Stockport, Cheshire, and
printed and bound in Great Britain by
CPI Antony Rowe, Chippenham and Eastbourne

A CIP record for this book is available from the British Library

ISBN 978 0 7486 2081 4 (hardback)
ISBN 978 0 7486 2082 1 (paperback)

The right of Peter Hames
to be identified as author of this work
has been asserted in accordance with
the Copyright, Designs and Patents Act 1988.

Published with the support of the Edinburgh University Scholarly Publishing
Initiatives Fund.

CONTENTS

TRADITIONS IN WORLD CINEMA

General editors: **Linda Badley and R. Barton Palmer**
Founding editor: **Steven Jay Schneider**

Traditions in World Cinema is a series of textbooks and monographs devoted to the analysis of currently popular and previously underexamined or undervalued film movements from around the globe. Also intended for general interest readers, the textbooks in this series offer undergraduate- and graduate-level film students accessible and comprehensive introductions to diverse traditions in world cinema. The monographs open up for advanced academic study more specialised groups of films, including those that require theoretically-oriented approaches. Both textbooks and monographs provide thorough examinations of the industrial, cultural, and socio-historical conditions of production and reception.

The flagship textbook for the series includes chapters by noted scholars on traditions of acknowledged importance (the French New Wave, German Expressionism), recent and emergent traditions (New Iranian, post-Cinema Novo), and those whose rightful claim to recognition has yet to be established (the Israeli persecution film, global found footage cinema). Other volumes concentrate on individual national, regional or global cinema traditions. As the introductory chapter to each volume makes clear, the films under discussion form a coherent group on the basis of substantive and relatively transparent, if not always obvious, commonalities. These commonalities may be formal, stylistic or thematic, and the groupings may, although they need not, be popularly identified as genres, cycles or movements (Japanese horror, Chinese martial arts cinema, Italian Neorealism). Indeed, in cases in which a group of films is not already commonly identified as a tradition, one purpose of the volume is to establish its claim to importance and make it visible (East Central European Magical Realist cinema, Palestinian cinema).

Textbooks and monographs include:

- An introduction that clarifies the rationale for the grouping of films under examination
- A concise history of the regional, national, or transnational cinema in question
- A summary of previous published work on the tradition
- Contextual analysis of industrial, cultural and socio-historical conditions of production and reception
- Textual analysis of specific and notable films, with clear and judicious application of relevant film theoretical approaches
- Bibliograph(ies)/filmograph(ies)

Monographs may additionally include:

- Discussion of the dynamics of cross-cultural exchange in light of current research and thinking about cultural imperialism and globalisation, as well as issues of regional/national cinema or political/ aesthetic movements (such as new waves, postmodernism, or identity politics)
- Interview(s) with key filmmakers working within the tradition

ACKNOWLEDGEMENTS

For a variety of practical reasons I have consulted few people while writing this book. No one other than myself can therefore be blamed for any short-comings. However, many people have helped me over the years and without this foundation, the book would have been impossible to write. In particular, I would like to thank: in Czechoslovakia and the Czech and Slovak Republics, the National Film Archive, Prague (Národní filmový archiv), the Slovak Film Institute (Slovenský filmový ústav), Finále Film Festival Plzeň, Karlovy Vary International Film Festival, the Bratislava International Film Festival and the Summer Film School at Písek held in the second part of the 1980s; in United Kingdom, the Slade School of Fine Art at University College London, the British Federation of Film Societies, the National Film Archive, the National Film Theatre London, the Czech Centre London, the London Film Festival, Stoke Film Theatre and Staffordshire University. All have facilitated both access to films and opportunities for study. The opportunity to meet and interview Czech and Slovak directors through my work for the London Film Festival and the Czech Centre London has proved particularly valuable.

I would like to acknowledge the support of those who have encouraged me to write on these subjects over the years, including Birgit Beumers (*KinoKultura*), Peter Cargin (*Film*), Andrew James Horton (*Kinoeye*), Penelope Houston (*Sight and Sound*), Nick James (*Sight and Sound*) and Mehelli Modi (Second Run DVD), together with those editors, co-editors and publishers who have sup-ported my previous work: Yoram Allon (Wallflower Press), Ernest Callenbach (University of California Press), Daniel J. Goulding (Oberlin College), Dina

Iordanova (University of St Andrews), Catherine Portuges (University of Massachusetts, Amherst), and Matthew Stevens (Flicks Books).

I am not listing here the directors and film personalities who I have interviewed. I must however mention all those who have been of key importance in providing practical assistance and insight in different circumstances: Liz-Anne Bawden, Renata Clark, Myrtil Frída, Dana Hábová, Věroslav Hába, Jenny Hames, Nick Hames, Sandra Hebron, Eva Kačerová, Ľubica Mistríková, Vladimír Opěla, David Phillips, Shaun Richards, Zdena Škapová and Miroslav Ulman. Original stills, where it has been possible to identify the photographer, are by Karel Ješátko (*The Party and the Guests*), Jaromír Komárek (*Loves of a Blonde*), Jiří Kučera (*Cutting it Short*), Vladimír Souček (*Marketa Lazarová*), Zdeněk Tichý (*It's Gonna Get Worse*) and Vlado Vavrek (*Birds, Orphans and Fools*). Stills are reproduced with the permission of Karel Ješátko, Jiří Kucera, Vladimír Souček, Zdeněk Tichý, and Athanor Film (*Conspirators of Pleasure*), Jan Němec Film (*Toyen*), Krátký Film Praha (*An Invention for Destruction*), National Film Archive, Prague (*Desire*), and the Slovak Film Institute, Bratislava (*Birds, Orphans and Fools*). I would further like to acknowledge the assistance of Athanor Film (Jaromír Kallista, Jan Švankmajer, Pavla Kallistová), Bonton Films (Aleš Novák, David Budský), Jan Němec Film (Jan Němec, Iva Ruszeláková), Krátký Film Praha (Barbora Wohlinová), the National Film Archive, Prague (Vladimír Opěla, Vanda Jarošová, Karel Zima), První veřejnoprávní (Čestmír Kopecký, Anna Kopecká), the Slovak Film Institute (Peter Dubecký, Miroslav Ulman) and the State Fund of the Czech Republic for the Support and Development of Czech Cinematography (Přemysl Huňa).

I would like to thank Linda Badley and R. Barton Palmer for their careful reading of the final text and all those at Edinburgh University Press for their efficient and detailed help and advice: Jackie Jones, Sarah Edwards, James Dale, Patricia Marshall, Máiréad McElligott, and Padmini Ray Murray.

Peter Hames
Stone, Staffordshire
February 2009

INTRODUCTION

The idea for this book originated with the flagship volume in this series *Traditions in World Cinema*. While many of the chapters in that book chart important developments in post-World War Two cinema, it struck me that many of the themes discussed – Italian Neo-realism, the French New Wave, the Czechoslovak New Wave and so forth – represented significant and influential movements rather than traditions as such. Were there, perhaps, more long-lived traditions in national cinemas? In the case of Czech and Slovak cinema, what connections could be made across time, between pre-war and post-war, Communist and post-Communist cinema? It also seemed to me that such an approach might serve to foreground neglected but nonetheless significant areas in the history of these cinemas.

The following introduction attempts to situate Czech and Slovak cinema within its overall context and, in the process, also examines the historical relations between Czechs and Slovaks and their relevance for the subsequent development of Czech and Slovak cinema, a culture that has been described as simultaneously common and separate.

CENTRAL AND EASTERN EUROPE

It has always struck me as odd that Central and East European cinemas (with or without Russia and the countries of the former Soviet Union) should be perceived within a collective image, in the post-World War Two period described as cinemas of 'the socialist bloc' and sometimes as Second Cinema.

After all, despite parallel experiences of Communism in the period 1948–89, the films of Czechoslovakia, Poland, Hungary and the Balkan countries have very different identities and histories. Also, while the pre-Second World War cinemas of France and Germany have been well covered by English-language historians, the cinemas of Central and Eastern Europe have been ignored. As nearly twenty years have passed since the fall of the Berlin Wall, the generalised exclusion of these cinemas from mainstream discussion can no longer be attributed to censorship, Communism or the effects of the Cold War.

It seems that we are still living with ways of thought that have inaccurately divided European heritage and culture between East and West. The idea of 'Eastern Europe', Larry Wolff suggests, was created by the Enlightenment – 'a synthetic association of lands, which drew upon both fact and fiction'.[1] It extended from Bohemia and Moravia (the present Czech Republic) to include Russia all the way to Siberia. Functioning in a manner similar to Orientalism, this perception, he argues, is not unrelated to Hitler's desire to impose a superior *kultur* and the post-war division of Europe into 'East' and 'West' at the Yalta conference in 1945. It is worth noting that Western politicians still find it difficult to shake off this mental perception of the world and that it remains a staple ingredient of tabloid journalism.

Geographically and historically, a number of states can be considered to be part of Central Europe. Martin Votruba points out that Germany, Poland, the Czech Republic, Slovakia, Switzerland, Austria and Hungary are all in Central Europe and that it is quite simply geographically illiterate to describe any of them as being in 'Eastern Europe'.[2] Other countries, including the Baltic countries (Lithuania, Latvia, Estonia) and Slovenia and Croatia might also make the same claims on historical and/or cultural grounds.

In addition to geographical and historical realities, there is also the concept of a 'cultural' Central Europe – a sense that, whatever the differences and conflicts, these countries have a shared set of cultural references. In his famous essay, 'A Kidnapped West or Culture Bows Out', Milan Kundera argued that Central Europe was part of an indivisible European culture – that the cultures of countries such as Czechoslovakia, Poland and Hungary had always been in constructive interplay with that of Western Europe.[3] Indeed, one only has to examine the terms of reference of books, exhibitions, theatre and film in those countries to realise that this is the case.

If we turn to 'Western' perspectives on culture, the same kinds of mental assumptions seem to be applied as in the world of politics. Despite highly significant contributions to the history of painting, sculpture, design and photography, relatively few major exhibitions from Central and Eastern Europe are mounted in Western countries. In the History of Art, works from Central and Eastern Europe are frequently perceived as reflections of Western

Europe. Artists become famous only when they locate to Western Europe or North America. To quote Czech examples, the work of Alfons Mucha, Frank (František) Kupka, Josef Šíma, Toyen and Jindřich Štyrský is known because of work done outside of Czechoslovakia. The same could be said of writers such as Josef Škvorecký and Milan Kundera who have established themselves respectively within English and French language cultures. Miloš Forman is primarily known for his English-language films *One Flew Over the Cuckoo's Nest* (1975) and *Amadeus* (1984) rather than for his earlier Czech films. Perhaps the most obvious example is the Polish director Krzysztof Kieślowski, who is now known primarily for his French films rather than his Polish ones.

While the expansion of the European Union and the increase in East–West co-production will, one assumes, begin to change these perceptions within cinema, this is not yet the case. Access to North American and West European consciousness seems to depend on the rare and unlikely prospect of winning a Hollywood Oscar or, more significantly, attracting the attention of West European film festivals. Films are not seen by the majority of critics (still less audiences) before they have passed through these preliminary selection filters.

Despite the Berlin award to the Bosnian film *Esma's Secret* (*Grbavica*, Jasmila Žbanić) in 2006 and the Cannes award to the Romanian film *4 Months, 3 Weeks, 2 Days* (*4 luni, 3 săptamâni şi 2 zile*, Cristian Mungiu) in 2007, there is a tendency to underestimate films from 'the East' unless they exhibit some unusual or exceptional appeal. One wonders if the Cannes Festival would have picked up on the Romanian 'New Wave' without the previous critical championship of the magazine *Positif*.

Furthermore, films that win awards at festivals are not typical. They tend to exhibit particular aesthetic characteristics – that is, they tend to conform to the innovative requirements of art cinema. While not denying the importance of this, there remains a wide range of films – apart from the crassly commercial – that do not aspire to be 'auteur' films and yet have a considerable wider significance. While these win major awards more rarely, it is noticeable that West European representatives in this category enjoy wider circulation than their Central and East European equivalents. Here, again, one comes up against the continuing 'wall in the head'. This is not so much a matter of audience response, which is frequently positive, but more a matter of the gatekeepers – the critics and the distributors who make the decisions.

This is one of the reasons why, nearly twenty years on from the fall of the Berlin Wall, the post-Communist cinemas of the Czech Republic, Poland, Hungary and the Balkan countries continue to be unknown and uncharted territory. This is one of the areas, in the case of the Czech Republic and Slovakia, that I will try to address.

3

CZECHOSLOVAKIA AND THE CZECH AND SLOVAK REPUBLICS

Czechoslovakia, a state formed after the disintegration of the Habsburg Empire at the end of the First World War in 1918, was often described as being at 'the heart of Europe' with Prague, its capital, at its centre.

If, after forty years of Communist rule, the concept of Central Europe still seems novel, the origins of the Czech and Slovak republics (and of Czechoslovakia) are even more remote. Prior to 1918, the last time that the Czechs and Slovaks had been part of a common independent state had been under the Greater Moravian Empire at the beginning of the tenth century. Under the Habsburg Empire, which dominated both nations, the Czech lands of Bohemia and Moravia had come under Austrian control and were ruled from Vienna while Slovakia had been under Hungarian domination. The Slovak capital, Bratislava (Hungarian: Pozsony; German: Pressburg) was the capital of Hungary from 1526 until 1784 when it was moved to Budapest. The notion of Czechs and Slovaks as constituting a single nation was resurrected at the time of the nineteenth-century national revival and assiduously promoted at the time of the creation of Czechoslovakia.

It is certainly questionable whether a sense of common identity could have been maintained over a thousand-year period and it should also be recognised that issues of ethnic identity and nationality would not have had the same connotations in the tenth century as in the nineteenth. As in all history, and especially national history, one is in the position of projecting meaningful stories on to complex pasts in order to justify origins, identity and belonging.

These are wide-ranging issues and there is little space to deal with them here. However, I shall attempt to give a brief account of Czech and Slovak histories, beginning with the Czech perspective since it is based not only on longer periods of independence but also greater degrees of political and economic development.

As Hugh LeCaine Agnew has pointed out, notions of national consciousness can be related to various periods of history without carrying with them the ideology of nineteenth-century nationalism.[4] National consciousness is also routinely associated with the development of a written literature. From these perspectives, the notion of Czech national consciousness can be linked to a number of historical periods – the era of Duke Václav I, the patron saint, in the tenth century, the rule of the native Přemyslid dynasty from the ninth to the thirteenth centuries and the period of Jan Hus and the Hussite 'revolution' in the fifteenth century among them. Czech became established as a literary language in the thirteenth century and was consolidated in the fourteenth century.

The traditional view of the Habsburg period (1526–1918), particularly after the Battle of the White Mountain in 1620, is as a 'period of darkness'. At that time, the Catholic Habsburg army of Ferdinand defeated the Protestant Czech Estates. The most serious aspects of the defeat were their consequences: the destruction of the Czech aristocracy (who mostly lost their property and went into exile); the forced re-catholicisation of the country; and the ending of Czech as a language of state. Twenty-seven Czech noblemen were executed in Prague's Old Town Square. Comenius and other intellectuals left the country, leaving it in the hands of a German-speaking elite.

The period of Habsburg rule that followed is generally considered to have prevented the development of a free, independent and democratic tradition. This is undoubtedly a simplified perspective and, as Petr Pithart has argued, Tomáš G. Masaryk, who was following in the tradition of František Palacký's *History of the Czech Nation* (*Dějiny národu českého v Čechách a v Moravě*, 1848–75)[5] in his *The Meaning of Czech History* (*Česká otázka/The Czech Question*, 1895) was less concerned with the accuracy of his history than its role as analogy. In asserting a tradition essentially rooted in the period of Jan Hus and the Hussite movement, which led to intellectual freedom, equality, justice, brotherhood and democracy, he was concerned with '*the truth of that history*, that is, the challenge, the inspiration . . . he was concerned with "the continuity of the national ethos"'[6] As René Wellek puts it:

> The past for Masaryk must stay alive to shape the future. Thus selection from the past of a 'usable' past, the creation of a tradition that would become a force in the present and future, seems an overriding duty to Masaryk.[7]

Palacký was a Protestant but the Catholic historian, Josef Pekař adopted a different perspective, seeing Germanisation as a positive influence leading to economic and cultural prosperity and a triumph of the European and the universal. Czechs and Germans in Bohemia had, to some extent, experienced shared destinies and influences did not all flow in one direction. However, while praising the splendours of the baroque, Pekař also recognised the spiritual and material decline that followed in the aftermath of Battle of the White Mountain.[8]

The Czech claim to independence in 1918 was based on the issue of historical or state rights. Since, in 1526, the Czechs had elected the Habsburg Ferdinand I to the Bohemian throne, the Czech state could be claimed to have a legal existence. Initially, political initiatives were directed toward the achievement of autonomy within the Habsburg Empire in a form similar to that enjoyed by Hungary since 1867 when the Empire had become the Austro-Hungarian Empire. This change in relationship (at any rate with Austria) was almost achieved in 1871.

The Slovaks, in contrast, had never been part of Bohemia. In the *Claims of the Slovak Nation (Žiadosti slovenskieho národu)*, formulated in 1848, political autonomy as a separate nation was sought under the Hungarian crown. Hungary recognised Croatian autonomy in 1868, which was a status to which other non-Magyar nations ruled by Hungary also aspired. The situation was further complicated by a German claim for an independent Bohemia within the Empire based on majority population. Hence, the Czech claims were analogous to the Hungarian and the Slovak to the German. The precise balance of populations also depended on where the borders might be drawn. However, while the Austrian half of the Empire pursued the idea of a multi-ethnic state from the 1860s onward, the Hungarian half did not and the Slovaks were subject to policies of enforced Magyarisation.

While there are important linguistic links between Czechs and Slovaks, they were, nonetheless, developing as separate nations. A codification of literary Slovak based on the West Slovak dialect (the one closest to Czech) was established by Anton Bernolák in 1787. Numerous works were published in this form although most Slovak writing at this time was in Czech. A codification based on the Central Slovak dialect was established in 1843 by Ľudovít Štúr and it was this that contributed to the development of a course of national revival separate from that of the Czechs. However, had the Czechs and Slovaks not presented themselves as one 'Czechoslovak' nation, it would not have been possible to argue for independence for the new state in 1918. Here, it is worth recalling that the 'founding fathers' of the new state were: the philosopher Tomáš G. Masaryk (President 1918–35), who was born in Moravia and whose father was Slovak; Edvard Beneš (President 1935–38 and 1945–48), born in Bohemia; and Milan R. Štefánik, a Slovak astronomer and a general in the French air force. Štefánik died in a plane crash in 1919. The Czechs and Slovaks had also established themselves as combatants in the war, fighting in both France and Russia. In particular, the Czechoslovak legions, formed from units that had deserted from the Austro-Hungarian armies, established a formidable reputation in Russia, with their epic journey to the West via Siberia entering the realms of myth.

According to H. Gordon Skilling, Masaryk (although not Beneš) realised that the creation of a single ethnic nation was not a possibility since this would have meant the assimilation of the Slovaks by the Czechs.[9] For Masaryk, the Czechoslovak nation consisted of two ethnic and linguistic wings. However, perceptions after independence differed between the two nations. According to Jan Rychlík, most Czechs saw the state as a reconstitution of the Bohemian independence that had been lost at the Battle of the White Mountain in 1620 but with Slovakia an additional province and Slovak as a different dialect.[10]

On the other hand, while there were undoubtedly Slovaks who accepted this conception, the majority, Rychlík argues, saw things differently. Czechoslovakia was Czecho-Slovakia, the union of two nation states. The argument for

Slovak autonomy was there from the beginning and based on the Pittsburgh Declaration of May 1918. This agreement between Czech and Slovak fraternal organisations in the USA signed in the presence of Masaryk had foreseen a dual state in which Slovakia would enjoy political autonomy. However, Masaryk did not consider this to be legally binding. While nationalist parties such as the Hlinka Slovak People's Party (*Hlinkova slovenská l'udová strana*/HSĽS) and the Slovak National Party (*Slovenská národná strana*, SNS) espoused the cause of autonomy, there were also autonomist views in other parties, including the Communists. In 1927, Slovakia (together with the other constituent provinces of Bohemia, Moravia, and Ruthenia) received administrative autonomy.

Given this background, it is perhaps easier to understand the various Czech–Slovak conflicts and political crises that have subsequently developed. Following the Munich diktat of 1938, the government was forced to cede the German speaking areas of the country (a third) to Germany, when France and Britain capitulated to Hitler's demands. At that time, the government accepted Slovak autonomy and Father Tiso became the first prime minister of Slovakia. While this was fairly obviously the first stage in a progression toward independence, when the declaration came in March 1939 (coinciding with the Nazi invasion of the Czech lands), this was a direct result of German pressure. Slovakia could either proclaim independence under German protection or Hungary would be given a free hand to reclaim her lost territories. As it was, the Hungarian speaking areas of Slovakia reverted anyway and Hungary occupied Ruthenia. In the Czech lands, the Germans established the Protectorate of Bohemia and Moravia.

None of this is intended to draw a veil over the activities of the Hlinka Slovak People's Party which, after 1936, rejected democracy and adopted totalitarian states as its model. The independent state established in 1939–45, despite being headed by a Catholic priest, was certainly fascist in the popular sense of the word and virtually liquidated the Jewish population. The Slovak National Rising (1944), coordinated by Communists, Russians, non-Communists and the Czechoslovak government in exile in London, although suppressed by the Germans, provided the final verdict on this regime. Tiso himself was executed for treason in 1947.

The allies had accepted that, in the post-war world, the integrity of the former Czechoslovakia would be sustained, with the exception of Ruthenia, which was transferred to Ukraine (that is, the Soviet Union). Although the democratic government was reinstated, it already had strong socialist commitments and, after the experience of Munich, a stronger relationship with the Soviet Union was thought to be inevitable. Nonetheless, despite a Communist prime minister (Klement Gottwald) and Communist control of the Ministries of the Interior and Information as well as the trades unions, many thought that a democratic system might survive. This was no doubt because the Communist

Party had been a legal party before the war and Gottwald had always stressed a Czech road to socialism.

However, this was not to be and, after a government crisis in 1948, in which democratic ministers had resigned in protest at Communist penetration of the police forces, President Beneš was forced to accept a Communist government. Prior to this, there were strong indications that the Communists would have lost significant ground in the forthcoming elections. The consequent purges of non-Communists were excessive and draconian but, as early as 1952, the Soviet Union felt it necessary to assert control through purges of the Party itself. The Secretary-General of the Czechoslovak Communist Party, Rudolf Slánský, and fourteen other leading Communists were arrested and accused of treason, and a trial ensued aided by Soviet 'advisors'. Eleven of the accused were executed and three given life imprisonment. Eleven of the fourteen were also Jewish.

The death of Stalin in 1953 and Khrushchev's denunciation of the cult of personality in 1956 led to some liberalisation but Czechoslovakia, having endured purges that had claimed some 136,000 victims, was in no position to make radical changes. However, throughout the 1960s, there were significant indications of change, particularly in the cultural sphere (including cinema), finally leading to the Prague Spring reforms of 1968 which, to quote the new Party secretary, Alexander Dubček, sought 'the widest possible democratisation of the entire socio-political system'.[11]

This attempt to introduce the kinds of reforms later espoused by Gorbachev led to the armed invasion of the Soviet Union and her Warsaw Pact allies in August 1968. After all, no one knew where this might end. The response of the Soviet Union was to provide Czechoslovakia with an army of occupation for the first time. The new government, purged of reformers, attempted to institute a return to normality – the policy of so-called 'normalisation'. The new Party leader from 1969, Gustáv Husák, had himself been a victim of the purges of the 1950s. While this time the purges were not physical, around half a million people left or were expelled from the Communist Party and it is estimated that 170,000 went into exile. The next twenty years were indeed a 'time of darkness' with writers, artists and film-makers blacklisted and/or forced once again to confine themselves to simplified or ideological subjects. Milan Šimecka accurately characterised it as an 'age of immobility'.[12] Given the fact that the attitude of the West was, to use Ľubomír Lipták's phrase, one of purely 'platonic sympathy', it was clear that change could only occur after changes in the overall balance of power or within the Soviet Union itself. As Lipták puts it:

> The *nomenklatura* system was consistently applied. For every more important position . . . an appropriate party organ was determined, which approved candidates. The higher positions in the party, state, army, and security were subject to approval by Moscow. The nomenklatura system

supported cynics, or at best pragmatists. In either case, the illusion of a
revolutionary party came to an end.[13]

The sole reform to survive was the federalisation of the country.

After the Velvet Revolution of 1989, which followed earlier events in Poland
and East Germany, Czechoslovakia returned to democracy. While this was
inevitably the result of the crisis in the Soviet bloc as a whole (since there was
no repressive support available from the government of the Soviet Union for
the 'normalised' Czech government), civil dissent did precede this. One should
mention here the activities of Charter 77, the human rights movement, for
which the new president, Václav Havel, had been one of the spokespersons.
Dubček, a non-person for twenty years (under permanent police supervision),
made a symbolic return as Chairman of the National Assembly.

In reflecting on the final separation of Czechoslovakia into the Czech and
Slovak Republics in 1993, it is important to recall the preceding debates
on autonomy. However, it is equally important to recognise that, in public
opinion polls, an absolute majority of both Czechs and Slovaks was opposed to
separation. It was essentially a political decision made within the ruling elites.
The ruling party in the Czech lands, the right-wing Civic Democratic Party
(*Občanska demokratická strana*/ODS) led by Václav Klaus, and the superficially left-wing Movement for a Democratic Slovakia (*Hnutie za demokratická
Slovensko*/HZDS) of Vladimír Mečiar in Slovakia had different agendas. If
the split was partly the result of Slovak nationalism, it was also a matter of
economic and political convenience on the Czech side. Significantly, with new
political structures on the horizon (NATO and the European Union), there was
less political need to maintain the union.

If one moves beyond these issues to perspectives on history and culture, it
seems fairly clear that, from most conventional viewpoints, the two nations
have been seen as separate. It has been quite normal for separate histories of
Slovakia to be published while most histories dealing with Czechoslovakia as
a whole will treat the histories of the Czech lands and of Slovakia as separate
issues. Critical studies of Czech and Slovak literature routinely treat the two as
separate. Josef Škvorecký's *All the Bright Young Men and Women* (1971) is
specifically an account of Czech and not Slovak cinema. This is not to suggest
that there are not studies that deal with both but it is quite normal to consider
them separately.

I would go further and simply argue that these are separate nations, histories
and cultures, between which there have been important links and connections,
and that these were clearly fostered in various ways during 1918–38 and
1945–93 in the periods of the common state. But it should also be recognised
that virtually the sole reform of the Prague Spring to remain in place was the
Federal Constitution recognising the independent status of Slovakia.

CINEMA

In cinema, there were few Slovak films in the pre-Second World War period while Czech cinema was highly developed. Regular film production began in Prague as early as 1910 and, by the beginning of the First World War, over a third of the cinemas in Austria–Hungary were based in Bohemia and Moravia. The silent period saw the creation of two important studios, the American and Biografia (AB) studios (1921) and the Kavalírka studios (1926) and an average yearly production of over twenty-six features. The viability of Czech language production in the sound era was obviously an issue and production dropped to only eight features in 1930. However, by the end of the decade, the annual average had risen to over forty. In 1932–33, the Barrandov film studios were constructed in Prague by Václav and Miloš Havel (the future president's father and uncle) and they were intended as a centre for international production.

The first international interest in Czech and Slovak cinema followed the success of three films at the Venice Film Festival in 1934: *The River* aka *Young Love* (*Řeka*, Josef Rovenský, 1933); *Ecstasy* (*Extase*, Gustav Machatý, 1932); and *The Earth Sings* (*Zem spieva*, Karel Plicka, 1933). Other films from the 1930s to attract international interest were *Heave-Ho!* (*Hej-rup!*, Martin Frič, 1934), featuring Jiří Voskovec and Jan Werich, *Jánošík* (Martin Frič, 1936) and *The Guild of Kutná Hora Maidens* (*Cech panen kutnohorských*, Otakar Vávra, 1938). Only one of them (*The Earth Sings*) was Slovak but three of them featured Slovak locations. The notion of 'Czech lyricism' was born. Czech cinema was also characterised by the development of comedy as a genre, with films starring Voskovec and Werich, Vlasta Burian, Hugo Haas and Oldřich Nový. Attacks on the rise of fascism were apparent in Frič's *The World Belongs to Us* (*Svět patří nám*, 1937) and Haas's film of Karel Čapek's play *The White Disease* (*Bílá nemoc*, 1937). Voskovec and Werich and Haas were to spend the war years in the United States, with Voskovec and Haas eventually staying permanently.

During the Nazi protectorate, film production continued but at a much reduced level, with the number of films dropping from forty-one in 1939 to eleven in 1944. One film was made in 1945 but not released until after the war. A majority share in all companies was to be German with Czech production cut back to allow for the production of German films and the AB company renamed Prag-Film. Nonetheless, Czech film was allowed to continue provided it avoided, in Goebbels' phrase, 'stupid nationalism'. Films were to avoid criticism of the Habsburg Empire and reference to the Czech Legion and Jews were not to be presented in a positive light. Czech language films were to have German subtitles. While the emphasis was to be on entertainment, the period saw some interesting work by Frič, Vávra and Václav Krška. The National Film Archive was formed in 1943 and a group that included Vávra, the novelist and film-maker Vladislav Vančura and the film-maker Elmar Klos planned the future nationalisation of the film industry.

It was only after the nationalisation of the industry in 1945 that regular Slovak feature production was initiated. Film studios and laboratories were established in Bratislava at Koliba in 1950 and were to provide the basis for future Slovak production. The Slovak industry was always separate in the sense that the films were in Slovak and not Czech and, with the exception of early films by Martin Frič and Václav Wasserman in the 1940s, they were made by Slovak directors and based on scripts by Slovak writers.

The film school, FAMU (Filmová a televizní fakulta, Akademie múzických umění) was established in 1947 and Czech cinema again attracted attention with Venice awards given to *The Strike* aka *The Siren* (*Siréna*, 1947) and to Jiří Trnka's puppet film, *The Czech Year* (*Špalíček*, 1947). Following the Communist takeover in 1948, there was a fairly swift adoption of the restrictive formulae of Soviet Socialist Realist cinema – that is, classical narrative with an explicit ideological or class basis. Yet Czech cinema was to continue to achieve international recognition in the field of animation and cracks began to appear in 'the system' especially in the late 1950s, following Khrushchev's denunciation of Stalin in 1956. The 1960s inaugurated Czech and Slovak cinema's golden age, culminating in the films produced during the Prague Spring, which were released in 1968 and 1969 and, of course, its first two Oscars, for *A Shop on the High Street* (*Obchod na korze*, Ján Kadár and Elmar Klos, 1965) in 1965 and *Closely Observed Trains* (*Ostře sledované vlaky*, Jiří Menzel, 1966) in 1967. Although, in the early 1960s, cinema was still struggling against repressive formats, it was these years that saw the emergence of new directors such as František Vláčil, Vojtěch Jasný and Štefan Uher. Subsequent years saw the appearance of Miloš Forman, Věra Chytilová, Jaromil Jireš, Jan Němec, Jiří Menzel, Ivan Passer, Evald Schorm, Juraj Jakubisko, Dušan Hanák and many others.

The suppression of the Prague Spring in 1968 led to the banning of well over a hundred features from the sixties, widespread purges and the introduction of a production programme that conformed to an officially sanctioned view of popular entertainment or presented naive ideological perspectives in which hardly anyone believed. Of course, some good films continued to be made – by Vláčil, Menzel, Chytilová, Uher, Hanák and others – but they were often not promoted and international interest was often actively discouraged.

In 1969, after the Federal Constitution was introduced, 'Czechoslovak Film Bratislava' (Československý film Bratislava) became 'Slovak Film Production' (Slovenská filmová tvorba), emphasising the fact of Slovak difference. 'Czech' and 'Slovak' films were always separately identified in publicity from that point onward – and, in fact, this had frequently been the case even earlier. Even in the late 1960s, Slovak film had made a number of co-productions with France and Italy (as well, of course, as with Central and East European partners) that had no Czech involvement. Czech production in the immediate post-war period (which included the Stalinist years) averaged around sixteen to eighteen features a year until the 1960s, when it rose to thirty features a year, and thirty-plus in the 1970s and 1980s. Slovak production began at around four features a year in the 1950s, rising to eight in the 1960s, nine in the 1970s and eleven in the 1980s.

Some Slovak directors, notably Ján Kadár and Juraj Herz, had pursued their careers in the Czech industry. This led, particularly in Kadár's case to a number of what might be termed, genuine Czecho-Slovak films. In 1963, he directed *Death is Called Engelchen* (*Smrt si říká Engelchen*) based on the novel by Slovak novelist Ladislav Mňačko about the Slovak National Uprising and, in 1965, *A Shop on the High Street*, shot in Slovakia with Slovak actors – effectively a Slovak film originating in the Czech studios. In Herz's case, his spell in the Slovak studios in the 1980s was prompted by his banning from the Czech studios. One of the three films, *I Was Caught by the Night* (*Zastihla mě noc*, 1985) was a co-production between the Barrandov and Koliba studios.

There has been a much greater overlap between the Czech and Slovak industries in areas such as cinematography and, more especially, acting and this has continued in the period since the division of the country in 1993. Indeed, most Slovak films have been co-productions with the Czech Republic. Slovak actors such as Emília and Magda Vášáryová and Marián Labuda have been as much stars of Czech films as Slovak. And, of course, while the films may have been Czech or Slovak in terms of production, the audience was common. While we are here considering links between individual industries within a single country, there are nonetheless clear parallels with similar production links in Western Europe.

The fall of Communism inevitably created a crisis in production, particularly since all government subsidies were virtually removed and, in the famous words of the current president, Václav Klaus, the film industry was 'a business like any other'. In 1991, the number of films released dropped to only four features which was lower than the previous crisis years of 1943 and 1951 with eight features each. However, by the late 1990s, production had risen to around twenty features a year. In contrast, while Slovak production was at two to four features in the early 1990s, it had dropped to one a year by the late 1990s. Here, one has to bear in mind that neither the Czech Republic, with a population of ten million, nor the Slovak Republic, with a population of just over five million, has any prospect of breaking even in the domestic market. However, with more adequate support currently in place (albeit temporary in the Czech case), the future seems more optimistic. Czech production in 2007 numbered some twenty-seven-plus films and Slovak production was at its highest for ten years with six features.

The various genres, tendencies and traditions examined in this book are subjectively based in that they are areas that I have found significant as an outside observer. Most are fairly straightforward. The chapters on animation and the avant-garde examine significant areas of production. Comedy can be regarded as an important genre, while realism and surrealism reflect important artistic categories or movements. The chapters based around history, politics and the Holocaust are defined in terms of their subject matter. The examination of lyricism and the absurd is, perhaps, more idiosyncratic.

In adopting these approaches, I am clearly focusing on some aspects of films at the expense of others. For instance, there are comedies that could also be considered under the headings of politics, lyricism and the absurd, animated films that are avant-garde, surrealist and political and so on. Very few films are specific to one heading. Each of the subjects is worthy of more extensive study and there are areas not covered here – romance, melodrama, Socialist Realist films and films about the Second World War. Given the fact that, since 1918, Czech feature production has numbered over 2000 films and Slovak production over 350, there are many subjects, areas and directors that have not been considered.

While I have included a separate chapter entitled 'Slovak Directions', this is a discussion of a particular set of developments within Slovak cinema rather than an account of Slovak cinema as such. Slovak films are also discussed in most of the remaining chapters. However, the intention is not to provide a comprehensive account of Czech and Slovak cinema but to raise a number of issues worth further examination and development.

NOTES

1. Larry Wolff, *Inventing Eastern Europe: The Map of Civilization on the Mind of the Enlightenment* (Stanford: Stanford University Press, 1994), p. 356.
2. Martin Votruba, 'Historical and National Background of Slovak Filmmaking', in Martin Votruba (ed.), *Slovak Cinema*, special issue of *KinoKultura*, December 2005. http://www.kinokultura.com/specials/3/votruba.shtml [Accessed 07/01/06]
3. Milan Kundera, 'A Kidnapped West or Culture Bows Out', translated by Edmund White. *Granta*, 11, pp. 93–118.
4. Hugh LeCaine Agnew, *Origins of the Czech National Renascence* (Pittsburgh: University of Pittsburgh Press, 1993), pp. 10–11.
5. Originally published in German as *History of Bohemia* (*Geschichte von Böhmen*, 1836–67).
6. Petr Pithart, 'Recognising a Prophet in the Czech Lands: T. G. Masaryk and Our Society', *Kosmas; Journal of Czechoslovak and Central European Studies*, 5, no. 2 (1986): p. 47; emphasis in the original.
7. René Wellek, Introduction to Tomáš G. Masaryk, *The Meaning of Czech History*, ed. René Wellek, trans. Peter Kussi (Chapel Hill: University of North Carolina Press, 1974), p. *xvii*.
8. See Josef Petráň and Lydia Petráňová, 'The White Mountain as a symbol in modern Czech history', in Mikuláš Teich (ed.), *Bohemia in History* (Cambridge: Cambridge University Press, 1998), p. 159.

9. H. Gordon Skilling, *T. G. Masaryk: Against the Current, 1882–1914* (Basingstoke: Macmillan, 1994), pp. 79–80.
10. Jan Rychlík, 'Czech-Slovak Relations in Czechoslovakia', in Mark Cornwall and R. J. W. Evans (eds), *Czechoslovakia in a Nationalist and Fascist Europe 1918–1948* (Oxford: Oxford University Press for the British Academy, 2007), pp. 18–19.
11. Alexander Dubček, 22 February 1968, quoted in Paul Ello (ed.), *Dubček's Blueprint for Freedom: His original documents leading to the invasion of Czechoslovakia* (London: William Kimber, 1969), p. 20.
12. Milan Šimecka, quoted in Ľubomír Lipták, 'Slovakia in the 20th Century', in Elena Mannová (ed.), *A Concise History of Slovakia* (Bratislava: Historický ústav SAV, 2000), p. 292.
13. Ľubomír Lipták, 'Slovakia in the 20th Century', in Mannová, p. 292.

1. HISTORY

History – Czech and Slovak history prior to the creation of Czechoslovakia in 1918 – has been the subject of many important Czech and Slovak films and the founding myths legitimising national identities have been of predictable importance. If the role of historical literature in the nineteenth century had been the creation of national consciousness then, according to Marketa Goetz Stankiewicz, such tendencies were encouraged after 1918, reaching their climax in the 1950s with the Marxist emphasis on the importance of history.[1] While historical literature and films had the function of promoting national and social cohesion, they could also, of course, provide a means of commenting on the present. It was not without significance that the first government-supported film was *St Václav* (*Sváty Václav*, Jan S. Kolar, 1929), marking the one thousandth anniversary of the murder of the country's patron saint, and that the first colour film, *Jan Roháč of Duba* (*Jan Roháč z Dubé*, Vladimír Borský, 1947), based on Alois Jirásek's play, should have told the story of one of the radical leaders of the Hussite movement. It was also not surprising that the Communist establishment should tap into this national history in the 1950s, in particular, by committing itself to the figure of Jan Hus, whose statue had been unveiled in the Old Town Square in Prague in 1915. Significantly, it faces the site where the Bohemian nobles were executed after the Battle of the White Mountain.

The director most associated with the historical film is Otakar Vávra, the only Czech director to pursue a career from the 1930s through to the present, in the process continuing to work under both the Nazi Protectorate and during the worst years of Stalinism. It is often argued that his emphasis on classical literature and historical themes allowed him to survive these various historical reverses and there is no doubt that such an approach was less likely to trouble the censors. On the other hand, he was clearly attracted by such themes from the beginning, with early films adapted from work by the historical novelists Alois Jirásek and Zigmund Winter. In 1937, he adapted Jirásek's *A Philosophical Story* (*Filosofská historie*), which was set against a background of the revolutionary year 1848. This was followed in 1938 by *The Guild of Kutná Hora Maidens*, a comedy set in the sixteenth century, and both were shown at the Venice Festival. In the last year of the war, he adapted Winter's novel *Rosina the Foundling* (*Rozina sebranec*, 1945), set in the seventeenth century, which was followed by another Winter adaptation, *The Mischievous Tutor* (*Nezbedný bakalář*, 1946), set in the sixteenth century.

Vávra was one of the key figures in the founding of FAMU (The Prague Film School) and numbers leading directors of the New Wave cinema of the 1960s such as Věra Chytilová, Jiří Menzel and Jan Schmidt among his former pupils. Despite his early involvement in the avant-garde, he soon argued that film was an immature art form and consequently evolved a 'system' or approach heavily dependent on literature. In a sense, the screenplay or the source material plays a dominant role. Menzel, who is unstinting in his praise for Vávra's teaching, has clearly been influenced by this although Chytilová moved in quite other directions.

During his career, Vávra has covered major themes in Czech history, with films about Jan Hus, Comenius and the Munich betrayal among others. Given his Left commitment, he has also had no difficulty in providing his interpretations with an appropriate ideological framework. One is frequently tempted to see Vávra as someone who is riding two horses – on the one hand, supporting Communism and doing little to rock the boat and, on the other, maintaining a commitment to the country's history and traditions. If his monumental Hussite trilogy, made in the 1950s, can only be viewed as an officially sanctioned project, it is difficult to see his chilling account of seventeenth-century witch-hunting, *Witchhammer* (*Kladivo na čarodějnice*, 1969), as anything other than a response to the political realities of the post-invasion period.

'The Hussite revolutionary trilogy' – *Jan Hus* (1954), *Jan Žižka* (1955) and *Against All* (*Proti všem*, 1956) – with its large budget and help from the army could hardly have been made without full official support. In adopting the national martyr, Jan Hus, as an official hero, the Communists promoted his demands for religious reforms and equality as part of the great medieval bourgeois revolution and as a precursor of the revolutions of the twentieth century. Thus the Bethlehem chapel in Prague, where Hus had preached his sermons, was reconstructed in the same year that Vávra directed *Jan Hus*.

From the Communist perspective, the Hussite revolution was primarily social and the Communists were its logical descendants. In one of the more extreme interpretations, the historian and musicologist Zdeněk Nejedlý noted:

> It is therefore ahistorical to think that Hus would today . . . be in any way a theologian. Today Hus would be the head of a political party . . . And his party would be very close – about this we can be certain – to us Communists.[2]

The first part of the trilogy tells the story of Hus, who used his sermons at the Bethlehem chapel to speak against the selling of indulgences, championed biblical over Church authority and also preached in the vernacular. Forbidden to preach, he was summoned to the Council of Konstanz to defend his ideas, with a promise of safe conduct from the Holy Roman Emperor Zigmund (Sigismund). He was arrested, accused of heresy, which was never proved or admitted, and burned at the stake. At the end of the film, Jan Žižka swears to remain faithful to his teachings.

In *Jan Žižka*, Václav IV defies the Utraquists (moderate Hussites) and returns the churches and monasteries to Catholic control. After the first defenestration of Prague in 1419, when seven members of the Prague Town Council were thrown to their deaths by Hussites, the country splits into opposing parts with Jan Žižka head of the 'people's movement'. At the end of the film, he defeats the lesser nobility at the battle of Sudoměř.

Against All is adapted from Jirásek's 1893 novel dramatising the life and conflicts within the radical community of Tábor. The Hussite cause has been successfully spread throughout the country when Tábor is beset by internal conflict and threats of attack from Emperor Sigismund. The film narrative includes Žižka's defeat of an attack on Tábor and his subsequent defeat of the Emperor's forces at the hill of Vítkov in Prague. Being based on Jirásek, the film also tells the more individual story of Zdena, who marries the priest Jan Bydlínský and who together die at the hands of extremists.

The three films are inevitably condensed accounts of the events but, with the benefit of hindsight, their conventions seem little more distorted than those of the standard historical epic. Indeed, in some ways, they recall some of those Pandro S. Berman/Richard Thorpe productions for MGM in the same era – for example, *Ivanhoe* (1952) and *The Adventures of Quentin Durward* (1955), both adapted from novels by Sir Walter Scott. Since Jirásek is sometimes referred to as the Czech Walter Scott, this is not so fanciful. However, Vávra is much more serious and much less prone to the promotion of spectacle for its own sake.

The approach is essentially that of the conventional historical epic, with carefully lit interiors and theatrical acting. But, although Vávra does not stint on spectacle or sets, they are not exploited in a grandiose manner. The costumes (and, in *Jan Hus*, the art direction as well) by Jiří Trnka impose their own unity of style and there is a relatively low-key, almost matter-of-fact attitude to fanfares and entrances, while Jiří Srnka's music makes no attempt to emulate the epic style of Miklós Rósza. The Hussite hymns are sufficient. The climactic battle of Sudoměř at the end of *Jan Žižka*, while clearly recalling Olivier's Agincourt, avoids exaggerated aesthetic spectacle. Also, the characterisation of Jan Hus in the first film of the trilogy is restrained and persuasively acted by Zdeněk Štepánek.

The first film is the most impressive, principally because the story of Hus, his ideas, his persecution, his defiance and betrayal, provide the ingredients for a coherent and dramatic narrative. The second is much more a sequence of dramatised incidents leading to the triumph of Jan Žižka. The third, since it is based on Jirásek, boasts a more complex but also a more classical narrative structure.

Writing of Hus in 1955, Miloš Kratochvíl, who collaborated on the screenplays of all three films, provided the following summary of Hus's ideas:

> He saw the decline of the Church through its worldliness, its devotion to the acquisition of wealth and secular power. He demanded that the clergy be satisfied with a normal income for their maintenance, like all other people, and that their property and lands be confiscated, as it was the strife over possessions that had led to the corruption of the Church: the acceptance of bribes for appointments to great State and Court offices, the sale of vacant benefices to the highest bidder and the like.
>
> Hus likewise attacked certain dogmas of the Church and the authority which the Church and clergy exercised over their believers, forcing them to blind obedience and forbidding them to use their own judgement. Hus maintained that every man had the right to use his own powers of reasoning in deciding what was right or wrong.[3]

One is tempted to look for omissions and distortions. The first is undoubtedly the absence of any reference to the central issue of communion in both kinds (bread and wine) until the second film, when it is shown without explanation. It is tempting to look at the conflict between Czechs and Germans and the emphasis on the exploitation of the serfs as a reflection of the preoccupations of the 1950s but both were, of course, also aspects of historical reality. One could point to the many historical films made in the USA or the UK (to say nothing of westerns) that have interpreted historical subjects in terms of a path to freedom, equality and democracy.

The story of the Hussite movement had been absorbed into the narrative of Czech history long before the Communists and had been promoted by both Palacký and Masaryk. Jirásek's novels, written in the late nineteenth and early twentieth centuries, themselves contributed to the centrality of the myth.

In adapting Hus and the Hussites as precursors of Marxist revolution, the Communists were merely promoting what was already there – and, of course, the formation of communes and the demand for social justice were part of the historical reality. To support what was already a defining myth was hardly surprising.

The films are not entirely clear without knowledge of the background. The relationship between Václav IV, King of Bohemia and Sigismund, his brother and the Holy Roman Emperor, is not a familiar matter and the views of Jakoubek, Hus's successor, of Jan Želivský and the priests of Tábor, whether fictional or real, are given only cursory coverage. On the other hand, the films chart most of the key events and work well as a summary of conventional accounts of the movement. *Jan Hus*, in particular, was well received by international critics, who interpreted it as a film about religion and conscience rather than a justification for the Cold War. The fact that its subject still provoked religious controversy was confirmed by the Vatican interference that resulted in its withdrawal from competition at the 1955 Venice Film Festival. The Catholic Church did not acknowledge any error until John Paul II's apology for Hus's death in 1999.

It is certainly permissible to classify the films as Socialist Realist. The heroes are positive, the villains negative, the sacrifices (particularly by women) are many and people fight for the cause of truth until death. Of course, the truth at this time was that of the Holy Bible versus the ecclesiastical establishment and not that of Communism. On the other hand, since it was the Catholic orthodoxy that had suppressed the Hussites, the film hardly lent support to the church in its confrontation with Communism. Logic and reason, in the context of the film, lead to equality and justice and the assertion that all are equal. By analogy, the cause of Communism can be seen to be promoting similar ideals and requiring parallel sacrifices and commitment.

Another historical figure to feature in Czech and Slovak fiction films, although this time much more in the area of legend, was Juraj Jánošík, 'the Slovak Robin Hood'. No less than four feature films were devoted to him in the former Czechoslovakia, to which one might add the Slovak–Polish epic, *The True Story of Juraj Jánošík and Tomáš Uhorčík* (*Pravdivá história o Jurajovi Jánošíkovi a Tomášovi Uhorčíkovi*), co-directed by Kasia Adamík and Agnieszka Holland and Viktor Kubal's animated feature, *Jurko the Outlaw* (*Zbojník Jurko*, 1976). Jánošík also features as a legend within Polish culture and was the subject of a feature and thirteen-part TV series in 1974. Adamík and Holland's film, based on a screenplay by the Slovak writer-director Eva Borušovičová, commenced shooting in 2002, ran out of money in 2003 and was taken on by the Polish producer Dariusz Jabloński in 2008.

Jánošík was born in 1688 in the village of Terchová in northwestern Slovakia. Recruited into the Habsburg army, he met the imprisoned outlaw Tomáš

Uhorčík and they later created a band of robbers, Jánošík becoming their leader at the age of twenty-three. They also operated in other parts of Slovakia and extended their activities to both Poland and Moravia. Reputedly, they robbed the rich, never killing their victims, and gave to the poor. Jánošík was tried and sentenced to death in 1713. The method of execution, reserved for leaders of robber bands, was to be pierced through the left-hand side on a hook and to be left hanging. The subject of innumerable works of (mainly Slovak and Polish) literature and poetry, the legend has remained very much alive until the present. He also featured in Jirásek's *Old Czech Legends* (*Staré pověsti české*, 1884) and was the subject of the Czech writer Jiří Mahen's play *Jánošík* in 1910.

The first – in fact, the only genuine Slovak feature film of the interwar period was Jaroslav Siakel''s *Jánošík* (1921). Siakel' and his brother Daniel, who acted as cinematographer, were based in the USA and the film was produced by the Slovak-American Tatra Film Company. Starring the Czech actor Theodor Pištěk, one of its sources was Gustav Maršall-Petrovský's novel *Jánošík, Captain of the Mountain Lads – His Tumultuous Life and Horrific Death* (*Jánošík, kapitán horských chlapkov – jeho búrlivý život a desná smrt'*), which was first published in Slovak in the USA in 1894. However, only half the screenplay was completed before shooting and the film also drew upon popular legends and Jiří Mahen's play. As Martin Votruba points out, the film:

> greatly reinforced the suggestions in 19th century Slovak Romantic poems about Jánošík that his heroic rebellion was directed against the overlords. The film fused feudal exploitation in the more distant past with the drive by the Hungarian-speaking government in Budapest in the 19th century to suppress the Kingdom's other languages and cultures . . . Unlike feudalism, this experience was still very fresh in people's memories and was among the reasons Slovaks immigrated to the United States.[4]

The Siakel' brothers, who came from a background in film-making and technical innovation in Chicago, had originally planned to make a series of films in Slovakia and *Jánošík* is not without historic interest. It uses a full range of narrative and film techniques which, according to Votruba, relate to their familiarity with the Hollywood mainstream.

The story is explicitly presented as legend, with a group of contemporary figures being told the story by an old peasant. In this version, Jánošík returns home after studying for the priesthood to find his mother dead. His father is then beaten to death for failing to turn up for work. After an encounter with the bandit Hrajnoha, Jánošík joins the outlaws and becomes their leader – but there will be no killing since, in his words, 'death does not change anybody'. In Jánošík's absence, his girlfriend Anka is the subject of advances from the squire, Count Šándor, but she manages to find sanctuary with the local priest.

The film devotes as much time to its story of the corruption of the Hungarian nobility as it does to Jánošík's free life in the mountains. To repay a debt, Šándor exacts further demands on the peasants in either money or (mainly) goods. An unmasked Jánošík leads his masked men into the Count's mansion where he announces, 'You shall not escape my revenge.' When he is tried, the sentence is that he be hung by the rib on a hook and that his body be quartered after his death. The final credit refers to him as 'the first fighter for the freedom of the Slovak people'.

The second *Jánošík*, based directly on Jiří Mahen's play, was directed by Martin Frič in 1935 and is formally a Czech film. The extensive exteriors were, however, shot in Slovakia and Pal'o Bielik, later to become a key figure in the development of Slovak film, played the lead part of Jánošík. Technically, the story does not differ greatly from its predecessor although all critics agree that this is very much a romanticised version, with a singing and dancing Jánošík, who repeats the act in defiance while on the scaffold. (According to legend, he danced round the gallows four times.) Before mounting the hook himself, Jánošík utters the famous words, 'As you have baked me so you shall eat me.'

In some ways, the film is a rather odd mixture of ballad, swashbuckling entertainment and national (Slovak) epic. While the music resembles operetta, Frič once described it as an art film. Here perhaps he was referring to a number of virtuoso sequences in which he combines extreme close-ups, rapid montage and superimposed images. Often impressive in all of its registers, it nonetheless walks an unusual tightrope.

The film was screened at the 1936 Venice Film Festival in the face of Hungarian objections. This international exposure led to wider interest and distribution in France, Germany and Britain among other countries. In his review in *The Spectator*, Graham Greene noted:

> it is treated in such a romantic rollicking tuneful way that we are reminded of *The Maid of the Mountains*, until the effective final sequence of Jánošík's capture and his cruel death, hung like butcher's meat with a spike in his ribs. Romance and robber-tunes and lyrical shots of a long-legged Fairbanks hero don't go with the spike.[5]

Pal'o Bielik is often considered one of the founders of Slovak film, in particular for his key work on the Slovak Uprising, *Wolves' Lairs* (*Vlčie diery*, 1948), which was co-scripted by Leopold Lahola.

In a sense, his return to the theme of *Jánošík* in 1963 was not typical of his work. But this handsome two-part film in colour and cinemascope was an altogether grander affair than its predecessors. The added length allows for the development of much more elaborate storylines, with part one largely devoted to Jánošík's youth and part two to his life as an outlaw. Part two is reminiscent of a western, with maximum attention given to impressive landscapes and action sequences. Although the new Jánošík (non-actor František Kuchta) is suitably sober, the robbers' hideout in the mountain heights, with its hand-winched lift and wooden escape pole and shute, requires considerable gymnastic skills.

Relationships between Jánošík and the other bandits are developed in greater detail with the characters of his close friend Uhorčík, his lieutenant Ilčík and the treacherous Gajdošík well to the fore. In both parts of the film, there is also light relief in the character of Uhorčík's father, played by Jozef Kroner, a sympathetic and comic figure whose unfamiliarity with weapons provides a running gag. Gajdošík kills old Uhorčík before betraying the group. Here, the plot developments also recall the conventions of the western. On Jánošík's death, smoke signals appear in the surrounding mountains and shots of the new young rebels who will take his place indicate that his death has not been in vain. (In Viktor Kubal's animated version of the story, Jánošík survives and his execution is faked.)

All of the films essentially hold to the same interpretation of the Jánošík legend. All include the episode in which an old woman throws peas on the floor, thus preventing his escape (although in all cases, this appears to be just a concession to tradition). Many of the other bandits mentioned by name either lived at different times or were members of different groups. On the other hand, although Jánošík was almost certainly a more conventional outlaw, the trial records indicate that he was never convicted of murder, giving substance to the high moral code adopted in the films. Like Hus, Jánošík could easily be assimilated into Communist historiography.

If Vávra's films of the 1950s were, according to the Liehms, a faithful imitation of Soviet styles,[6] the 1960s encouraged changing attitudes towards history. According to Antonín J. Liehm, historical topics which, under Stalinism, had served 'merely as a vehicle for bombastic political propaganda and to stress or create myths, gradually began to change into odd versions of the present'. As viewers increasingly adapted to this new language, 'the more facile the historical subjects became at speaking the language'.[7] Two directors who took the historical film in these new directions were František Vláčil and Oldřich Daněk.

Vláčil's *The Devil's Trap* (*Ďáblova past*, 1961) was the first of his three historical films from the period and was adapted from a novel by Alfréd Technik by František A. Dvořák and Miloš Kratochvíl, the latter of whom had scripted Vávra's Hussite trilogy. Set at the time of the Counter-Reformation, it tells the story of the conflict between Spálený, a miller, and his son, Jan, and the regent Valecsky. Respected for his wisdom and understanding of nature, particularly underground caverns and the sources of water, Spálený warns against the construction of a new barn. Rumours are spread that the miller and his family are suspected of witchcraft and a Jesuit priest is sent to investigate. The attempt to persecute and convict them fails since both the regent and the priest lose their lives in an underground tunnel. Vláčil noted that he was attracted by the theme of 'the fight against dogmatism and obscurantism', although he felt that it was not perfectly realised.[8] While characterised by Vláčil's habitual visual flair, it also has a sense of history as present that was developed to greater lengths in his subsequent two films, *Marketa Lazarová* (1967) and *Valley of the Bees* (*Údolí včel*, 1967).

Marketa Lazarová, which was voted the best Czech film ever made in a poll by both Czech and Slovak critics in 1999, goes from strength to strength in terms of its critical reputation and Vláčil's films, eight years after his death, are finally beginning to attract international attention. The film itself is a remarkable achievement in terms of its aesthetic appeal and originality, which was certainly inspired by the original novel by Vladislav Vančura.

The film was based partly on Vančura's novel, first published in 1931, and partly on his unfinished study, *Pictures of the History of the Czech Nation* (*Obrázy z dějin národa českého*, 1939–40) but, while Vančura's novel provided no historical clues and was intended as an 'autonomous' work, Vláčil deliberately tried to create a sense of the thirteenth century. The film was even set during a specific reign, that of Václav I (1230–53) – not to be confused with St Václav (921–35), also Václav I, who ruled as Duke. The original screenplay located the action between 15 February and 1 August 1250, with a detailed calendar specifying the time and place of the action. While none of this is readily apparent in the completed film and the 'royal sequences' were finally omitted, it nonetheless contributed to the film's shaping and conception.

Vláčil has commented that, in historical films, he always felt that he was watching actors dressed up in costume, where frequently inaccurate externals mattered more than the history. In *Marketa Lazarová*, like the Bergman of *The Seventh Seal* (*Det sjunde inseglet*, 1957) and *The Virgin Spring* (*Jungfrukällan*, 1960), he made an essential attempt to project himself into the mentality and feelings of a past age. He wanted to present the characters as contemporaries – 'I wanted to understand them, see through the eyes of their lives, their failings, their desires.'[9] Thus, aided by his historical advisors, he attempted to recreate their world with maximum verisimilitude – but, ironically, it was one that was primarily imagined since little documentary evidence of the reality of everyday life at that time has survived. In attempting to think himself back into the thought processes of the time, Vláčil studied contemporary groups living at the same level of development.

The film tells of the conflicts between the rival clans of the Kozlíks and the Lazars and the doomed love affair between Mikoláš Kozlík (František Velecký) and Marketa Lazarová (Magda Vášáryová). Alongside this is the relationship between Mikoláš's sister, Alexandra, and the captive son of a Saxon count, Kristián. Interlaced with this narrative is the overall historical context – that of paganism versus Christianity and the struggles between the rival clans and the controlling claims of the king. While organised religion is, to some extent,

Figure 1.1   František Vláčil: *Marketa Lazarová* (1967)

conveyed as a repressive force – Marketa rejects the convent in favour of Mikoláš – the world of the Kozlíks is both pagan and Christian and, in this way, analogous to many 'adaptations' to Christianity.

The film's bleak reality (much of it was shot in winter) suggests a genuine 'dark age' – yet this was a period in which Bohemia became one of the most important powers in Europe, with the development of towns and agriculture, written Czech literature, the movement of Germans into the Czech lands and the development of national consciousness.[10]

Vančura's novel had itself been designed as a polemic with the Czech conception of national history and of historical prose, with its notion of suffering for its faith and language. Having said that, while it thrusts us into an alien world rather than giving us a sanitised history lesson, the film does not offer an allegory of the present. Perhaps its greatest significance lies in its resolute rejection of anything resembling Socialist Realism. Here, there is no right path, no progressive solution – people remain imperfect and motivated by primitive instincts, passions and fears.

Given the film's aesthetic status – which is as much 'avant-garde' as historical – it is worth giving a brief summary of its approach. Vláčil is not interested in narration in the conventional sense – unlike his next two films, *Valley of the Bees* and *Adelheid* (1969). The focus is much more on the subjective and psychological world and the reaction and interplay of character in specific situations. The action is 'explained' by intertitles, which function in much the same manner as old chronicles. A range of narrative approaches is used – stories, monologues, subjective perception, an omniscient narrator – but there are few concessions to convention as we are immersed in a highly unusual world.

The film is beautifully visualised, with a striking use of composition in depth and Vláčil's cinemascope format encompasses a wide range of techniques ranging from extreme close-ups to contradictory and parallel actions within the frame and an extreme use of subjective camera. Zdeněk Liška's music uses a range of percussive effects and even specially created instruments. The film allows us to see and experience feelings suppressed by conventional forms. Above all, it is, as many Czech critics have noted, a film without moral and ideological messages and, in this sense alone, it is a step into new terrain.

In his adaptation of Vladimír Körner's novel, *Valley of the Bees*, Vláčil adopted a more conventional narrative form but maintains his authentic costumes and atmosphere and the attempt to project himself into a past age. Here the Czech–German oppositions, an implicit element in *Marketa Lazarová*, become more apparent. The film tells the story of Ondřej of Vlkov, the son of a Czech noble, who is raised as a member of the order of Teutonic Knights. As a child, Ondřej secretes a collection of squirming bats under the rose petals presented to his father's new teenage bride. His father flings him against a stone wall and, fearing that he may die as a result, vows to dedicate his life to the service of the Virgin if it is spared.

The Knights' castle on the Baltic – like the Knights' costume itself – is conveyed with a geometric and repressive perfection. When Ondřej takes his vows, he is required to renounce his father and mother and to resist the temptations of man, woman and his own body. The film then focuses on the relationship between Ondřej and the handsome knight, Armin von Heide. Ondřej decides to return home and the film follows the course of his journey and its results, the resurrection of his love for his stepmother, Lenora, and Armin's pursuit.

In its evocation of the early years of Christianity, the film again deals with pagan/Christian oppositions but also demonstrates the reality of human passions suppressed by formal systems. Lenora's love for her stepson counts as incest and Armin comments to a blind girl on his arrival in Bohemia – apparently his first encounter with the opposite sex – that, if she were to touch him, she would lose her hand. There is little doubt also that Armin's vehement pursuit of Ondřej and attempt to return him to the Order is the result of his own passion and love. Armin – who is also explicitly likened to a werewolf – cuts Lenora's throat and is subsequently devoured by dogs. But Ondřej nevertheless returns to the Order.

Despite the film's dramatic oppositions between Czech and German, this is still a world of contrasting historical currents. While Bohemia – again, the film is set in the thirteenth century – had already been a Christian kingdom for two centuries, Vláčil clearly indicates the positive elements in pagan survivals and the accommodating attitudes of the local priest, who is prepared to sanction the marriage of Ondřej and Lenora. He likens their union to the activity of the bees who, when one hive is destroyed, immediately build another.

In the years following the Soviet invasion, *Valley of the Bees* was seen to carry a doubtful allegorical message but the hunt for subversion had, by then, become exhaustive. Vláčil's plans to make a film about the Czech-born general of the Thirty Years' War, Wallenstein (Valdštejn), came to nothing – as, of course, did his plans to analyse the origins of the Prague Spring.

Oldřich Daněk, the other director to take historical film in new directions, was also a novelist, stage producer and dramatist. He made two historical films in the 1960s, *The Nuremburg Campaign* (*Spanilá jízda*, 1963) and *The King's Blunder* (*Královský omyl*, 1968), but subsequently found his film-making career at an end. He went on to write historical novels and the highly regarded play *You Are Jan* (*Vy jste Jan*, 1987), in which he returned to the subject of Jan Hus.

In his interview with Antonín Liehm, his interest in historical film was clearly apparent. While acknowledging that Czechoslovakia lacked the resources to make films employing casts of thousands, he also saw low budgets as an advantage that allowed for a different kind of film. Although interested in what might be termed the lessons of history, he noted that it made little sense to regard his films as allegories. All history did was to set his subjects, in a sense, beyond time. Speaking of *The King's Blunder* he noted that 'the film takes place in the present, or – to be more accurate – takes place in the present, too'.[11]

Daněk's films essentially set personal stories against historical backgrounds. *The Nuremburg Campaign* takes place during the Hussite wars where, against the broad currents of history, the crusade against the Hussites, the Hussite victory and subsequent invasion of Germany, Ondřej Keřský searches for and finally discovers the man who abducted and raped his bride and murdered his relatives. The Hussites allowed into Nuremburg to pursue their teachings are nonetheless betrayed.

The King's Blunder is set in the fourteenth century during the reign of Jan (John) of Luxemburg. The king's vice-chamberlain, Jindřich of Lipá, the real holder of power, is resented by other nobles, who persuade the queen to imprison him. Realising her errors, she attempts to get Jindřich to capitulate and admit his guilt in exchange for freedom but he refuses. Eventually, the king releases him out of political necessity.

Another important historical film made in 1968 was Hynek Bočan's *Honour and Glory* (*Čest a sláva*), which was released in 1969. It was adapted from a novel by Karel Michal and set during the Thirty Years' War following the Battle of the White Mountain. The film provides a portrait of a Czech noble-man, Václav Rynda (Rudolf Hrušinský), whose property was lost after the

defeat at the White Mountain and who now ekes out a living with his followers, more peasant than nobleman. He receives messengers from abroad who
want him to organise a revolt against the Habsburgs that will be matched by
an offensive from Protestant armies in the West. When he finally agrees, news
arrives of the Treaty of Westphalia that finally ended the conflict. He leads his
troops off in a fated rebellion. As played by Rudolf Hrušínský, the character of
Rynda moves from one of Švejkian acquiescence to one of proud but doomed
resistance – from a kind of moral suicide to a physical one.

According to Bočan, the period in which the film was set – 1648 – had
an immense effect on the formation of the national character. The educated
quarter of the nation had gone into exile, leaving 'a nation of Švejks', survi-
vors who were somehow able to continue and regenerate. Indeed, the parallels
resonate throughout history. 'I read something interesting some place: in 1938
the Germans had an internal directive to allow the emigration of the Czech
intelligentsia, and top people in general. They knew that a nation without
these people is much more easily controlled'.[12] This was a situation that was
to recur in both 1948 and 1968. As Bočan notes, the novel, which appeared in
the early 1960s, and the film itself produced an evolving historical resonance
as the political changes of the 1960s progressed.

Although *Honour and Glory* is a low-budget film, with an orthodox narrative based on character and dialogue, there are also echoes of *Marketa
Lazarová*. The opening scenes, with the burning cross and hanging bodies
accompanied by the music of Zdeněk Liška recall Vláčil's film as does Rynda's
run-down fortress, with its unimpressive drawbridge. Here again, in contrast to
the romantic historical epic, the characters are virtually dressed in rags.

It would be fair to say that the low-budget black-and-white historical film
was a characteristic of the 1960s, not only looking at historical parallels
but also relevant moral and political issues. In 1969, Otakar Vávra made
his contribution with one of his best films, *Witchhammer*, dealing with the
seventeenth-century witchcraft trials. While, like most of his films, it is reliant
on dialogue, it was made with a relentless precision, rhythm and logic. It is also
beautifully staged in cinemascope, with stylish photography (Josef Illík) and a
compelling score by Vávra's regular collaborator, Jiří Srnka.

The narrative begins when an old beggar woman hides the Host in her scarf at
Communion. She has agreed to take it to another woman whose cow is failing
to give milk. Despite the views of the enlightened priest Dean Lautner that such
superstitions should not be taken too seriously, a young priest, alert to heresy,
persuades the Countess de Galle to send for an inquisitor. Summoned out of
retirement, the inquisitor Boblig unleashes a process from which no one is safe.

The procedures of the inquisition tribunal routinely use torture to extract
confessions in a progression that moves from the ignorant old women with
whom it all begins through to the local dignitaries, the sheriff himself and

Dean Lautner. While there is much discussion about the methods used on the accused, officialdom consistently turns a blind eye. For instance, torture is only supposed to be used with the permission of and in front of the tribunal. Despite the evidence of bleeding fingers and limbs, the fiction is maintained that this is not taking place. Later, the comment that they use thumbscrews and the Spanish boot is dismissed as minor and a matter of routine practice.

The trials have to be paid for and, as the process continues, the inquisitor increasingly targets those with significant resources. In order to gain accomplices, he suggests that rumours could be spread and offers benefits for those who collaborate. Eventually, he targets Dean Lautner, an educated and generous man, who sees through Boblig and offends him with his learning and capacity to play the violin. Boblig asserts that he needs only one Bible, the inquisition's guide, *The Hammer Against Witches* (*Malleas malificarum*, 1486), which is dismissed by Lautner as ungodly.

Appeals against the trials to the Countess fail, appeals to the Bishop fail and further appeals fail to reach the Emperor. The Emperor, we are told, is preoccupied with the Turkish threat to Vienna, while others prefer to protect themselves against any charges of having aided or assisted anyone accused of witchcraft and heresy.

Vávra, who wrote the script together with Ester Krumbachová, based it not only on Václav Kaplický's novel but also actual trial records in the region of Šumperk. Quite apart from this maximum concern with historical accuracy, he also intended it as a commentary on the political trials of the 1950s. Given the Czech concern to regard everything as political, particularly at this time, it could not be seen any other way.

While the film follows the process of interrogation and condemnation, it also examines the consciences of those who watch and feel powerless in an extended chain of responsibility. Thus there is the judge who is sacked for doing his job, the priest who sits on the commission knowing that he will receive no support for any dissenting view and Lautner's 'friend' who resigns from the commission as a matter of conscience but will not stand up for him. We learn that the lay members of the commission are poorly educated, that everyone is watching everyone else, that the walls have ears and that anyone who stands up for heretics can be suspected of being a heretic himself.

The film makes its points with absolute precision, intercut with the shaded eyes of a priest reciting the 'facts' about witches and the practices of the devil. At the time, Vávra noted, 'In historical records I came upon sensible, hard-working people who fell quite unexpectedly into the clutches of the revived medieval witch trial machine, which swallowed and crushed absolutely innocent people, ordinary and educated alike'.[13] It was the mechanism of the trials that attracted him, not only evoking the trials of the 1950s but also, of course, referring to the possibility of what might now happen in the present.

In 1968, the Czech poet, František Hrubín, wrote a new play entitled *Oldřich and Božena* (*Oldřich a Božena*) with the subtitle, *A Bloody Plot in the Czech Lands*. The story is that of the Bohemian Prince Oldřich who takes the peasant girl Božena as his mate. Oldřich's marriage was childless and the offspring of his liaison with Božena was later to rule as Břetislav I. The child represents the hope of national survival in opposition to the forces of the Emperor. Hrubín observed that everyone has his model of history 'but the inner actions, passing through our consciousness . . . are always contemporary'.[14]

Taken by many at the time of its production in September 1968 as a reference to contemporary events, Vávra, who had made two films with Hrubín in the 1960s, originally planned to make it into a film. He only gained permission in 1985, fourteen years after the author's death. In the 1970s and 1980s, the kinds of historical speculation typical of the 1960s were not encouraged.

Vávra continued to operate in the fields of history and literature during the 'normalisation' period, working principally with the author of the Hussite trilogy, Miloš Kratochvíl, including an adaptation of his novel about Comenius in *The Wanderings of Jan Amos* (*Putování Jana Amose*, 1983). In *A Meeting with Love and Honour* (*Příběh lásky a cti*, 1977), he dramatised the relationship between the nineteenth-century poet and writer, Jan Neruda, and the early feminist, Karolina Světlá, and, in *Veronika* (1986), he focused on the pioneer novelist and patriot, Božena Němcová.

Vláčil turned to the more immediate past with a bleak epic adapted from Josef Čapek's novel *The Shades of Ferns* (*Stín kapradiny*, 1984) and to the Romantic poet Karel Hynek Mácha for his last feature film *The Magus* (*Mág*, 1987). While the films themselves are of varying quality, these products of the 'age of immobility' reveal a continuing concern with the national tradition.

Since 1989, of course, with the rise in production costs and the need for production values to be seen on screen, there has been little emphasis on historical subjects (particularly given the relative absence of state support). This contrasts rather markedly with Poland and Hungary, where historical epics have proved among the most successful with local audiences.

Strangely enough, epics seem to have appealed (to producers) rather more strongly in Slovakia despite the dramatic fall in production. As mentioned earlier, there was a new version of *Jánošík* and Juraj Jakubisko's Slovak–Czech–Hungarian–British *Báthory* (2008) – 'the most expensive film in Central European history' – was released in the year prior to this book's first publication. Jakubisko's film presents an alternative history of the story of Erzsébet Bathory, the countess who was alleged to have bathed in the blood of village maidens. In Jakubisko's version, Báthory is the richest noblewoman in Hungary, an important figure in the defence of Europe against the Ottoman Empire in the late sixteenth century but also a highly educated, cultured woman and a loving wife. The legend of the 'Bloody Countess', it is suggested, is at least partly circumstantial. Strikingly shot and written, directed, designed (and painted, an unusual credit) by Jakubisko, it certainly falls outside of the 1960s tradition of realist historical drama. While Jakubisko is undoubtedly confronting a period of Central European history that has been largely unexplored, the film is also a mix of personal cinema and blockbuster (shot in English). The film has been the most successful at the box office in Slovakia since 1990 and has also performed successfully in the Czech Republic. Interestingly enough, the Hussite trilogy, the various *Jánošíks* and *Witchhammer* have all been successfully released on DVD.

Despite the more critical stance adopted by the historical films of the 1960s – the fact that history becomes a living and relevant reality – they do not contradict notions of Czech and Slovak identity. Perhaps it is worth adding a footnote here on the similar use of classical music. The Czechs are rightly proud of a heritage that includes Smetana, Dvořák, Suk and Janáček among others. As with other aspects of national identity, both democrats and Communists have shown an interest. In the 1950s, Václav Krška made a biography of Smetana – *From My Life* (*Z mého života*, 1955) – to be followed the next year by a version of his opera *Dalibor* (1956), both projects that coincided with the Hussite trilogy. Similarly, in the years of normalisation, Vláčil turned to Dvořák with *Concert at the End of Summer* (*Koncert na konci léta*, 1979) and Jaromil Jireš to Janáček with *Lion with a White Mane* (*Lev s bílou hřívou*, 1986). Jiří Krečjík's *The Divine Emma* (*Božská Ema*, 1979) was a biography of the famous opera singer Emmy Destinn (Ema Destinnová), who was a star in the United States before the First World War. Her refusal to act as a spy for the Austrian secret police was considered to have political parallels, although the controversy was less apparent to foreign audiences.

The identification of Czechs with music is made explicit in Jan Svěrák's *The Elementary School* (*Obecná škola*, 1991), adapted from his father's semi-autobiographical script about the immediate post-war years and one of the first post-Communist films. Zdeněk Svěrák's script refers to Smetana, Dvořák and the popular operetta composer, Rudolf Friml (*Rose Marie* and *The Vagabond King*), who had studied under Dvořák. Here the reference is, with some irony, to *The Donkey Serenade*. The Czechs, he suggests, conquered the world with their music. Similarly, at the end of Svěrák's Oscar-winning *Kolya* (*Kolja*, 1996), the central character, František Louka (Zdeněk Svěrák), an unemployed musician during the years of normalisation, ends up playing Smetana's *My Country* (*Ma vlast*) in an orchestral performance under the statue of Jan Hus in Prague's Old Town Square. (He is actually cut into real footage of a concert that took place under the baton of the former exile, Rafael Kubelík.)

The Second World War must also now be regarded as part of history – indeed, it is now being reconstructed by writers and directors with no experience of the historical reality. This was an important theme in Czech and Slovak cinema under Communism, particularly since there was a continuing representation of the threat of Nazism, in turn linked to the threat from the West during the Cold War. This is not a subject that I have addressed, except with reference to the Holocaust, but a number of films in the late 1960s began to raise repressed issues. One was Vláčil's *Adelheid* (1969), adapted from a novel by Körner, which was, in some ways, an extension from the themes of his earlier films. It was the first film to deal explicitly with the expulsion of the Germans from the Sudetenland after the war but, more importantly, it deals with ethnic and ideological identities and the ways in which relations between individuals become distorted. In 1968, Jindřich Polák made *Riders in the Sky* (*Nebeští jezdci*), a tragic study of the sacrifices of Czech and Slovak pilots in the British Royal Air Force. In 2001, Jan Svěrák made *Dark Blue World* (*Tmavomodrý svět*), an epic and more romanticised approach to the same subject which became the most successful film to date with Czech audiences. The number of Czech pilots was in the region of 500 and their contribution was not acknowledged until 1991. Under the Communists, many had been rewarded by imprisonment.

NOTES

1. Marketa Goetz-Stankiewicz, *The Silenced Theatre: Czech playwrights without a stage* (Toronto: University of Toronto Press, 1979), p. 224.
2. Zdeněk Nejedlý, *Komunisté-dědici velikých tradic českého národa* (*Communists: The Inheritors of the Great Traditions of the Czech Nation*) (Prague: Práce, 1978), p. 43, quoted in Bradley F. Adams, *The Struggle for the Soul of the Nation: Czech Culture and the Rise of Communism* (Lanham: Rowman & Littlefield, 2005), p. 101.
3. Miloš Kratochvíl, 'Jan Hus', *The Czechoslovak Film*, VIII, 6, 1955, pp. 4–5.
4. Martin Votruba, 'Historical and National Background of Slovak Filmmaking', in Martin Votruba (ed.), *Slovak Cinema*, special issue of *KinoKultura*, December 2005. http://www.kinokultura.com/specials/3/votruba.shtml [Accessed 07/01/06]
5. Graham Greene, *Janosik*, in *The Pleasure Dome: The Collected Film Criticism 1935–40*, ed. John Russell Taylor (London: Secker and Warburg, 1972), pp. 86–7.
6. Mira Liehm and Antonín J. Liehm, *The Most Important Art: East European Film After 1945* (Berkeley: University of California Press, 1977), p. 106.
7. Antonín J. Liehm, *Closely Watched Films: The Czechoslovak Experience* (New York: International Arts and Sciences Press, 1974), p. 159.
8. František Vláčil, interviewed in Antonín J. Liehm, p. 175.
9. Ibid.
10. See Zdeněk Měřínský and Jaroslav Mezník, 'The making of the Czech state: Bohemia and Moravia from the tenth to the fourteenth centuries', in Mikuláš Teich (ed.), *Bohemia in History* (Cambridge: Cambridge University Press, 1998), p. 50.
11. Oldřich Daněk, interviewed by Antonín J. Liehm, *Closely Watched Films*, p. 161.
12. Hynek Bočan, interviewed in *Closely Watched Films*, p. 340.
13. Otakar Vávra, interviewed in *Czechoslovak Film*, 6, 1969, p. 8.
14. František Hrubín, Programme to *Oldřich and Božena*, quoted in Goetz-Stankiewicz, p. 224.

2. COMEDY

Comedy is a genre that is prominent in most national cinemas and Czechoslovakia has been no exception. In all cinemas, comedy takes on specifically national forms and references in addition to its more universal characteristics. But comedy does not automatically 'travel' – it is difficult to think of major international comic successes from Russia, Poland, Hungary and Germany to name but four countries. The same is true of French comedy post-Jacques Tati and he was in many ways an exception. In effect, with the exception of the 'silent clowns', it has been normal for comedy not to travel.

In this context, Czech comedy is arguably unusual. Judging purely in terms of Czech Oscar-winners and nominations, comedies have always been prominent. Comedy has been well to the fore in such films as: *Loves of a Blonde* aka *A Blonde in Love* (*Lásky jedné plavovlásky*, 1965); *The Firemen's Ball* (*Hoří, má panenko*, 1967); *Closely Observed Trains* (1966); *My Sweet Little Village* (*Vesničko má, středisková*, 1985); *The Elementary School* (1991); *Kolya* (1996); and *Divided We Fall (Musíme si pomáhat*, 2000). All were Oscar nominated and two, the Oscar-winning *Closely Observed Trains* and *Kolya*, were to prove the most successful Czech films ever made. Even during the interwar period, we can find *Heave-Ho!* (1934) achieving screenings in New York, London and Paris.

While it has often been observed that British audiences respond well to Czech films because of some indefinable similarity in the sense of humour, this fails to explain the much wider appeal of Czech comedy, which has become almost synonymous with the ways in which the Czech cinema has been perceived.

The issue of comic tradition is a tricky one and it is by no means clear that there is any simple form of progression. If one examines British cinema, also renowned for its comedy, one often looks in vain for any references – or indeed consciousness – of the films of the 1920s or 1930s in current productions. The tradition of Ealing comedy from the 1940s and 1950s lives on but, even here, it is via circuitous routes, a sensitivity passed on via television.

In small countries such as Czechoslovakia, the paths traced between theatre, literature, cinema, television and life itself have been even more closely intertwined. A number of younger directors such as Alice Nellis, Saša Gedeon and Jan Hřebejk have expressed their admiration for the New Wave of the 1960s. But, as Gedeon once put it, he is more influenced by the society in which he lives and its traditions, as were the directors of the wave, than by individual films and directors.

Although Miloš Forman observed that the films that he and his colleagues produced in the 1960s were influenced by the 'bad' films they saw around them rather than by any deeper tradition, they also acknowledged the influence of Jiří Voskovec and Jan Werich, whose comic vision had dominated Czech theatre in the 1930s and had also led to four feature films. Forman also stated that he felt almost obliged at some stage to adapt Jaroslav Hašek's classic novel *The Good Soldier Švejk and his Adventures in the Great War* (*Osudy dobrého vojáka Švejka za světové války*) which had been published in the 1920s.

Jiří Menzel, perhaps the most significant of Czech comedy directors, has acknowledged himself to be a student of comedy and an admirer of the classic Hollywood comedies, as well as of the leading comedy director of the pre-war period, Martin Frič. His frequent collaborator in the post-1969 period, Zdeněk Svěrák – *Seclusion Near a Forest* (*Na samotě u lesa*, 1976), *My Sweet Little Village* (1985), *The Life and Extraordinary Adventures of Private Ivan Chonkin* (*Život a neobyčejná dobrodružství Ivana Čonkina*, 1993) – is also a student of the genre. Indeed, the absurdist Jára Cimrman Theatre that Svěrák established with his co-writer and performer, Ladislav Smoljak, has often been seen as a continuation of the tradition of Voskovec and Werich. Svěrák has spoken of how he often 'tries out' ideas in the theatre in order to find out what will work.

This complex and highly developed strand in the story of Czech cinema is certainly worthy of a full-length study. However, I want to restrict this chapter very largely to considering: the early work of Martin Frič; Forman's *The Firemen's Ball*; the work of Menzel; a more slapstick post-war tradition associated with the comedies of Oldřich Lipský and Václav Vorlíček; and Vladimír Morávek's more recent *Bored in Brno* (*Nuda v Brně*, 2003). Many of the other 'comic' films that might have been considered here – the work of Ivan Passer, Hřebejk, and Nellis – are discussed in other chapters which serves as an indication of the ways in which films habitually cross between genres and themes.

The Good Soldier Švejk is arguably the best known of all Czech novels. Initially based on Hašek's experience of the Austrian army in 1915, its anarchistic and apparently idiotic hero was clearly a Czech making fun of his masters. Its effective use of irony and satire as a weapon was something that became 'ingrained in the Czech psychology and artistic imagination'.[1] It gave birth to a film version, *The Good Soldier Švejk* (*Dobrý voják Švejk*, Karel Lamač, 1926), and three sequels in 1926–27 (by Lamač, Svatopluk Innemann and Gustav Machatý). Other versions appeared in 1931 (Martin Frič), 1954 (Jiří Trnka's puppet version) and 1956–57 (Karel Steklý). Piscator's stage version appeared on the Berlin stage in 1928 and there were even Russian – Sergei Yutkevich's *New Adventures of Švejk* (*Noviye pokhozdeniya Shveika*, 1943) – and English – Lamač's *It Started at Midnight*, 1944 – film adaptations.

It has been alleged that many Czechs know passages of the novel by heart but others have come to see its idiotic hero as characteristic of the stupidities of bureaucratic rule under Communism. A much more positive influence is Voskovec and Werich's company, Liberated Theatre (Osvobozené divadlo), which was a regular feature of Prague theatre from 1927–38. Brought together by a shared interest in American westerns and Mack Sennett comedy, Voskovec referred to the American slapstick comedians as 'our Stanislavskys'.[2] Their mixture of circus, jazz, vaudeville and dadaism gave birth to what the novelist Josef Škvorecký described as 'a kind of intellectual-political musical'.[3]

While they initially set out to create a world of 'pure fun', the economic crisis of the early 1930s, which had hit Czechoslovakia badly, and the progressive rise of Nazism soon gave their work a political edge. Their first two films *Powder and Petrol* (*Pudr a benzin*, 1931) and *Your Money or Your Life* (*Peníze nebo život*, 1932) were both directed by their stage director, Jindřich Honzl. Reflecting their world of absurdism and slapstick humour combined with wordplay ('semantic clowning', to use Roman Jakobson's words), disguised tributes can be found in later films such as Jan Němec's *Martyrs of Love* (*Mučedníci lásky*, 1966), which evokes the mood of the early 1930s, and Menzel's version of Václav Havel's *The Beggar's Opera* (*Žebrácká opera*, 1991).

Their subsequent two films, *Heave-Ho!* (1934) and *The World Belongs to Us* (1937), took on a more committed role, with the first confronting the issue of unemployment and capitalist corruption and the second a fascist attempt to overthrow the government. The negative of the second was destroyed during the Nazi occupation. Both were directed by Martin Frič.

Heave-Ho!, which was the only pre-war Czech comedy to attract international attention, tells the story of the head of a firm, Jakub Simonides (Jan Werich), who is ruined by a ruthless rival. The latter is a cripple who makes comments such as, 'Business is slow. Don't be sentimental about the workers. Fire them or go broke.' Voskovec plays a workers representative, Filip Kornet, who is supposed to speak on the radio about the unemployment situation. He speaks from a prepared script. 'It is my privilege to speak for the unemployed. Smiling we gaze into the future . . .' But, when he rejects this misrepresentation of reality and starts to tell the truth, he is dragged away from the microphone.

Circumstances bring Voskovec and Werich together, leading to a number of traditional slapstick routines. These include cutting a hedge at different levels from opposite directions, ironing trousers with a steamroller and accidentally burying a car and a display of kissing techniques learned from popular films.

When Werich inherits a half-built house that has escaped the attention of his creditors, he completes it with the help of unemployed labour. They decide to form a co-operative (the 'hejrupaci') and produce milk products that succeed in putting Werich's rival out of business. As business increases, the results are presented through the use of split-screen techniques. The return of their first lorry, where the milk in churns has turned to butter, launches a parody of the cream separator sequence from Eisenstein's *The General Line* (*General'niya Linya*, 1929). Voskovec speaks in a kind of Russian and a procession of lorries echoes the multiple tractors that fill the screen in Eisenstein's film. The sequence was criticised by the ultra left but, perversely, also presented by others as pro-Soviet propaganda.

As Václav Kofroň has pointed out, Voskovec and Werich had just enjoyed a stage success with their *Donkey and its Shadow* (*Osel a stín*), 'a relentless anti-fascist satire' in which they 'poked fun at political dilettantism, demagogy and various types of fanaticism, and pointed to the funding of the Nazi movement, and the links between German big capital and the Nazi Party'.[4] But while *Heave-Ho!* was hailed as Czechoslovakia's first social film, the overall mood was one of fun, that of a film which Voskovec and Werich noted in a 1937 interview 'defended the optimistic solidarity of young people against the woes of economic depression'.[5]

Kofroň is right to point to the ways in which the film oscillates between cinematic narrative and the vaudeville 'turns' of Voskovec and Werich. Their comic style, which is fundamentally based on improvisation, never entirely escapes its theatrical origins and provides the key justification of the film's narrative. But this is hardly a unique failing and, it has to be said, not one likely to worry their intended audience. The film was immediately compared to works such as René Clair's *A nous la liberté* (1931) and Chaplin's *City Lights* (1931). Shown in Venice, Moscow, Paris, London and Brussels, it was sold to most European countries before its banning after the Nazi invasion.

In their play, *Obverse and Face* (*Rub a líc*, 1937), Voskovec and Werich had treated the increasingly militant Fascist threat and *The World Belongs to Us*, produced in the same year, was partly adapted from this source. The film begins in a waxworks museum, where Drexler is exhibiting Lionel, supposedly a freak who is half man and half beast. Some years later, during the Depression,

Drexler has become propaganda chief and recruiting agent for a Fascist political party and Forman, the former Lionel, has become a strike leader in a factory. Voskovec and Werich are newspaper sellers who are hired to paint rival slogans on the factory walls. The workers learn that the fascists are planning to overthrow the government using weapons that have been stockpiled in the factory. The plot is thwarted but not before Voskovec and Werich have accidentally detonated a weapon, mistakenly thinking that the words 'Krupp Essen' have something to do with food. They are assumed to have died in the explosions and find themselves attending their own memorial service. The film includes many impressive gags including the scene where Voskovec attempts to free Werich from iron bars fixed around his neck with the help of industrial tools, including a giant circular saw. The scene, they affirmed, was *not* taken from Chaplin's *Modern Times*. Among other planned film projects were adaptations of their plays *The Golem* (*Golem*, 1931) and *Ballad of Rags* (*Balada z hadrů*, 1935), about the French fifteenth-century poet, François Villon. The second was prepared but never made and the first was made in 1936 without them, after differences with its French director, Julien Duvivier.

Another leading comic phenomenon of the period was the genius of Czech cabaret, Vlasta Burian, who appeared in thirty-two films between 1926 and 1956, including eight by Karel Lamač and nine by Martin Frič. Comparing him to Groucho Marx, Josef Škvorecký comments, 'He had the same mercurial energy, was capable of similar verbal floods, and stupefied the audience with wise-cracks, explosive gags, aggressive conquests of women, fantastic mimicry.'[6] For Frič, he also appeared in a number of classics, including Gogol's *The Inspector General* (*Revizor*, 1933) and a Czech-Polish version of Ilf's and Petrov's *The Twelve Chairs* (*Dvanáct křesel*, 1933).

Frič, arguably the most talented director of his generation, made some eighty-five features in a career that extended until his death in 1968. He also made many films with the comic actors Hugo Haas (later in Hollywood) and Oldřich Nový, as well as working in a whole range of genres. Comedy was obviously his forte and his command of pace and timing would have served him well had he ever moved to Hollywood. Undoubtedly a commercial director, his work was defined by an absolute professionalism and the level of his work over such a long career is probably unequalled anywhere. In the Communist era, he again worked with Jan Werich – on the two-part film *The Emperor's Baker* and *The Baker's Emperor* (*Císařův pekař* and *Pekařův císař*, 1951), produced at the height of Stalinism – and also on a highly acclaimed version of Chekhov's *The Bear* (*Medvěd*, 1961) for television.

In *The Emperor's Baker* and *The Baker's Emperor*, Werich stars as the Emperor Rudolf II (1552–1612) who, alongside his patronage of Tycho Brahe, the English alchemist Edward Kelley and a host of other inventors and scientists, is also searching for the Golem and the elixir of life that will return his lost youth. He imprisons his double, the baker Matěj, also played by Werich, who has allocated the daily supply of bread to the poor. A succession of comic gags leads to his replacing the Emperor, outwitting his advisors and discovering the secret of the Golem. Scripted by Werich, Frič and Jiří Brdečka, with impressive design and costumes by Jiří Trnka, it is a film of some elegance and wit that primarily provides a frame for its performers. While it also supports sound socialist principles, revealing the corruption of the court and supporting ideals of equality and justice, it is scarcely an ideological work and has obvious links to the pre-war collaborations between Frič and Voskovec and Werich.

However, I would like to briefly discuss three of the films that Frič made with Oldřich Nový – *Kristian* (1939), *Valentin the Kind* (*Valentin Dobrotivý*, 1942) and *The Poacher's Ward* (*Pytlákova schovanka*, 1949). Works of pure entertainment, they were, given their years of production, films of considerable sophistication.

A comedy of mistaken identity, *Kristian* tells of a humble clerk in a travel agency, Alois Novák (Nový), who dreams of a more sophisticated life, working overtime so that, once a month, he can pretend to be a millionaire and visit the Club Orient. Here, as 'Mr Kristian' he tips lavishly, chats up and dances with pretty girls and then leaves to return to a humdrum home life. However, he meets his match in the charming Zuzana (Adina Mandlová), who is also seeking *her* escape from routine and who tracks him down. In the process, he pretends to be two people (Alois and his 'brother' Kristian), Zuzana pretends to be his wife and he is accidentally impersonated by his friend, Josef. His wife, Marie, leaves him but, in the end, everything is resolved – he receives promotion at work and Marie decides that she will no longer force him to play dominoes at home. Alois and Zuzana have had their eyes opened and everyone is reasonably forgiven.

Apart from the sophisticated charm of Nový and Mandlová in the main roles, the film is beautifully timed. The opening sequence is something of a tour de force as the Bar Orient prepares for opening. The camera pans across the space of the nightclub as waiters prepare the tables and the band readies itself. Kristian's arrival is portrayed in small details and through the reactions of others until we finally see his face. Movements around the space are orchestrated with an almost balletic skill.

Valentine the Kind, made during the Nazi Protectorate, provides a similar exercise in reassurance and escapism. This time, Nový is a clerk in an insurance office who is tricked by two colleagues into believing that he has won a fortune on the lottery. As the winnings are due in three days, he spends all his savings, buys a new house and car and gets seriously in debt. In the end, by a trick of fate, it turns out that he really *has* won the lottery. The film is a partial continuation from *Kristian* in that people's behaviour towards the new 'millionaire' is determined entirely by his status.

In *The Poacher's Ward*, the beautiful but poor Elén meets René, a millionaire (Nový) on a train, who is attracted by the beauty of her singing. They fall in love but Elén mistakenly believes that he has been unfaithful to her and rejects him, eventually marrying the violinist Pavel. Desperate, René loses his fortune and begins to make a living writing the libretto for a musical play. He falls seriously ill and, when Elén hears of it, she runs to his deathbed. Her singing brings him back from almost certain death and her marriage proves to be invalid.

The subject matter of these three films – wealth, fantasy, love – has much in common. But they are full of comic incident and played with considerable style. Frič apparently intended *The Poacher's Ward* to be a satire on *kitsch* which many took at face value. But while it exaggerates these conventions (with some affection), the film is not a world away from the previous two and the Communist censors were not entirely happy. The three films seem to inhabit a world where politics is absent but they also reflect the work of an obsessive film-maker. As Liehm suggests, cinema became Frič's 'very life, the meaning of his life, he was incapable of thinking in any other terms'.[7]

It might have been thought that the traditions linked to Hašek and Voskovec and Werich would have flourished during the Communist period (1948–89) as they were both anti-war and pro-working class. However, despite the fact that Hašek had been praised by Czech Communist writers before the war, it was only after positive evaluations from the Soviet Union and the German Democratic Republic that there was a revival of interest – and the Liberated Theatre as such had to wait somewhat longer. But, quite aside from the film versions of *Švejk* produced in the 1950s, these comic traditions lived on in more indirect ways and also transferred to the Czech New Wave directors of the 1960s. Forman once said to Voskovec, 'We could not have existed without you two . . . we learned how to improvise on the screen, how to speak a living language'.[8]

The comic flavour of Czech films of the 1960s was identified principally with the work of Forman and Menzel, with Forman making his debut three years before Menzel in 1963. However, Forman's work can also be identified with the move toward the observation of the everyday and the use of non-actors and, while the films include scenes drawing upon classic comedy, it is an emphasis on observation that takes precedence.

In both *Black Peter* aka *Peter and Pavla* (*Černý Petr*, 1963) and *Loves of a Blonde*, he features scenes in dance halls, which become set pieces in their own right. These films are discussed in the chapter on realism. However, in *The Firemen's Ball*, a dance provides the framework for the whole film, which is much more deliberately designed in its comic sequences and in providing a kind of metaphorical commentary on reality.

It was originally inspired by the example of someone Forman (and his collaborators, Ivan Passer and Jaroslav Papoušek) had known at Prague's Lucerna ballroom and who organised dances. However, while writing the script in the mountains, a visit to a real firemen's ball transformed their vision into something even more compelling. The film again used non-actors, with the vast majority coming from the local community. However, many of the key characters had already made their debuts in Forman's previous films.

The action centres on an annual firemen's ball where a dance, a beauty competition and a raffle are to be provided. The narrative is structured around two main developments – the progressive theft of the raffle prizes and the firemen's abortive attempts to organise a beauty contest. At the end of the film, a fire siren goes off, the brigade fail to put out a fire and an old man is left homeless. As a gesture, they decide to donate all the raffle tickets to him – but, by now, the prizes have been stolen. The ceremonial hatchet which they are planning to present to their president (who is dying of cancer) has also been stolen. The film ends with two old men – the man whose house has been burned down and the fireman assigned to guard his remaining belongings – climbing into an abandoned bedstead outside the old man's house. Beside them is a discarded crucifix in a wastebasket.

This somewhat bleak take on everyday socialism was not appreciated by the authorities, who took an even less favourable view of the incompetence displayed by the firemen who, as officials and organisers, could be interpreted as representing the Party itself. It was one of a number of films banned 'forever' following the Soviet invasion.

Cinematographer Miroslav Ondříček has spoken of how the set was constructed to create a warm atmosphere in which the large cast was able to interact naturally. Among the comic set pieces is the film's opening sequence where the banner advertising the event goes up in flames as two firemen argue about responsibility. The parade of largely unwilling beauty contestants takes place in front of a group of excited old men (the firemen's committee), who compare them with some disappointment to the more glamorous examples in a magazine spread, marching them around the room like prize animals. The raffle prizes fall over to the consternation of their guardian as a couple embrace under the table, the president is sent forward to collect his award in place of a young girl and so on. The humour is abrasive and prompted the leader of the Surrealist Group, Vratislav Effenberger, to describe it as 'vicious, dangerous, concealed, and explosive', striking out against 'spiritual wretchedness' and the petty bourgeois Czech.[9]

In his terms, it presented the real absurdity of contemporary life to public gaze. The film is, of course, extremely funny but, at the same time, Forman's sharp look at his fellow countrymen is here critical rather than affectionate when compared with his earlier films. In important respects, it also verges on caricature. However, when a public screening was organised to condemn the film, the local people approved of it. Needless to say, Italian producer Carlo

Ponti, its co-producer, agreed with its Communist critics – as apparently did some of its US exhibitors.

The links between film and literature continued in the post-war period and, where comedy was concerned, the most influential writer was Bohumil Hrabal, eight of whose books or stories have been adapted for the screen. Jiří Menzel directed five of them, as well as contributing to the New Wave's collective 'testament' based on Hrabal's collection of short stories, *Pearls of the Deep* (*Perličky na dně*, 1965). Hrabal was not only considered the most important writer of his generation but was to become a legend in his own life-time. The image of him holding court at his favourite Prague pub – the Golden Tiger (*U zlatého tygra*) – as well as reflecting reality, is worthy of Hašek and of *Švejk*.

While Hrabal's largely unpublished pre-war work had come under the influence of the avant-garde, his experience of the Nazi occupation and of post-war Stalinism was to lead in other directions. A graduate in law, his life as a railway linesman and train dispatcher, at the Kladno iron works, and as a wastepaper baler gave him a rich resource from the everyday. The direct life experience, he concluded, could become a poetic act. The privately published *People's Conversations* (*Hovory lidí*, 1956) revealed his obsession with authentic speech in a representation of the working class that was at odds with the simplifications of Communist ideology. In searching for 'the little pearl at the bottom', he appeared to have tapped into the suppressed consciousness of an era.

Based on Hrabal's collection of short stories first published in 1963, *Pearls of the Deep* came to be regarded as the manifesto of the new wave. The emphasis on conversations is apparent in Jan Němec's section, 'Imposters' ('Podvodníci'), where two old men on the brink of death construct artificial pasts in which one claims to have been a successful opera singer and the other a famous journalist. In Jiří Menzel's 'The Death of Mr Balthazar' ('Smrt pana Baltazara'), set at a motorcycle race meeting, a conversation is constructed entirely from motorcycle lore (make, cubic capacity, year of manufacture) interspersed with the sounds of passing engines. The autobiographical origins of Hrabal's work are apparent in 'At the World Cafeteria' ('Automat svět'), Věra Chytilová's contribution. Set in a café near his flat, it includes a wedding and a corpse and features his friend, the 'explosionalist' artist, Vladimír Boudník. In Jaromil Jireš's 'Romance', the film evokes the romance Hrabal once had with a gypsy girl. In Evald Schorm's 'House of Joy' ('Dům radosti'), two insurance salesmen (another of Hrabal's jobs) attempt to interest the primitive painter, Václav Žák, whose visions come from inside him 'like the inside of a goat'.

This obstinate investigation of reality was, of course, a characteristic of many Czech films of the time, notably those of Forman and Passer. However, while they share Hrabal's concern with irony and the absurd, they lack his obsession with the eccentric and the surreal, his philosophical references and his literary links with such unlikely influences as William Faulkner and T. S. Eliot.

In *Closely Observed Trains* (the novel), Hrabal constructed his most orthodox narrative, drawing from a number of earlier works based on wartime experiences, two of them dealing with the subject of suicide. While his new emphasis lay on the hero's quest for sexual initiation, he retained much of the earlier versions' taste for morbid imagery. In Jiří Menzel's film adaptation, however, it was given the kind of humanist flavour that won a Hollywood Oscar and made the film popular all over the world.

It is hardly surprising that the hero no longer sits down on a dead horse and that his sexual triumph is no longer lit by the allied firebombing of Dresden. But this is a comedy that remains highly unusual. When its adolescent hero, an assistant at a sleepy railway station, experiences an unsuccessful night of love-making, he attempts suicide. After the discovery of his sexual problem – premature ejaculation – he finally achieves success in the arms of the glamorous resistance fighter, codenamed 'Viktoria Freie'. But his achievement of manhood is also linked to his death. Entrusted – by accident – with the explosives to blow up a Nazi munitions train, he is equally accidentally shot.

The central theme is complemented by the observation of the station staff: the station guard, an 'immoral fellow' who entertains young women at night; the stationmaster, who keeps pigeons and dreams of becoming an inspector; the telegraphist who allows the guard to stamp her backside; and the old porter who dreams of more glorious days under the Habsburgs.

While Menzel is an undoubted admirer of Hrabal, the strength of the film derives from an unusual degree of collaboration. Hrabal noted that he rewrote the screenplay six times in order to re-conceive it visually and ended up preferring the film to his novel. Writing of their collaboration, Hrabal observed that they kept 'complementing each other, like two mirrors flashing at each other with the reflections of our poetic vision'.[10] In fact, a striking aspect of the film is the way in which Menzel often finds a visual form for the original imagery – 'the twittering of telegraphs and telephones', the chime of a clock and the image of scissors when Miloš 'cuts off' his relationship with the past.[11]

The collaboration between Hrabal and his young admirer was extremely close, giving rise to a complex work that not only mixes comedy and tragedy with a story of young love but also intersperses it with powerful and often magic imagery. Combined with this is the careful timing of key comic scenes – for example, the scene where Miloš waits open-mouthed for a kiss from his beloved as she leans from the back of a train and Hubička whistles it out of the station, Hubička's pursuit of the telegraphist prior to the bottom stamping scene and the confrontation of officialdom with a station master covered in goose feathers during the official inquiry. In this film, Menzel began at the top and it has remained unsurpassed in his subsequent work.

There is no doubt that Menzel's collaborations with Hrabal have constituted his main contributions to cinema and this film was followed by *Skylarks on a String* (*Skřivánci na niti*, 1969, released 1990), *Cutting it Short* (*Postřižiny*, 1980) and *The Snowdrop Festival* (*Slavnosti sněženek*, 1983). In the first of these, which was filmed after the Soviet suppression of the Prague Spring in 1968, Menzel and Hrabal explicitly addressed the subject of Stalinism in the post-war period. Set in the 1950s, the action takes place in a scrap metal yard, where remnants of the bourgeoisie are being re-educated and introduced to the benefits of the new utopia via forced labour. The prisoners include a librarian who refused to destroy books, an attorney who insisted on upholding the law and a saxophonist who played decadent music. The male 'counter-revolutionaries' are matched by a group of women prisoners who have been arrested for trying to escape to the West. This group of misfits pay little attention to work since they are, ironically, engaged in a strike against an increase in work norms which, under the legendary Stakhanovite system, are leading to an increase in unusable product.

Skylarks on a String differed from its predecessor in that its narrative was no longer focussed on a central character. Here, the subject is the group and the multiple characters are treated with a great deal of finesse as a complex web of plotlines interact. The erotic relationships that develop between the two groups become focused on the character of Pavel (Václav Neckář, who played the hero of *Closely Observed Trains*) who actually manages to get married via an array of bureaucrats and surrogates but is unable to consummate it due to his premature arrest. Menzel even manages to humanise the oppressors since the prison guard engages in an absurd but comical marriage to a Roma girl. In a comic performance of some political precision, Rudolf Hrušínský plays the camp overseer, mouthing meaningless platitudes and carrying an empty briefcase. His real enthusiasms are reserved for a lascivious sponging of young Roma girls in a campaign for cleanliness and the denunciation of inmates to the secret police. Many felt the subject was not one for comedy – and neither did the compliant post-invasion regime which, for quite different reasons, banned it.

After this, Menzel was not allowed to work again until 1974, when he made *Who Looks for Gold* (*Kdo hledá zlaté dno*), an empty Socialist Realist piece about a construction site that was no more than an obligatory act of penance. Hrabal, who had supported the Prague Spring, was not allowed to publish until 1976, when his 1970 novella, *Cutting it Short*, appeared. An evocation of his childhood memories of the provincial town of Nymburk, it presented the authorities with few problems. Here, Hrabal himself emphasised the lyrical touch, a search for a time 'filled with the joyful discovery of the world'. Menzel and Hrabal collaborated on the film in 1980.

The heroine, Maryška (Magda Vášáryová), based on Hrabal's mother, is

Figure 2.1 Jiří Menzel: *Cutting it Short* (*Postřižiny*, 1980)

the personification of female sexuality. Her presence gives quiet pleasure to the inhabitants of a provincial town dominated by the local brewery. The film's comedy is triggered by the arrival of Uncle Pepin, a character based on Hrabal's real uncle. A former cobbler who came for a two-week visit, he stayed for forty years. 'He sat there at the table and stared at the ceiling and saw what he was talking about up there. He merely reproduced it', wrote Hrabal.[12] Pepin's spontaneous narrations were to exercise a key influence on on Hrabal's work. In the film, his stories deal with pet raccoons, Austrian officers, aunts and uncles and dentists who pull out one another's teeth.

Menzel reserves his 'magic' for the beautiful Maryška. Her tender beauty is emphasised with a predictable emphasis on her billowing dress as she cycles through town or stands on a phallic chimney in the wind. There are a number of explicitly erotic scenes – her night time bath in the brewery, the marital massage with a strange piece of medical equipment and the public spanking of her backside. In another chauvinist scene, her beautiful hair turns out to be a horse's tail. When her hair is cut, one of the references embodied in the film's title, it is a symbol of inevitable change and of a move beyond the film's frozen fantasy.

References to silent comedy become explicit in Menzel's treatment of the volunteer fire brigade who state that they 'are not a Keystone Cops comedy with Lupino Lane'. Uncle Pepin, as Jan Uhde has pointed out, provides a parallel with Tati's Monsieur Hulot, particularly in the running gag where one of the members of the brewery becomes permanently accident-prone after meeting him.[13] Full of references to silent comedy, *Cutting it Short*, despite the pig slaughtering with which it begins (a key element in Hrabal's memories), remains one the best post-Tati comedies.

With *The Snowdrop Festival*, Menzel and Hrabal produced a film with a more bitter flavour. Set in the countryside near Prague – the area of Kersko, where Hrabal had his own cottage and did most of his writing – it deals with the life and characters in the local community and the discovery of a wild boar. The initial incident with the boar is filmed like a silent comedy but the unfortunate beast is tracked down to a classroom at the local school and shot dead in front of the children. The hunting associations from the two local villages squabble over their right to the corpse and the honour of having killed it while the children sing 'My Bohemia'.

There is plenty of observation of multiple characters and some typically Hrabalian dialogue and humour – the man who inhabits a junkyard and plays a clarinet in the woods, the policeman who deflates the cycle tyres of the drunken inmates of the pub, discussions on the 'healthiest water' in Central Europe, how to run a Trabant and so forth. Yet these characters are not particularly likeable and the killing of the boar and its aftermath provides a bleak portrait of human relations. The one positive character, the permanently enthusiastic Leli, is killed when his bike is knocked into the ditch by the local bus.

While, of course, Hrabal's comedy is always laced with surrealism, physical cruelty and an ironic approach to life's games with individual destiny, the softening effects of Menzel's comic mechanisms and 'humanist' perspective are less in evidence than in earlier films. Here, perhaps, the influence of Hrabal prevails over that of Frič.

Nonetheless, there are some witty scenes – the opening where the woods are full of the sounds of gunshots which turn out to be echoing from television screens in adjacent dwellings. The panning and crane shots establish a contradictory lyricism. An odd juxtaposition of moods, the film seems ultimately to be full of comic elements that have ceased to be funny, serving only to provide a more bitter message.

Both Menzel and Hrabal adapted their perspectives to the requirements of the new regime and much of Hrabal's work was either unpublished or published in censored editions. Similarly, the majority of films had become almost inane as, having learned the lessons of the 'subversive' New Wave, scripts were laundered of anything that might be considered offensive or critical. In these circumstances, as Jan Uhde once wrote, *Cutting it Short* appeared like a flower on the desert of Barrandov.[14] There is little doubt that the collaboration between Menzel and Hrabal represents one of the crowning achievements of Czech cinema and, in relative terms, the films produced during the years of 'normalisation' are more important than is currently recognised. They kept alive a creativity, a humour and a poetry that everything around them seemed set to deny.

Although Menzel has worked closely on all his scripts and imposed his own characteristic flavour on the results, he has always been dependent on his literary collaborators or literary sources. In two films, *Capricious Summer* (*Rozmarné léto*, 1967) and *The End of Old Times* (*Konec starých časů*, 1989), he drew on the work of the avant-garde novelist and film-maker Vladislav Vančura. In 1976, he collaborated with the comic writers, Ladislav Smoljak and Zdeněk Svěrák on an original script for *Seclusion Near a Forest* and he later worked with Svěrák on the Oscar-nominated *My Sweet Little Village* and *The Life and Extraordinary Adventures of Private Ivan Chonkin*.

All of these films have a different flavour from his Hrabal films. The most impressive is probably *Capricious Summer*, a film that won the main award at Karlovy Vary in the year of the Soviet invasion and his first film after his success with *Closely Observed Trains*. The film remains extremely close to its original, characterised as a 'prose of a remarkable parodying humour, a sparkling tension between pathos of delivery and pettiness of material'.[15] Of course, this cannot be conveyed in another language, yet the performances of Rudolf Hrušínský, Vlastimil Brodský and František Řehák, as the film's three main characters, are full of dry humour and flashes of interplay that take the film beyond any mere dependence on language.

The film examines the provincial world of three ageing members of the bourgeoisie, whose routine of fishing, eating and drinking is interrupted by the arrival of a travelling conjuror (played by Menzel) and his beautiful blonde assistant. They each harbour their own illusions and become involved in abortive liaisons with the glamorous assistant, whose mundane contributions to the conjuror's act achieve a magic of their own. The whole is suffused in a reflective mood, a sense of late summer and a past age. In fact, the film sometimes recalls the Jean Renoir of *Une Partie de campagne* (1936), not least with the sudden squall of rain that affects their attempted idyll.

But there are plenty of neat comic episodes – the boat that sinks after Antonín's wife attempts to interest the Canon in her charms, Antonín's night with Anna when he massages her foot, Arnoštek's stumbling but magic performance on the high wire. There's even a rather Hrabalian episode when the Canon's torn ear is sewn back on with a fish hook – a scene of gory intensity lightened by a discussion on class struggle and decadent poets.

In the period following 1989, Menzel has been much less active primarily because he dislikes the financial struggles of the marketplace. His first film, an adaptation from his successful stage production of Václav Havel's *The Beggar's*

Opera (1991), was produced under the nationalised industry but was more of a theatrical record than a genuine film adaptation. Of course, Menzel has always tried to remain close to his originals and this was also true of his *The Life and Extraordinary Adventures of Private Ivan Chonkin* (1993), which was adapted by Zdeněk Svěrák from the Russian novel by Vladimir Voinovich.

However, his long-nurtured project was a film version of Hrabal's *I Served the King of England* (*Obsluhoval jsem anglického krále*, 2006), which was finally completed after a gap of over ten years. Written very much in Hrabal's characteristic stream-of-consciousness style, the action of the novel is seen from the perspective of its central character. In an afterword to the Czech edition, Hrabal wrote, 'I didn't have any control over what I wrote; so I wrote in the luminous intoxication of the automatic method.'[16] In the novel itself, he writes, 'I covered page after page while the pictures in front of my eyes went by faster than I could write.'[17]

Dítě (which translates as 'child') is an apprentice waiter in a Prague hotel who tries to learn the trade and hopes to realise his dream of owning his own hotel and rising to worldly success. Like Švejk, he is a simpleton but inordinately impressed by wealth and women. He discovers that, contrary to popular perception, the rich really do enjoy their ill-gotten gains. Curiously, following the Nazi occupation of the Sudetenland, he seems to perceive only the Czech mistreatment of Germans and falls in love with a German teacher and champion swimmer. They marry and produce a mentally defective child called Siegfried. Finally, Dítě realises his dream with the help of a fortune gained from his wife's sale of stamps amassed from Jewish homes in the Łódź ghetto in Poland. At the end of the novel, Dítě's property is confiscated during the Communist takeover of 1948, when he argues that he deserves to be imprisoned with the other millionaires. But he is never accepted by them. Here, Hrabal describes an absurd prison with a locked gate and no fence in which the millionaires and the militia conspire to improve their cuisine and swap places.

An extensive final section reveals a reflective Dítě working in the Sudetenland repairing roads. After an initial encounter with an ex-professor of French literature and a girl of loose morals, he ends up alone with a dog, a cat, a goat and a horse for company. He looks back on his life, interrogating himself as if he were a public prosecutor. In the final pages, he begins to write his story of 'how the unbelievable became true'.

As James Wood puts it, the novel is 'a joyful picaresque story, which begins with Baron Münchhausen-like adventures, and ends in tears and solitude, a modulation typical of Hrabal's greatest work'.[18] The novel develops in five separate blocks, each dealing with Dítě's move to a separate location and hotel. His character and appearance emerge only gradually and his blond hair and blue eyes are only emphasised in the third section, when he has to prove his Aryan origins. He becomes progressively aware of the irony of his marriage to a German at a time when his countrymen are being murdered. But his primary concern is that his simple-minded collaboration should be covered up and that he should survive.

Tim Beasley-Murray argues that the novel draws on the traditions of the avant-garde, especially surrealism. Indeed, one might add that the French literature professor spends a whole evening talking about Robert Desnos, Alfred Jarry, and Georges Ribemont-Dessaignes. Hrabal's approach is based on montage, a technique that Beasley-Murray characterises as 'the deployment of fragmentary material in order to break down the barrier between traditional, organic art and the empirical and fragmentary experience of reality'.[19] The shift between conscious and unconscious is indicated by the constant repetition of the phrase 'and the incredible became fact' or 'the unbelievable became true', a phrase that is also repeated in Menzel's film adaptation.

The film version, of course, owes nothing to the avant-garde and is concerned primarily to extract the novel's principal narrative elements. However, while Menzel remains remarkably faithful to Hrabal's text, he ends up with a film narrative that seems paradoxically both too long and too short. While Hrabal's stream-of-consciousness approach is difficult to accommodate in itself, the fact that he originally described the novel as 'stories' indicates the episodic (and, in fact, contradictory) elements of the totality. The most difficult section is clearly Ditě's romance with Lise and his temporary accommodation with the Nazis. Virtually a subject in itself and contradicting the earlier sections of the book, Menzel deals with it speedily when it seems to require, in film terms, a much greater elaboration.

On the contrary, Menzel reserves his flair and enthusiasm for Ditě's service at the Golden City of Prague, the Hotel Tichota and the Hotel Pařiž. His worm's-eye view of the rich and their beautiful women remains at the heart of the film. The early sequence of Ditě serving frankfurters at Prague railway station is filmed as a black-and-white silent film complete with subtitles and this slapstick approach is continued through other sequences. The film exhibits a visual love affair with the designs and fashions of the pre-war Republic and a superb period score by Aleš Březina. At times, Menzel's approach recalls the choreography of a Hollywood musical.

The Bulgarian actor, Ivan Barnev, in a characterisation clearly based on Chaplin, is excellent in the main role and is supported with some style by Martin Huba as the maître d' of the Hotel Pařiž and Pavel Nový as an eccentric general. The juxtaposition of scantily clad young ladies from the 'Golden Paradise' with lecherous older men, taken direct from the original, will no doubt be the subject of dissertations offering further discussion of the 'male gaze'.

The novel's final section, perhaps inevitably, becomes a framing device for the whole film as Ditě, the road-mender, looks back on his path through life.

Again, this does not entirely work, partly because it unintentionally cuts into the mood of the other episodes, but also because the older Dítě is played by a different actor (Oldřich Kaiser).

Needless to say, there is no attempt to incorporate Hrabal's more abrasive elements – Dítě's mentally defective son who spends his time hammering nails into the floor, the decapitation of Lise when she dies in an air raid, the shooting of his dog at the end of the novel. Instead, in a scene of wish fulfilment, Dítě again serves his first customer (who has actually been transported to the concentration camps) and raises his glass to the camera.

Ladislav Smoljak and Zdeněk Svěrák were associated with a particular brand of absurdist humour deriving from their Jára Cimrman Theatre, which was established in the 1960s. According to Škvorecký, it offered 'a hugely sophisticated, irreverent, nonsensical and often socio-politically critical dramaturgy, with roots in the "decadent" dada and pataphysical mystification'.[20] Jára Cimrman, who gave the theatre its name, is an imaginary character and universal genius, equally adept as a writer, inventor and film-maker. In a recent newspaper poll, he was voted the most famous Czech of all time. The absurdist humour to which the plays gave birth found its way to the screen in a number of guises with Smoljak and Svěrák frequently doing star 'turns' in other people's films.

Together, they scripted a number of films, including two for Oldřich Lipský – *Joachim, Put it in the Machine* (*Jáchyme, hod' ho do stroje!*, 1974) and *Mareček, Pass Me a Pen* ('*Marečku, podejte mi pero!*', 1976). Their work for Menzel on *Seclusion Near a Forest* was probably their best from this period although it is not typical. It was a gentle comedy about 'weekenders' from Prague who decide to buy a country cottage and discover that they must share their new idyll with its ageing owner whose own father remains healthy at the age of ninety-two. The retreat to the country was very much a national obsession in the normalisation years but the film's reconciliatory comedy nonetheless contained some sharp observations.

In the 1980s, Smoljak himself turned director with *Ball Lightning* (*Kulový blesk*, co-directed by Zdeněk Podskalský, 1978), *Run, Waiter, Run!* (*Vrchní, prchni!*, 1980), *Jára Cimrman, Lying, Asleep* (*Jára Cimrman, ležící, spící*, 1983), *Dissolved and Let Out* (*Rozpuštěný a vypuštěný*, 1984) and *Uncertain Season* (*Nejistá sezóna*, 1987). *Ball Lightning* is a brilliant ensemble comedy about how to change flats in Prague. *Run, Waiter, Run!* tells of the exploits of a bookshop assistant and father of several illegitimate children, who impersonates head waiters in a number of restaurants in order to supplement his income. Set at the end of the nineteenth century, *Jára Cimrman, Lying, Asleep* concerns Cimrman's attempts to turn the Austro-Hungarian monarchy into an Austro-Hungarian-Czech monarchy but both the Archduke Ferdinand and the Emperor turn out to be doubles. The title of *Dissolved and Let Out* refers to a body dissolved in a bath of acid. A turn-of-the-century detective drama, it features a hero (sometimes represented by a clockwork replica) who is constantly frustrated by an unseen superior.

During the 1980s, Svěrák also worked with Menzel on *My Sweet Little Village*, in some ways a development from *Seclusion Near a Forest*. Set in a small village, it is a multifaceted comedy with a rich variety of intertwining subplots and a number of illicit affairs. It centres on the story of the simple-minded Otík, who causes a number of minor disasters and whose Prague-based boss plans to take over his village house. Full of witty observations and some mild criticism of ideological excesses, it reveals both Menzel and Svěrák to be working within the major traditions of screen comedy. It also boasts a gentle and lyrical style.

They adopted a similar approach to *The Life and Extraordinary Adventures of Private Ivan Chonkin* (1993), which remains very close to the original. The story of a Russian Švejk sent to guard a crashed plane during the Stalinist era, it is a funny story that somehow came outside of its time and did not enjoy any kind of success. It was, of course, shot in Russian with a Russian cast which was, no doubt, the reason for lack of success in Czechoslovakia and the Russians were not that keen on a satire coming from outside. But it remains a perfectly legitimate version of a novel widely regarded as a classic and deserves reassessment.

Besides these more high-profile comedies, there has been a whole range of apparently less ambitious works based around popular genres and references to 'Western' culture – for instance, Oldřich Lipský's *Lemonade Joe* (*Limonádový Joe*, 1964), Václav Vorlíček's *Who Would Kill Jessie?* (*Kdo chce zabít Jessii?*, 1966) and *End of an Agent* (*Konec agenta W4C prostřednictvím psa pana Foustky*, 1967), which are satires on westerns, strip cartoons and Bond films respectively. A more recent example from this particular genre would be Václav Marhoul's elaborate take on Philip Marlowe, *Smart Philip* (*Mazaný Filip*, 2003) or even Marek Dobeš's zombie comedy *Choking Hazard* (2004).

Lemonade Joe enjoys an almost iconic status in Czech cinema and it is not uncommon to hear its theme song being played in cafes to this day. The story was adapted from the work of Jiří Brdečka, famed as a leading animator as well as writer. His *Lemonade Joe* stories were written for magazines in the early 1940s and were subsequently adapted as a stage play in 1946. His script for the 1964 feature film has much in common with his earlier work on Jiří Trnka's puppet film, *Song of the Prairie* (*Árie prérie*, 1949), where the theme song also made its debut.

Of course, a peculiarly Central European fascination with the American West has been long standing, not least via the Western novels of the German writer Karl May, many of whose novels were adapted as films in Germany and proved very popular in Czechoslovakia. *Lemonade Joe* is an attractively naive musical parody whose provenance is really the 'B' westerns of stars like William S. Hart and Tom Mix through to singing cowboys like Gene Autry (with plenty of yodelling to prove the point).

Set in the town of Stetson City, it charts the victory of good over evil as the protagonists fight over the right to promote whisky or lemonade and compete for the hand of the delectable Winifred Goodman. The film begins with a brawl in the Trigger Whisky Saloon (owned by Doug Badman). Dressed like a member of the Salvation Army and representing the Arizona Revival, Winifred and her father enter the saloon and campaign against the demon drink. Lemonade Joe enters the room dressed in white from head to toe. Apart from demanding lemonade ('Colaloka'), he is a superb marksman and foils a bank raid with his casual under-the-arm shooting. He is soon locked in combat with the black-caped figure of the legendary Hogo Fogo (in reality, Horace Badman), who seeks to turn the town back to its whisky-drinking ways.

Although Lipský's direction is rather functional, the film has plenty of ideas, many of them derived from animation. Smoke rings provide secret clues in a card game, dotted lines represent Joe's bullets and there are frozen shots as he appears on both ground and rooftop level. Extreme close-ups seem almost like a parody of Sergio Leone before they became familiar and there is a widescreen close-up of Joe's tonsils as he practises his yodelling. But there are also some affectionate genre references – Doug Badman balancing his feet on the hitching rail like Henry Fonda in *My Darling Clementine* (1946) and the bar girl Tornado Lou recalls Frenchy in *Destry Rides Again* (1939). The film is affectionate and witty in a way that outdoes any other European parodies.

Who Would Kill Jessie? again draws on popular culture – this time cartoons. Miloš Macourek's story tells of a scientist who invents a machine that can see and influence dreams. An unexpected side effect is their practical materialisation. The scientist's husband reads a comic strip in a scientific magazine and, when his wife injects him with the serum, the characters of a seductive blonde, a western gunman and a Superman figure enter the world of 1960s Prague. While the film is shot in the tradition of crazy comedy, its cartoon-based characters can only speak in 'speech bubbles' and are otherwise mute. The film contains some light debate on people's freedom to dream, how to deal with fantasies that have become reality and how to re-educate them – or, alternatively, incinerate them.

Lipský and Václav Vorlíček, who directed *Who Would Kill Jessie?*, continued to make films in this kind of genre during the 1970s and 1980s. Lipský worked again with Brdečka on *Nick Carter in Prague* aka *Adela Hasn't Had Supper Yet* (*Adéla ještě nevečeřela*, 1977), complete with a man-eating plant designed by Jan Švankmajer, while moving to a new collaboration with Smoljak and Svěrák and Vorlíček continued to direct scripts by Macourek with titles such as *Girl on a Broom* (*Dívka na koštěti*, 1971) and *What Do You Say to a*

Plate of Spinach? (*Což takhle dát si špenát?*, 1977). The equivalent to popular comedies in other countries, they are distinguished by their idiosyncratic and original plot ideas rather than their sense of cinema or aesthetic sophistication.

While comedy in the conventional sense is omnipresent in post-1989 Czech cinema and, in this more 'commercial' form, is no different from films produced elsewhere, one film with a specific 'Czech' resonance is Vladimír Morávek's *Bored in Brno* (2003). It was a film that not only crossed generations in terms of audience but also achieved an unusually unanimous critical response, going on to win five Czech Lions, including one for Best Film.

A debut film by the stage director Vladimír Morávek, he co-wrote it with the leading actor Jan Budař. It apparently grew out of conversations in a bar between them and producer Čestmír Kopecký about their first experiences with women. While this eternal theme, treated with a good deal of slapstick, no doubt kept audiences entertained, one suspects that its real resonance lies elsewhere – in its recognisable characters, links to daily life and social commentary. In this sense, it could also be compared to Miloš Forman's early films not least because, like them, it is filmed in black and white. Unlike the majority of Czech comedies (or, indeed, feature films), it is also set in the Moravian capital of Brno.

The film takes place over a single Saturday night and juxtaposes the quests of four separate couples, with its primary emphasis the relationship between Standa Pichlik (Budař) and Olinka Šimáková (Kateřina Holánová). Both suffer from minor mental disabilities and are, in conventional terms, 'simple-minded'. While the humour is sometimes at their expense, it is mainly they who have the last laugh and provide the film's sole example of a continuing and successful relationship. Standa merely wants to end his virginity but Olinka is set on a course for true love. The other couples comprise: Norbacher, an ageing actor and Vlasta, an uptight psychologist; a young couple with differing ideas about sexual technique; and two male friends whose discussions about women lead them to a final acceptance of their homosexuality.

In a perceptive review of the film, Jana Nahodilová points to the ways in which it signals its preoccupation with sex.[21] In the early part of the film, Norbacher appears in a TV sketch prefaced by the words 'Do you know how much sex there will be in Brno tonight?' In a sense, the film provides the answer. Nahodilová also suggests that it is a film in which women dominate. It is Olinka who takes the initiative when she invites Standa to stay with her. The psychologist, Vlasta, makes all the overtures to Norbacher while another forty-something, Jitka, targets Standa's brother, Jarda. The men in the film are variously shy, pathetic or self-obsessed.

An important element of the film's interwoven plotlines is their common location, a housing block, where everyone seems to share a world whose material and psychosocial limitations have not changed much since the time of

Forman's *Black Peter* and *Loves of a Blonde*. But, as Nahodilová suggests, the social cohesion that might once have existed is no more. The film also draws consciously on the notion of provincialism. As the second largest city in the Czech Republic, Brno is a provincial city with pretensions to sophistication. As Morávek puts it, everyone carries the sense of provinciality and a simultaneous desire to escape within them.[22]

The film has a number of similarities with another film produced by Kopecký, Petr Zelenka's *Buttoners* (*Knoflíkáři*, 1997). It focuses on separate stories with a tangential overlap, which together provide a portrait of life in the contemporary city. It even has a key dramatic incident – the death of Norbacher. Hit by a baker's van driven by the two young men at 4.02 in the morning, he has faced his failure – drunk, impotent and condemned to a life of provincial anonymity. The film gives a sense of having evolved from characters, observation and improvisation rather than any fundamental literary concept. It continues a tradition of social commentary and observation combined with the traditional Czech ingredients of slapstick and irony – more of that obstinate investigation of reality that Ivan Passer once said characterised the sixties.

At the time of writing, two comedies, *I Served the King of England*, scripted and directed by Menzel, and *Empties* (*Vratné lahve*, 2007), directed by Jan Svěrák, from a script by Zdeněk Svěrák, seem set to break all Czech box-office records. The first has already been discussed but it is worth considering *Empties* in conclusion. Curiously enough, despite Jan Svěrák's collaboration with his father on four previous projects, including the Oscar-nominated *The Elementary School* and the Oscar-winning *Kolya*, this was the first that could genuinely be categorised as a comedy.

The success of *Empties* is, on the surface, puzzling since it is a low-key work without any surprising or outrageous elements. Like *Kolya*, *Cosy Dens* (*Pelíšky*, 1997), and *Bored in Brno*, it is a film that appeals to all generations via its subject – in this case, the problems of a retired couple and their daughter. The second, less specific factor is that its mixture of laughter and tears is executed with considerable precision and balance.

The theme of the film is basically that of adjusting to retirement. Post-retirement-age schoolteacher Josef Tkaloun (Zdeněk Svěrák) finds that he can no longer make contact with his pupils and decides to resign. However, he is unable to settle for a life of idleness, initially taking a job as a cycle messenger and then as the man who looks after the bottle returns at the local supermarket. At the same time, his marriage has become an affair of habit and his wife feels excluded from his new-found activities. We also discover that he has been having an affair – although, due to a set of comic coincidences, his attempt to continue it in retirement proves abortive. Nonetheless, he retains his sexual fantasies about being a ticket inspector meeting willing young ladies in a railway carriage.

Zdeněk Svěrák, who originally began his life as a teacher, undoubtedly sympathises with the under-recognised and underpaid reality and builds his story from a sequence of small events and observations. Much is developed from Tkaloun's relationships with a variety of his customers in the supermarket and his work alongside his monosyllabic colleague, Mr Rezáč (Pavel Landovský), who attempted to murder his wife because of her infidelity, and for whom Josef arranges a new marriage. Other memorable characters include the old lady to whom he makes special deliveries and the young woman with a strange array of ticks on her naked midriff (it later transpires that they do not refer to lovers, as Josef and Rezáč speculate, but to pints of beer sold in her job as a waitress).

Many of the film's observations will register with older audiences – for instance, the assumption that someone is bidding Josef good morning when they are really speaking on their mobile phone or the fact that he has been hoarding books for his 'declining years' which, his wife tactlessly suggests, have now arrived. The film reaches its climax with a surprise for her birthday – a trip in a balloon that ends the film with a whole set of farcical elements and a final reconciliation (although the actual ending is a repetition of Josef's ticket inspector fantasy). It is the performance of Daniela Kolářová as the wife (she played the same role in Menzel's earlier *Seclusion Near a Forest*) that gives the film its tougher qualities. But, despite the problems in their relationship, they continue through their slightly uneasy mixture of 'laughter and tears'.

The Svěráks' slightly mundane but recognisably human story, together with the fact that Svěrák senior is something of a national institution, clearly registered with Czech audiences and has delighted foreign audiences as well. But, film marketing being what it is, it is unlikely to reach the same numbers as their earlier *Kolya*.

Of course, humour and comedy permeate many Czech films from Jan Němec's *The Party and the Guests* aka *Report on the Party and the Guests* (*O slavnosti a hostech*, 1966) to Jan Švankmajer's *Faust* aka *The Lesson of Faust* (*Lekce Faust*, 1994). What is significant about Hašek, Voskovec and Werich, Hrabal, Smoljak and Svěrák and their film equivalents is that they are 'seen' to be part of a tradition. Voskovec and Werich were loved because of their links to 'liberty and democracy' and Hrabal was hailed as a 'glorious incarnation of the Czech spirit' (Kundera). Even the American parodies have their own special qualities and one can genuinely speak of a kind of social cement in the face of adversity.

NOTES

1. František Daniel, 'The Czech Difference', in David Paul (ed.), *Politics, Art and Commitment in the East European Cinema* (London: Macmillan, 1983), p. 55.
2. Jiří Voskovec, quoted in Cecil Parrott, 'The Liberated Theatre: Voskovec and Werich', in Alan Ross (ed.), *The London Magazine 1961–1985* (London: Paladin/ Grafton, 1989), p. 250.

3. Josef Škvorecký, *All the Bright Young Men and Women: A Personal History of the Czech Cinema* (Toronto: Peter Martin Associates, 1971), pp. 23–4.
4. Václav Kofroň, *Hej-rup!/Heave Ho!*, in Peter Hames (ed.), *The Cinema of Central Europe* (London: Wallflower Press, 2004), p. 17.
5. Jiří Voskovec and Jan Werich, 'Interview s Voskovcem a Werichem', *Pressa*, 157, 30 July 1937, p. 3., quoted in Kofroň, p. 18.
6. Josef Škvorecký, *All the Bright Young Men and Women*, p. 22.
7. Antonín J. Liehm, *Closely Watched Films: The Czechoslovak Experience* (New York: International Arts and Sciences Press, 1974), p. 13.
8. Miloš Forman, quoted in Antonín J. Liehm, 'S Jiřím Voskovcem o čemkoli', *Listy*, 5 July, 1975, quoted in Danièle Montmarte, *Le Théâtre Libéré de Prague* (Paris: Institut d'études slaves, 1991), p. 100.
9. Vratislav Effenberger, quoted in Antonín J. Liehm, *The Miloš Forman Stories* (NewYork: International Arts and Sciences Press, 1975), p. 86.
10. Bohumil Hrabal, 'Introduction', in Jiří Menzel and Bohumil Hrabal, *Closely Observed Trains* (screenplay), translated by Josef Holzbecher (London: Lorrimer, 1971), p. 8.
11. Hrabal, quoted in Radko Pytlík, *The Sad King of Czech Literature: Bohumil Hrabal, his Life and Work*, translated by Katheleen Hayes (Prague: Emporius, 2000), p. 8.
12. Hrabal, op. cit.
13. Jan Uhde, Západ, 3, p. 27, discussed in Josef Škvorecký, *Jiří Menzel and the History of the Closely Watched Trains* (Boulder: East European Monographs; New York: Columbia University Press, 1989), p. 91.
14. Ibid., p. 86.
15. Milan Kundera, quoted in Jan Hořejší, 'Jiří Menzel', *Czechoslovak Life*, July 1968, pp. 12–13.
16. Bohumil Hrabal, *Obsluhoval jsem anglického krále*, Prague, 1993, p. 188, translated in Tim Beasley-Murray, 'The Avant-garde, Experience and Narration in Bohumil Hrabal's *Obsluhoval jsem anglického krále*', in David Short (ed.), *Bohumil Hrabal (1914–97): Papers from a Symposium* (London: School of Slavonic and East European Studies, University College London, 2004), p. 87.
17. Bohumil Hrabal, *I Served the King of England*, translated by Paul Wilson (London: Chatto and Windus, 1989), p. 239
18. James Wood, *The Irresponsible Self: On Laughter and the Novel* (London: Jonathan Cape, 2004), p. 149.
19. Beasley-Murray, pp. 85–6.
20. Škvorecký, *Jiří Menzel and the History of the Closely Watched Trains*, p. 9.
21. Jana Nahodilová, Bored in Brno (Nuda v Brně), in Peter Hames (ed.) *Czech Cinema*, special issue of *KinoKultura*, November 2006. http://www.kinokultura.com/specials/4/boredbrno.shtml [Accessed 16/11/06]
22. Vladimír Morávek, quoted in ibid.

3. REALISM

Of all the 'isms', the various manifestations of realism have been the most discussed and theorised. What is clear is that the terms realism, naturalism, critical
realism, Socialist Realism, Neo-realism and even surrealism have been applied
to situations in which that particular artistic movement has been regarded
as more 'real' or 'authentic' than others. Frequently, of course, the notion of
realism has been linked to portrayals of working-class life, an analysis of the
real nature of class relations, the economic relations of the present or visions
of an improved or idealised future. Particular forms of realism tend to develop
in response to particular forms of falsity. In this chapter, I shall primarily consider films that conform to the traditions of social realism or which attempt to
approximate the appearance of everyday life.

Realism in Czech cinema has primarily been seen as a 1960s' development
and was certainly a preoccupation of the New Wave in the early sixties. Its
relative rarity in the pre-war period can be seen in the response of Czech critics
to Voskovec and Werich's film *Heave-Ho!* (1934) as the first 'social' film. It
was not, of course. Many dramas and melodramas of the 1920s and 1930s
could be said to have dealt with social subjects. Přemysl Pražský's *Battalion*
(*Batalion*, 1927) is set against a background of a Prague pub whose regulars
include thieves, prostitutes and other unfortunates. Carl Junghans' *Such Is
Life* (*Takový je život*, 1929), which includes the subtitle 'the days of the poor
have no end', is an extremely powerful portrait of the life and death of a
poor washerwoman. Karel Anton's *Tonka of the Gallows* (*Tonka Šibenice*,
1930) is based on the true-life story of a Prague prostitute. Social injustice and

deprivation form the background to a number of films operating in popular genres.

Many of these films can be linked to left-wing tendencies in the German cinema of the early 1930s, a movement that began with Piel Jutzi's *Mother Krausen's Journey to Happiness* (*Mutter Krausens Fahrt ins Glück*, 1929), *Berlin – Alexanderplatz* (Jutzi, 1931) and *Kuhle Wampe* (Slatan Dudow, 1932) from the script by Bertolt Brecht and Ernst Ottwald. It is also useful to recall that Erwin Piscator's stage production of Jaroslav Hašek's classic Czech novel *The Good Soldier Švejk* (1928) formed part of this 'progressive' trend.

Carl Junghans' *Such is Life* began its life in Germany and production was only moved to Prague when he was unable to raise the money. It is a technically striking film and one of a number that looked forward to the principles of Italian Neo-realism. Featuring the Russian actress, Vera Baranovskaya, who appeared in Pudovkin's *Mother* (*Mat'*, 1926), its story is divided into six major parts corresponding to themes of work, pleasure, sadness, rest, bitterness and final days. She faces the problems of a drunken and unfaithful husband, who is sacked from his job, and a daughter made pregnant out of wedlock. Although the immediate cause of her death is an accident, her physical and mental exhaustion lies at the root. Besides Baranovskaya, the film stars the Czech actor Theodor Pištěk and the German actress Valeska Gert.

The film's most striking qualities are the use of location and its almost documentary feeling. Although the situation of the mother is difficult, she is initially upbeat and life is not experienced as unremitting gloom. The film's use of understatement provides a quiet force, with elements of humour and observation worthy of Miloš Forman. There are dramatic shots and an increased use of montage towards the end but its overall effect is low-key and leaves critical conclusions to the viewer. The titles given before the funeral nonetheless note that 'the days of the poor have no end'. Of course, unlike *Heave-Ho!* (released in 1934 and discussed in the chapter on comedy), *Such is Life* did not command an audience. Social criticism and the exposure of capitalist inequalities were no more popular with audiences and producers in the 1930s than they are now.

However, after the nationalisation of the film industry in 1945, left-wing film-makers began to take the cinema in new directions. Karel Steklý's *The Strike* (1947), adapted from Marie Majerová's popular 1935 novel set in the mines of Kladno, where poor working conditions lead to a strike and its suppression, won the Golden Lion award at the Venice Festival. Mira Liehm and Antonín Liehm note that it was a film that brought together a number of members of the pre-war avant-garde, including the producer and composer, E. F. Burian, whose music also won an award at Venice. It was 'a film that joined social pathos with avant-garde poetics and period color'.[1] It offered a classic Socialist Realist theme, one might argue, but this was before the imposition of official policies, and one of the main characters leaves for a better life in the USA. It did, however, serve as a prototype for similar films in the 1950s.

Many films did not require distortion to render them pro-socialist but the overall effect of the imposition of Socialist Realism following the Communist takeover in 1948 was to rule out any criticism of the present in favour of the class struggles of the past and resistance against the Nazis – the two were often associated and given similar priorities in the production plan. Accessibility also dictated the use of orthodox narratives and clearly established plot development. Films set in the present promoted falsely optimistic viewpoints, ignoring the persecution of both non-Communists and Communists during the 1950s.

It was the distortions of Socialist Realism that were to become one of the main targets of the film-makers of the 1960s. Some films challenged the status quo on thematic grounds (for example, the films of Ladislav Helge, which I discuss in the chapter on politics). However, the main impulse to put 'real life' on the screen was to come from New Wave directors like Jaromil Jireš, Věra Chytilová, Miloš Forman and Ivan Passer. Jireš, Chytilová and Forman made their first films in 1963 and effectively marked the beginning of the New Wave.

Jireš's *The Cry* (*Křik*, 1963), adapted from a story by Ludvík Aškenazy, tells of a television repairman whose wife is expecting their first child and whose calls bring him into contact with elements of contemporary society. His chance encounters introduce him to the threat of war, the promise of sexual infidelity, the cynicism of bureaucrats and the existence of racism. Yet, while there are many shots set in the street and even, possibly, the use of hidden camera, Jireš is more interested in making a poetic film. Already, there are the flashbacks, flashforwards and imaginary scenes that came to characterise his later work.

In her debut feature, *Something Different* (*O něčem jiném*, 1963), Chytilová followed the cinéma-vérité inclinations of her short film *A Bagful of Fleas* (*Pytel blech*, 1962). It follows the training of a real gymnast, Eva Bosáková, and ends with her success in the world championships. But, while there is a great deal of emphasis on the struggles that lie behind media success, the limitations of her existence and the rigidity of her training programme, Chytilová juxtaposes this story with a fictional account of a married woman who begins an affair. In one scene, Bosáková appears on the woman's television screen but the two stories are otherwise unrelated, juxtaposed for formal and critical reasons. While the power of the cinéma-vérité sequences is undeniable, Chytilová soon moved in the direction of the avant-garde with her succeeding films.

Forman began his work with *Talent Competition* (*Konkurs*, 1963), also a film of two stories but, this time, not planned as such. It began as an amateur project designed to record the Semafor Theatre of Jiří Šlitr and Jiří Suchý – in some respects, the spiritual successor to Voskovec's and Werich's Liberated Theatre. Started on 16mm, the film began as a record of teenage auditions which somehow managed to encapsulate the insecurity, cruelty, humour and beauty of youth all at the same time. Most notable here is a montage of different girls singing the same song, each image and face cut to different phrases (a sequence that Forman reconstructed for his first American film *Taking Off* in 1971). The second story, *If There Were No Music* (*Kdyby ty muzicky nebyly*), was designed simply to give the film an overall feature length. This time, he focuses on the annual brass band competition in the town of Kolín. Both films expand their cinéma-vérité approach to include simple story ingredients, giving birth to a combination that was to form the basis of later films. Also, many of the actors and non-actors who were to appear in Forman's feature films appeared here for the first time.

When talking of the cinéma-vérité influences on these early films, it is worth recalling that none of them conform to the rigorous definition of the term. Stephen Mamber notes that cinéma-vérité is the act of 'filming real people in uncontrolled situations . . . the film-maker does not function as a "director" nor, for that matter, as a screenwriter . . . no one is told what to say or how to act'.[2] On the other hand, Forman has recounted how he virtually 'salivated' at the sight of the faces of real people on the screen. Ultimately what the films do – and this is particularly true of the films of Forman and Passer – is to use elements of these techniques to give their scripted and directed films a sense of relevance and conviction. Equally, the characters and locations presented in films such as Forman's *Black Peter* (1963) and *Loves of a Blonde* (1965) were recognisably authentic and no one could say that about any other films purporting to deal with contemporary Czech life.

The style of Forman's Czech films was also a group style that owed much to his regular collaborators, Ivan Passer, Jaroslav Papoušek and cinematographer Miroslav Ondříček. Passer and Papoušek collaborated on all three of Forman's subsequent films and Papoušek contributed the original story for *Black Peter*. Ondříček worked on *Talent Competition*, *Loves of a Blonde*, *The Firemen's Ball* and on Passer's first feature *Intimate Lighting* (*Intimni osvětlení*, 1965). Papoušek also worked with Passer on *Intimate Lighting* before taking solo writer/director credit on his *The Best Age* (*Nejkrásnější věk*, 1968). Papoušek once said, 'Each of us was an equal among equals'.[3] But, despite formal similarities, there were also differences.

Both *Black Peter* and *Loves of a Blonde* share a background that could be described as working class. Petr, the hero of the first, works in a grocery store while Andula, the central character in *Loves of a Blonde*, works in a shoe factory. Neither has career prospects or wider ambitions and their only outlets lie in romance and in music. Neither conforms to the Socialist Realist stereotype with its positive attitudes, political motivation and utopian vision. The films also reflect the Italian Neo-realist view of seeking out the value in the 'everyday', those lives in which nothing extraordinary is ever likely to happen. While controversial, the films were approved by the more liberal wing of the

Communist Party as a new development in socialist art. *Loves of a Blonde* had a significant impact on the young English director, Ken Loach, who commented, 'It made a great impression on me when it first came out; its shrewd perceptiveness, irony, warmth. It allowed characters time to reveal themselves.'[4]

The films are not only reflections on contemporary life, they are also comedies, and this is why Forman believes he was allowed to get away with a lot – the social and political criticism was partially submerged. In *Black Peter*, the criticism is fairly general, touching on lack of motivation, petty thieving and sexism, portrayed through characters locked in a situation from which there appears to be no escape. In *Loves of a Blonde*, it is more extensive. One of the principal themes concerns the problems of young girls condemned to work in the provinces in order to meet the needs of the economic plan. This was a subject that had already been aired in Chytilová's *A Bagful of Fleas*. There is little concern for their social (or sexual) needs and the temporary import of a contingent of middle-aged reservists for a dance is presented as a major breakthrough in bureaucratic thinking. The film's sharp portrait of authority culminates in an address on morality by the female warden of their hostel. The scene functions as a brilliant exposure of hypocrisy, acquiescence and fake democracy.

While the films nominally focus on boy-meets-girl relationships, these are given a mundane and de-dramatised quality. Their authenticity and casual cruelty is much closer to life than the simplifications of either Hollywood or Socialist Realism. While it is often assumed that Forman exclusively used non-actors, he, in fact, uses actors as well. These included Vladimír Pucholt, who plays Petr's friend in *Black Peter*, and Míla, the object of Andula's affections in *Loves of a Blonde*, and Vladimír Menšík, who plays the lead army reservist in the same film. But Jan Vostrčil, who plays Petr's father, was a conductor of brass bands they found in Kolín while Míla's mother was found on a Prague tram. Significantly, it is these subsidiary characters who often become the main focus of the films. While clearly fascinated by the qualities that non-actors could bring to their parts, Forman also noted that they had to be selected with extreme care. In fact, while the films have the appearance of improvisation because of their somewhat relaxed concern with narrative structure, they were quite rigorously scripted. In order to 'capture those fleeting moments that will never come again',[5] he was concerned to provide maximum space for interaction and to keep the camera subservient to his characters.

Whether the style of Forman's and Passer's films derived from their experiences on *Talent Competition* or not, they certainly mark a shift away from conventional narrative. If compared with classic Neo-realist films such as the de Sica/Zavattini *Bicycle Thieves* (*Ladri di bicyclette*, 1948) and *Umberto D* (1952), it is apparent that they are very different. Both the Italian films emphasise social problems – the first of them unemployment and the second poverty in retirement. But, while they use non-actors, they also employ conventional script devices focusing on relationships between father and son in the first and the old man and his pet dog in the second. In the first, the father becomes a thief but repents and is accepted by his son; in the second, Umberto plans to commit suicide with his dog because he cannot afford to feed him but the relationship is re-established. Neither film solves the problems of injustice but their humanist values are confirmed. Despite taking us through a range of differing situations, the films also hold firmly to a straightforward linear narrative.

In *Black Peter* and *Loves of a Blonde*, none of the characters is wealthy but they all have jobs. They go through romances that have a brief intensity but mean little and move back to a world of routine work without much hope or interest. Here the narratives serve only to provide a progression to which audiences are accustomed while the real emphasis is on situations in which Forman can observe his non-actors, their faces and their interactions. He also constructs situations, particularly dances, where the films can take on a cinéma-vérité quality. As Forman once said, when writing a screenplay, he was not concerned so much in the logical development of a story but with

Figure 3.1   Miloš Forman: *Loves of a Blonde* (*Lásky jedné plavovlásky*, 1965)

what he found to be interesting – a sequence of 'interesting' moments. '[T]hey don't have the weight of a "classic", logical construction; but they do have the advantage of a certain nonsense with its own strict rules, depending on the behaviour of the characters who are involved.'[6]

In a recent study of *Loves of a Blonde*, Andrew Klevan introduces Stanley Cavell's concept of 'unknownness', a quality used to emphasise separateness and isolation. These are, indeed, qualities to be perceived in both films. Writing of Andula, Klevan notes:

> The feeling that she remains unknown arises from her facial blankness: her lack of expressive range has been caused by her face being caught, and then hardening, somewhere in limbo between expectancy and disappoint-ment. She has learned not to feel too deeply, floating instead between the possibilities of both.[7]

Hana Brejchová, who plays Andula, is the sister of Jana Brejchová, at that time Czech cinema's most popular female star and married to Forman. She was obviously not picked off the street like other characters and it can be assumed that she is giving a directed performance. But, while Forman's films may indeed convey 'separateness and isolation', this is arguably presented as a fact of life rather than a social problem, an antidote to the self-conscious control and artificiality of the entertainment film. While the glum and down-at-heel surroundings may, indeed, reflect life under 1960s Czechoslovak socialism, these realities can be found almost anywhere – one has only look at British equivalents such as Karel Reisz's *We Are the Lambeth Boys* (1959). The degree to which early Forman influenced early Ken Loach is a matter for conjecture – more than likely they were set on parallel paths in supposedly different societies that had more than a little in common. But what *is* notable is the fact that Loach admired Forman because of his respect for ordinary people. The boredom and dislocation identified by Klevan is also matched by a kind of stubborn individuality, a capacity to go on regardless, a fundamental resilience. While there is not much spontaneous laughter in the films, they are comedies and the Czech audience is provided with a mirror both for itself and its everyday bureaucracy.

Forman once described his main film influences as Chaplin and Walt Disney, noting that he was particularly attracted to Chaplin's mixture of laughter and tears. He often introduces comic elements or comic timing into scenes that are apparently serious and uses a number of key comic sequences that are struc-tured with a great deal of formal care.

In *Loves of a Blonde*, the key sequence is the dance hall scene where the group of army reservists are matched up against the young factory girls. The sense of the dance floor as an arena where male and female must meet is strong and soon becomes a throng of bodies to be traversed. Forman sets up a very formal arrangement between a trio of men and two trios of girls. The trio of reservists was made up of two of Forman's old school friends with the dominant part played by Vladimir Menšík. On the opposite side of the hall sit Andula and her two friends. Both Andula and Menšík sit in the centre of their respective groups. Close by them sit another trio of older woman, two of them 'plain' with an attractive one in the centre.

The men decide to send their 'chosen' girls a bottle of wine but the waiter delivers it to the wrong group. Menšík retrieves the situation and the waiter is dispatched to collect the bottle and deliver it to the right group. Much play is made of acknowledgments and looks across the dance floor, the waiter's half circuit to reach them and Menšík's quarter circuit to reach the waiter. As Klevan notes, '[B]y not settling into any consistent point of view, the film is arranged so that the characters are not in charge of the narrative movement.'[8] All the time, we have the sense of events casually observed and, indeed, much of the dance seems be a spontaneous affair that just happens to include a film crew.

Another important aspect of both films is their attention to the older generation, who have more strength of personality than the younger. In *Black Peter*, there is an emphasis on the character of Petr's father (Jan Vostrčil), who consistently subjects his son to well-meaning monologues about work, women and sex that are full of non sequiturs and contradictions. Forman said that he originally conceived the character as half old-style patriot and half Social Democrat – someone who really does not yet know how to explain the contradictions of life under the existing form of socialism. Yet Vostrčil's character is much less specific than this and, despite a sense of powerlessness and apathy, he can still escape to his brass bands at the weekend.

In *Loves of a Blonde*, one of the key scenes involves Míla's father and mother, who engage in an extended dispute after Andula turns up at their flat in search of Míla following their night of love in the provinces. Andula's arrival (initially she just leaves her case and departs again) provokes a sustained and neurotic diatribe by the mother. When Andula returns she becomes the subject of an inquisition by the mother, with the father constantly trying to take her part. As Forman remarked, the interaction between these two non-actors kept getting better and better and, in the final scene, when the returning Míla is taken into their bed for protection, the words were their own. They are people who have slaved all their lives for next to nothing but the father is likeable and positive and the mother is anything but downtrodden despite her endless complaints.

Passer's *Intimate Lighting* deals with a more 'middle-class' subject since his protagonists are musicians and the setting is a house in the country. However, such distinctions are, to some extent, artificial, especially in Czechoslovakia where the working class was often privileged over traditional middle-class professions. Formally, the film is constructed on much the same principles as Forman's films – this time using entirely non-actors (although Jan Vostrčil could now perhaps be termed something of a professional). The film gives the appearance of simply 'happening' in front of the camera, although Passer has pointed out that it was entirely scripted. Writing of his short film, *A Boring Afternoon* (*Fádní odpoledne*, 1964), adapted from Bohumil Hrabal's story, Jaroslav Boček described Passer's unique talent as being able to create a 'plurality of happening'. He describes a scene in which everything 'discharges in contacts, promptings, small sparks, in one word: in an atmosphere both lyrical, fragile and captivating'.[9]

Intimate Lighting was apparently suggested to Passer by scriptwriter Václav Šašek and Passer directed it as a favour. They were a little worried that the executive producer might find elements of the completed script politically unacceptable but instead he remarked that he found the whole thing totally boring and couldn't imagine how anyone could sit through it. Indeed, nothing much seems to happen. It describes the visit of Petr, a classical musician, to the country house of his friend, nicknamed Bambas, who is head of a provincial music school. During the weekend, they go to a village funeral where they provide the music. They practice a quartet, compare past and present and make a drunken attempt to 'escape' from the mundaneness of their lives but, by Sunday morning, the status quo has returned. In fact, from a conventional story point of view, nothing *does* happen. Passer simply observes the interaction of his characters during a day in the country.

In the opening scene, a conductor rehearses the local orchestra for a performance of Dvořák's cello concerto, in which Petr is to be the soloist. Bambas is seen from behind, sitting at a typewriter. He walks through to the rehearsal where they discuss ticket sales and tells them that Petr is arriving a day early. The camera pans across the room as they play the concerto, revealing that the orchestra consists mainly of old men. The camera ends on a boy and then the window, moving outside to continue along the side a railway car. We see the shadow outline of a cello case and two figures moving along the inside.

The absence of anything other than a generalised story content means that, as viewers, we watch the action, reflect on the characters, observe the age of the orchestra, notice the quality of the playing – in other words, there is space for the action and space for the observer. The film never deviates from this approach. When Petr and his girlfriend Štěpa arrive at Bambas's house, they first meet his children and then his wife and mother-in-law, who are preoccupied with preparing the meal and looking after the children.

The next day's mealtime is apparently unstructured but centres on the exchange of food. The meal degenerates into a minor dispute as portions of chicken are handed out. Štěpa offers her drumstick to one of the children as Grandad (Vostrčil) watches enviously. In quick succession, Bambas's wife transfers her food to Štěpa and Grandmother passes her food to the mother. When Grandad ends up with the drumstick (which he wanted) and the two children treat the leg as if it is a wishbone, Štěpa retreats to the kitchen in a fit of giggling. The scene does no more than observe a mundane situation that most have experienced, with the women engaging in a form of polite sacrifice.

The musical quartet gives rise to squabbles between Bambas and his father-in-law while Štěpa talks to Grandmother about her past and then parades in the garden outside and discovers some kittens. She holds one of the kittens up at the window as the four men rehearse. Of course, it is not just a meaningless combination of events. We discover that Grandad and Grandmother had met in a circus and eloped together and we watch the beautiful Štěpa with the young kittens against a rural background with the sound of Mozart. The juxtaposition of themes and images is both poetic and reflective.

The earlier funeral scene is more knowingly poetic with its reflections on life, death and sexual conquests (by Grandad). The beautiful Štěpa evokes erotic reverie as she walks behind the funeral procession; an old man and a female haymaker in a bikini are juxtaposed in a wheatfield; the three men talk of Smetana against a background of the Bohemian landscape; a sneeze echoes from the church; a congregation of old men come out to urinate against a wall. How much was made up and how much inspired by the situation it is difficult to tell.

The two heroes are disillusioned and middle age has doubtless given them a lesson in unpalatable political realities. At the same time, the grandparents had experienced a better world before the war and Štěpa is still hopeful. But the audience has to look very hard for this kind of message and it is the film's affection and humour that dominate. The photography (by Ondříček and Josef Střecha) also takes the film away from the drab interiors of *Black Peter* and *Loves of a Blonde* towards an overall mood of lyrical reconciliation. For Passer, the experience of the everyday can also be positive.

Miloš Forman's most famous and controversial Czech film, *The Firemen's Ball* (1967), discussed in the chapter on comedy, was shot in the provincial town of Vrchlabí and, despite the repertory company of 'actors' from his previous films, drew heavily from members of the local community. However, he has, by now, moved beyond the 'observation' of his earlier films to produce a more complex comic script in which everything is closely manipulated and pointed. It is something of a classic but is not based in the observation of the everyday in quite the same ways.

Jaroslav Papoušek, who had collaborated with both Forman and Passer, made his directing debut with *The Best Age*, and followed this with his series about the Homolka family (1969–72). The first has much in common with the work of Forman but, by this stage, the unfamiliar faces of the earlier films have begun to resemble a repertory company. Hana Brejchová (*Loves of a Blonde*), Josef

Šebánek, Milada Ježková and Josef Kolb (*Loves of a Blonde*, *The Firemen's Ball*), Věra Křesadlová (*Talent Competition*, *Intimate Lighting*), Ladislav Jakim (*Talent Competition*, *Black Peter*) and Jan Stöckl (*The Firemen's Ball*) are all on hand in *The Best Age*, while Šebánek was to play the eponymous Homolka. In addition to this more self-conscious 'presence', Papoušek's solo scripts are, like *The Firemen's Ball*, much more self-consciously structured and pointed than the earlier films.

In *The Best Age*, Papoušek, who had originally studied as a sculptor, draws on his experience of art school life in a film that opts for multiple character observation. Structured around the use of three different models in the sculpture studio, it focuses on which of them, the young, the middle-aged or the old, can contemplate the best life – which, in effect, enjoys the 'best age'. However, Papoušek does not require his characters to act and they are used for much the same qualities that they revealed in films such as *Loves of a Blonde*. In *Ecce Homo Homolka* (1969), however, the comedy and performances become much more overt, critical, and even vicious. A kind of desperate farce that examines the perpetual martyrdom of a family living in an overcrowded flat, it is also set against a background of prejudice, apathy and fear. In some ways, it can be seen as the last film of the Forman group, the end of a style which, for many foreigners, had come to characterise Czech cinema in the 1960s.

There was no real equivalent to this brand of low-key realism in the years of normalisation principally because, especially in the 1970s, reality was presented in a relentlessly sanitised and naive manner. It was not until the mid 1980s that official production programmes allowed a genuine focus on social issues such as crime, drugs and soccer hooliganism. Věra Chytilová's critical take on contemporary reality, *Prefab Story* (*Panelstory*, 1979), was not only premiered outside of Prague but effectively 'buried' by the authorities. In any case, her abrasive approach could hardly be described as being within the realist tradition.

Unsurprisingly, the reflection of reality again became the task of documentary. While this book focuses on feature films, it is worth mentioning here the documentaries of Helena Třeštíková who, from the 1970s, has concentrated on documenting the lives of ordinary people.

Třeštíková, who graduated in 1974, made her first post-FAMU documentary with *The Miracle* (*Zázrak*, 1975), a documentary following the pregnancy of a young woman from the first months until a few days after birth. Gradually, she was able to create a space in which she could work and developed an approach based on 'long term shooting' or 'time collecting', to use Zdena Škapová's terms, in which she constantly returns to the same subject over a period of years.[10]

In 1980, Třeštíková found six young couples and filmed them over the five years that followed their marriages. Largely by accident, her subjects reflected a cross section of society and the results were presented in six documentaries. In 1999, she returned to the subject, recording her couples for a further six years. Eventually, six feature-length documentaries appeared, combining both sets of material and providing a unique personal record of the years of normalisation and of adaptation to the new capitalism.

With *Marriage Stories (Manželské etudy*, 1987–2005), Škapová suggests that Třeštíková has come closer than any other director to the ideals of Cesare Zavattini – filming the life of the everyday, 'ordinary' person whose life is anything but ordinary.[11] In recording the social and psychological realities of the 1980s and the transitions of the 1990s, Třeštíková has produced a unique document that shows up the inevitable failures of the feature film. Yet this progressive and inconspicuous – even austere – approach to film is not the normal approach to film-making and reveals the emphases of a particular personality. Most recently, Třeštíková's *Marcela* (2007) and *René* (2008), developments from *Marriage Stories*, enjoyed international critical success as free-standing works for cinema.

In the post-Communist period, after nearly ten years experience of the new realities of capitalism and globalisation, the feature film again began to show interest in realism and social reality. The New Wave directors have many admirers among the younger post-Communist directors, including Saša Gedeon, Jan Hřebejk, Alice Nellis and Roman Vávra (the so-called 'Velvet Generation'), although most have used more explicit, elaborate and also conventional scripts than those of Forman and Passer.

Perhaps closest to their approach have been Alice Nellis's two films *Eeny Meeny (Ene bene*, 2000) and *Some Secrets (Výlet*, 2002), both of which focus on the micro-world of family relations with great sensitivity and insight. Like Forman and Passer, Nellis focuses on small groups of people against unassuming backgrounds. In both films, the main role is taken by Iva Janžurová playing a mother – in the first, opposite her daughter, Theodora Remundová (also a documentary director), and, in the second, with both her daughters, Theodora and Sabina. This already allows for a resonance and intimacy that extends outside of the film itself.

Eeny Meeny is set against a background of the national elections. Jana (Theodora Remundová) returns home to her small town in order to take her mother's place on the election committee. In the meantime, her mother, Helena (Janžurová), is taking care of her husband, Jan, who is recovering from a stroke, and trying to persuade him that he is fit enough to go and vote for her preferred candidate. However, the polling station is only occasionally troubled by visitors anxious to assert their democratic rights and the committee members have ample time to consider their real interests, which range from bungee jumping to poetry, and to listen to Mrs Laskoňová's speculations on the origins of the common cold virus.

The primary emphasis in *Eeny Meeny* is on the relationship between mother and daughter and their problems of communication. Helena's concern for Jana has a suffocating effect and their discussions remain superficial, with the mother unable to see beyond the obvious and the practical. In contrast, Jana enjoys a more open relationship with her father and it is only after his unexpected death that she and her mother begin to establish any real contact.

Significantly, Nellis comments that she was concerned to make a film focusing on her parents' generation, a generation who had lived their lives under Communism. She also notes that 'because their personal problems are so connected with the situation around them, that's why the film is also about politics'.[12] This balance between the personal and the political is relevant and interesting but hardly reassuring. Helena is active in a determined manner born of long-held conviction while Jan is apathetic and cynical. Not only has the new system failed to live up to expectations but the electorate, who once complained about their lack of freedoms, can now scarcely be bothered to vote.

The film observes a cross section of society but avoids being schematic or heavy-handed. Like Passer, Nellis touches lightly on her subjects with understanding and humour, a bitter-sweet approach that shares their fears, losses and hopes. While the film's low-key approach has prompted the comment that the film might have worked just as well as a radio or TV play, it is notable that Nellis and her cinematographer, the Lithuanian-born Ramunas Greicius, spent three months preparing the film's colour scheme and visual style.

Some Secrets is very much a sequel to *Eeny Meeny* and is again concerned with the minutiae of family relationships. Following the death of her husband, who was Slovak, Milada (Janžurová) decides to fulfil his supposed dying wish to have his ashes buried in a graveyard in Slovakia. Accompanied by her mother-in-law, two grown-up daughters, a son-in-law and a grandchild, they embark in two cars on a family journey through the Czech Republic.

Like *Eeny Meeny*, the film focuses on mother–daughter relations. Each member of the family has secrets, ranging from the dramatic to the trivial, with the world perceived through the unexplained assumptions of four generations. The world of the family trip, with its arguments, detours, ice creams and carefully nurtured supply of toilet paper, is beautifully observed and is certainly not exclusively Czech. During the course of the film, the characters reach the same kinds of reconciliation as Jana and her mother in *Eeny Meeny*. Zuzana, who is having an affair, reaches an understanding with her husband, the pregnant Ilona, who feels fat and unloved, learns to feel positive about her forthcoming child, and the daughters come to understand their mother better.

This journey into the heart of the family is matched by the film's physical journey. While this is a classical device, it is also a journey from the Czech Republic to Slovakia, through countries that were once one. Like *Eeny Meeny*, this gives the film a political context, although it again receives a gentle and ironic treatment, with personal relations ultimately the more important. Both films are noticeable for the diminished role of the father, who dies in the first film and is already dead in the second. This allows their emphasis on mother–daughter roles. Ultimately, both films provide an analysis of family relations and misunderstandings, frequently banal but also significant. And, although there is reconciliation through discussion, it is clear that this can only be a stage. Nellis's two studies of communication reveal that good intentions cannot work without understanding. Iva Janžurová, in particular, gives an outstanding performance in both films, each of which is based on a close perception of the everyday.

Other directors to bring a critical focus to contemporary life have been: Bohdan Sláma with *Wild Bees* (*Divoké včely*, 2001) and *Something Like Happiness* (*Štěstí*, 2005); Marek Najbrt with *Champions* (*Mistři*, 2004); and, surprisingly, Martin Šulík with *City of the Sun or Working Class Heroes* (*Sluneční stat aneb hrdinové dělnické třídy*, 2005). All three have set their films away from Prague, examining life in the industrial town of Ostrava (in Šulík's case) or in smaller towns or villages. Sláma's films, like Nellis's, have attracted a degree of international attention, winning awards in both Rotterdam and San Sebastian.

Wild Bees, with its examination of life in a Moravian village, signalled a new direction in post-Communist feature films. The location itself, a run-down village apparently without hope, is unusual, as is Sláma's approach to narrative. His many-faceted portrait, although not without use of comic stereotypes, has the stamp of authenticity, while the multiple characters provide a variety of points of identification, allowing the film's low-key boy-meets-girl story to evolve almost by accident.

Eighteen-year-old Kája, a dreamer, seems to lack any ambition or dynamism and lives with his grandmother and a disillusioned and philosophising father. His brother, Petr, who has left home and dropped out of university, returns home for a visit. Both sons are a disappointment to their father in that they lack any interest in 'the inner meaning of existence'. When Petr tells Kája that he should leave the village or he will go mad, his father notes that, in his case, it led to no marked success. To the grandmother's comment that the father didn't graduate either, he replies that he was fighting Communism.

Božka, who serves in the village shop, has a kind of relationship with Láďa, who is practising for his Michael Jackson impression at the village dance. But she gradually and imperceptibly moves towards Kája and ends up sleeping with him after the dance. However, the film's emphasis is less on narrative and more on the characters and their environment – Božka's shack of a shop, her mother's apartment (where she entertains male visitors for money while Božka's younger brother does his homework), Kája's repetitive and sterile world, the apparently dynamic but actually naïve and vulnerable Láďa and the Roma apartment beneath Božka's.

In the main, we see unhappy and unsuccessful people without any 'rosy' qualities, left behind in the mainstream world's pursuit of affluence. However, the end of the film, when Kája sleeps with Božka and Petr with Jana, provides something of an upbeat note. The next morning, the two brothers leave while Božka rides Láďa's bike with him on the pillion. Božka and Jana share an exchange about the previous night with a friend who shouts out that last night she had 'celebrated sadness'. But, for once, Božka is not glum. Perhaps, after all, small pleasures can be found amongst the poverty, in a world far removed from the glamour of the media (in a significant early scene, Božka had thrown a stone at the village loudspeaker, which had been spouting music and advertising).

Sláma insists that the theme (or themes) of his second feature, *Something Like Happiness*, found *him*, rather than being something he 'chose'. Yet again, the overwhelming reality of theme and context is that of a world of unsuccessful and ordinary people who have derived little or no benefit from the new economic realities. Nobody, it seems, is fundamentally happy, no one enjoys success, but they are still hoping for 'happiness'.

The film is set in the north Bohemian town of Most, where the natural world has clearly been marked by the effects of acid rain. Sláma examines the intertwining lives of three families. Monika lives with her parents in an apartment block, has a Czech boyfriend in the US and plans to emigrate. Toník lives in relative poverty with his aunt on a run-down farm. Dáša also lives on the block together with her two small children.

Monika works in a supermarket, her father is out of work and her mother works shifts. While no one utters any laments for the past, there appears to be precious little personal or economic satisfaction in the present. Yet Monika and Toník, former childhood friends, are decent people and, when Dáša suffers a breakdown and is confined to a psychiatric ward, they look after her children. Sláma's script and direction provide a deeply felt insight into his characters and hold up a sharp mirror to a society where, as Jiří, Monika's US-based boyfriend puts it, he could never live again, where people have a special talent for ruining their lives.

Mr Souček, who is out of work, seems much the most balanced of the characters but is condemned by his wife as a failure. She wants the best for her daughter, Monika, doesn't want her to waste her time on another loser like Toník and is all for her leaving to marry Jiří, who has a job in the USA. Toník's parents are also fundamentally decent people, although worried by his lack of prospects. The father works in a factory and is committed to the conventional world of regular hours and work which, while it provides him with a certain stability, is hardly fulfilling. Toník lives with his aunt on the family farm, with its leaking roof, trying to survive by keeping goats and selling potatoes. But their attempt to scrape a living seems to be quixotic in the face of prevailing realities and 'the factory', after all, is willing to buy the land off them.

Dáša, a single mother with two children, is unable to cope and lives on the verge of collapse and insanity. Her affair with Jára seems to give her sexual satisfaction but her insecurity is palpable and it seems that she will be unlikely ever to fulfil her role as a mother or find a supportive partner. Jára, the one economic success, is cheating on his wife and, while 'human' like the other characters, is certainly the most selfish and least likeable.

The film's narrative focus is on the developing relationship between Monika and Toník. They come together in order to care for Dáša's children and the scenes between them and the children are remarkably affecting. After Monika is committed for treatment, Jára wants to move into her flat (since he pays for it) with his new girlfriend so Monika and Toník move the children to the farm, where they begin to reconstruct the house. Briefly, a positive (even idyllic) life begins but it is soon doomed to collapse. Dáša reclaims her children, Toník's aunt dies and Monika leaves to visit Jiří in the USA. Toník is left with nothing – alone in a half completed bathroom. At the end of the film, Monika returns to the farm in time to witness it being bulldozed and discovers that Toník has disappeared. Here, the film ends but there is the sense that she may find him. As in *Wild Bees*, there is no resolution to the characters' lives. We do not know what will happen to them in the future but there is at least hope based on their continued searching.

Something Like Happiness has a more direct narrative than *Wild Bees* and less humour. On the other hand, its characters are arguably more likeable. Despite its depressive opening, with characters sunk in despair in a café (to a melancholy Roma song), the film has its moments of lyricism – particularly the final scene where children play and a dog runs alongside Monika's departing train. But it is frequently an ironic lyricism – snow that momentarily transforms a stunted industrial landscape, a boat trip on a pond and the discovery of birds' eggs on the trunk of a dead tree. The film gains a great deal from its acting and Sláma emphasises that the project was one to which the whole cast were committed. Tatiana Vilhelmová (Monika), Anna Geislerová (Dáša) and Pavel Liška (Toník) all give remarkable performances.

Marek Najbrt's *Champions* has something of the flavour of *Wild Bees* but it is a much more bitter and acerbic work, providing a sharp look at contemporary society through an examination of life in a run-down town in the former Sudetenland. The central focus of the film's characters mirrors the national obsession with ice hockey. The celebrated defeat of the Soviet Union in the 1969 world championships the year after the suppression of the Prague Spring has entered the realm of myth. Here, however, there are no heroes. A representative bunch of misfits gathers in a pub to watch the contemporary championships on television: Karel, the owner of the failing pub; the bigoted invalid, Jarda; the neurotic Pavel; Josef, who hopes his father wasn't a Roma; and Milan, the bus driver who constitutes the only link with the outside world.

Bohouš, an alcoholic, believes he can foresee the outcome of future play-offs. Najbrt's bleak portrait of a world of alcoholism, debt, bigotry, racism and infidelity trails far behind dreams of national glory and bears little resemblance to the fantasies of the new consumerism. A clever and multilevel film, it provides a strong antidote to the reconciliatory charms of conventional Czech comedy.

Champions is sharply observed and precisely directed and edited. However, its main deviation from what might be termed 'theatrical realism' (in the group scenes inside the pub) lies in Bohouš's alcohol- and substance-fuelled premonitions of the results of the matches combined with his visions of 'real' ice hockey players. Although this gives the film a stylistic distinction and helps to frame and present its critical observations, it does sometimes seem as if it is from another film.

The decrepit village and its penniless occupants and visitors live in a world of hopeless illusion and aspiration. They behave as if they were part of the crowd at the ice hockey match, join in the chant of 'When Czechs are near, the world shakes in fear' and observe that ice hockey players achieve more than all the politicians put together. But the poverty, the racism, the infidelities, the broken relationships, the lack of hope, the despair and the cynicism go hand in hand with this national pride.

The Czechs win the championships but Karel has lost his wife, Jarda has lost his son, the bus driver has ceased to be a lodger and the bus will soon stop calling at the village. Karel will soon lose the pub, Pavel is divorced and living on pills and only Josef 'the gypsy' obsessed with proving his Czech identity remains. The German, Ziege, who still lives in his old house (which was given to Pavel after the war) has, we assume, blown himself up with a wartime grenade.

The treatment of racial prejudice is interesting. Pavel's hatred of Ziege (and Germans) goes well beyond everyday prejudice but his friends try to ignore his attitude and pass it off. At the same time, while they constantly 'reassure' Josef that he is not a gypsy, the prejudice and jokes consistently resurface. On one level, it is an absurd and black comedy but with few laughs. Gypsies and coloured people (suspected gypsies) and Germans have no place in the greater Czech nation. As Pavel says to Ziege, speak Czech in the Czech Republic and German in Germany (so much for the two million plus Germans expelled from Czechoslovakia in 1946).

While these films are, perhaps, closest to the realist tradition in terms of observation (Nellis) and social criticism (Sláma and Nabrt), it would be wrong to suggest that other films are uncritical. Other films focus on the problems of the middle classes in a more stylised manner, as in Petr Václav's *Parallel Worlds* (*Paralelní světy*, 2001). Václav also directed the most powerful account of Roma life in his *Marian* (1996), a subject also taken up very effectively in Zdeněk Tyc's more commercial *Brats* (*Smradi*, 2002). Other films of social criticism have followed, including Benjamin Tuček's *Girlie* (*Děvčátko*, 2002) and Karin Babinská's *Dolls* (*Pusinky*, 2007). Directors such as Jan Hřebejk have provided critical films within a more commercial format – *Up and Down* (*Horem pádem*, 2004) – or, like Zelenka and Gedeon, within the framework of a more auteurist cinema.

However, I would like to end this chapter with a discussion of Martin Šulík's *City of the Sun or Working Class Heroes*. The film is polemical in two obvious ways – firstly in the use of its subtitle and, secondly, in presenting itself as a 'Czechoslovak' film. In fact, it began as a Slovak project scripted by Marek Leščák, who had previously worked with Šulík on *The Garden* (*Záhrada*, 1995) and *Orbis Pictus* (1997), and became a joint project for the usual financial reasons. It was the first Czech or Slovak feature film to really address the problems of unemployment resulting from economic restructuring. Šulík, who has remarked on his admiration for Ken Loach, has here moved to a quite different subject from his earlier work, which falls more within the art or folk-inspired traditions of Slovak cinema.

Set in the once-rich industrial town of Ostrava, on the Czech–Slovak border, the film examines the aftermath of an industrial closure when an unspecified company is sold to the Italians. The workforce is laid off and the film opens with a violent confrontation between workers and management. It says much for the negative heritage of Socialist Realism that it took fifteen years for a feature film to readdress such issues.

The screenplay is very direct, opting for an immediate focus on four of the men who have lost their jobs, their attempts to find alternative work and the effects on their personal lives. Initially, they club together to buy a van and set themselves up in the removal business but their attempts are doomed to failure. They transport sheep unsuccessfully, strip the contents of an abandoned church and end up in a fight, and make their first real money as bailiffs' assistants repossessing the belongings of one of their colleagues. Eventually, disaster strikes when their lorry is stolen and they are unable to trace it.

The four men have differing personal lives. Milan is divorced and is trying to raise his son, Bandy, on his own. His wife has visiting rights and Bandy also stays with her but he is failing at school and taking to drink. Milan makes the pertinent observation to Bandy that, these days, dropouts 'don't even get a decent burial'. Lack of a regular income means that Milan is unable to care for him properly. In the meantime, his wife makes a living by answering a telephone sex line. When Bandy is found drunk at night in the city, Milan finally decides to leave for Slovakia (despite being Czech) in search of a changed environment.

Perhaps the most extreme and dramatic story involves Tomáš, who is emotional, violent and loyal. At the beginning of the film he is seen struggling with the police and management, where he confronts his wife's brother, who is part of management. Tomáš is unable to adjust to this betrayal or to his brother-in-law's offer of preferential treatment. When his wife, unsurprisingly, gets work at a local restaurant, he is unable to accept that she will have to give up her role of looking after the children. He is the one who is most upset by their role as bailiffs' assistants and it is he who has the lorry stolen from him. An absurd chase after the lorry results in the thief escaping and Tomáš being arrested. When his wife accuses him of being a 'loser', he attempts suicide, his wife leaves and he loses his children. When he is released from mental hospital, he is again rejected.

The unmarried Vinco has had multiple relationships but is unable to settle down with anyone. Eva, a former girlfriend who works in a bar, asks him to come and help her break with her present partner. A passionate affair begins between them that looks as if it may develop into a permanent relationship. In a rather predictable encounter, Tomáš's wife visits him and entices him into bed, where Eva discovers them. When Tomáš finally finds out, there is a fight between him and Vinco.

The most stable relationship is that of the good-humoured Karel, who looks after his three daughters when is wife is injured in a road accident. Despite his misfortunes, he still clowns around and reduces his children to laughter. He is also the author of the immortal line (to his wife) that 'quality sex is a poor man's only joy'. They are from Slovakia, came to Ostrava in search of work and now fear that they will be stuck there forever. His daughter's attendance at her first Holy Communion provides a positive and lyrical interlude and is attended by all of his friends.

All is not negative on the work front as the new employers begin to take on labour, although requalification is required. Towards the end of the film, there is a scene in which some of them test each other on their progress in learning English. At the end, Vinco and Karel, who are helping Milan and Bandy on their journey to Slovakia, meet up with Tomáš, who is planting out flowers in a public park. They join together in bouncing on a trampoline in a defiant and utopian assertion of their friendship.

Although *City of the Sun* can be characterised as a realist film, the performances of all four actors are decidedly charismatic. They are all decent men who feel deeply the assault on their work and dignity. The film is also a compelling portrait of masculinity as full of bravado and occasional violence but also deep emotion and vulnerability. Alongside this is a more subdued but ever practical and adaptable female response to life's changes.

Apart from the alternation and integration of the four stories and the balancing of mood, Šulík also intercuts almost still shots of Ostrava and idle factories in a regular montage of the town they inhabit, complemented by an original and highly effective score by the leading Slovak composer, Vladimír Godár. Although the film was awarded the prize for best 'Czech' film at the Finále

Festival of Czech Film in Plzeň, it was not a great commercial success. But then, like Loach's films in the United Kingdom, the everyday subject does not allow for audience escapism and, like Loach's films, it was probably under-promoted. Perhaps it was also seen as a primarily Slovak project. But, beyond this, it is a film that is intensely relevant and human.

The subject matter for films rooted in social realism is, of course, ever present and, in this respect, the return of Czech and Slovak cinema to such subjects is not unique. Stylistically, though, it is interesting to note the influence of British 'kitchen sink' realism on Czech cinema in the 1960s, Forman's influence on Loach and other international directors and Loach's influence on Šulík. It is a reminder that the world of aesthetic exchange is frequently much wider than commonly assumed by audiences and critics. In terms of stylistic continuity, the links between past and present are somewhat less, with the low-key tradition of the 1960s best reflected in the films of Alice Nellis. But such continuities are rarely overt and are much more linked to cultural and social experiences that have been essentially internalised.

NOTES

1. Mira Liehm and Antonín J. Liehm, *The Most Important Art: East European Film After 1945* (Berkeley: University of California Press, 1977), p. 99.
2. Stephen Mamber, *Cinéma Vérité in America: Studies in Uncontrolled Documentary* (Cambridge, MA: The MIT Press, 1974), p. 2.
3. Jaroslav Papoušek, quoted in Josef Škvorecký, *All the Bright Young Men and Women: A Personal History of the Czech Cinema*, trans. Michal Schonberg (Toronto: Peter Martin Associates, 1971), p. 93.
4. Ken Loach, National Film Theatre Programme Note, quoted on the video cover of *A Blonde in Love* (London: Connoisseur Video, 1993).
5. Miloš Forman, in Antonín J. Liehm, *The Miloš Forman Stories* (New York: International Arts and Sciences Press, 1975), p. 138.
6. Ibid., 108–9.
7. Andrew Klevan, *Disclosure of the Everyday: Undramatic Achievement in Narrative Film* (Trowbridge: Flicks Books, 2000), p. 103.
8. Ibid., p. 112.
9. Jaroslav Boček, *Looking Back on the New Wave* (Prague: Československý Filmexport, 1967), p. 27.
10. See Zdena Škapová, *Marriage Stories (Manželské etudy, 1987–2005)*, in Peter Hames (ed.), *Czech Cinema*, special issue of *KinoKultura*, November 2006. http://www.kinokultura.com/specials/4/marriagestories.shtml [Accessed 16/11/ 2006]
11. Ibid.
12. Mark Preskett, 'A Little Bit of Money and a Lot of Love: Alice Nellis's *Ene Bene*', *Central Europe Review*, Vol. 3, No 21, 2001. http://www.ce-review.org/01/21/kinoeye21_preskett.html [Accessed 15/05/2007]

4. POLITICS

All films are political, it has been said, but some more political than others. There is some truth in such a bland assertion. After all, those films that avoid political issues, ignore everyday reality or provide simplistic solutions to social problems have political consequences almost by definition. Most commercial films come into this category since their prime objective is to please audiences and producers most of whom are not interested in confronting or changing reality. However, it can also be argued that most films produced in the eastern bloc under the banner of Socialist Realism, in its pure form, come into the same category. Their purposes were propaganda, the reality and the characters presented were artificial, the solutions preordained and any deviation from approved opinion was considered subversive.

In the 1970s, most exponents of film studies were Left-inclined and often viewed political film solely in terms of the modernist tradition of Eisenstein and Vertov and the political theatre of Bertolt Brecht. Political film, almost without exception, was perceived as exposing the realities of imperialism or the contradictions of capitalism. Radical ideas, it was thought, could only be presented in a radical form. Thus the work of Godard and the Dziga Vertov group and Latin American Third Cinema was approved of and the political films of Costa-Gavras were held to be questionable (mainly because of their conventional narrative form). While First Cinema (Western commercial cinemas) and Third Cinema (the 'underdeveloped' world) were the focus of study, Second Cinema (the 'socialist' bloc) was ignored. East and Central European political cinema in general, and Czech and Slovak cinema in particular, was not held to be of interest.

There were a number of reasons for this. First of all, its political attacks were not on capitalism but on 'actually existing socialism' and arguably harboured illusions about the virtues of western democracy. Second, they were not 'underground' films produced on behalf of the working class or in 'resistance' to the system but films paid for by the government. (Here, it must be remembered that the production of any films *outside* of the system was a virtual impossibility.) The worst sin of all was that many of them were perceived to be 'art' films produced by an intellectual elite, engaging in self indulgent expression and designed for consumption by similar elites. Finally, of course, the aberrations of East European socialism were something that radicals preferred to ignore – they provided evidence of a less than ideal practice. In fact, one of the surprising consequences of the collapse of the Soviet Empire during the late 1980s and the early 1990s has been the decline of Left politics as such – as if there was some form of subterranean psychological link between the two.

Particularly in view of the above, it is worth considering the very different attitude to politics that was taken in Czechoslovakia in the 1960s. In a Czech context, the plays of Beckett, Ionesco and, above all, Václav Havel had a political resonance that was missing for Western audiences. The Czech theatre critic Zdeněk Hořínek puts it well:

> In the 1960s, politics meant something different than it does to an English readership today. In the 1960s, Havel wasn't writing about politics exclusively, he was criticizing the whole society in general. After all, at that time, a man had to live in a society with which he did not agree. So everything in the 1960s had a political context and meaning, intentionally or unintentionally. And the view that everything was political worked both ways – not only from the authorities' point of view, but also from the audience's. In the 1960s, everything was interpreted politically.[1]

Milan Kundera observed that, in a world that was suffocating under art that was 'educational, moral, or political', the impact of a writer like Ionesco was explosive. His plays fascinated because of their anti-ideological stance. 'They returned autonomy to art and beckoned it to take again the path of freedom and creativity.'[2] In other words, 'autonomous' art itself took on a political function since it represented a dissent from official policy. Here one can easily see how films such as *The Party and the Guests*, *The Firemen's Ball* or *Daisies* (*Sedmikrásky*, 1966) were seen to have an immediately political meaning that might be invisible to foreign audiences. However, it would be untrue to say that there were not more overtly political films and some of these even dated back to the 1950s.

There are obvious parallels between the problems of making political films under the commercial system and under a nationalised system where production content is controlled. Criticism could be slipped into commercial or, in the case of Czechoslovakia, officially approved genres provided it did not derail the overall thrust. Similarly, subjects once deemed unacceptable or dangerously radical can be confronted 'after the event', when history and governments have moved on. For instance, the British film of Walter Greenwood's novel about the depression, *Love on the Dole* (John Baxter, 1941) was filmed in the 1940s when the government had determined the importance of national unity in the face of the Nazi threat. Similarly, in 1968 in Czechoslovakia, Jasný's *All My Good Countrymen* (*Všichni dobří rodáci*), Jireš's *The Joke* (*Žert*, 1968) and Menzel's *Skylarks on a String* were produced when the Prague Spring sanctioned a critical perspective on the political excesses of Stalinism in the 1950s.

The politically significant films that appeared in Czechoslovakia immediately after the war were not all intended as simplified propaganda. Films such as *The Strike* (1947), which won the main prize at Venice, Jiří Weiss's *The Stolen Frontier* (*Uloupená hranice*, 1947) and Otakar Vávra's adaptation of Karel Čapek's *Krakatit* (1948) were by no means negligible works. Also, even if one dates the imposition of Socialist Realism from the Communist accession to power in 1948, it can be argued that cracks in the system were already beginning to appear by the late 1950s (even the mid 1950s if Václav Krška's adaptations of Fráňa Šrámek are considered). This, at a time when many believed in the system, can be linked to genuinely changing views on the role and evolution of socialism that many saw as culminating in the Prague Spring. However, the period 1970–89 was much less susceptible to the emergence of any critical voice following the extensive purges of the Party. Of course, it is critically unfashionable to study either of these periods partly because they were aesthetically orthodox and partly because searching between the lines for relatively minor examples of political dissent is not especially rewarding.

Not surprisingly, the first criticisms of the system came from within the ranks. When Ladislav Helge, a committed Communist, began to make critical films from the mid 1950s on, he was determined to avoid the falsifications of propaganda. Virtually unknown in the West, his films were fairly conventional in form although often powerfully dramatic. His first two features, both written by the novelist Ivan Kříž, were *School for Fathers* (*Škola otců*, 1957) and *Great Seclusion* (*Velká samota*, 1959). Regarded pretty much as a breakthrough, *School for Fathers* tells the story of a teacher, Jindřich Pelikán (Karel Höger), from the Moravian capital of Brno, who takes up a position in the border village of Milonice. Committed to real education, he finds that the local school's shortcomings are covered up by platitudes about 'class consciousness' and other ideological slogans. His predecessor confesses that the children are not very bright and neither are their parents and advises him to give good grades and settle for a quiet life. Pelikán retorts that the children should not start out their lives with lessons in dishonesty.

The headmaster, who is primarily concerned with his own position and the school's reputation and owes his position to his 'connections', is only too willing to listen to the complaints of the parents' committee and suggest that Pelikán be transferred. Malicious rumours soon circulate that Pelikán has been sent to the village as a punishment (presumably for political misdeeds) and that he is having an affair with a fellow teacher. An anonymous letter is sent to his wife who has remained in Brno.

When one of the pupils is denounced as a 'reactionary', Pelikán befriends him and attempts to integrate him with the rest of the school community. The sins of the fathers (significantly, we learn nothing about the boy's absent father), he argues, should not be visited on the children. Similarly, he announces to the local Party chairman that his son's failings at school are due to a privileged lifestyle and parental neglect.

Pelikán's example of integrity attracts the grudging admiration of his colleagues, the love of his pupils and the eventual support of the parents. But their conversion comes too late. Pelikán, disillusioned, returns to Brno, leaving behind the woman colleague who has fallen in love with him and a community that now has to resolve its own problems.

Of course, we are not looking here at the failure of socialism or of the Party but of individuals. It is notable that the chairman, in his wisdom, accepts Pelikán's criticism and supports his views at the parents' meeting, turning the discussion in his favour. But the film nonetheless questions simplified slogans and dogma and provides a critical account of an everyday reality. Filmed in a classical form – Helge was never an exponent of the auteur style – it is an understated, sensitive and attractive film that definitely marked out new directions.

Great Seclusion, released two years later, tells the story of the director of a village co-operative who is a hard worker and a sincere Communist. When he returns to his home village he finds himself facing a situation in which everything is in decline as a result of idleness, drink and theft. He confronts the problems with a zeal that alienates him from both his girlfriend and the villagers. At the end of the film, he takes to drink and denounces the concept of the 'new man' for which he has worked so hard. After it was viewed by a special committee, Helge changed the ending to substitute another in which the villagers come to him in sympathy, turning it into a mockery of what he had intended. Kříž's novel with the same title was published the following year and was viewed as a development within the schema of the Socialist Realist novel – the emphasis was to be shifted to the human participants and their relationships.

Of course, there was nothing inherently subversive about these films. If cinema was to encourage the building of socialism, it does not seem unreasonable to suppose that there should be criticism of existing practice. If the objectives were adhered to, then the criticism could be argued to place its emphasis on human fallibility. However, the films' downbeat endings, in particular the original 'black' ending of *Great Seclusion*, while they ensure a moral message, fight shy of any purely mechanical resolution.

In *Shame* (*Stud*, 1967), Helge extended the theme of *Great Seclusion* with greater sophistication. It focuses on the situation of a local party secretary, Arnošt Pánek (played by Július Pántik who also played the hero of *Great Seclusion*). Again, corruption is endemic and again he ends up drunk and alone in the village square. But the film now touches on wider issues – the conflict between 'old' and 'new' Communists, the morality of denunciation and the nature of democracy. These were films that genuinely marked the movement of criticism from the inside.

Another Communist who cut his teeth on the Socialist Realist novel was Jan Procházka. His *Green Horizons* (*Zelené obzory*, 1960), which was filmed by Ivo Novák in 1962, was also an attempt to extend the range of Socialist Realism. He was also a prolific writer of screenplays and the head of one of the production groups at the Barrandov Studios. Procházka, who came from a farming background and spent his early years as an activist in the Communist youth organisation, seems to have got away with a substantially more critical approach than most with the result that many of his films, particularly the twelve titles that he made with the director Karel Kachyňa in the 1960s, were frequently dismissed as officially approved criticism.

Green Horizons, which was hailed by the literary critic Václav Černý as one of the few successful Socialist Realist novels, told the story of a young man who runs a depressed collective farm and experiences an unsuccessful love life. His first films with Kachyňa initially attempted broad humanist subjects but became progressively more critical. With *Long Live the Republic* (*At' žije republika*, 1965), *Coach to Vienna* (*Kočár do Vídně*, 1966) and *Night of the Bride* (*Noc nevěsty*, 1967), they treated three officially approved subjects – the liberation of the republic in 1945, the partisan war against the Germans and the collectivisation of agriculture – but in a highly unconventional manner.

Both Procházka and Kachyňa came from Moravia and there seem to be strong autobiographical elements in many of the films they made together in the 1960s. In an essay on Kachyňa, Boris Jachnin pointed out that he preferred to work with someone else's script but frequently changed it radically in order to turn words into images.[3] Procházka provided him with themes of strength and substance and, together with composer Jan Novák, a fellow Moravian and pupil of Bohuslav Martinů, and cinematographers such as Josef Vaniš and Josef Illík, they formed a strong and consistent team.

In *Long Live the Republic*, they made a partly autobiographical work that was supposed to celebrate the liberation from the German occupation. But it is a far cry from the ideological simplifications normally associated with the genre. It is presented as the subjective experience of a twelve-year-old boy and, as such, it is free of any interpretative historical framework.

The film's highly inventive use of cinematography and editing, in which present, past and dream merge in a continuous flow, provides a child's-eye view of the world as something frequently oppressive and dangerous. After being regularly beaten by his father, Olda sees adults primarily as threats. Russians and Germans appear in isolated incidents and overall developments are experienced in an oblique and half-understood manner.

When the Soviet troops enter the village in triumph, the event is undercut by negative connotations. Following the slogans 'Long live the Republic!', 'Long live the Soviet Union!' and 'Long live Stalin!', the villagers stone Cyril, the only man who had befriended Olda, and accuse him of being an informer and he commits suicide. Olda is beaten by other boys. In the context of the simplified politics then promoted, these contrasts were clearly intentional – but less explicitly 'subversive' than suggestive that real history is a world away from wishful thinking and political propaganda. Perhaps Kachyňa's and Procházka's grim-faced community is closer to reality than the community of friends we find at the beginning of Jasný's *All My Good Countrymen*.

Coach to Vienna is a film of classical dimensions. The heroine (Iva Janžurová) has resolved to kill Germans in retaliation for the murder of her husband. She is commandeered to drive two Germans, one seriously wounded, towards safety. In the process, she drives them through endless pine forests, which serve both as a labyrinth and a means of insulation from the world outside. Eventually, her relationship with Hans, the young Austrian who only wants to be friends, turns to one of human understanding. However, at the end of the film, they are discovered by partisans who take them to be lovers, rape the woman and kill Hans.

The film adopts a simple humanist theme and non-propagandist approach to war and, although it is primarily a poetic and epic work, *Coach to Vienna* again seeks to undermine the simplifications of propaganda. Not all Germans are 'bad', the acts of the partisans were not always 'heroic' and, without human understanding and the rejection of simplified political oppositions, genuine progress is impossible.

With *Night of the Bride*, based on Procházka's novel *Holy Night* (*Svatá noc*), they turned their attention to the collectivisation of agriculture and the conflict between Communist and non-Communist. The opening sequences record the beginning of the process. An inventory of livestock is taken. Picin, the local Communist leader, addresses the crowd but no words come from his mouth and the vision of a future paradise is represented only in images.

A conflict is established between Picin and the rich farmer, Šabatka, when the latter asks what the farmers will receive in exchange for giving up their belongings to the collective. We learn that one of the landowners has committed suicide and killed all his cows. His daughter (Jana Brejchová), who had left him as a young girl in order to become a nun, returns as his suicide is discovered. From the beginning, there is a strong sense of 'us' (the farmers) versus 'them' (the Communists). The daughter plans to celebrate a midnight Mass but her plans are opposed by both Picin and the village priest. Šabatka and his friends plan to kill Picin, who they regard as no more than a tool of the Kremlin, but it is Picin who kills Šabatka.

The central religious theme makes an odd match with the subject of collectivisation but it is developed at some length, suggesting an extraordinary inbuilt sense of religion in the community. Although Communist triumphs over non-Communist, Picin is not a man of vision or charisma. On the contrary, he is mean and vindictive – someone who suffered under the previous political system and lives with a sick wife.

Yet again, the film avoids simplification – it just seems to observe its characters, their belief systems, their conformities and their differences as part of a historical situation in which no single person can be said to possess all of the truth.

The films bluntly confront official mythologies and it is difficult to see why their critical nature was not more recognised both internally and internationally. As someone who had been involved both politically and practically with many of the realities portrayed, Procházka seems to be reflecting the contradictions of a lived experience. Perhaps this helps to explain the official acceptance of these films, when the criticisms of others would have been directly suppressed. But he also, of course, enjoyed a senior position within the Party. His outspoken support for the reform programme was made apparent at the Writers Congress of 1967 when he spoke out against subordination to doctrines and dogmas.

In 1968, Procházka, together with Václav Černý, was accused by the KGB of heading an anti-Party group aimed at the destruction of socialism. It is not surprising therefore that the Kachyňa/Procházka films *Funny Old Man* (*Směšný pán*, 1969) and *The Ear* (*Ucho*, 1970) should have been suppressed, the first after its release, the second before it could be shown. *Funny Old Man* deals directly with the effects of the political trials of the 1950s through the story of a man who had been imprisoned and disclaimed by his daughter. *The Ear*, which received its first screening in 1989 and made its international debut at Cannes in 1990, provides a compelling insight into the mental framework of a totalitarian society and has gone on to receive considerable critical acclaim.

It tells a story about Ludvík (Radoslav Brzobohatý), a deputy minister, and his wife, Anna (Jiřina Bohdalová), and links recrimination over domestic issues to a wider political and moral framework. After leaving a government reception at Prague Castle, the couple return home to find that their gate is open, the electricity cut off and the phone dead. The secret police have paid them a visit. Gradually, through flashbacks, a picture begins to be formed – the Russian general who was 'in the know', the colleague surprised to see Ludvík at the reception, the enquiries about the heating in their house and the new ministerial chauffeur. It transpires that most of Ludvík's colleagues had been arrested as they arrived at the reception. The ostensible reason is that the plans for a new brickworks are now considered against the Party line. An obscure technical issue becomes the excuse for a sinister and incomprehensible exercise in terror.

In this Kafkaesque bureaucracy, guilt is preordained and no rational explanation is required. Even those at the centre of the power structure are expendable. When Ludvík decides to commit suicide, he discovers that his gun has been taken (*they* will decide when the time is appropriate). In a final irony, the phone rings and he is appointed Minister. But the authorities also know, as does his wife, that her husband is self-obsessed, will change his views for the sake of survival and can easily be manipulated.

The film's style is almost that of film noir – the flashbacks to the castle are shot in semi-Expressionist style, with faces thrust towards the camera. The whole film takes place at night, with only the final scenes at dawn. As the couple explore their house, they use lighted candles, matches and lighters, increasing the justification for Kachyňa's noir style. Ludvík's face repeatedly confronts us or meets his own reflection. The film's mixture of marital squabbling and comedy with the style of the thriller makes it more than just a criticism of political errors. It is a journey into the atmosphere and mind of an era.

The work of Helge and Kříž and Kachyňa and Procházka provides ample evidence of some of the critical thinking going on inside the Communist Party – but, of course, criticisms were coming from outside as well, with two of the most profound films of the 1960s coming from new wave director Evald Schorm. Schorm, who played the man who refused to compromise his principles in Jan Němec's *The Party and the Guests* (1966) which was, incidentally, produced with the support of Procházka, enjoyed precisely this reputation and was regarded as the 'philosopher' of the New Wave. He also believed in the importance of his scripts and the writer's ideas.

If President Novotný defended Kachyňa's *Long Live the Republic* against its critics in the following year, the same was not true of Schorm's *Everyday Courage* (*Každý den odvahu*, 1964), which he had banned. Scripted by another member of the New Wave, Antonin Máša, it followed in the footsteps of Helge in that it provoked a critical reflection on the role of a Party worker, Jarda Lukáš, who finds the world he has created beginning to collapse around him. The film gains considerable strength from its use of the documentary tradition (Schorm was also a major documentary director), particularly in its portrayal of factory life and youth culture. However, it combines this with powerful dramatic performances (by Jan Kačer and Jana Brejchová) and a modernist score by Jan Klusák. The lack of morale, the materialism and the failure to achieve the socialist dream are readily apparent all around Jarda, provoking a harrowing self-analysis that was received as one of the most profound criticisms yet made. It is, as Josef Škvorecký remarked, 'a frontal attack against the betrayal of ideals, and the fact that the President and his advisors labelled this truly revolutionary work of art as a slander against the revolution, is just another Czechoslovakian paradox'.[4]

Schorm's next film, *Return of the Prodigal Son* (*Návrat ztraceného syna*, 1966), told the story of an architect who attempts suicide and his efforts to adjust to the reality he finds about him. Confined to an asylum, he escapes several times and is finally released, on each occasion failing to adjust to the world he discovers about him. In a sense, we are taken on a journey through society and its ills – relationships with his wife and her family, the hypocrisies of his working environment, the threat of war, injustice. The doctor recommends him to adopt an attitude of 'humble indifference' while Jan regards this as a recipe for 'continuous suicide'. This graded portrait of a society based on compromise is one of the most profoundly critical films of the New Wave and, while its portrait of alienation could have been set in other industrial societies, it extends the criticism already made in *Everyday Courage*.

His following three films were contrasting in their styles and subjects. *Saddled with Five Girls* (*Pět holek na krku*, 1967) was a story of young love set against a background of visits to the opera. Nataša is a beautiful and sensitive girl, daughter of a prominent official, who is tricked and exploited by her less well-off friends, who effectively destroy her growing romantic attachment to a young boy. Again, the film focuses on failures in communication and, ultimately, Nataša decides to use her position to achieve revenge. Although less radical in its criticism than his previous films, it was also, said Schorm, a film about the point where a person begins to become warped or deformed. His film of Josef Škvorecký's script *End of a Priest* (*Farářův konec*, 1968) was a contemporary morality play, interspersed with quotations and parables, which told the story of a sexton who successfully passes himself off as a priest. Increasingly, he takes his role seriously and poses a threat to the town's Communist mayor, engaging him in mock-intellectual debates. At the end of the film, he finds himself hanging from the church rafters, with the mayor on one side and a member of the secret police on the other.

End of a Priest was banned and *Seventh Day, Eighth Night* (*Den sedmý, osmá noc*, 1969), scripted by Zdeněk Mahler, was banned before release. An allegory set in an archetypal Czech village, it tells of what happens when a sequence of mysterious events take place, including the disappearance of the stationmaster. While everything has a rational explanation, collective paranoia takes hold and everyone's worst instincts are released. Interrogations, the abolition of rights and the search for scapegoats ultimately lead to murder. The intercutting of aerial shots of the village, suggesting surveillance or an alien presence, led to rumours that the film was 'about' the Soviet invasion. In 1969, Schorm also put together a compilation of secret footage of the Soviet invasion, *Confusion* (*Zmatek*), which was finally released in 1990.

The two most critical political films were Jasný's *All My Good Countrymen* (1968) and Jireš's *The Joke* (1968), based on the novel by Milan Kundera. Both films were, of course, products of the more open atmosphere of the Prague Spring, which allowed the possibility of more analytical approaches to political history. While Kundera's novel was first published in 1967, Jasný's film had, in fact, been in preparation since the mid fifties. Based on his mother's recollections of village life, the script had been completed in 1956 but was only passed for production in 1967.

While being a work of political criticism, *All My Good Countrymen* is also a lyrical poem in the tradition of *Desire* (*Touha*, 1958), with many images shared by the two films. According to Jan Žalman, the film expressed Jasný's belief in 'the eternal course of Life and Nature' in which the essential certainties are 'birth, love, labour, and death'.[5] Throughout the film, the landscape provides an enveloping beauty as the seasons advance and human endeavours, both good and bad, are progressively superseded.

The film focuses on the experiences undergone in a single Moravian village between the years 1945 and 1958, together with an epilogue set in 1968. While it bluntly exposes the horrors and failures of agricultural collectivisation, its originality lies in the way in which it concentrates on a group of seven friends whose lives and relationships become fragmented. The tragedies remain within a community that continues to meet on social and official occasions. Like a number of other films from the same period, it analyses social interaction and the ways in which problems are the responsibility not just of individuals but of a whole society.

The film begins with the ending of the war and moves forward to the process of collectivisation and the imposition of Stalinism. Dispossession, collectivisation that is all but compulsory, careerism, vindictiveness and incompetence are the end result of a policy that had no economic justification. While the film consists of a collection of stories and characters, its narrative gradually begins to focus on František who heads the opposition to the collective. This leads to his imprisonment and escape. Finally, he agrees to help the collective when it fails as a result of gross mismanagement.

The film is critical of Communist policies from the very beginning and the two 'positive' Communists disappear from the narrative at an early stage. Bertin, the postman, is shot by mistake by anti-Communists who mistake him for Očenáš, the local leader (and church organist and music teacher). Očenáš, who means well, is eventually forced to leave the village because of continued threats. František's daughter becomes a successful musician as a result of her lessons with Očenáš. At the end of the film, Očenáš returns to the village and, with reference to the Prague Spring, notes that everything is now changing.

The film's clear political statements are what made it significant in 1968 and led to its eventual banning after the Soviet invasion. But, as a work of art, the film goes well beyond its political analysis with a whole range of strong characters who only accidentally become involved in politics. Besides the idiosyncrasies of the seven friends, we meet the local femme fatale, 'the merry widow', and her two sons and a village painter who produces Chagall-like images. There is also the appearance of a ghost as a separate character. In Jasný's film, enmeshed in the beauties of nature, life consists of fantasy and myth and the imaginative and emotional world plays its role alongside the political.

Although *The Joke* was made the year after the publication of the novel, Jireš and Kundera had already developed the film script before its publication. Kundera once criticised the 'political' interpretation of his book, arguing that it was, above all, a love story. However, the film eliminates the love story and it is impossible to view it as anything other than political in its objectives. Entirely set within a range of political references, it can be summarised as a film about the futility of revenge.

Ludvík Jahn (Josef Somr), a former Communist, comes from a small town in southern Moravia. As a student in the 1950s, he decided to outrage his militant girlfriend, Markéta, who opts for a weekend of collective euphoria rather than a weekend of love with him. He sends her a postcard with the phrase 'A healthy spirit reeks of idiocy. Long live Trotsky!' For this political joke, he is expelled from both the Party and the university and ends up enduring two years forced labour, three years in the army and one in military prison. The prime mover in this process is his former friend and comrade, Pavel. On his return to his home town, Ludvík plans to revenge himself on Pavel by seducing his wife. Unfortunately, things have changed. Pavel no longer cares about his wife as he has a young mistress and he has moved with the times and become a reform Communist.

Jireš provokes a critical response to his subject through the intercutting of past and present – but this is not just a matter of flashbacks since the two realities are contrasted and frequently comment on each other. The film is set in the present and, as Ludvík visits his old town, he thinks back to his love affair with Markéta, his condemnation by his fellow students and his years of forced labour. This 'dialogue with history' begins in 1949, with young people in folk costume dancing in the streets to the slogan 'Long live Gottwald!' (ironically, these scenes were shot during the invasion of 1968).

The face of Markéta is picked out from the crowd. 'Your smile is so funny,' she remarks to him. 'I'm rejoicing,' he replies ironically (in the present). 'It looks like private thoughts,' (a sin in those days) her voice replies as we return to him in the present, looking down an alley. Markéta, he tells us, was the embodiment of the time, 'naive, joyful and severe'.

As he continues on his journey through the town, the flashbacks continue. A ceremony welcoming newly born children is intercut with the words of Ludvík's 'joke' and those of the Communist martyr, Julius Fučík. The flashbacks to forced labour concentrate on the characters of the committed Communist, Alexej, who has denounced his own father and whose literal and unquestioning devotion to the cause leads to his own destruction, and on Čeněk, a former Cubist painter, whose erotic painting is explained away as an allegory on peace. Throughout these scenes of past injustice, joyous hymns to work and officially approved folk music strike an ironic counterpoint.

While the first part of the film emphasises the past, the second forsakes this critical interplay to focus on the acting-out of Ludvík's revenge. In this section, Helena, Pavel's wife, a radio reporter who still speaks in the rhetoric of the past, becomes a kind of substitute Markéta. She is the victim of her delusions as well as of Ludvík's revenge through sex (accompanied by the words, 'We're building a brand new world! We're looking to the future.') When he finally meets Pavel, he is treated to a new commentary in which Pavel himself condemns the illusions of the 1950s and the ways in which they disguised injustice and the persecution of the innocent.

The film not only exposes the injustice of the 1950s but also remains true to Kundera's spirit of scepticism. Pavel's reformist zeal seems to be little more than an accommodation to the spirit of the times and, of course, given the Soviet response in reality, the film was made in the knowledge that the Prague Spring could not be sustained. Filmed in black and white, it completely avoids the lyricism normally associated with Jireš's work.

Following the suppression of the 1968 reforms, the kinds of criticisms that evolved during the 1960s were to prove completely impossible and the critical search for minor evidence of criticism or subversive comment becomes something of a fine art. The first sign of any return to the injustices of the Communist past came with the preparation, in 1989, of Jiří Svoboda's *Family Matters* (*Jen o rodinných záležitostech*, 1990), which dealt with the political trials of Communists in the 1950s. In many ways, it revisited the territory explored by Costa-Gavras with his *The Confession* (*L'Aveu*, 1970), in which he had adapted the memoirs of Artur London, one of the few Communists accused in the 1950s to escape with his life. The main parts were played by Yves Montand and Simone Signoret. By the time *Family Matters* was released, the regime had fallen and the film's concern with only the unjust treatment of Communists was no longer sufficient.

In the post-Communist period, few films have treated the historical complexities of the 1948–68 period – or indeed the 'normalisation' years of 1968–89 – with any great sophistication. Two of the most popular films of the immediate post-war period were Vít Olmer's *The Tank Battalion* (*Tankový prapor*, 1991) and Zdenek Sirový's *The Black Barons* (*Černí baroni*, 1992). Adapted respectively from the novels of Josef Škvorecký and Miloslav Švandrlík, the first deals with national service and the second with service in the 'black units', the special army units reserved for political undesirables. Both opted for a frontal assault on Communism and its stupidities as broad farce. The only film that attempted a more nuanced approach was Jan Schmidt's *Rebounds* (*Vracenky*, 1990) but this was passed for production prior to denationalisation. Two more orthodox but powerful accounts of the early Communist period were Hynek Bočan's *Boomerang* (*Bumerang*, 1997) and Petr Nikolaev's *A Little Piece of Heaven* (*Kousek nebe*, 2005).

The most substantive accounts of the later years of the Communist era have been Jan Hřebejk's *Cosy Dens* (1999) and *Pupendo* (2003). Both were scripted by Petr Jarchovský and adapted from stories or motifs by Petr Šabach and both of them were major box office successes. However, they approach the subject through the lives of people without significant influence or importance, reflecting everyday experience. The films provide little political analysis and the themes are principally those of surviving Communism.

In *Cosy Dens*, set during the year of the Prague Spring, Hřebejk and Jarchovský examine two families, one Communist and one anti-Communist, who live almost side by side in the same apartment block. One family is headed by Šebek, a military officer and committed Communist who is in charge of the army canteen, the other by Kraus, a former resistance fighter whose brother fought in the Royal Air Force. Their sterile confrontations seem far from the everyday concerns of their wives and children. The Prague Spring is barely mentioned prior to the invasion, at which point both families come together, with Šebek making a serio-comic attempt to commit suicide. The film is, in effect, more a memoir of family life than an analysis of 1968. Nonetheless, political realities determine those lives and the film is dedicated to those 'whose friends and parents left'.

One of the few films to touch on the subject of 'dissidence' and the 'normalisation' years, *Pupendo* provides a portrait of the 1980s through the story of a discredited sculptor, Bedřich Mára (Boleslav Polívka), who has fallen foul of the regime. He is not a dissident or representative of the avant-garde but his refusal to conform leads to a lifestyle quite different to that of his conformist ex-lover, Magda, and her husband who have maintained their Communist Party membership. On the initiative of Alois Fábera, an unemployed art historian, Magda is persuaded to bring Mára back to prominence but the Voice of America intervenes with the reading of an article by Fábera praising their efforts to circumvent the system. At the end of the film, both families end up in the same boat – a holiday at Hungary's Lake Balaton in place of the hoped-for visits to Yugoslavia.

In both films, Communists and non-Communists share the same fates and are caught in the same political traps. The films have been criticised for ignoring certain realities but they are both concerned with the lives of men and women without real influence, caught in impossible situations, to reveal partially hidden ironies and contradictions. While the films can stimulate interaction and debate, there is no direct consideration of political events – in which most people's participation seems to be ineffectual or non-existent.

Jan Svěrák's Oscar-winning *Kolya* (1996) is also a film set in the years of normalisation. Its basic story is that of a middle-aged cello player, Louka (Zdeněk Svěrák), and his relationship with a young Russian boy, who he adopts by entering an arranged marriage with his mother. A former member of the Czech Philharmonic Orchestra, he is banned from performing due to his brother's misdemeanours. In the meantime, he makes a living by playing at funerals and putting gold leaf inscriptions on tombstones. There are various references to the realities of the times – the bureaucracy, serio-comic contact with the secret police, putting up flags for the latest Communist anniversary, ironic comments about resisting the regime and so on. As in *Cosy Dens*, it is a world to be endured.

A more recent film, *It's Gonna Get Worse* (. . . *a bude hůř*, 2007), provides a more significant, although less balanced and inclusive, portrait of the Communist era. Based on part of a long underground novel by Jan Pelc published in samizdat in the early 1980s, it examines the lives of a group of dropouts during the 1970s and their ongoing battle with and victimisation by the police. The central character, Olin (Karel Žídek), has been released from a mental institution after slashing his wrists. However, the motive was the not-uncommon objective of avoiding national service in the armed forces, generally regarded as a demeaning and brutalising experience. Without employment, he is soon taken to the local police station where he is beaten up and told to find a job by the end of the week. Olin and his friends live in a world of drugs and casual sex, in which they listen to banned music, viewing their dissident lifestyle as a protest against the Communist regime.

Here it is worth recalling the fact that, under Communism, there was no unemployment, even if the work was purely nominal. Those without work would be declared social parasites and were subject to jail sentences. All public activities had to be approved and private gatherings were automatically assumed to be actually or potentially subversive (one English academic was once held in a police cell overnight for giving an unauthorised lecture on Plato). In the context of this film, Olin is warned against his repeated attempts to organise unapproved football matches.

This was also the period that saw the founding of the human rights group, Charter 77. This was in response to the public trials of the rock groups, The Plastic People of the Universe and DG 307 in 1976. After playing at the wedding of The Plastic People's artistic director, Ivan Jirous, twenty musicians were detained and a hundred people were interrogated. The Communist

Figure 4.1   Petr Nikolaev: *It's Gonna Get Worse* (. . . *a bude hůř*, 2007)

Party daily, *Rudé pravo*, described the musicians and their followers as drug addicts, alcoholics and criminals (8 April 1976). DG 307 took its name from the provision that excused people from national service on mental health grounds. It is significant that the film uses music by both DG 307 and The Plastic People and that Pavel Zajíček of DG 307 and Vratislav Brabenec of The Plastic People, who had both been imprisoned as a result of the trials, play roles in the film.

Jirous had incurred the wrath of the authorities by championing an underground culture. Writing in 1975, he argued that the role of the underground was 'the creation of a second culture: a culture not dependent on official channels of communication, social recognition, and the hierarchy of values laid down by the authorities'.[6] However, Olin and his friends can hardly be regarded as in any way organised but, as dropouts and drug addicts, they meet most of the authorities' criteria for repression.

One of director Petr Nikolaev's principal achievements is the way in which he has drawn performances of almost documentary authenticity from his young cast. Setting the film in an industrially deprived area of northern Bohemia, he uses both non-actors and unknowns but, having told them the situations, was very much dependent on them drawing on their own experiences. Karel Žídek is leader of a local heavy metal band and had previously appeared in Břetislav Rychlík's documentary *God's Stone Quarry*

(*Kamenolum Boží*, 2005). Any similarities between past and present are, as they say, purely coincidental.

The film's further criticism of its times is continued through the central character of the 'wild man', a vagrant who is actually an ex-RAF pilot whose face was severely burned during a crash over the English Channel. During the film, Brabenec arrives with an invitation for him to receive a medal in the United Kingdom – purely a formality, he notes, since 'the bastards won't let him go anyway'. Other than demonstrating their opposition to the regime through their lifestyle, Olin and his friends also attempt to escape the country. At the end of the film, it briefly becomes a genre piece as they make an abortive effort to cross the border. Eventually, we learn that Olin has escaped but that the wild man has committed suicide in an asylum and that Olin's friend, Olga, has thrown herself out of the window of a reform school.

The film is full of crudity – one of the characters, Pig Pen, constantly refers to the state of his penis, sex is considered almost as a public service and Olin impregnates two would-be lesbian mothers. But there is also a sense of partnership and brotherhood which, rather perversely, echoes that of a political underground. Here the personal lives of these 'hippie' outcasts have a rather more direct political implication than their western equivalents. The film also provides a salutary reminder that it was not only politicians and intellectuals who suffered under Dr Husák's regime of 'normalisation'.

Filmed on 16mm and in black and white, the film is deliberately constructed to provide an 'underground' feel and producer Čestmír Kopecký conceived the idea of releasing it only though pubs and clubs (complete with a toilet break) in order to reach its target audience and avoid the commercial framework of the multiplex. Although it is arguably the best film to have been made about that era, its lack of production values or exotic appeal means that it is unlikely to register with international audiences on any significant level.

If one turns to criticism of the post-Communist period, the political film is relatively less evident. Here, as in the pre-war period, it is social realism that is the preferred mode. This is discussed in more detail in the chapter on realism but it is noticeable that these approaches did not begin to emerge with any degree of significance until the work of Bohdan Sláma in the early years of the new century. Even here, though, criticism often remains implicit. In a world where, to echo Margaret Thatcher, there was no alternative to the doctrines of economic liberalism, to suggest otherwise was to risk being labelled a crypto-Communist, especially in Central and Eastern Europe.

One of the few directors to take a hard look at the new realities in the early post-Communist years was Věra Chytilová. *Inheritance or Fuck-Boys Gutntag* (*Dědictví aneb Kurvahošigutntag*, 1992), her comedy about a peasant who inherits a fortune, has the memorable final shot in which the central character turns to the audience and threatens to 'buy them all'. In the arguably unique black comedy *Traps* aka *Traps, Traps, Little Traps* (*Pasti, pasti, pastičky*, 1998), she makes a tenuous connection between a story about rape and the values of the new political system. Her heroine, a veterinary surgeon, is raped by two men and enacts a severe revenge (castration). The main focus of the film's humour lies in the men's hopes of becoming reattached, but the film is also an allegory about male power. One of the men is a government minister and it is the men who have the last word.

But, for considered criticism of the new system, one has to turn to documentary and here it is relevant to consider the work of Karel Vachek who, in any case, considers his work to be neither feature nor documentary but filmnovel. A member of the New Wave generation, he made only two films in the 1960s – the short *Moravian Hellas* (*Moravská Hellas*, 1963) and the full length *Elective Affinities* (*Spřízněni volbou*, 1968), a cinéma-vérité-style record of the presidential elections in that year. There then began a long absence from filmmaking that lasted until 1991.

Extremely influential in the world of post-Communist documentary, Vachek attracts both disciples and opponents. What is clear, however, is that his films engage in a multilevel debate about contemporary society, culture and tradition using a collage of discussions, images and observations. In his first post-Communist film, he again followed an election campaign, this time the parliamentary elections, in his film *New Hyperion or Liberty, Equality, Fraternity* (*Nový Hyperion aneb Volnost, rovnost, bratrství*, 1992). His other titles include *What is to be Done? Or How I Journeyed from Prague to Česky Krumlov and Formed my Own Government* (*Co dělat? Cesta z Prahy do Českého Krumlova aneb Jak jsem sestavoval novou vládu*, 1996), *Bohemia docta or the Labyrinth of the World and the Paradise of the Heart [A Divine Comedy]* (*Bohemia docta aneb Labyrint světa a lusthauz srdce [Božská Komedie]*, 2001), *Who Will Guard the Guard? Dalibor or the Key to Uncle Tom's Cabin* (*Kdo bude hlidat hlidače? Dalibor aneb Klíč k Chaloupce strýčka Toma*, 2003) and *Záviš, the Prince of Pornofolk Under the Influence of Griffith's 'Intolerance' and Tati's 'Monsieur Hulot's Holiday' or the Foundation and Doom of Czechoslovakia (1918–1992)* (*Záviš, kníže pornofolku pod vlivem Griffithovy* Intolerance *a Tatiho* Prázdnin pana Hulota *aneb vznik a zánik Československá, 1918–1992*, 2006). With their scarcely everyday references to Hölderlin, Chernyshevsky, Comenius, Smetana, Dante and Bohuslav Balbín to name but a few, they signal themselves as something outside the normal run of film consumption. With the exception of the last, they all run for over three and half hours.

Alice Lovejoy suggests that Vachek's films chart a journey from the centre to the periphery, from those at the heart of political power to those artists and intellectuals who 'exemplify the questions and complications of the political transition'.[7] His outsider figures listen to an inner and intuitive wisdom – they 'say important things even when the time does not want to listen'.[8]

His films are filled with long conversations – often in symbolic locations – between the director and 'minor' characters. In *Who Will Guard the Guard? Dalibor or The Key to Uncle Tom's Cabin*, Vachek bases the film firmly in the rehearsals for Smetana's opera *Dalibor* at the National Theatre. The fifteenth-century story gives the film a specific 'Czech' context, with the film's three acts focussing on attitudes to the past, prospects for salvation and the transition to capitalism. Topics include discussions on how the conductor Václav Talich preserved Smetana and collaborated with the Nazis, the links between the National Theatre and the ideals of Masaryk, Havel and Dubček, the anti-charter, globalisation, the role of former Communist apparatchiks, advertising and many other subjects. In fact, it is quite impossible to watch his films without engaging in the kinds of dialogue he demands.

His influence on young documentary film-makers has been quite significant with many of them taking on his particular approach based on dialectic and analysis. Perhaps most noteworthy here has been *Czech Dream* (*Český sen*, 2004). Made by Filip Remunda and Vít Klusák, it went on to achieve international acclaim. The film follows the process of the marketing and promotion of a fake hypermarket as a means for analysing the realities of the consumer society and provides a compelling examination of the manipulations of the commercial world. Besides organising a provocation that attracted international media coverage, Remunda and Klusák reveal a world in which consumption and shopping have become ends in themselves. At the conclusion of the film, 'real' advertisements replace the 'false' ones to which we have become accustomed.

In 1991, Peter Pišt'anek's novel *Rivers of Babylon* was published in Bratislava. This was, of course, before the break-up of the country, although his subject is recognisably Slovak. The novel was a phenomenon in Slovak literature and, as Peter Petro and Donald Rayfield point out in their introduction to the English translation, many were shocked by its iconoclasm. 'A literature that once showed Slovaks as a nation of wise bee-keepers and virtuous matriarchs now presents the nation stripped of its myths and false esteem.'[9]

Set between August 1989 and the spring of 1990, it charts, in allegorical fashion, the transition from normalised Communism to wild west capitalism. It is fundamentally the story of Rácz, an obscure boiler man who uses his power, brutality and charisma to rise in the world. Initially he achieves power through blackmail – switching off the power at the Hotel Ambassador, where he works, and turning it back on for an appropriate fee. His skill at manipulation and intimidation soon has the hotel staff in the palm of his hand and the manager isolated. By the end of the novel, he has become owner of the hotel and has acquired the services of a crooked lawyer and a protection firm run by former members of state security. But the novel's criticism goes much wider, with a rich range of subsidiary characters, all of them corrupt, selfish and far removed from higher thoughts or ambitions.

The novel became part of a trilogy, with two further novels published in 1994 and 1999. However, it was the first novel that was filmed in 1998 by Vladimír Balco. Perhaps, inevitably, the range of the novel is lost and the film concentrates almost exclusively on the character of Rácz. The film suffers from the usual problems inherent in any faithful adaptation – it includes all the major characters however briefly and all of the major incidents with insufficient motivation. The film had less impact than anticipated, principally because the novel is almost impossible to adapt.

Nonetheless, it is certainly true that, if the novel challenged a world of philosophical bee-keepers, the film does the same. The sordid reality of the boiler room and the gloomy rain-soaked streets of winter counter the folkloric and poetic traditions of Slovak cinema. Welcoming 1990, Lenka the language student, observes that, now that Slovaks have freedom, 'everyone will develop according to his own nature and enrich the life of everyone else'.

The grander, multilevel satire of the novel tends to be lost in a sequence of unpleasant incidents but the film does make a commendable effort to maintain the 'anti' stance of the novel. It was also criticised for making its parallels between Rácz and the then prime minister, Vladimír Mečiar, much too overt but, as Andrew James Horton notes, 'The return to subversive political allegory as a cinematic form of expression makes it unique, not just in Slovakia but in Central and Eastern Europe generally.'[10]

I realise that this chapter does not deal with political cinema in the 1920s and 1930s but the films from these periods that might be considered political are considered in other chapters – Comedy (Voskovec and Werich), Realism (Carl Junghans), The Avant-Garde (Vladislav Vančura). Perhaps unsurprisingly, a direct concern with politics has been much more a characteristic of the Communist period and its aftermath.

NOTES

1. Zdeněk Hořínek, quoted in Carol Rocamora, *Acts of Courage: Václav Havel's Life in the Theater* (Hanover, NH: Smith and Kraus, 2004), p. 397.
2. Milan Kundera, 'Candide Had to be Destroyed', in Jan Vladislav (ed.), *Václav Havel or Living in Truth* (London: Faber, 1987), pp. 258–60.
3. Boris Jachnin, 'Karel Kachyňa: Four Decades of a Great Czech Director', *Kinema*, Fall 1990, http://arts.waterloo.ca/FINE/juhde/jachnin952.htm [Accessed 21 January 2003].
4. Josef Škvorecký, *All the Bright Young Men and Women: A Personal History of the Czech Cinema* (Toronto: Peter Martin Associates, 1971), p. 144.
5. Jan Žalman, 'Everyone a Good Fellow Countryman', in Peter Cowie (ed.), *International Film Guide 1970* (London: Tantivy Press, 1969), pp. 83–4.
6. Ivan Jirous, 'Underground Culture', *Index on Censorship*, 12, 1, February 1983, pp. 32–4.
7. Alice Lovejoy, 'Center and Periphery, or How Karel Vachek Formed a New Government', in Peter Hames (ed.) *Czech Cinema*, special issue of *KinoKultura*,

November 2006, http://www.kinokultura.com/specials/4/lovejoy.shtml [Accessed 16 November 2006].

8. Robert Krumphanzl and Zdeněk Vašiček, 'O Radosti, důstojnosti a několika dalších věcech', interview with Karel Vachek in *Revolver Revue*, 52, April 2003, p. 170. English translation in Lovejoy.

9. Peter Petro and Donald Rayfield, 'Introduction' to Peter Pišt'anek, *Rivers of Babylon*, translated by Peter Petro (London: Garnett Press, 2007), p. 5.

10. Andrew James Horton, 'Slovakia Rediscovered (Part II): Vlado Balco's *Rivers of Babylon*, *Central Europe Review*, 0, 10, 30 November 1998. http://www.ce-review.org/kinoeye10old.html [Accessed 21/04/08].

5. THE HOLOCAUST

The Jewish-born Slovak film-maker, Ján Kadár, director of the Oscar-winning *The Shop on the High Street* aka *The Shop on Main Street* (1965), once said that, subsequent to the war, he had never encountered racial discrimination either in his work or in his private life. Although he had been imprisoned in Auschwitz and 'chose' his Jewish identity as a result of the Nazi Race Laws, he nonetheless regarded anti-Semitism as a matter of degree, remarking that, in the Czech lands, it had been a peripheral influence. This comment could, of course, be regarded as merely tactical but he also observed that it was one of the reasons that he had regarded the persecution of others as 'mistakes'.

The issue of anti-Semitism in the post-war period in Czechoslovakia has, as far as I know, not been addressed in the feature film but, in its treatment of the Holocaust on film, the achievement of Czechoslovakia is probably unequalled in its range and persistence. Undoubtedly, there was a strong Jewish representation within the intelligentsia – writers such as Jiří Weil, Arnošt Lustig, Norbert Fryd, Ludvík Aškenazy, Ladislav Grosman and Ladislav Fuks and directors such as Alfréd Radok, Jiří Weiss and Ján Kadár, all of whom were to receive international recognition. Furthermore, there was a strong Jewish element within the post-war leadership of the Communist Party itself.

In the Stalinist show trials and purges of the 1950s, there was a clear anti-Semitic element. As pointed out earlier, of the fourteen leading Communists arrested at that time, which included the Secretary-General of the Party, Rudolf Slánský, eleven were executed and three sentenced to life imprisonment. Eleven of the fourteen accused were Jewish and labelled as working for the West. The official verdicts expressly used the term 'of Jewish origin'. The trials of the 1950s, apart from eliminating the leadership of a party which pretended a degree of independence from Soviet control, also reflected a change in Soviet policies toward Israel. Kadár also noted that, in 1967, anti-Semitism again manifested itself when the government took a consciously pro-Arab stance.[1]

But it would be wrong to simplify these oppositions as the post-war Communist Party had already carried out its own purges. After the Soviet invasion of 1968 following the Prague Spring reforms, when the government was 'kidnapped' and taken to Russia for 'negotiations', the Soviet captors reserved particular venom for the 'Galician Jew', František Kriegel, who maintained a constantly principled stance. Kept in seclusion during the negotiations, his fellow government members refused to return to Prague without him. As the regime was directed away from reform toward the neo-Stalinist 'normalisation' that was to prevail for the next twenty years, it is worth noting that Lustig, Weiss and Kadár emigrated to the USA, Grosman to Israel and Radok to Sweden (although the total emigration at the time was calculated to be of the order of 170,000). The Holocaust themes that had made up a major element of 1960s cinema virtually disappeared.

One of the first notable Holocaust films to be produced after the war was the Polish *The Last Stage* (*Ostatni etap*, 1948), directed by Wanda Jakubowska. As Ewa Mazierska has pointed out, Jakubowska was a committed Communist and the film can be regarded as both a Holocaust and a Socialist Realist film, conforming to the style and aesthetics of the approved dogma.[2]

The first of the Czech Holocaust films was quite different. Alfréd Radok's *Distant Journey* aka *The Long Journey* (*Daleká cesta*, 1949) was begun before the era of aesthetic dogma had been instituted. Radok, who had served his theatrical apprenticeship with the avant-garde stage director, E. F. Burian, adapted a highly stylised – almost Expressionist – approach to the subject that is virtually unique. Jiří Cieslar suggests that he might have been influenced by *Citizen Kane* (1941), which was shown in Prague the previous year. The film received a good critical reception when it was shown in New York in 1951. Bosley Crowther described it as 'the most brilliant, the most horrifying film on the Nazis' persecution of the Jews' that he had seen.[3]

Radok's style did not meet with official approval and resulted in the film being shelved for forty years – until it was shown again on Czech television after the fall of Communism. The unacceptability of style may have been the official excuse but Radok no doubt also had his enemies. Nonetheless, he made two further features, continued to work in the theatre and was the principal force behind the experimental *Laterna magika*.

The film is centred on the Terezín (Theresienstadt) ghetto, which was established by the Nazis in November 1941. Terezín, a small town about 60 km from

Prague, was built as a military fortress town during the reign of the Habsburg Emperor Josef II between 1780 and 1790. After the German occupation, it was established as a transit camp from which Jews would be transported to concentration and extermination camps such as Auschwitz and Buchenwald. As Karel Kosík put it, it was a 'transfer point for human material', treated like cement, lumber, or cattle.[4] Its objectives were to remain secret and it was presented to the Jews as a labour camp.

As Jiří Cieslar has pointed out, conditions were mild compared with those of the extermination camps but, nonetheless, 35,000 perished from starvation, disease and other causes. During the war, 150,000 were imprisoned there and about half were transported to the east.[5] For a time, the Nazis granted the Jews limited self-government in order to create an illusion of freedom. Terezín developed a considerable culture, with concerts, cabarets and operas performed in its lofts and cellars. The Nazis pretended that Hitler had 'given the town to the Jews' and it was famously provided a beautification for a visit by the international Red Cross, successfully representing everyday life as almost normal. The visit inspired the infamous propaganda film *Theresienstadt: A Documentary from the Jewish Settlement Area* (*Theresienstadt: ein Dokumentarfilm aus dem Jüdischen Siedlungsgebiet*, 1945), also known as *The Führer Gives a Town to the Jews* (*Der Führer schenkt den Juden eine Stadt*). When shooting finished in the autumn of 1944, many of those filmed were transported east. By the time the film was shown to another Red Cross delegation in Terezín in April 1945, Auschwitz had already been liberated and the true horrors revealed.

Distant Journey begins with the early years of the German occupation when the first signs of discrimination against Jewish people were beginning to emerge. The story centres on an intellectual Jewish family, the Kaufmanns, whose daughter, Hana Kauffmannová, is a doctor. Gradually, they are deprived of their rights and forced to wear the yellow star and Hana loses her job. The Kauffmanns are deported to Terezín but Hana's marriage to an 'Aryan' fellow doctor, Antonín Bureš, saves her from joining them. Finally, her husband is arrested and she also ends up in Terezín, only to discover that her family has been transported east.

Radok's approach to his subject was to present the experience as a nightmare and to emphasise the personal experience of his characters. As Cieslar describes it

> [H]e created a vision of Terezín that resembled a large, crazy and grotesque railway station, a waiting room or antechamber for the extermination camps – a world of chaos. The lofts of the houses are constructed like a stage set, without visible floors or ceilings, made up of steps, oblique walls, and black wooden bars . . . a complex labyrinthine area of enclosed spaces and pools of light.[6]

In addition to this, Radok uses unusual images such as a puppet descending a staircase and the sound of a saxophone and plays a grotesque variant on Ravel's *Boléro* as Jews enter one gate with their luggage and coffins are carried out the other.

Perhaps the most radical element of Radok's approach lies in his juxtaposition of the fictional story with documentary inserts. This is effected by using a small screen in the bottom right-hand corner of the frame, where one image is imposed on the another. The images, which sometimes represent the previous sequence and sometimes the next, mix fictional footage with propaganda newsreels. The device not only draws attention to the wider context of the film but also plays an important part in its rhythmic and formal structure. One example follows the suicide of Professor Reiter, which is linked to images of Himmler, Heydrich (Reichsprotektor of Bohemia-Moravia) and K. H. Frank – the direct or indirect controllers of the political reality. It was Heydrich who issued the instructions for the creation of Terezín.

Made only three years after the war and using Terezín locations, the film was based on a synopsis by Erik Kolár who had himself been imprisoned in Terezín. Both Radok's father and grandfather had died there. An important part of his objective was to reveal not only the evil in others but 'the evil in us' – that is the hidden or open anti-Semitism within the Czech people. This was not as fully developed as intended but a number of elements remain (the caretaker who steals Jewish possessions and Antonín's father, a representative of 'everyday Semitism', who refuses to attend his son's wedding). Yet both the father and Antonín's brother also perish in the camps. According to Cieslar, a scene was planned juxtaposing German students watching the execution of Jewish professors with Czech nationalist students fighting Jewish sympathisers. He suggests that Communist censorship might have eliminated it.[7]

Cieslar identifies three narrative layers in the film: the central story of Hana and Antonín, whose mixed marriage is set against the background of progressive anti-Semitism; the tragic story of Jewish life in Prague and Terezín; and the parallel use of the documentary inserts. He suggests that, in the second level, many scenes take on the role of ceremonies or rites, in which the characters lose their individual character and take on the role of symbols, with metaphorical scenes filmed with deliberate stylisation.

While Radok's approach creates a powerful sense of involvement, his techniques also produce a tension between involvement and reflection. This links to Radok's concept of film as an 'artistic report' in which different points of view can be compared. He said that much of what he wanted to communicate in the film derived from Hitler – a name which, he said, for him evoked the image of a little girl offering Hitler a bunch of wild flowers, as he bent over her with a benevolent smile. In *Distant Journey* he wanted to stress:

the paradox that so many people . . . simply don't see things, don't want to see things, or see only the picture of Hitler and the little girl. And that is the horror of it. Everything that they wrote about in the newspapers was depicted as the best . . . Hitler promised Czechoslovakia the only possible salvation . . . If you really want to get a picture of that period, you have to see the one and the other, not one but two, both sides.[8]

Radok was clearly working within the pre-war traditions of the experimental avant-garde which, by 1949, had become politically unacceptable. Radok noted that he was himself regarded as a 'cosmopolitan' and a 'formalist', someone who, according to the Stalinist cultural watchdog Ladislav Štoll, was 'a person standing on the other side'.[9]

In the 1960s, Holocaust films became a significant strand in Czech cinema, ranging in style from realist to expressionist, intimate to experimental, to tragi-comedy, black comedy and horror. The most famous include *Romeo, Juliet and Darkness* (*Romeo, Julie a tma*, Jiří Weiss, 1959), *Transport from Paradise* (*Transport z ráje*, Zbyněk Brynych, 1962), *The Fifth Horseman is Fear* (*. . . a pátý jezdec je Strach*, Zbyněk Brynych, 1964), *Diamonds of the Night* (*Démanty noci*, Jan Němec, 1964), *The Shop on the High Street* (Ján Kadár and Elmar Klos, 1965), *A Prayer for Kateřina Horovitzová* (*Modlitba pro Kateřinu Horovitzovou*, Antonín Moskalyk, 1965), *Dita Saxová* (Antonín Moskalyk, 1967) and *The Cremator* (*Spalovač mrtvol*, Juraj Herz, 1968).

While this undoubtedly reflected the increasing liberalisation that affected the film industry in the years preceding the Prague Spring of 1968, the roots of the development lie as early as the late 1950s when many of the novels and stories on which they were based were first published. In some cases, the novels marked a progression beyond Socialist Realism towards more individual-based stories and, despite obvious parallels with the Jewish victims of the 1950s show trials, they also fitted the official preoccupation with Nazi war crimes and the threat from the West. However, on a more profound level, whereas Socialist Realist novels – novels of 'socialist construction' – had asked the reader to identify with the ruling ideology, the new literature, as Alfred French has argued, concentrated on the victims of power and ideology and 'called the reader to participate in the fear experienced by the hunted, the little people crushed between powerful conflicting forces'.[10] And, of course, as Radok noted, the phenomena he described in *Distant Journey* (that is the inability or unwillingness to see beneath the surface) were also phenomena of Communist as well as democratic societies. Certainly, in the film versions, there were often deliberate attempts to universalise the subjects or render them as allegory.

The second major Holocaust film was Jiří Weiss's adaptation of Jan Otčenášek's novel *Romeo, Juliet and Darkness*. Otčenášek, who had begun with Socialist Realist novels, had broadened his scope with the novel *Citizen*

Brych (*Občan Brych*, 1956), which examined the dilemmas of a bourgeois intellectual during the Communist takeover of 1948. It was filmed by Otakar Vávra in 1959 and again by Ladislav Helge – as *Spring Breeze* (*Jarní povětří*) – in 1961. *Romeo, Juliet, and Darkness,* which was published in 1958, bears many parallels with *The Diary of Anne Frank*.

In May 1942, the Jewish family Wurm are sent to join a transport. Their neighbour, the student Pavel Rumler (Ivan Mistřík), is one of the few to bid them goodbye. In the empty flat he finds a Jewish girl, Hanka (Dana Smutná), who had come to visit them and has escaped the transport. Pavel hides her in the attic while a German officer's mistress moves into the Wurms' flat. Pavel and Hanka fall in love but martial law is declared following the assassination of Heydrich. After a confrontation with Kubiasová, the mistress, who is also interested in Pavel, Hanka runs into the street and is shot down.

Weiss, who had begun his career in documentary before the war (he won an award at Venice for his *People in the Sun* (*Lidé na slunci*, 1935) spent the war years in Britain, where he made his first fiction film. He was to become one of the most important Czech directors of the post-war period with such films as *The Stolen Frontier* (1947) and *The Wolf Trap* (*Vlčí jáma*, 1957), both of which attracted international interest. His powerful and dramatic approach often recalls British cinema of the same era but his background in documentary is also evident. *Romeo, Juliet and Darkness* is striking for its low-key observation of everyday life under the occupation and its simplicity of plot and construction.

When the Jewish family leave at the beginning of the film to report for their transport, the whole episode is understated while, at the same time, conveying fear and irony. The routine of daily life is also convincingly displayed during a family evening as Pavel studies, his mother sews and his grandfather works on his inventions, with Ketèlbey's 'In a Persian Market' on the radio. Reactions to the death of Heydrich are conveyed solely in looks. A reference to the Nazi destruction of the village of Lidice is referred to only in the phrase 'they killed a whole village'.

Weiss's loving portrayal of the central romance and the beauty of the young woman are the film's dominant factors. Focusing on the attic room, the centre of Pavel's childhood fantasies, it is a world isolated from the Nazi terror that rules outside. The face of Dana Smutná provides the film's emotional focus – sad, melancholy, reluctantly drawn into the young man's obsession. Her final smile and their silent waltz convey the depth of their feeling and the pathos of the situation. While the reactions of the world outside are graduated and contrasted much like Petr Jarchovský's script for the more recent *Divided We Fall*, it is this visual portrait that carries the film's emotional force.

In keeping with its classical style, violence is kept off screen and it is the small points of observation that contribute most to its overall effect. When

Heydrich is assassinated, the previously empty streets echo with the visual and aural shock of military carriers. Nothing more explicit is needed to convey the resultant terror which threatens the central characters. The film went on to win numerous international awards.

Zbyněk Brynych's *Transport from Paradise* (1962) was the first film to be adapted from the stories of Arnošt Lustig. Lustig, who was sent to Terezín and subsequently Auschwitz and Buchenwald, was a foreign correspondent during the 1948 Israel–Arab conflict, reporting from the Israeli side. Falling under official disapproval during the Stalinist trials, his collection of stories *Night and Hope* (*Noc a naděje*) was published in 1957 and followed in 1958 by *Diamonds of the Night*, a second collection. His fiction has been continuously based on the Holocaust and remains so to this day. He has said that he believes in writing as memory – 'my inclination is this responsibility to the dead, but I cannot describe them as dead. I have to share the illusion that writing about these people is like writing about the living'.[11]

> The Jewish catastrophe was one of the most important events in history, not because it happened to Jews – because it could happen to Czechs, or to Russians, or to Americans – but because it happened at all. It proved that man is able to destroy his fellow man for a very small reason or without reason, for some demonic prejudices.[12]

The screenplay of *Transport from Paradise* was adapted by Brynych and Lustig from the stories in *Night and Hope*, which are reworked to form a single narrative. They are unified through the visit of a German SS general charged with organising a transport to the death camps. Near the beginning of the film, we witness the shooting of the Nazi propaganda film, *Theresienstadt: A Documentary from the Jewish Settlement Area* (*The Führer Gives a Town to the Jews*). Its Jewish director, Kurt Gerron, is introduced to the general and key scenes are rehearsed in which various inmates repeat the words 'I am all right in Theresienstadt' or 'I lack nothing in Theresienstadt' in a variety of languages.

In welding together themes and incidents from the original stories, Brynych and Lustig attempt a broad portrait of the realities and different moral choices, ranging from sacrifice to collaboration. Did the Jewish elders collaborate? Was resistance impossible? In a rather obvious image in the opening scenes, sheep make way for a motorcycle and sidecar, preparing the ground for the film's moral, 'Never again like sheep'.

The film uses a predominantly 'realist' approach with an initial portrait of the details of community life filmed in an almost cinéma-vérité style. When the Jewish chairman of the town council, Löwenbach, refuses to sign the document for the latest transport to Auschwitz because he has heard about the gas chambers, it becomes apparent that the Jews have access to forbidden sources of information. (The Nazis announce proudly that the Jews have the right to self-government, under supervision, and that *they* make the decisions on who will be transported.) A poster is revealed proclaiming 'Death to Fascism' and the hunt begins for an underground printing press and radio. Löwenbach is, however, soon replaced by the compliant Marmulstaub and the limited resistance is rewarded by death and transportation. There is some stereotyping here but also a sophisticated range of characterisation.

While working principally on a 'realist' level, the film is underlined by strong formal elements. It is punctuated by the patrol of the empty ghetto streets by Obersturmführer Herz in his motorcycle and sidecar, the scenes of the young people before the transport are accompanied by the sound of a guitar played in their quarters and, finally, the whole ghetto is paraded and counted in order to find a wounded conspirator. Here the endless lines of inmates standing on the Apfelplatz are accompanied by the insistent repetition of a train whistle and repeated shots of them splashing through mud towards their Nazi oppressors. The film ends with the departure of the train for Auschwitz, moving on rail tracks that run through the town's streets.

Brynych followed *Transport from Paradise* with the rather different *The Fifth Horseman is Fear* (1964). Adapted from the novel by Hana Bělohradská (*Without Beauty, Without Collar/Bez krásy, bez límce*), it tells the story of a Jewish doctor in Nazi-occupied Prague who pays with his life for sheltering a wounded Resistance fighter. Originally designed as a realist account, Brynych and his screenwriter Ester Krumbachová deprived it of its topical references, including the Nazi insignia, in order to represent fascism as 'an international disease' whose symptoms were to be found in many countries. A world of fear and of informing is evoked and the words 'Let Dr Braun take the blame. Blame the Jew for whatever the police want' are spoken. The film begins and ends with dark figures waiting in the streets and, as in his earlier film *Skid* (*Smyk*, 1960), written by Jiří Vala and Pavel Kohout, Brynych uses Expressionist imagery and lighting to create an overbearing sense of foreboding. As Jan Zalman wrote, 'Everything in this film takes place in an atmosphere of intense anxiety . . . The narrow lanes, the ill-lit yards, and mysterious backwaters of old Prague are the landscape of Fear.'[13]

But, while Brynych widens the range of reference, his hero remains Jewish and the early scenes of the film where he moves from room to room through objects assembled by class – pianos, violins, clocks, china – confiscated from the Jews sent to the camps, hardly need abstraction to make their points. The film evokes a sense of hallucination and nightmare. The film's central scenes in which Braun (Miroslav Macháček) searches for morphine from a former colleague take him to a decadent late night party and a mental asylum, which become stylistically associated. The sustained and grotesque party is initially lit like a stage set but finally illuminated by a lighted ceiling. In one scene, Braun is provided with an extended soliloquy accompanied by the sound of violin. The arrival of the wounded fighter on his bike is backed by cheerful music and is initially perceived as comedy by a watching boy. Shots of neighbours on the stairs or peering over the stairwell – hardly a new device – here achieve a strange intensity and unique composition. From the opening scenes, where we see confiscated pianos, the sound of the piano plays a key role. The opening scenes are accompanied by the sound of a piano tuner, which are later replaced by piano scales and music emanating from a piano teacher's flat. The part of the teacher is played by Olga Scheinflugová, the widow of the writer, Karel Čapek. This is not without its own resonance given Čapek's strong anti-Fascism and the death of his brother, Josef, the well-known painter, in Auschwitz. While Brynych remains faithful to his subject, this search for wider symbolism, besides evoking Kafka, is clearly linked to the contemporary world, the persecutions, denunciations and informing that characterised the Stalinist years.

The same symbolic approach is adopted in Jan Němec's first feature, *Diamonds of the Night*, which was made the same year. Adapted from Arnošt Lustig's novella *Darkness Casts No Shadow* (*Tma nemá stín*), it tells the story of two Jewish teenagers who escape from a Nazi death train and flee through the woods. Němec creates an intensely emotional film that identifies with their emotional state and uses the full range of film technique to create a hallucinatory dream world. More experimental than Lustig's original, we do not discover whether the boys live on or die – we are given two endings, either of which could be imaginary. The film will be discussed further in the chapter on avant-garde film but, lest we convert it entirely into an 'auteur' film, it is worth recalling that the story is rooted in Lustig's own experience. He himself escaped from a death train and was recaptured three times and three times was sentenced to death.

> I can tell you the story of two of these almost executions, but the third escaped from my memory, and I am still trying to remember . . . I know that it happened during the trip, but what really happened, I don't know. My memory plays with me. My memory suppresses what is very unpleasant – it comes here and there; it jumps out like a devil from a box.[14]

Lustig, who once said that his verbal attempts to describe his experiences in the camps came across as hallucinations and that this was what prompted him to write, described *Diamonds of the Night* as the best of the adaptations from his work.[15]

The most famous of all the Czechoslovak Holocaust films is *The Shop on the High Street* (1965). One of a sequence in the partnership of Ján Kadár and Elmar Klos, it was the first Czechoslovak film to win an Academy award. Based on a novel by Ladislav Grosman, it is set during the period of the 'independent'

Slovak state during the Second World War. It takes place in a small town and focuses on the relationship between an old Jewish woman, Mrs Lautmannová (Ida Kamińská) and a Slovak carpenter, Tono Brtko (Jozef Kroner), who is allocated her button shop as an 'Aryan controller'. The shop, however, is worthless – Lautmannová is supported by the Jewish community – and she is stone deaf. She is under the impression that Tono is her shop assistant while he has to maintain the fiction that he is in charge. The mutual misunderstanding is initially comic, as a strange form of interdependence develops prior to the deportation of the Jewish community. However, when Lautmannová is left off the list, Tono is scared that he will be accused of sheltering a Jew and tries to get her to join the deportees. He fails and pushes her into the cellar. When the transport is over, he finds that she is dead and hangs himself.

The film is a grim moral fable that works on a number of levels. Tono is the proverbial 'little man', whose main object is to stay out of trouble, and he wants life to continue as normal. His brother-in-law is, however, a leading member of the Hlinka Guards and Tono's wife is anxious to make the most of her new financial opportunities. The development of 'everyday Fascism' towards its eventual horrors finds its parallel in a wooden pyramid ('the Tower of Victory') that is slowly being constructed in the town square. Its completion, together with the slogan of the clerical-Fascist state 'Life for God, Liberty for the Nation', coincides with the transportation of the Jews.

The film shows how Tono's minor compromises take him on a path leading to virtual collusion but it avoids simple moral statements through its emphasis on the central relationship. This almost has the character of a romance as Mrs Lautmannová cooks for him and plays her dead husband's favourite record and Tono reconditions her furniture. She gives him her husband's old suit and bowler hat, making him look like Charlie Chaplin. In one scene, in which he 'promenades' with his wife and her brother, Kroner develops this into a comic turn that constantly deflates and undermines their pretensions. In an episode of wish fulfilment at the end of the film, Tono, dressed as Chaplin, escorts Lautmannová in a bitter-sweet dance to the sounds of the town band.

As mentioned earlier, Slovakia achieved its formal independence in March 1939, coinciding with the German occupation of the Czech lands of Bohemia and Moravia. Slovakia signed an agreement that effectively recognised German protection of its political independence and territorial integrity. Behind its Christian facade, the state implemented Nazi laws against the Jews without restriction. The film is set in 1942, the year of the Nuremburg Laws, which Slovakia was among the first to implement. Indeed, as Ľubomír Lipták put it, it was as if the government was compensating for its servility toward Germany by concentrating a frustrated ambition for power on the Jews.[16]

Ľubica Mistríková has admirably analysed the complexity of the film's approach and the ways in which it moves from comedy to tragedy, creating

Figure 5.1   Ján Kadár and Elmar Klos: *A Shop on the High Street* (*Obchod na korze*, 1965)

a continuous tragic-comic mode. Despite the fact that many of the scenes are comic, it is essential that they also contain the elements that will build towards a tragic ending. Kadár referred to the film as a comedy set within the classic structure of ancient tragedy. In his interview with Liehm, he noted his interest in 'a comic, grotesque, tragic scenario that grows entirely out of a misunderstanding' and 'the possibility of showing the whole problem from the inside out, in one drop of water. Talking about millions is, indeed, always easier than showing one human fate'.[17]

While the film is fundamentally cast in the form of a classic narrative, it is a work of considerable sophistication. The performances of Kroner and Kamińská (a Polish actress and co-founder of the Yiddish Art Theatre of Warsaw) are masterly and sensitively convey the shifting nature of personal and community relations. Vladimír Novotný's camerawork and Zdeněk Liška's music also play significant roles in creating the film's atmosphere and emotion.

While based on Slovak sources, featuring Slovak actors and being spoken only in Slovak, the film was, in fact, produced by the Barrandov Film Studios in Prague so that, while it is a key film in the history of Slovak film culture, it is officially a 'Czech' film because of its production history. But, as Mistríková notes, it is perhaps the first genuine Czech–Slovak production, made at a time when the concept of co-production did not exist. Like *Distant Journey*, the film deals with both individual destiny and the wider political reality but, here, it is through individual destiny that the broader historical and political points are made manifest.

Between 1965 and 1967, there were two further adaptations from works by Arnošt Lustig – Antonín Moskalyk's television adaptation of his *A Prayer for Kateřina Horovitzová* (1965) and his feature film *Dita Saxová* (1967). *Dita Saxova* is concerned with the trauma of survival. Dita is the only one of her family to have survived the camps and lives in a women's home run by the Jewish community of Prague. Courted by three men, she loses her virginity to one who merely treats her as one of his conquests. She loses her three friends, emigrates to Switzerland, celebrates her nineteenth birthday and disappears (we assume) to certain death in the mountains.

The film concentrates on her failure to find emotional reassurance and love. Dita, played by the Polish actress Krystyna Mikolajewska, is stunningly beautiful but curiously detached and unemotional. While this is no doubt the result of her experiences, the film also emphasises this through an approach reminiscent of Antonioni's early 1960s' trilogy of *L'Avventura* (1960), *La Notte* (1961) and *L'Eclisse* (1962). She is primarily a component of Moskalyk's widescreen compositions set against walls, textures and buildings. The scope images, filmed in sepia by Jaroslav Kučera, are remarkable in themselves but the slow pace and extensive dialogue scenes fail to achieve the intensity of, for instance, *Romeo, Juliet and Darkness*.

A different approach to the Holocaust theme was taken in Juraj Herz's adaptation of Ladislav Fuks's novel *The Cremator* (1968). Fuks had made his reputation with his first novel, *Mr Theodor Mundstock* (*Pan Theodor Mundstock*, 1963), in which his Jewish hero prepares himself both psychologically and physically for his eventual transportation to a concentration camp. First published in 1967, the novel of *The Cremator* tells the story of Karel Kopfrkingl, a worker in a crematorium who rises to the position of director. He is proud of his mastery in his trade and takes mystical pride in the incineration of the dead, who are therefore rapidly speeded towards reincarnation. He wants to spare people the pain of life and is preoccupied with the *Tibetan Book of the Dead* and the Dalai Lama. He is opposed to suffering which, he believes, should have no role in the modern humanitarian state.

Karel's progressive fantasies lead to total madness when he encounters a German friend who points out that Hitler, like Karel, also wishes to eliminate suffering and converts him to Nazi racist ideology and the need to eliminate those of Jewish origin. Eventually, he realises that his wife, Lakmé, is half Jewish and that his two children are therefore also tainted.

Herz, who had been assistant director on *Transport from Paradise* and *A Shop on the High Street*, had been imprisoned in Ravensbrück concentration camp during the war. He originally studied puppetry alongside Jan Švankmajer, appearing in both Švankmajer's *The Last Trick* aka *The Last Trick of Mr Schwarzwald and Mr Edgar* (*Poslední trik pana Schwarcewalldea a pana Edgara*, 1964) and *The Flat* (*Byt*, 1968). *The Cremator* was his third film as a director. Not surprisingly, it has been marketed and appreciated largely as a horror film and has, courtesy of DVD, subsequently come to acquire a cult following.

The film is something of a tour de force with Stanislav Milota's cinematography employing a wide-ranging use of camera techniques and an impressive use of depth of field and the wide angle lens. The whole story is accompanied by a remarkable performance by Rudolf Hrušínský as Karel, whose melodious and unctuous voice is both hypnotic and insidious. The credit sequence – a montage of hands, portions of bodies and faces sinking into an infernal holocaust – is accompanied by a ghostly female voice. The film goes much further than Radok in its descent into nightmare. Here, the hero murders his own family and any sense of logic, order and realism is stripped away to reveal a political world where only a madman can remain with some form of control. Michael Brooke suggests that the Nazi theme is a kind of diversion from the film's experimental and aesthetic journey,[18] yet it is the discovery of the Holocaust reflected in microcosm and in personal relations that provides its unique horror and there is little doubt that this reflects Fuks's own aesthetic. The continued parallel with contemporary realities is also there – although Herz leaves out the book's ironic conclusion when Karel observes victims returning from the camps and promises a new order without persecution, injustice or suffering.

Herz planned to work with Fuks on two further scripts – *The Story of a Police Commissioner* (*Příběh kriminálního rady*) and *Natalia Mooshaber's Mice* (*Myši Natálie Mooshabrové*) – but, although the scripts had been prepared, the Soviet invasion ensured that the time for such experiments was over. In 1985, Herz took on another 'holocaust' subject with *I Was Caught by the Night*. Based on a story by Jaromíra Kolářová, Herz adapted it to tell the story of Milena Jesenská, Kafka's girlfriend, who was not Jewish, and also drew upon his own experiences in Ravensbrück. But, generally speaking, the flowering of Jewish subjects that characterised the 1960s, whether used symbolically or not, had come to an end. There were films dealing with the war theme on a kind of analogous level. Moskalyk's film of Vladimír Körner's script *Cuckoo in the Dark Forest* (*Kukačka ve temném lese*, 1984) told the story of a Nazi officer who adopted a Czech boy because of his Aryan appearance and Karel Kachyňa adapted Jewish writer Ota Pavel's *The Golden Eels* (*Zlatí úhoři*, 1979) and *Death of the Beautiful Roebucks* (*Smrt krásných srnců*, 1986). In 1989, he filmed another Terezín story, the Anglo-Czech *The Last Butterfly* (*Poslední motýl*), featuring Tom Courtenay, which was released in 1990. Vojtěch Jasný had planned to film Lustig's *The Unloved* in the USA but this came to nothing as well.

The Jewish theme in post-1989 cinema has not been any more prominent but it has had a presence. Two films were adapted from Ivan Olbracht's collection *Golet in the Valley*, which were about pre-war Jewish life in sub-Carpathian Ruthenia. Zeno Dostal directed *Golet in the Valley* (*Golet v údolí*, 1995) and Karel Kachyňa made *Hanele* (1999), which was adapted from the well-known story *The Sad Eyes of Hanna Karajich* (*O smutných očích Hany Karadžičové*). Olbracht himself had, of course, collaborated on Vladislav Vančura's film *Faithless Marijka* (*Marijka nevěrnice*, 1934) which, unlike Dostal's and Kachyna's films, was filmed on location in Ruthenia. Both *Golet in the Valley* and *Hanele* were low-budget films designed primarily for television. Vladimir Körner continued the race theme of *Cuckoo in the Dark Forest* with Milan Cieslar's *The Spring of Life* (*Pramen života*, 2000). Dealing with the Nazi Lebensborn programme, the film's central character falls in love with a young Jewish boy.

Two films deal directly with the theme of the Holocaust – Slovak director Matej Mináč's *All My Loved Ones* (*Všichni moji blízci*, 1999) and Jan Hřebejk's *Divided We Fall* (2000). Mináč also directed a documentary about the English diplomat Nicholas Winton, who saved 669 mainly Jewish children from the Nazi death camps. *Nicholas Winton – The Power of Good* (*Sila ľudkosti Nicholas Winton*, 2001) won an Emmy award. *All My Loved Ones* tells the story of the destruction of a rich Jewish family against the background of the growth of Nazism. Despite a certain degree of international success, the script by Jiří Hubač was schematic and the characters rather one-dimensional. The eighty-seven-year-old Jiří Weiss had fared rather better with his sensitively realised and more personal film of his own script *Martha and I* (*Martha a já/ Martha und Ich*, 1990). Czech made but German produced, it featured Michel Piccoli and Marianne Sägebrecht in the roles of a Jewish gynaecologist who marries his Sudeten German housemaid. It was based on his childhood memories of his own uncle who ended up in a concentration camp.

However, the most impressive of the later films is undoubtedly *Divided We Fall*, which was shortlisted for an Oscar and enjoyed wide international distribution. The team of writer Petr Jarchovský and director Jan Hřebejk has been the most successful in post-1989 Czech cinema with films such as *Cosy Dens*, *Pupendo* and *Up and Down*. While *Divided We Fall* was their biggest international success, it was the least successful of their domestic releases – although it was still well into the top twenty Czech releases.

Jarchovský and Hřebejk seem to have set out to provide their own parallel to Czech history with films that dealt with the Second World War – *Divided We Fall* – the fifties – *Big Beat* (*Šakalí leta*, 1993) – the year of the Prague Spring – *Cosy Dens*, 1999 – the years of normalisation that followed – *Pupendo* – and the contemporary situation – *Up and Down*, 2004.

Unlike the sixties films, which dealt directly with situations of which their writers and directors often had personal knowledge, *Divided We Fall* was made by film-makers who had not even been born at that time. The theme of the Jewish man hidden during the war had obvious parallels and the fine line sometimes drawn between opposition and collaboration are themes familiar from a number of the 1960s films. In a press conference, Jarchovský also recounted how he had asked the novelist Josef Škvorecký, who had lived through the war years, if his plot was plausible. Škvorecký's reply was in the affirmative.

Jarchovský's script takes on the subject of the relationship between Czechs, Jews and Sudeten Germans during the Nazi occupation of the country. In a pre-credit sequence, we see three friends from before the war, the Czech Josef Čížek (Boleslav Polívka), the German Horst Prohaska (Jaroslav Dušek) and the Jewish David Wiener (Csongor Kassai) whose father employs them all. The Jewish family is expelled from its home and sent to Terezín. The opening sequence ends with the escaped Jewish man, David, looking for help from his former friends. The Czech title of *Divided We Fall*, which translates as 'We must help each other', is ironic and is spoken by Horst to Josef.

Josef and Marie agree to hide David in a secret room and keep him there until the end of the war. The film's central plot then centres round Marie's pregnancy by David. However, this is not an affair. Josef, who has been diagnosed by a collaborationist doctor as infertile, needs a child in order to prevent their having to share his flat with a Nazi bureaucrat and comes up with the scheme himself. It is the only way to prevent David's discovery.

Horst, who collaborates with the Nazis – but draws a distinction between Sudeten Germans like him and Reich Germans like his wife – persists in his efforts to maintain his pre-occupation contacts with the Čížeks, bringing them gifts and attempting to encourage their involvement with the new realities. Horst suspects that they are hiding David but keeps his suspicions to himself while Josef (at Marie's insistence) joins Horst in his work and is soon regarded as a collaborator by the neighbours. Horst teaches him how to adopt the dead facial mask that indicates 'an irreproachable expression of loyalty'. In fact, albeit by chance, Josef is defending the lives not only of David but also of those on his street who might be associated with the harbouring of a Jew. At the end of the film, Josef is only saved by David's testimony and Horst is only saved by Josef's intervention. The Czech who appears to be a collaborator is revealed as sheltering a Jew and protecting the lives of his neighbours while Horst, who has collaborated, assists at the birth of a part-Jewish child.

Both Josef and Horst are shown, in their different ways, as victims of events rather than individuals devoted to a cause. They represent the choices of those without power, those who wish to survive. The choice faced by most people under tyranny is either conformity or the pretence of conformity and no choice is without its risk of harming someone. In another irony, Šimáček, one of the neighbours, who is earlier introduced as a helpful and reliable man, attempts to denounce David on his first appearance after his escape. He fears for his life. Later on, he joins the resistance and denounces Josef as a collaborator. He reacts with obvious shame when he learns the truth.

David has an unchanging situation – save for the fact that he is required to make love to his friend's wife in order to ensure his survival. The film functions primarily as an analysis of the adjustments of those who find themselves hiding him (since it can hardly be presented as a decision). One of the few explicit references to Nazi racism is the comment by the Nazi official who inherits the Wieners' house that, according to a scientific study, the life of one German is equal to that of twenty Slavs or one hundred Jews.

Jarchovský's approach in all of his scripts is to avoid simplification and suggest ambiguity – to indicate that almost everyone 'has his reasons'. Thus even the Germans, whose ideology is never presented as anything other than vicious, remain people whose lives are affected and who retain human rather than merely symbolic properties. At the end of the film, Josef happily pushes the pram with his new Jewish-Czech child against a background of the damage caused by the Prague uprising, imagining the return of the Wiener family and of a world that has now gone forever. Unusually, the film also reveals the violence and vengeance wreaked on the Nazis and their collaborators – something that would never have been shown in a film in the Communist era.

The Jewish subject will probably not figure largely as a continuing theme in Czech feature films and *Divided We Fall* is really about the adjustments likely to be made under any form of tyranny. However, Arnošt Lustig points out that, despite the fact that his own and sole subject is the Holocaust, he regards the term as a label, a simplification. The genocide of other races has occurred both before and since the Second World War. He is really writing 'about people under pressure. Under certain circumstances, this subject encompasses subjects like love, friendship, courage, cowardice, pride. So it doesn't limit me in any way'.[19] The theme of the Holocaust may continue in some form but, like *Divided We Fall*, it will be the analysis of a particular situation by creators for whom it has become a part of history.

NOTES

1. Ján Kadár, interviewed by Antonín J. Liehm, *Closely Watched Films: The Czechoslovak Experience* (New York: International Arts and Sciences Press, 1974), p. 408
2. See Ewa Mazierska, 'Wanda Jakubowska: the Communist Fighter', in Ewa Mazierska and Elżbieta Ostrowska (eds), *Women in Polish Cinema* (New York and Oxford: Berghahn Books, 2006), pp. 149–65.
3. Bosley Crowther, *New York Times*, 28 August 1950, quoted in *Closely Watched Films*, p. 41.
4. Karel Kosík, 'What is Central Europe?', in Kosík, *The Crisis of Modernity: Essays and Observations from the 1968 Era*, ed. James H. Satterwhite (Lanham, MD: Rowman and Littlefield, 1995), pp. 174–5.
5. Jiří Cieslar, 'Daleká cesta (Distant Journey)', in Peter Hames (ed.), *The Cinema of Central Europe* (London: Wallflower Press, 2004), p. 46.
6. Ibid., p. 47.
7. Ibid., p. 51.
8. Alfréd Radok, interviewed in Liehm, *Closely Watched Films*, pp. 44–5.
9. Ibid., p. 39.
10. Alfred French, *Czech Writers and Politics 1945–1969* (Boulder: East European Monographs; New York: Columbia University Press, 1982), p. 128.
11. Arnošt Lustig, in Jeffrey Young, 'A Conversation with Arnošt Lustig and Miroslav Holub', *Trafika* (Prague), 1, Autumn 1993, p. 161.
12. Ibid.
13. Jan Žalman, *Films and Filmmakers in Czechoslovakia* (Prague: Orbis, 1968), pp. 32–3.
14. Lustig, 'A Conversation with Arnošt Lustig and Miroslav Holub', p. 165.
15. Arnošt Lustig, 'A Small Stone in a Big Mosaic', interviewed by Pavlina Kostková, *Central Europe Review*, 3, 28, 22 October 2001 http://www.ce-review.org/01/28/kostkova28.html [Accessed 02/03/02].
16. Ľubomír Lipták, *Slovensko v. 20 storočí* (Bratislava: Kalligram, 1998), quoted in Ľubica Mistríková, *Obchod na korze/A Shop on the High Street*, in Peter Hames (ed.), *The Cinema of Central Europe* (London: Wallflower Press, 2004), p. 99.
17. Ján Kadár, interviewed by Antonín J. Liehm, quoted in Ľubica Mistríková, 'Obchod na korze/A Shop on the High Street', in Peter Hames (ed.), *The Cinema of Central Europe* (London: Wallflower Press, 2004), p. 101.
18. Michael Brooke, 'The Flame and the Flesh', *Sight and Sound*, 16, 6 June 2006, p. 88.
19. Lustig interviewed by Pavlina Kostková.

6. LYRICISM

In 1934, during the Venice Film Festival, the City of Venice gave a joint award to four Czechoslovak films, Gustav Machatý's *Ecstasy* (1932), Josef Rovenský's *The River* (1933), Karel Plicka's *The Earth Sings* (1933) and Tomáš Trnka's short film, *Storm Over the Tatras* (*Bouře nad Tatrami,* 1932). It is interesting that the name of the avant-garde film maker Alexander Hackenschmied (Alexander Hammid) was associated with two of them, as assistant director on *Ecstasy* and as editor of *The Earth Sings.* Two of the films were Slovak (*The Earth Sings* and *Storm Over the Tatras*) and *Ecstasy* used both Slovak and Ruthenian locations. All of the films, with the exception of *The Earth Sings*, were photographed by Jan Stallich. Here, in the world's first international film festival, one could argue that the notion of 'Czech lyricism' was born. Whether this was due to the accidental appearance of three films by Stallich or three films foregrounding the Slovak landscape is a matter for conjecture. But there is, indeed, a sense that much Czech (and Slovak) cinema reveals a continuing concern with the lyrical evocation of landscape and that this has been conveyed primarily through the sensibility of cinematographers.

If one accepts the dictionary definition of lyrical, then it is something that is like poetry or aspiring to the condition of poetry, with poetry itself defined as the expression of elevated thought or feeling in a metrical form. Thus the presence of nature and of landscape, although frequently associated with lyricism, is not a necessary element. Nonetheless, the term 'lyrical' is invariably used to describe Czech films or cinematographers whose work contains these elements.

They are also, of course, characteristics that increase the films' emotional and aesthetic intensity.

The presence of landscape in Czech films is not unique to that art form and, of course, is to be found elsewhere, most notably in painting and music. One has only to think of Dvořák, Smetana or Suk, who (like Sibelius and Vaughan Williams) ally the musical evocation of landscape with a strong sense of national identity. One of movements of Smetana's patriotic *My Country* is, after all, called *From Bohemia's Woods and Fields*. In Jan Svěrák's 1991 film *The Elementary School*, the music of Dvořák and the landscape come together in a film that is, on one level, about national identity. The same phenomenon is to be found in most European cultures, particularly in times of war, threat and occupation.

In discussing lyricism in Czech cinema, the essential elements comprise the visual image (cinematography), the evocation of landscape as a positive force and a sense of the countryside as a homeland and of a paradise lost or regained. The scene in Menzel's *Closely Observed Trains* where the hero thinks he is about to be killed and thinks about 'the world he is about to leave' creates just this sense. Vojtěch Jasný, whose films *Desire* and *All My Good Countrymen* (1968) strongly embody these qualities, called his revisiting of these locations after his foreign exile *Return to the Lost Paradise* (*Návrat ztraceného ráje*, 1999).

For a tradition that implicates the role of the cinematographer so strongly, it is important to reconsider the notion of authorship. As Cathy Greenhalgh argues, in conventional criticism, the director is normally viewed as responsible for a film's content – 'its conception and the formal relation of both story and performance'. For Greenhalgh, '[t]he cinematographer's realm is perceived as relating to the "style" of the film, and to the techniques and tools which serve it. This separation of duties reinforces beliefs about roles which in reality considerably overlap'.[1] She suggests that alternative histories could be written via the work of key cinematographers – for example, Boris Kaufman who worked with Jean Vigo, Elia Kazan and Sidney Lumet; Sacha Vierny who worked with Alain Resnais and Peter Greenaway; and Freddie Francis who, as well as directing horror films, photographed films for Jack Clayton, Karel Reisz, Martin Scorsese and David Lynch.

The work of a particular cinematographer often provides a sequence of films by a director with a particular 'look' but a cinematographer's style may also change according to director or subject. The Czech cinematographer Otto Heller, who went on to pursue a career in the United Kingdom after the Second World War, had worked before the war with Martin Frič, Voskovec and Werich, and Hugo Haas. However, the 'styles' adopted for Laurence Olivier's adaptation of Shakespeare's *Richard III* (1955), Alexander Mackendrick's comedy *The Ladykillers* (1955), Michael Powell's psychological horror *Peeping Tom*

(1960) and Sidney J. Furie's thriller *The Ipcress File* (1965) proved to be very different. To state the obvious, the 'styles' he adopted for different directors and cinematographers interact and complement each other in different ways.

A feeling for lyricism and landscape is a characteristic of the work of many Czech and Slovak cinematographers and directors. Here one can point to the work of Jan Stallich, Ferdinand Pečenka, Jan Čuřík, Jaroslav Kučera, Dodo Šimončič, Martin Štrba, and Jaromir Kačer (cinematographers) and directors such as Gustav Machatý, Josef Rovenský, Václav Krška, František Vláčil, Vojtěch Jasný and Jaromil Jireš, among others.

Gustav Machatý was one of the few Czech directors of the interwar years to gain an international reputation. He directed his first film in 1919 and worked in Hollywood during 1920 and 1921 but made his reputation after returning to Czechoslovakia with an impressive adaptation of Tolstoy's *The Kreutzer Sonata* (*Kreutzerova sonata*, 1926). In the late 1920s and early 1930s he worked with the poet Vitězslav Nezval on two films, *Erotikon* (1929) and *From Saturday to Sunday* (*Ze soboty na nědeli*, 1931). Nezval was one of the founders of the Czech Poetist movement in the 1920s, which converted into a strong Surrealist movement in the 1930s. Nezval's name has also been linked to Machatý's *Ecstasy*. However, one suspects that, while Nezval may have contributed creative impulses and ideas, the real creative input was indeed that of Machatý, who was certainly a director of ambition.

Ecstasy is today remembered as the film that enjoyed a certain *succès de scandale* at the 1934 Venice Film Festival, outraging the Vatican with its shots of a naked Hedy Lamarr (then Kiesler) and, for its time, outspoken sex scenes. While its plot was not as strong as either *Erotikon* or *From Saturday to Sunday*, its formal elements made it one of the foremost films of its time. Its simplifications were intended to produce an early sound film with international appeal.

The fundamental story is quite simple. The heroine, Eva (Hedy Kiesler), gets married to a dull and self-centred older man who treats her as little more than a material acquisition, neglecting her both personally and sexually. She leaves home and returns to her father's estate and the freedom of the countryside. She asks for a divorce but, in the meantime, begins an affair with Adam (Zvonimir Rogoz), a handsome engineer. When her husband eventually comes to fetch her, his chance of reclaiming her has passed. It seems as if he may murder her lover but eventually opts for his own suicide.

The American poet, Parker Tyler, comes close to the film's essence in his comment that:

> poetry not plot is the pith of the matter, [as] is evident from the work's general looseness of structure . . . I fancy that, as an impressionist poem rather than a modern triangle drama . . . *Ecstasy* has influenced the world's experimental film movement more than is suspected.

In the erotic scenes, Machatý's 'vision of Hedy Lamarr seems one of lyric enchantment'.[2] Paul Rotha argued that Machatý's direction 'put him with the best directors of the period'.[3]

Although a sound film, *Ecstasy* has only a few spoken lines and is, to all intents, a silent film as far as speech is concerned. Stallich was already an experienced cinematographer but Machatý had been particularly impressed by his work on *Storm Over the Tatras* (1932). *Ecstasy* was his only film with Machatý since the director made no more films in Czechoslovakia. Zoë Bicât points out that Stallich differed from the influential German cinematography of the time by using less chiaroscuro and elaborated a low-key lighting style to a much greater extent than the Americans. His images, she remarks, 'have an eloquence which is almost independent of sound. Their lyricism relies on Stallich's arrangement of light, lens diffusion and camera movement'.[4] The jury of the European Federation of Cinematographers, which selected *Ecstasy* as one of the key films in the history of European cinematography in 2003, described the exterior photography as outstanding – 'full of romantic vision and unconventional shots'.[5]

When Eva is carried into her new house at the film's opening, we see erotic statuettes in her husband's collection but she is already framed behind the bars of a chair and the reality of her imprisonment is suggested. She looks in the mirror at her husband, smiles and then turns to see him walk out. She undresses flirtatiously but he pricks his hand on her necklace and retreats in discomfort. As the camera moves fluidly around her bed, his feet stretch out stiff and life-less, emphasising his polished shoes. She waits as the camera moves along her body and moves to close-ups of greetings telegrams.

Her husband's repressive (and repressed) nature is emphasised by the con-stant shadow of his hat and his involvement in routine actions. A repeated mirror shot precisely foreshadows that of Kane (Orson Welles) in *Citizen Kane* (1941) (and, indeed, the hall of mirrors sequence in Welles's *Lady from Shanghai*, 1948). When Eva departs, images of his shadow and reflection are cut together, emphasising a sense of psychological disruption.

When Eva lies in bed in her father's house, horses are seen on the skyline, dawn light pierces a crack in the curtains and is cast over one of her eyes. She rises and opens the curtains and the doors to the outside. When she rides out into the country, the opening up of the landscape creates an enormous sense of liberation. The celebrated bathing scene has a predictable premise – as she swims, her horse runs off, attracted by a mare. She runs after it in the nude and then hides in the bushes when the engineer arrives. She dresses and Adam band-ages her ankle after she has fallen. But this physically powerful and attractive man, unlike her husband, is gentle.

One might argue that the names of the lovers, Eva and Adam, the 'para-dise' of the landscape and the symbolism of horse and mare are heavy handed by contemporary standards. But the scenes of the naked woman against the landscape or merged with the patterns of water certainly create Tyler's sense of lyrical enchantment – the romantic merging of man and nature is strikingly achieved. Machatý's sense of the form and rhythm of landscape has, like Jasný's work, been compared with Dovzhenko's *Earth* (*Zemlya*, 1930).

The truly erotic scenes, recalling Machatý's treatment of a similar subject in *Erotikon*, follow this and are nothing like as physically explicit. Back in her father's house, Eva plays the piano amidst heavy and ornate décor, her face reflected in the piano top. A storm blows the curtains through the open window and there are repeat images of the horse. This is followed by an impressive sequence where Eva approaches her lover's cabin. The camera moves forward in jump cuts towards the lighted window at increasing speed, 'so that a rectangle of light at the lower right corner of the frame pounds outwards like a beating heart'.[6] Again her eyes are caught in the light. The following love scene is conveyed almost entirely by lighting and montage, with the camera shooting from above, below and the side. It is, of course, voyeuristic. Close-ups of her hand and arm trailing on the rug, her knees and her face from the front and side are followed by the image of Adam looking on.

One of the most noted sequences is the car journey at the end of the film when the husband gives Adam a lift. As the car progresses towards a level crossing, montage is used expressively – the cross cutting of close-ups between the two men, the increasing sound of the engine breaking in over the music, the replacement of this by the sound of a train whistle and the low angle shot of her husband through the driving wheel.

The final episode of the film is a visualisation of František Halas's poem 'Hymn to Work' ('Píseň práce'). This virtually abstract section features a low-angle montage of muscular workers edited to an increasing rhythm, intercut with ripening corn, wheels, water, cables and fountains and ending with the poetic image of mother and child. A continuous movement past raised picks juxtaposed with a constant single pick recalls the single scythe in Eisenstein's *The General Line*.

The film broke new ground in a number of directions, not least in its delicate handling of situations open to potential parody. And, as Tyler points out, it was 'an unusual gesture, in an unusual direction, when its subject – viewed seriously as I think its maker viewed it – required courage to film.'[7]

In Rovenský's *The River* aka *Young Love* (1933), Stallich's photography is again very much to the fore. The film tells a simple story about a young boy, Pavel, and his battle to catch a large pike that has been keeping fish away from a pool on the river, his relationship with a young girl, Pepička, and his suspected drowning. It depends centrally on its lyrical photography of the river and was photographed in the Sázava region of what is now the Czech Republic.

The opening scenes provide a powerful impact, with images of streams running through woods, tracking shots of the river, images of a man steering his raft through the waves and foam, culminating in a calm surface and shimmering light. A church sermon pronounces, 'First there was nature, and then there was man, who came to tame nature.' Shots of birds and trees and of deer swimming in the water give way to men, stripped to the waist, chopping up trees and tree roots. Man's evil side is represented by the shot of a man firing a gun. A poacher catches a rabbit but the lyrical tone prevails, as a singing reaper moves through the fields, his scythe over his arm.

The juxtaposition between romantic imagery and a harsh reality is maintained throughout the film. Pavel finds an animal's skeleton in a poacher's trap and peasants, recalling images from Eisenstein's *The General Line*, dig out buckets of stones as they try to turn impossible hill soil into arable land. A man pushes a plough as women pull it like human cattle.

The relationship between Pavel and Pepička develops during their last days at school. In a sentimental goodbye to the school, the now-adolescent children sing a folk song about parting. On the night of his departure, we see a Roma caravan against the skyline and a horse in the moonlight. A man plays an accordion and a girl sings a popular song of the period about nomadic life.

Although Pavel goes to the town, his emotional and imaginative world draws him back to the countryside and to his climactic duel with the pike. The sequence in which he catches the pike, as he ties the line around his waist, is very much like a prototype for the catching of the alligator in Robert Flaherty's *Louisiana Story* (1948). In the ensuing drama, the pike drags him underwater in a dramatic struggle.

The film does not seek the same stylistic heights as *Ecstasy* and its poetry is more restrained and balanced by the realities of life. Released internationally under the title of *Young Love*, the romantic relationship provides a key element in the film's poetic development, concentrating on small details and fantasies. The final schoolroom scene, for instance, focuses on flowers in vases and close-ups of the boys' and girls' feet under the desks. In one of their scenes in the countryside, Pavel gives Pepička four berries wrapped in a leaf. In another scene, they make a crown of daisies as he plays the mouth organ and she taps a bandaged big toe. He promises to buy her boots if he is successful in catching a large fish. Later, these elements trigger his return to the river which, of course, also carries its symbolic reference to life (as it does in Jean Renoir's film adaptation of Rumer Godden's *The River*, 1950).

Another director strongly influenced by these trends was Václav Krška who, with *Fiery Summer* (*Ohnivé léto*, 1939), in collaboration with František Čáp, made a strongly lyrical and erotic work. Set in the countryside of southern Bohemia and the town of Písek, where Krška was born and which provided the background of many of his later films, it was based on his own novel. Its story of young love and seduction is set against a luscious landscape, with plenty of opportunity for the exposure of attractive bodies. It won several Czech awards in 1940, a year in which such fantasies had become part of a lost reality. When I first saw it many years ago, I noted that it seemed almost like a cross between Machatý and D. H. Lawrence. It featured Lída Baarová in one of the leading roles and also shots of happy workers stacking the corn sheaves. His second film *Magic of the River* (*Řeka čaruje*, 1945) was the only film made during the last year of the war and was finished after the liberation. An ageing commercial advisor forsakes his life of routine and returns to the river of his youth, supporting himself with casual labour. If the film has any ideology at all, writes Peter Demetz, 'it is a lyrical populism favoring the people on the riverbanks, vagabonds, fishermen, farmhands, and millers, over bourgeois city residents. The river keeps flowing and rejuvenates, almost mystically'.[8]

These forms of lyrical film, with their appeal to the countryside and their sense of homeland, provided one of the first challenges to the straightjacket of Socialist Realism that had been enforced after 1948. Mira Liehm and Antonín Liehm noted that Krška had been torn away from 'his poetic, imaginative lyricism, his striking pictures of the Czech countryside, and his tense sensualism'.[9] But, if one moves to the mid 1950s, it was Krška again who reasserted the tradition of lyricism, albeit in a more refined manner, in his adaptations of Fráňa Šrámek's works, *Moon over the River* (*Měsíc nad řekou*, 1953) and *The Silver Wind* (*Stříbrný vítr*, 1954), this time photographed in colour. *The Silver Wind* was banned for two years apparently because of objections by a minister's wife.

Šrámek, also from Písek, who died in 1952, was a poet, novelist and dramatist who certainly dealt with themes of sexual awakening and rebellion set against petit bourgeois life. *Moon over the River* was based on Šrámek's play and *The Silver Wind* on his novel but both exhibit a reflective lyricism that is strikingly amplified by Ferdinand Pečenka's photography and Jiří Srnka's music. Krška's interest in young male bodies was certainly a matter of contention in the early fifties (although Czechoslovakia was one of the first countries to legalise homosexuality). However, memory leaves one with the film's moods rather than its themes – the small town of Písek and the lyrical evocation of youth against the background of the river and its gentle landscape. But, of course, neither film reflected the concerns and prerogatives of Socialist Realism.

Soon after this, in the late 1950s and early 1960s, a strong emphasis on lyricism developed in a sequence of films that, while they did not directly challenge the system, asserted quite different human values than those required by the prevailing ideology. Karel Kachyňa has noted how his early films with Jan Procházka comprised 'general humanistic ideas with a strongly lyrical note'.[10] Films such as *Fetters* (*Pouta*, 1961), *Stress of Youth* (*Trápení*, 1961) and *The High Wall* (*Vysoká zed'*, 1964) certainly reflected these qualities.

However, if we except Štefan Uher's Slovak film *Sunshine in a Net* (*Slnko v sieti*, 1962) which is discussed elsewhere, the most notable films were undoubtedly Jasný's *Desire* (1958) and Vláčil's *The White Dove* (*Holubice*, 1960). Jasný and Kachyňa, who worked together on a range of documentaries and one feature – *It Will All Be Over Tonight* (*Dnes večer všechno skončí*, 1954) – in the 1950s, had both studied cinematography and Vláčil, besides studying art history, had also worked as an assistant on animated films. In other words, their terms of reference lay with the potentiality of the image.

Jasný's principal collaborator on *Desire* was the cinematographer, Jaroslav Kučera, who was once described by the director Martin Frič as 'the most extraordinary cameraman this country has ever had'.[11] In fact, Kučera worked on two of Jasný's and Kachyňa's joint films and all of Jasný's subsequent features prior to his exile following the Prague Spring. Kučera's powerful use of the image reveals itself in the work of other directors but it is most notable in his work for Jasný and Věra Chytilová – *Daisies* and *The Fruit of Paradise* (*Ovoce stromů rajských jíme*, 1969) – to whom Kučera was married and whose work is discussed in the chapter on the avant-garde.

In Jasný's two films *Desire* (1958) and *All My Good Countrymen* (1968), there is a remarkable celebration of the Moravian landscape and of the eternal verities of the seasons. However, in the first of these, the emphasis on the human qualities of the lyrical film was of major significance since it was a time when such virtues in themselves represented a challenge to the status quo.

Scripted by Vladimír Valenta, who was later to play the stationmaster in Menzel's *Closely Observed Trains*, *Desire* consists of four separate and contrasting stories, corresponding to the four seasons of the year and the four ages of man. Its cyclical structure moves through an examination of the magic and wonder of childhood, the loves and illusions of youth, the struggle and hardship of middle age, through to the loneliness and sadness of old age. At the end of the film, an old woman dies and there is news that a child has been born.

Many of the scenes in the film have a strong sense of enchantment, deriving in large degree from the use of landscape. In the first episode, 'About the Boy Who Sought the Edge of the World' ('O chlapci, ktený hledal konec světa'), the film admirably conveys the immediacy and innocence of childhood experience. Small boys run across fields, then up a hill towards the camera. As they continue, their movement is intercut with shots of crows flying against the sky and trees outlined on the horizon. When the boys reach the horizon, they realise that it is not the edge of the world and the birds fly on across another landscape. As in *All My Good Countrymen*, much of the film's effect derives from evoking the textures of landscape – elements more often associated with the qualities of still photography.

The mood of magic and enchantment associated with the first episode gives place in the second to a spirit more in the mood of romantic pastiche. 'People on the Earth and Stars in Heaven' ('Lidé na zemi a Hvězdy na nebi') recounts

Figure 6.1   Vojtěch Jasný: *Desire* (*Touha*, 1958)

the story of the love between a young astronomer and a beautiful young girl. The stylised and stereotyped dialogue takes place against a background of strongly pastoral settings and a mood of romantic exultation. Here Kučera's photography of the black-and-white contrasts in the swirling water of the river and the Viennese-style waltz on the woodland dancing stage are particularly notable.

The landscape changes with the seasons and its use becomes more dramatic as the year moves on. In the third episode, 'Anděla', the only one with any political content, we are told the story of a strong individual, Anděla, who refuses all the pressures put on her to join a collective farm. When the collective finally decides to use persuasion rather than coercion, we are clearly looking at a scene put in to please the censors since the whole thrust of the story goes against this. The shots of the unrepentant Anděla and her itinerant assistant reaping against an impressive landscape of hills and sky are full of lyrical nostalgia for a lost way of life.

In the final episode, 'Mother' ('Maminka'), the mother of two men who have left home lives alone in a small village, where she teaches at the village school. Her sole companion is a black Labrador dog. When she dies, much play is made of the snow-covered landscape and the dog searching for his dead mistress to the tolling of a bell. The dog later links the sons to the past at their mother's funeral.

A film of great sensitivity and charm, it not surprisingly has many qualities in common with Jasný's masterpiece, *All My Good Countrymen*. As I have indicated elsewhere, it was based on his mother's memories of village life in the 1950s, the period of the enforced collectivisation of agriculture. The film is unique in Czech film history (and possibly in film history as such), in the way it juxtaposes its lyrical vision with the harsh political realities of the period. In this sense, it marks a strong contrast with the Kachyňa/Procházka *Night of the Bride* and its bleak portrait of destructive conflict.

The film basically spans the period from 1945 to 1958 with an epilogue set at the time of the Prague Spring. The main narrative begins in May 1945 and ends in the winter of 1958. It moves through a sequence of eleven sections which, again, follow the seasons but in an approximate rather than rigorous manner. It focuses almost entirely on village characters, people known to each other, and their reactions and progression as they are shaped by events.

The film begins with a landscape of extraordinary beauty, as the village characters are presented to us in the aftermath of the German occupation. After a night in the village pub – a constant point of reference throughout the film – they sleep off the night before under a tree in the fields. As dawn breaks, small figures fan out from the horizon in images of breathtaking beauty to the sound of the birds' morning chorus. Jasný pointed out that, immediately after the war, it was a time of high spirits, when everyone relaxed. When the Communists take over in 1948, the tannoy system relays propaganda as the landscape is covered with a powdering of snow.

However, the film does not use landscape as a correlative to narrative events and is more concerned to show that the seasons and nature prevail regardless – it is a continuing reality despite the arrogance and conflict of human endeavour. Thus each section of the film is prefaced by virtually still images of the countryside that verge on abstraction and serve to 'enclose' the action that follows. The overriding emphasis is on landscape – the fields, the almost abstract lines of ploughed land or birds perched on the stems of grass. Many are elaborated from themes that first appeared in *Desire*. The incorruptible František, who is imprisoned for his failure to join the collective, is shown throughout ploughing with his horse against the skyline. The dog that runs through the snow to welcome him back from prison and the swirling camera of the village dance both recall scenes first used in *Desire*. As in the case of Machatý, it is relevant to mention the influence of Dovzhenko as an inspiration – an influence that Jasný himself acknowledges. The village painter, as mentioned earlier, is also given to Chagall-like visions.

The other main film of significance in the resurrected 'poetic' school of the late 1950s to early 1960s is Vláčil's *The White Dove*. The film is a simple story about a young boy, Míša (played by future film director Karel Smyczek), an artist and a dove. The bird is released and, instead of finding its way home to the shores of the Baltic, is blown off course to Prague. There, the crippled boy,

Míša, shoots it with an air gun. But the bird is, in fact, rescued and the artist and the boy nurse it back to health, preparing it for freedom.

This is the only feature film on which Vláčil worked with the cinematographer, Jan Čuřík. Vláčil, who was a strongly visual director as is evident from later films – particularly his masterpiece *Marketa Lazarová* – almost certainly controlled the imagery, given his concern, like Hitchcock and Eisenstein, for composition within the frame. However, *The White Dove* is the most lyrical of his films and it also shares characteristics of Čuřík's work with other directors.

As Bicât points out, the film emphasises a high depth of field, with very long shots framing actions in the far corners of the screen.[12] Vláčil constructs a polarity between the dove's owner, Susanne, in the Baltic, where these are vivid contrasts of blacks and whites and shots of sea and beach, and the bleak grey of the apartment blocks where Míša and the painter live. As Bicât observes, when Míša inches around his flat in a wheelchair, his 'relationship to sunlight is like that of an imprisoned bird' with the use of shadows on translucent screens emphasising his spiritual stuntedness.[13]

The Baltic scenes are absolutely stunning. When the bird first fails to appear to Susanne, she is left sitting in a black head scarf with the surf breaking round her deserted figure and the jetty on which she sits framed at the top of the screen. Later, with the cage empty outside her house, she wakes up and the camera rights itself as she turns over. An imaginary voice hypnotically whispers her name. There are delicate shots of her searching on the beach. She is framed in the doorway, walking in shallow water and almost appears to be walking on the water. Later, when the artist's drawing of the bird arrives from Prague, it reaches her as she sits among the shallows, sheltered by a black umbrella. The scenes in Prague are more complex and suffused with a sense of imprisonment – both physical and psychological. Indeed, it is the bird's return to freedom that is associated with Míša not only recovering his spiritual balance but also his physical health.

The fact that cinematographers do not carry what appear to be characteristic styles into other features is apparent from Čuřík's and Kučera's other works. Čuřík, for instance, also worked with Zbyněk Brynych on *Transport from Paradise*, Chytilová on *Something Different*, Juráček and Schmidt on *Josef Kilián* aka *A Prop Wanted* (*Postava k podpírání*, 1963) and Schorm on *Everyday Courage*, all films with very different objectives and visual styles. Similarly, Kučera, aside from his 'experimental' work with Chytilová discussed elsewhere, worked with Němec on the hallucinatory *Diamonds of the Night*, the Hrabal tribute *Pearls of the Deep*, with Moskalyk on the Antonioni-influenced *Dita Saxová* and, post-1969, on a whole range of more 'commercial' films.

Another director with a strong lyrical vein was Jaromil Jireš, who worked with both Kučera and Čuřík. Jireš's debut film was *The Cry* (1963), which is normally considered part of the 'New Wave' breakthrough of 'realist' subject matter in a year that also included Forman's *Black Peter* and Chytilová's *Something Different*. Adapted from Ludvík Aškenazy's collection of stories *A Little Black Box* (*Černa bedýnka*), the film reflects what Czech critics had come to describe as 'the Aškenazy view' of life and Jireš considered the film to be an excellent testimony on the contemporary world. To quote Jan Žalman:

> Aškenazy works with minute splinters of experience, even the most insignificant of which is made by ingenious artistic effort to represent a miniature universe. The screenplay of *The Cry* orders these small particles in such a way as to form a plot and to serve an underlying idea.[14]

The story centres on Slávek, a television repair man whose life brings him into contact with different clients and different experiences, leading to a reflective perception of the world in which he lives. Intercut with this is the story of his wife, Ivana, who is in hospital expecting their first child, and a whole sequence of memories which primarily concern their first meeting and early romance, in which the memories of the couple sometimes merge – in the sense that the flashbacks link them and it is not always clear who has thought what. Further interpolations include fantasy and newsreel sequences.

Sometimes represented as an exercise in style for its own sake, Jireš's film is much more ambitious than this, linking 'realist' observation with newsreel representations, fantasies, hopes, romance – a portrait of both inner and outer worlds. Kučera's camera enters into this world, fully rendering its differences and ambiguities. As Žalman puts it, 'The resultant film is a cascade rather than a mosaic, a swift succession of images, of things past and present, a stream of subjective meditation, commentary and introspection, faith struggling against doubt all the time, confidence with uncertainty.'[15] There are episodes where Slávek walks on his hands, a sequence of romance that intercuts kissing couples and statues and montage sequences of Ivana skiing or dancing linked to photos. There is plenty of opportunity too for the demonstration of Kučera's virtuoso skills, although this is far from the evocation of the Moravian countryside characteristic of his work with Jasný.

Čuřík worked with Jireš on six of his feature films. In his adaptation of Kundera's *The Joke*, Jireš very consciously avoided the lyrical style to which he was temperamentally attracted. However, in the very different *Valerie and her Week of Wonders* (*Valerie a týden divů*, 1969) and *And Give My Love to the Swallows* (*. . . a pozdravuji vlaštovky*, 1972), he gives this full vein. I shall discuss *Valerie and her Week of Wonders* more fully in the chapter on surrealism. However, it is fair to say that audiences were stunned by Čuřík's award-winning cinematography, not just for its conventional lyricism but for its extraordinary attention to colour and texture.

The story of a young girl's fantasies during the week in which she 'becomes a woman', *Valerie and her Week of Wonders* was based on the 'black' novel by Vítězslav Nezval. It concentrates on a mix of Gothic fantasy and *Alice in Wonderland*, in which Valerie meets figures of ambiguous (mostly male) sexual identity who provide both threat and reassurance. Foremost among these is the weasel-like Tchoř (literally, polecat), a vampiric creature who is perceived as both priest and father figure. The film was co-adapted by Ester Krumbachová, who was also responsible for the costume design.

The rich reds of the coach into which Valerie climbs for security, the velvety folds of Tchoř's cape, the textures of Valerie's hair and the almost painterly qualities of the meadows immerse the film in a wash of colourful imagery, making it into a magic world of dreams, but ones that are ultimately reassuring. Most importantly, the film is set in an apparently isolated town in the countryside, a timeless venue surrounded by summer landscape.

And Give My Love to the Swallows, by contrast, is the story of a young resistance fighter, Maruška Kudeříková, who was imprisoned, tortured and executed by the Nazis. Based on the real diaries of the heroine written in captivity, the story is quite simple, although Jireš fragments his narrative into intercut accounts of her life in prison, life with her family and her work for the resistance movement. Although landscape plays its part in the flashbacks, the film is essentially the portrait of a martyr, with a great deal of emphasis on the beauty of Magda Vášáryová in the central role.

Everything is dedicated to the thoughts and feelings of the heroine, with the film's visual symphony of grey and green precisely attuned to her blonde vulnerability. Her stance and figure provide a fragile beauty and, as in *Valerie*, there is an emphasis on her long hair which, here, acquires a symbolic value. There is one striking sequence that combines images of Maruška's hair blowing in the wind while she is leaning through the window of a train – a virtuoso combination of music, image and sound based on the rhythm of the train. When her hair is cut off in the final scenes, there is a strong sense of violation, as it is placed on the table in front of her. It will be passed on to her relatives.

The lyricism of the country setting is used throughout to symbolise her past. At the opening of the film, when she is in the death cell, there is a flashback to her childhood and she recalls asking her father for a ride. She holds a sunflower as it begins to thunder and her father quotes, 'In vain does thunder roar and hell spit fire.' The most emotionally affecting flashbacks are centred on a green field overlooking open country – a great fertile plain. It is there that she walks with her boyfriend, sings with her friends and imagines her family coming to meet her shortly before her death. In a scene where the cession of the Sudetenland is announced over Prague radio, peasants stand silent in the fields while a horse can be seen on the horizon. As the local names are changed from Czech to German, there is a further sense of violation. The whole reflects her final words, 'Give my love to the swallows, the birds, and the trees.'

And Give My Love to the Swallows was made under the post-Prague Spring management of the Barrandov Studios, when there was a return to the production policies of the past. Thus, its immortalisation of a resistance heroine clearly related to the restricted themes that had now become the norm. Yet, on a formal level, the film is as impressive as Jireš's earlier work and Čuřík's cinematography is no less striking or committed than his work on *The White Dove* or *Valerie and her Week of Wonders*. The complex interaction of present and past and the use of the heroine's point of view and narrative of events mirror the approaches in Jireš's previous films. The use of the textures of stone walls (particularly in the credits) and the foreshortened images of landscape recall those of Jasný and Kučera in *Desire* and *All My Good Countrymen*. In many ways, it is a remarkable visual poem.

Of course, one has to ask if this return to a lyrical view of revolution does not contradict Jireš's (and, more particularly, Kundera's) criticism of lyricism in *The Joke*. But it seems that Jireš was genuinely attracted by his heroine's innocence and conviction. While the authorities had sought to promote Kudeříková as a Communist martyr analogous to the cult of Julius Fučík, there was an irony in the fact that Kudeříková's relatives had apparently supported the 1968 reforms. In other words, she had not fought for Stalinism but for rather different ideals. Similarly, the shots of the condemned conspirators (which may, indeed, be based on genuine practice) show them each interspersed with their own guard and recalling public images of the political trials.

It is reasonable to argue that, in the post-1968 years, lyricism did provide some kind of refuge with directors, as in the late 1950s to early 1960s, seeking the simple humanist subject that could, at the same time, allow opportunity for personal expression. This is certainly true of the work of Jireš, Kachyňa and Vláčil. Jireš, like Kachyňa, had also trained in cinematography and can be said to have found refuge in the visual. He continued to collaborate with Čuřík and this sometimes led to a bizarre aestheticism applied to quite trivial scripts – for example, *People of the Metro* (*Lidé z metra*, 1974) about the building of the Prague metro. Other films such as *Incomplete Eclipse* (*Neúplné zatmění*, 1982), the story of a blind girl who regains her sight, were more successful.

Perhaps the sole director to successfully continue this tradition in these years was Vláčil, who certainly produced a sequence of films due for reappraisal. The visual force of his work was apparent in such films for children as *The Legend of the Silver Fir* (*Pověst o stříbrné jedli*, 1973) and *Sirius* (1974). When he returned to adult feature films, he hardly complied with the current demand for optimistic entertainment, producing such melancholic and downbeat films as

Smoke on the Potato Fields (*Dým bramborové natě*, 1976) and his adaptation of Josef Čapek's *The Shades of Ferns* (1984). His work continued to be accompanied by striking and atmospheric imagery.

Other directors and cinematographers share features of 'the lyrical' with its qualities becoming less dominant. One of these is Jiří Menzel, whose adaptations of Vančura's *Capricious Summer* (1967) and Hrabal's *Cutting it Short* (1980), both photographed by Jaromír Šofr, evoked the Czech landscape and small-town life with an undoubted concern for its beauties and sense of a lost era. Of course, the Czech concern with creating a rural idyll is not restricted to the arts since having a weekend cottage and being able to escape to a private world are almost considered as part of life's essentials. Menzel satirises this in his comic adaptations of the script by Ladislav Smoljak and Zdeněk Svěrák, *Seclusion Near a Forest* (1976), and in his Oscar-nominated adaptation of Svěrák's *My Sweet Little Village* (1985).

In the post-Communist era, there has been no overt return of lyricism, although elements are present in a wide range of films. Here, one can point to the work of Vladimír Smutný with Jan Svěrák (*Kolya*, *Dark Blue World*), Jan Malíř's work with Jan Hřebejk and, more particularly, with Slovak director Juraj Nvota on *Cruel Joys* (*Kruté radosti*, 2002) and Martin Štrba's work with Martin Šulík. More overtly, cameraman-turned-director F. A. Brabec made a heavily lyrical adaptation of K. J. Erben's fairy tales, *Wild Flowers* aka *A Bouquet* (*Kytice*, 2000). Štěpan Kučera (son of Jaroslav Kučera and Věra Chytilová) has also given considerable visual force to films such as Petr Václav's *Marian* (1996) and to Saša Gedeon's *Indian Summer* (*Indiánské léto*, 1995) and *Return of the Idiot* (*Navrát idiota*, 1999).

Gedeon's stories of small-town life, while sometimes reminiscent of Miloš Forman in their attention to young people's lives and their subtle observation, are also carefully constructed on a visual level. While they do not emphasise landscape to any degree, his careful evocation of location and atmosphere and of dance halls and city streets at night makes him the one genuine poet of his generation.

One film that does approximate the visual traditions of earlier periods is Ivan Vojnár's relatively seldom seen *The Way Through the Bleak Woods* (*Cesta pustým lesem*, 1997). Made on location in the Šumava forest and filmed entirely in black and white' scope, it inevitably echoes the photographic traditions associated with Jasný, Vláčil and Kachyňa.

Set just before the outbreak of the First World War, it is the story of a dentist who leaves Vienna to practise in a small and remote community. Initially dispassionate, he is gradually drawn into their lives and conflicts. While the plot has been described as minimal, it could be better described as elliptical. Relationships are unexplained and the narrative unpredictable, yet it is perfectly possible to reconstruct the story and relationships of the characters in retrospect.

But it is clear that landscape is the real subject, with the film dominated by the evocation and pace of winter. There are extraordinary scenes of snow-scapes – a village buried by snow, a figure skating on a frozen lake – against which the human participants are tiny and incidental. Rather than being a mere backdrop to the human story, the roles seem to be reversed. Jaromír Kačer's moving camera and crane shots and the evocative music of Irena and Vojtěch Havel together create a melancholic beauty and almost a sense of suffocation.

Like *Desire* and *The White Dove*, it is a film where the visual style prevails and it is deliberately based on the qualities of old photographs. Vojnár regards the photographic picture as a 'revived memoir'. His hypnotic images – shining windows in remote cottages, muffled figures against the snow – stem, he believes, from a collective unconscious. A work of considerable power and originality, it had little chance of achieving box office success in the com-mercialised 1990s and remains a relatively rare example of a Czech post-Communist 'auteur' film.

The black-and-white photography of Kačer is clearly central to this work and he has also made important contributions to Tomáš Hejtmánek's film about Vláčil, *Sentiment* (2003), and to Jana Ševčíková's documentary *Old Believers* (*Starověrci*, 2001), again with his distinctive and evocative use of black and white. In *Sentiment*, Kačer was responsible for the location photography, the landscapes and settings where Vláčil once shot films such as *Marketa Lazarová*, *Valley of the Bees* and *Adelheid*.

I have discussed a limited range of films here. There are arguably many more directors of photography who reflect the Czech gift for lyricism – Václav Hanuš, Jan Kališ and others. In fact, the 'Czech school' of cinematography, from Stallich, Vích and Heller in the 1930s through to the present, has remained a consistent element in Czech cinema. In the post-war period, Slovakia has found its equivalents in the work of Stanislav Szomolányi, Igor Luther, Šimončič and Štrba. It is a rich and important tradition that deserves an extended study in its own right.

NOTES

1. Cathy Greenhalgh, 'Shooting from the Heart – Cinematographers and their Medium', in Roger Sears (editorial director), *Making Pictures: A Century of European Cinematography* (New York: Abrams, 2003), p. 145
2. Parker Tyler, *Classics of the Foreign Film: A Pictorial Treasury* (London: Spring Books, 1966), p. 95.
3. Paul Rotha with Richard Griffith, *The Film Till Now* (London: Spring Books, 1963), pp. 607–8.
4. Zoë Bicât, 'Jan Stallich: *Extase* 1933' (*Ecstasy*), *Making Pictures*, p. 206.
5. Ibid.
6. Ibid.
7. *Classics of the Foreign Film*, p. 94.
8. Peter Demetz, *Prague in Danger: The Years of German Occupation, 1939–45:*

Memories and History, Terror and Resistance, Theater and Jazz, Film and Poetry, Politics and War (New York: Farrar, Straus and Giroux, 2008), p. 205.

9. Mira Liehm and Antonín J. Liehm, *The Most Important Art: East European Film After 1945* (Berkeley: University of California Press, 1977), p. 111.

10. Karel Kachyňa, interviewed by Antonín J. Liehm, *Closely Watched Films: The Czechoslovak Experience* (New York: International Arts and Sciences Press, 1974), p. 144.

11. Martin Frič, interviewed in Antonín J. Liehm, *Closely Watched Films*, p. 19.

12. Zoë Bicât, 'Jan Čuřík: *The White Dove* 1960 (*Holubice*)', *Making Pictures*, 1968, p. 260.

13. Ibid.

14. Jan Žalman, *Films and Filmmakers in Czechoslovakia* (Prague: Orbis), p. 63.

15. Ibid., p. 64.

7. THE ABSURD

'Cinema of the Absurd' is a phrase that came to mind in thinking about certain films of the 1960s. Films such as Pavel Juráček's and Jan Schmidt's *Josef Kilián* (1963), Jan Němec's *The Party and the Guests* (1966) and *Martyrs of Love* (1966), Antonín Máša's *Hotel for Foreigners* aka *Hotel for Strangers* (*Hotel pro cizince*, 1966) and Juráček's *A Case for the Young Hangman* (*Případ pro začínajícího kata*, 1969) could all be described as such. They also coincided with the popularity of theatrical productions of Beckett, Ionesco, Albee and other dramatists who had been referred to in Martin Esslin's book *The Theatre of the Absurd* (1962) as well as to Czech equivalents such as Václav Havel and Josef Topol. Also, in the mid 1960s, Kafka was republished in Czech and discovered for the first time by many.

The theory of the absurd can be linked to Albert Camus's study *The Myth of Sisyphus* (*Le Mythe de Sisyphe*, 1942) and its fiction equivalent *The Outsider* (*L'Étranger*, 1942). The experience of the absurd, he argued, was the result of man's search for meaning, the desire to impose meaning on a world which had none. It was this experience that led to rebellion, a view reflected in his *The Rebel* (*L'homme révolté*, 1951) and *The Plague* (*La Peste*, 1947). The films listed above can all be linked to such views since they all involve characters who attempt to impose meaning in a world that has become incomprehensible. In other words, they do not merely experience the incomprehensible, they are seeking to understand it or make some sense of it.

In *Josef Kilián*, a medium-length film that the authorities tried to submerge, the story follows that of a man who becomes involved in a sequence of increasingly absurd situations that lead to no logical end. One day, he discovers a shop in a side street that is offering cats for loan. He borrows one but, when he attempts to return it, he discovers that the shop has disappeared or – to be more precise – the shop is there but appears to have been closed for years. He attempts to find a means of returning the cat by recourse to a succession of bureaucrats who provide no explanation but require him to justify himself. The final office turns out to be empty but with a ringing telephone on the floor. In the film's penultimate scene, the hero has a conversation with another man who also turns out to have a cat on a lead.

While borrowing a cat may be absurd, it is no more so than many of the other things he might have chosen to do that weekend and the responses to his misdemeanours would have been no different. Much of the film has to do with problems of meaning and of understanding. For instance, when he approaches people in the street, his cat's head peeping from his briefcase, they direct him to various vets, and tell him stories about a woman who keeps cats. The sequence concludes with a statement in which a woman says 'I don't understand' in Russian. An earlier street sequence had also addressed the subject of meaning. Snippets of disjointed conversation address the subject of understanding, including both a teacher's question to his class and a taxi driver's contribution 'Don't you understand Czech?'

The film's prime target is, of course, the Kafkaesque world of bureaucracy which takes a variety of forms – the official sitting halfway up a wall of filing cabinets to which the man protests 'I am a normal man', the man who reminds him of his responsibilities and of the literacy rate in Brazil, and the labyrinth of corridors leading to the empty room. The sense of bureaucratic supervision seems to be embodied in the very buildings themselves but, apart from this Habsburg inheritance, the film explicitly addresses the present. On the wall of the waiting room outside the empty office is a folder labelled 'observations for workers' – it is empty. The newspaper he picks up to read is in Arabic. The room fills with clients each presumably with a query based on their own every-day experiences of the absurd.

In two scenes, there are explicit references to Stalinism. At the beginning of the film, the hero detaches himself from a funeral procession and enters a building, where he passes through a collection of posters and banners symbolising the Cold War (untranslated in the original English subtitles). Alongside such slogans as 'Cholera and plague are the allies of Truman', 'Still more coal for the Republic' and 'The Komsomol is our example' are cartoons of Truman and Uncle Sam and a portrait of Stalin. When he enters the next room in search of the eponymous Josef Kilián, he explains that he wanted to tell him that someone had just died. At the end of the film, the hero approaches the camera flanked by two pillars that had previously framed the largest statue of Stalin in Eastern Europe.

While *Josef Kilián* could perhaps be described as 'politicised Kafka', Juráček's next film, *Every Young Man* (*Každý mladý muž*, 1965), was much more directly based on his own experiences and made during his army service. It consists of two stories based on life in an army camp. In the first, a corporal accompanies a soldier on a visit to a doctor in the local town. The mood is not far removed from that of *Kilián*, although we are now in the provinces. The locals view them with hostility and remove the tablecloths in the restaurant before they arrive. The two soldiers are either isolated from or oppressed by their environment and end up in a peculiar scene where they see a noose in a window and try to break in and laughter echoes from the opposite side of the street.

In the second story, we are confronted with a sequence of scenes from army life: manoeuvres in which everyone exhibits an ostentatious lack of interest; tanks moving through a village; a lecture on nuclear fallout involving a flower and a pet mouse; and a camp dance to which only one girl turns up. The same girl had appeared during the first story and clearly she represents no more than fantasy. But while this second story contains some more 'realist' observation, its pacing suffuses it in a kind of endless boredom. While acting as a comment on the 'real' experience of national service, it is also a companion piece to *Josef Kilián*, strongly inflected with a sense of the absurd as well as of the pointless.

In connection with his film *The Party and the Guests* (1966), Jan Němec mentions Camus's *The Outsider* as a parallel. Just as the hero was arrested for failing to cry at his mother's funeral so Němec's collective hero has no idea why it is accused or what crime they have committed. This was a film placed on the famous list of four films banned 'forever' and has consequently almost always been interpreted in political terms. While Němec's views are a little ambiguous in this respect, he at least accepts that it is about the ways in which people adjust to dominant power – although not necessarily just Communist power.

The film opens with a group of well-dressed people enjoying a picnic in the countryside. The conversation is largely pointless – snippets of dialogue caught, according to the author of the original unpublished story and co-author of the screenplay, Ester Krumbachová, as if at a cocktail party. They see a group of people dancing through the woods and speculate as to whether it might be a wedding party.

Subsequently, as the party moves on through the woods, continuing to mouth platitudes, they are surrounded by a group of men and marched off into a clearing. There they are interrogated by an imbecilic, gap-toothed superior wearing plus fours. They appear to have been accused of something but it is unclear what. Finally, another figure appears – a diminutive figure in a white dinner jacket, with a trim beard – who welcomes the captives as his 'guests'. It seems that they had all been on the way to his birthday party before being intercepted by 'the boys', for whose behaviour he apologises.

They then proceed to the festivities – a banquet with open-air tables set out

Figure 7.1   Jan Němec: *The Party and the Guests* (*O slavnosti a hostech*, 1966)

by a lake. There, after some disorderly proceedings in which the guests end up sitting in the wrong places, it transpires that one of the guests has disappeared. He has left – he just didn't want to be here, explains his wife. It is soon decided that a search should be organised but one that involves the use of a real police dog and may end with the firing of a shot. With the exception of the 'guests', the whole party moves off in pursuit as the guests extinguish burning candles as an economy measure.

The film proved to be particularly controversial not least because Němec and Krumbachová cast their friends in virtually all the parts – and they were mostly members of the Prague intelligentsia. Here, it is instructive to consider their roles after the suppression of the Prague Spring. They included: film director Evald Schorm who was banned from the studios until 1988; the novelists Josef Škvorecký and his wife Zdena Salivarová (Škvorecká) who emigrated to Canada where they set up 68 Publishers and published banned Czech literature; the psychologist Jiří Němec who became a spokesman for the human rights group Charter 77; and Dana Němcová who became secretary of VONS, the committee to defend the unjustly prosecuted. There were also the theatre writer and producer Ivan Vyškočil, the composer Jan Klusák, pop music composer Karel Mareš and many others. The police dog handler was real and lost his job as a result of appearing in the film.

The film was immediately banned on the instructions of President Novotný who is reputed to have climbed the walls in rage. One of the main concerns was the fact that Ivan Vyškočil, as the host, bore an accidental resemblance to Lenin while Novotný saw it as an allegory about the banning of Schorm's film *Everyday Courage*. Quite apart from this, it was viewed as elitist and incomprehensible and, if it did contain any meanings, they were likely to be subversive ones. While Němec tried to pass it off as a statement about the exercise of power under capitalism (not entirely fanciful), the real targets were very close at hand.

To give it a one-to-one political interpretation, while recognising that this is only partial, the host is clearly the head of state (and presumably therefore leader of the Communist Party) and the guests are invited to join the celebration and offered flattery, bribes and promises of advancement in exchange for their support. The 'boys' are clearly the secret police and their leader, Rudolf (Jan Klusák), the host's adopted son, is responsible for using force when the host's speeches may fail. The guests (and the wedding party) and earlier guests represent a cross section of society that is being progressively incorporated into the new power structure. While the host mouths political platitudes and takes on postures recalling Socialist Realist paintings and propaganda newsreels and the secret police jump to attention when Rudolf plays the role of organ grinder, the film's real focus is the guests and how they adapt to the events that they encounter. In these ways, the film provides a precise parallel to the methods and structures of the state.

Josef (Jiří Němec), a well-dressed figure who could easily be a lawyer, readily and smoothly takes on the role of collaborator. During the initial interrogation, he organises his fellow guests in a line to 'tally with the documents'. He appears to offer evidence of secret identification and, when the guests are imprisoned in a circle drawn in the gravel, he is seized by Rudolf to engage in a march round the outside. When he arrives at the feast, he is seated on the right hand of the host and is granted the honour of delivering the speech proposing the pursuit of the errant guest.

Karel (Karel Mareš) speaks out for the guests, marches outside the circle without permission (and ignores the designated exit marked by two stones). As a result, he is roughed up by the thugs while Rudolf steals his bag and proceeds to cut off its decorative fringe with feverish enthusiasm. On the arrival of the host, the struggle is dismissed as fun and the host agrees that he too is a democrat. But Karel's oppositional stance is soon mollified by apologies and the return of his cigarette lighter. After a brief opposition, he too agrees to acquiesce in 'the system'.

The only established couple in the group are the guest who disappears (Evald Schorm) and his wife (Jana Pracharová). She talks a lot and is soon eager to adapt and to please the authorities, to enjoy whatever material goods are on offer. In fact, her main concern in connection with the 'hunt' is that her husband's new suit should not be spoilt. Schorm, on the contrary, says nothing either in response to the group's early platitudes or to the host's welcome. When everyone claims to be a democrat, he looks on in bemused disbelief. When his wife mentions human rights, he motions to her to keep quiet. His disappearance takes place off-screen. In this superficial and conforming world, principles have become mere words.

Apart from the manifest absurdity of the situation, the film is also absurd in terms of its dialogue. Acknowledging the influence of Ionesco, Krumbachová observed that she tried to create dialogue in which the characters said nothing meaningful about themselves – 'it was my intention to demonstrate that people generally only talk in terms of disconnected ideas, even when it appears that they are communicating with one another. I tried not to mimic real speech but to suggest its pattern.'[1] Škvorecký described it as a film 'in which people keep talking and talking – yet the resulting mood of the film is a strange deafness, an appalling apathy, and a peculiar alienation'.[2]

The film's emphasis on dialogue is somewhat surprising for a director with a strong visual sense but one suspects that Němec was drawn to it by the unusual use of language. Whereas in Hollywood films dialogue is usually used to confirm meaning, here it does the opposite. As Krumbachová put it, tragedy is revealed by pictures 'and our words have no relationship to what we see'.[3] Thus, Němec uses images deriving from photojournalism, emulating the style of Henri Cartier-Bresson, and also draws on images from the history of art, including Goya's *Capriccios*, while the seating arrangements for the banquet are based on those for Nobel Prize ceremonies. The deliberate use of photographic images with 'everyday' connotations links the absurd dialogue with political reality while an emphasis on close-ups establishes a strong sense of claustrophobia. The film not only creates the sense of a world in which weak people collaborate in creating the reality that oppresses them but also a world that has become absurd, where words have become slogans, principles have been emptied of meaning and the only possible moral stance has become one of silence and abstention.[4]

Juráček's *A Case for the Young Hangman*, made in 1969, had been planned for many years and shares themes with his earlier work. Adapted from the third book of Jonathan Swift's *Gulliver's Travels*, its hero finds himself in a world not unlike contemporary Czechoslovakia. Swift juxtaposes the declining state of Balnibarbi with the island of Laputa hovering above it, representing the isolation of power and aristocracy, and this symbolism is retained in Juráček's film version.

The film begins with Gulliver driving his car along a road in what appears to be contemporary Czechoslovakia. He is then transported via a mysterious tunnel and a car crash to the land of Balnibarbi. The parallel with Alice falling down the rabbit hole is reinforced when he comes across a dead hare (Hare Oscar) dressed in human clothes, from whom he inherits a watch. He then begins a journey through a world which Juráček described as both familiar and unfamiliar, where logical connections have been destroyed.

There are many links with the worlds of Kafka and of *Josef Kilián*. Throughout, Gulliver is required, like the hero of *Kilián*, to account for himself to various groups of authority figures. For instance, he is interrogated by students in a lecture theatre where he explains that he is not Oscar. He is examined by a group of 'simple people', whose chairman is a child, and is only saved by an unexplained call to see the Governor of Laputa. At the Academy of Letters (a parallel to Swift's Academy of Projectors), he is introduced to 'thinking machines' which will remove the need for unnecessary thought. Later he encounters an execution machine but it won't work and more conventional means have to be used. In one of the film's more pointed comments, a poet is condemned to death for writing a poem 'foreign to our spirit'. The hero of *Kilián* appears complete with his incongruous cat.

There is some prospect of an explanation of the absurdities experienced by Gulliver but explanation merely leads to different absurdities – the story of the performing hares that had been banished to the forests, the king who is really a hotel porter and the minister who is really a gardener. But these events are given tremendous force by their shifting location within Gulliver's memories and the desolate and abandoned streets of Laputa (the film uses a wide variety of distinctive locations).

Women are not absent from *A Case for the Young Hangman* but their role is unreal. Gulliver remembers his drowned love, Markéta, who, like the girl in *Every Young Man*, reappears in a number of incarnations, representing more of an eternal longing and an eternal absence. This emphasises the fact that the film is much more than a political parable or a transferring to film of the real absurdities of the bureaucratic world. As Juráček notes in his diaries, he had always experienced the everyday world as bizarre – 'the bizarre seemed to me self-evident'.[5]

All of these films could be said to represent visions 'foreign to our spirit'. After all, the bureaucratic world of real socialism was not supposed to be absurd, alienating, oppressive, to reduce people to little more than ciphers within a system, to encourage self-seeking, to produce a world in which honesty can only be maintained by silence and abstention.

It is tempting to see the films as linked to the strong theatrical tradition of the absurd that developed in the 1960s, notably the plays of Václav Havel – *The Garden Party* (*Záhradní slavnost*, 1963), with its satire on bureaucracy and Communist jargon, and *The Memorandum* (*Vyrozumění*, 1965), about the invention of an artificial language that no one can learn or understand. Then, in 1964, the Theatre on the Balustrade (Divadlo na zábradlí) produced its season of 'absurd' plays that included works by Ionesco, Beckett and Jarry. Perhaps more crucial was the Liblice Conference on Kafka in 1963, which undoubtedly led to the rediscovery of a writer whose work held close parallels with experience under totalitarianism. As Hável himself said, the absurd was something that was 'in the air'.[6]

If the influence of Kafka was, perhaps, most pre-eminent on the filmmakers, it was nonetheless clear that Krumbachová was, like Havel, influenced by Ionesco. Havel plays a small part as a fellow national service victim in Juráček's *Every Young Man*. Jan Němec, Havel's second cousin, was also planning a film based on his screenplay *Heart-Beat* aka Stolen *Hearts*, about criminals involved in the trading of stolen body parts. Along with other screenplays, it was confiscated by armed police when he was effectively forced to emigrate in 1974. All of this suggests a close interaction between theatre and cinema and a parallel development and often close personal connections as well.

Havel noted recently that even when he was a 'mere' writer, he was a political phenomenon. 'That's the way it works in totalitarian conditions: everything is political, even a rock concert'.[7] The mere fact of adapting an absurdist – that is an incomprehensible and therefore politically subversive – approach was, in itself, a political act. It was also 'anti-Marxist' in the sense that it denied the simplified slogans and explanations promoted by Communist orthodoxy. Despite directors' allegations to the contrary (which would have certainly been necessary at the time), it is impossible for the uncommitted outsider not to see films such as *Josef Kilián*, *The Party and the Guests* and *A Case for the Young Hangman* as anything other than extraordinarily powerful and precise commentaries on the nature of totalitarian power.

Antonín Máša, who had scripted Schorm's *Everyday Courage*, also found himself drawn to the more oblique commentaries offered by the 'art' film. His bizarre *Hotel for Foreigners* – 'a mummery about love and death' – shared a number of characteristics with the films already discussed, not least the work of Ester Krumbachová as art director and costume designer. Petr Hudec arrives at the Hotel World to visit his sweetheart Veronika, only to find himself increasingly drawn into a set of incomprehensible and undoubtedly absurd situations. The film is based on Hudec's diary and attempts to piece together the various 'reasons' for his eventual murder.

There are parallels with the Alain Resnais/Alain Robbe-Grillet (*Last Year at Marienbad/L'Annee dernière á Marienbad*, 1961), not least in the characters whose true nature is often ambiguous. For instance, Veronika once loved her stepbrother Willi, who is really Otomar, who she has never met. The waiters at the hotel include Vladimír, Veronika's brother and Willi, who is also a count with thirteen illegitimate children. The duke, who owns the hotel, probably does not exist. These plot elements also owe some resemblance to *A Case for the Young Hangman*, where the King of Laputa is also a hotel porter working in Monte Carlo and the chief minister is really a gardener.

While the film's reflections on life evoke a popular notion of Kafka – the hero dies for no good reason, he is treated with contempt by the staff, abandoned by his girlfriend and fawned on by an older woman – the film seems primarily to be, like *Martyrs of Love*, a witty evocation of silent cinema and of elusive and romantic moods. The desk clerk, who wants his new guest to join a 'happy family' where there are no closed doors, suggests some political points but the film seems primarily to be concerned with the acting out of its elusive game. Love, the film suggests, is the assassin. Máša's film is little known although the American critic, Kirk Bond, rated it one of the best of the 'New Wave' films.[8]

The absurd as reflected in these films effectively came to an end with the Soviet invasion when such 'decadent' themes and projects could no longer be supported. Despite the undoubted Czech love for the absurd, the clever and the witty, this kind of combination found little outlet during the years of normalisation. Perhaps the Jára Cimrman films, which were clearly identified as comedy, came closest. There was, of course, the unique example of Jan Švankmajer but his work also drew on different sources and, during this period, was also largely underground. Post-normalisation, the film that seems nearest to this tradition is *Wings of Fame* (1990), a Dutch-made English-language film by exiled Czech director Otokar Votoček.

In the past ten years, the director who most embodies the characteristics of the absurd, the clever and the witty is Petr Zelenka, with films such as *Buttoners* (1997), *Year of the Devil* (*Rok d'ábla*, 2002) and *Wrong Side Up* aka *Tales of Everyday Insanity* (*Příběhy obyčejného šílenství*, 2005). Zelenka, who has also written for television and theatre, was awarded the prize for best play of the year for his *Tales of Common Insanity*, which was later adapted as a film under the same title but with the English title of *Wrong Side Up*. While recognised in 'the West', his work has been particularly well received in 'the East' – that is Russia and, especially, Poland – and his latest film, *The Karamazovs* (*Karamazovi*, 2008), is that rarity, a Czech-Polish co-production.

Just as Zelenka would, with some justification, deny the direct influence of the 'New Wave' on his work, his work differs from that of Němec and Juráček. Whereas their films are set against no recognisable contemporary reality, Zelenka's films are immersed in it and have provided some of the sharpest commentaries on post-Communist realities. *Buttoners*, which won a Golden Tiger award at Rotterdam, attracted a good deal of international critical attention. On the surface, the themes of the film are merely eccentric: the Japanese learn how to say 'fucking weather'; a young couple are only able to make love in a taxi; another man has an obsessive desire to remove studs from upholstery with false teeth located in his backside; and another achieves success by lying between railway tracks and spitting at trains.

With *Buttoners*, Zelenka initiated what Christina Stojanova calls 'the mosaic narrative', involving multiple characters and overlapping stories, which she regards as a defining characteristic of the new Czech cinema.[9] It opens with black-and-white images recreating the last minutes before the dropping of the first atomic bomb in August 1945. Intercut with these are shots on the ground of a party of Japanese complaining about the incessant rain. In fact, since they are based in Kokura, it is only the weather than ensures that the bomb falls on Hiroshima and not, as intended, on them. In an incongruous juxtaposition, they learn to swear in English (or rather American), repeating the words 'fucking weather', with much emphasis on 'w's and 'th's. This emphasis on the unpredictable and the unexpected becomes the primary way in which the film's various episodes interconnect.

Zelenka's first story, 'Taxi Driver' ('Taxíkář') involves Franta, a driver on night shift (also on tranquillisers) and his various fares. The first are the aforesaid couple in search of somewhere to make love. The second turns out to be the woman's husband, who arranges to be driven to an address where he believes his wife to be meeting her lover. He proves to be wrong – the woman is, in fact, the driver's wife, although he remains unaware of this. In the second story, 'Rituals of Civilisation' ('Civilizační návyky'), a young man tells a psychiatrist that his wife has left him. The psychiatrist asserts that only 'the rituals of civilisation' (a synonym for his own antiseptic habits) can save him. In 'The Last Decent Generation' ('Poslední slušná generace'), Franta drives a middle-aged couple to the home of another couple, whose daughter is about to marry their son. The man is the one with a peculiar obsession with the buttons in upholstery but their hosts have an equally strange private obsession – the re-enactment of aerial combat. In 'Fools' ('Pitomci'), a working-class couple bicker incessantly about the man's incompetence and inadequacy while watching a television programme about a project to launch frozen human sperm into space. Finally, in 'The Ghost of an American Pilot' ('Duch amerického pilota'), four girls hold a séance and summon up the ghost of the American pilot who flew the A-bomber. One of the girls takes him to the radio station whose programme has been featured throughout the film, where he broadcasts a plea for forgiveness.

The radio programme offers a discussion in which the significance of cause and effect is rejected and the power of contingency is asserted. Thus, while the characters act as if they are in control of their lives, their words and actions are based on misunderstandings and their consequences unforeseen. The pilot does not know that he is going to drop the bomb; the psychiatrist is unaware that he will cause the young couple who are about to be married to die in a car accident; and the Japanese do not know that the bad weather they are trying to curse is saving them from extinction. There are, of course, also significant comments on aspects of contemporary life – serial infidelity, the strange power relations that exist within marriage and the obscure fantasies and desires that lie beneath the surface of the everyday.

Buttoners is a kind of tour de force in the ways in which it weaves its connections between disparate and unlikely stories, with a veritable network of visual and verbal connections. In the end, all attempts to impose unity and meaning are doomed to failure – love and relationships are temporary, illusory, and ultimately absurd. Simulated aerial combat, detaching buttons with one's backside and spitting at trains only go slightly beyond the peculiarities of the everyday. They illuminate contemporary reality in the same ways that the problems of Juráček's cat exposed bureaucracy. But, ultimately, it is the superficially adjusted psychiatrist, with his obsessions with hair combing and teeth cleaning, who produces the most lethal effects. No doubt the Communists would have objected had such a film been produced in that era but somehow Zelenka suggests a vision of human fate lying beyond the failures of particular socio-economic systems.

Zelenka's next script, *Loners* (*Samotáři*, 2000), something of a companion piece, was directed by David Ondříček. While Ondříček's direction gives the film a much more fluid, commercial and accessible form, the subject in many ways marks a continuation from *Buttoners*. The script links the lives of seven temporarily unattached 'loners' in a sequence of overlapping episodes made with great verve and humour. Here again are concerns with coincidence, language, radio, the generation gap, a car crash, the private face of the medical profession and a bemused Japanese investigation of family life in the Czech Republic. The film also adopts the perspective of an outsider – a Macedonian student, Vesna (played by Macedonian actress Labina Mitevksa) – who concludes that the reason Czechs are so nasty to each other is because they have such a horrible language.

This portrait of the new post-Communist generation of Czechs seems to centre on the lack of any stability or sense of commitment in their lives. Robert works in a travel agency and likes to record the dramatic crises of others on camera; Petr, who works as a DJ and also broadcasts snippets of 'real life', breaks with Hanka on the basis of the toss of a coin; Ondrej, a highly respected neurosurgeon, forsakes his family in an attempt to renew his previous relationship with Hanka; Vesna, who pretends to have come to Prague because of her interest in UFOs, is really looking for her father; while Jakub, a permanently stoned rock musician, helps others but has forgotten that he has a girlfriend. Her mother puts Hanka's break-up down to her 'lifestyle', a constantly repeated phrase that Hanka finally ends up repeating herself.

It is surely no accident that Jakub, when collecting his drugs, should fail to recognise the national anthem or that, in another scene when he walks at night like an alien apparition, lit by car headlights, it is to fragments of Dvořák. When the Japanese tourists observe a typical Czech meal as part of their travel itinerary, they accidentally witness a row between Hanka and her parents to the sound of Smetana's *My Country*. Of course, this kind of irony can be traced back to *Loves of a Blonde* but it is a markedly different use of musical reference to the positive associations implied, for instance, in Jan Svěrák's *The Elementary School* or *Dark Blue World*.

The film seems to focus on the empty lives of the superficially successful and it seems that only Vesna, the outsider, and Jakub, the dropout, have maintained any sense of moral value and commitment. But, at the end, Hanka is back with Petr and Ondřej has returned to his wife. The absurdities of *Buttoners* are rather less apparent here but Ondřej does hire a magician to make him disappear and there is some doubt as to whether he really wants to pursue Hanka or is primarily attracted by the plumber's disguise he adopts to follow her. Like *Buttoners*, the film also has its tragedy in the death of Robert's mother. While Ondříček's style is different and more obviously 'visual' than Zelenka's, its controlled pace works well in a film that is obviously more light-hearted and became something of a cult amongst young people in Central and Eastern Europe.

Zelenka's next film as writer-director was the mockumentary *Year of the Devil*. Zelenka had already used this form in his first feature, *Mňága – Happy End* (1996), the story of a fictitious rock band that became real, which was clearly influenced by Rob Reiner's *This Is Spinal Tap* (1984). In *Year of the Devil*, the legendary underground singer Jaromír Nohavica plays himself in a film about a singer and recovering alcoholic who goes on tour with the popular folk-rock band, Čechomor. The film is told through the eyes of a fake Dutch documentary film-maker who is making a film about an institution for recovering alcoholics and finds himself drawn into an increasingly curious and mystificatory experience.

The film's casual nature gives the impression that it has all come together by accident and the succession of interviews and concert footage only differ from the real thing by virtue of their absurd statements. Nohavica, the members of Čechomor – František Černý, who played the part of the taxi driver in *Buttoners*, Karel Holas, Michal Pavlík and Radek Pobořil – and the documentary film-maker, Jan Holman (Jan Prent), all become the focus of interviews and commentary. How much of the film was pre-scripted is difficult to assess since it frequently gives the impression of a group of friends making it up as they go. Zelenka's regular credit 'A Film by Petr Zelenka and his Friends' springs to mind.

Year of the Devil is prefaced with 'documentary' interviews about spontaneous human combustion set in various countries and the narrative proper begins with Nohavica in the alcohol clinic and Holman making his documentary about the treatment of alcoholics in the Czech Republic. Nohavica has apparently realised the need for a cure after forgetting the words to his own songs while his guitarist, Karel Plihal, who is not an alcoholic, likes the centre so much that he wants to stay.

The narrative seems of less consequence that the film's sequence of absurd observations many of which seem to be of the 'what if?' variety. What if Černý were the doorman at a transvestite night club? What if a serious film critic were to ask questions about Nohavica's underpants? But these funny and bizarre happenings only work in the context of a skit on the rockumentary – in tandem with the real folk appeal of Čechomor and Nohavica's own grotesque lyrics. The film is unique and unpredictable and one suspects that it was not only its musical appeal that made it a box office success with young Czech audiences.

With *Wrong Side Up*, adapted from *Tales of Common Insanity*, both titles tell their own apposite stories. Yet again, Zelenka is concerned with the absurdity of the world about him while *Wrong Side Up* refers to one of the character's suggestions that the best way to reach a woman is to dispatch yourself in a crate. The central character, Petr, who works in a dead–end job as an airport dispatch worker, has lost his girlfriend Jana to someone with more elevated prospects. The film's tight structure recalls its theatrical origins, although Zelenka wrote an entirely new script for the film version.

The film begins with newsreel footage of Fidel Castro being greeted at Prague airport by the Communist President of the 'normalisation' period, Gustav Husák. While it mirrors the film's ending when Petr is accidentally dispatched in a crate bound for Cuba, it also introduces us to one of the film's principal motifs – Communist newsreels.

Petr is someone to whom 'strange things happen'. First of all, a spare crate arrives and, when opened, reveals a female mannequin wearing a mask. His boss, it appears, is keen on sexy mannequins and 'Eva' is soon dressed up, sometimes wearing his wife's clothes. Intent on regaining Jana's love, Petr decides to practise a charm that involves cutting off some of her hair and boiling it in milk. Unfortunately, in drunken error, he cuts off the hair of her new partner's aunt instead. In the meantime, his neighbours, a composer and his wife, are unable to have sex without someone watching and pay him to help them out. After the boss's wife has angrily dismembered 'Eva' the mannequin, she is reassembled – in Petr's apartment.

Jana's oddities are more predictable. After their break-up, she finds new liaisons by deliberately ringing the local phone box and becoming involved with a variety of men as if 'by accident' (twenty, she says, unconvincingly). Her new boyfriend is the chance result of this deliberate strategy.

The theme of phone calls continues in Petr's relations with his parents. He receives a call at work from his mother, claiming that his father, David, is dying. In fact, he is not but his mind has moved into a state of virtually permanent apathy which his mother variously interprets as Alzheimer's or senile dementia. The evidence for this is his habit of gazing into his beer bottle and watching the bubbles disperse. He also fails to respond to his wife when she attempts to startle him by saying 'boo'. He has gone silent and his wife gives him 'two months at the most'.

Under the Communists, he did voice-overs for the weekly newsreels – he was the voice of the times. His voice is quite distinctive and it is now something he wishes to live down. His wife, however, thinks that recognition may help him and encourages him to make random phone calls to see if people recognise who it is. On one of these occasions, he makes contact with a female sculptor called Sylvia and this leads to an unusual (platonic) liaison.

Impressed by his instant recall of dates, subjects, and commentary – 'The General Secretary of the Central Committee of the Czechoslovak Communist Party Gustav Husák, who is on a two-day visit to North Moravia, arrived in Moravia' and so forth – she suggests that he makes recitations at social gatherings, like poetry. There is, after all, she notes, a growing nostalgia for those times. He is also introduced to the excitements of sky diving (where, perversely, his wife rings him on his mobile).

His wife is obsessed with the world's evils and problems – wars, famine and disasters – and obsessively collects for good causes, sending boxfuls of clippings to Petr about what is going on in the world. It is *her* obsessive behaviour that ultimately leads to madness and she ends up in the Prague streets in her husbands underwear and shouting 'boo' at passers-by.

So, it seems, as in *Buttoners*, we can never really foresee the consequences of our actions, the absurd reversals of fate and the strange effects of accident. While demonstrating the apparent impossibility of meaningful relationships among the young, the film also reveals the strange unities (and falsities) that are shared by the parental generation. Alienation in a world of technology is indicated not only by the continuing and largely unintended results of phone conversations but also in the miniature robots that surround David at the hospital, where his wife had gone to give blood, and the endless stream of cars, reminiscent of Godard's *Weekend* (1968) as Petr and his father hold a long conversation with David walking and Petr driving.

If one reads the play, it does not seem so far from the 'theatre of the absurd'. Yet Zelenka comes from a different generation and one could perhaps look more productively at his interest in American independents. If there is a similarity with earlier forms of absurdist cinema, it is no doubt an accidental one. Also, despite his acute observation of contemporary reality, the films cannot really be seen as an attack on 'the system'. The humour is Zelenka's own – or perhaps part of a shared perception and context, part of that black and sarcastic humour that Švankmajer considers typical of Prague itself.

Writing in 1962 in his *Theatre of the Absurd*, Martin Esslin argues:

> There are enormous pressures in our world that seek to induce mankind to bear the loss of faith and moral certainties by being drugged into

oblivion – by mass entertainments, shallow material satisfactions, pseudo-explanations of reality, and cheap ideologies. At the end of that road lies Huxley's Brave New World of senseless euphoric automata.[10]

Times have not changed for the better. Perhaps, like the theatre of the absurd, to follow Esslin's argument, absurd cinema also helps us to face the human condition as it is and to free us from the illusions that will cause 'constant maladjustment and disappointment'.[11] But, perhaps more importantly, it encourages us to view that condition with a sense of irony and humour.

NOTES

1. Ester Krumbachová, interviewed by Antonín J. Liehm, *Closely Watched Films: The Czechoslovak Experience* (New York: International Arts and Sciences Press, 1974), p. 280.
2. Josef Škvorecký, *All the Bright Young Men and Women: A Personal History of the Czech Cinema* (Toronto: Peter Martin Associates, 1971), p. 123.
3. Krumbachová, interviewed by Liehm, p. 280.
4. For a detailed discussion see Peter Hames, 'O *slavnosti a hostech/The Party and the Guests*', in Peter Hames (ed.), *The Cinema of Central Europe* (London: Wallflower Press, 2004), pp. 139–48.
5. Pavel Juráček, *Deník (1959–1974)*, edited by Jan Lukeš (Prague: Národní filmový archiv, 2003), p. 333.
6. Václav Havel, *Disturbing the Peace: A Conversation with Karel Hvížďala*, translated by Paul Wilson (New York: Knopf, 1990), p. 54.
7. Václav Havel, *To the Castle and Back*, translated by Paul Wilson (New York: Knopf, 2007), p. 4
8. Kirk Bond, 'The New Czech Film', *Film Comment*, 5, 1, Fall, 1968, pp. 78–9.
9. Christina Stojanova 'Fragmented Discourses: Young Cinema from Central and Eastern Europe', in Anikó Imre (ed.), *East European Cinemas* (New York and London: Routledge, 2005), p. 219.
10. Martin Esslin, *The Theatre of the Absurd* (London: Eyre and Spottiswoode, 1962), pp. 313–14.
11. Ibid., p. 313.

8. THE AVANT-GARDE

Czechoslovakia was one of the main pre-war centres for modernism and the avant-garde so it is only natural that this should be reflected in cinema. The desire to make 'independent' or 'experimental' films has extended from then to the present.

The notion of avant-garde film has been much debated but, in general, I would accept the views of Janet Bergstrom and Constance Penley that avant-garde film can be defined as 'apart from the mainstream' and is often seen primarily as an extension of painting, the graphic arts and performance.[1] The question of whether it is then 'avant-garde' within this context is another matter and, of course, innovation, particularly narrative innovation, often finds a reflection in more mainstream developments.

This raises the question of where one should place such major innovative directors as Dreyer, Bresson, Antonioni, Godard or Tarkovsky, whose work had mainly been achieved within the area of fiction film. The fact remains, of course, that absolute distinctions cannot be drawn between what has come to be known as 'art cinema' and the avant-garde any more than one can draw absolute distinctions between the avant-garde and the mainstream.

There are certainly overlaps in the case of Czech and Slovak cinema. If the roots of experimental cinema lie in the Devětsil movement of the 1920s and the surrealist movement of the 1930s, it is impossible to ignore the fact that many names associated with these movements (Voskovec, Werich, Frič, Vančura, Nezval, for instance) worked in feature films that could not primarily be considered 'experimental'. On the other hand, the 'avant-garde' feature films of

Vladislav Vančura in the 1930s and of Věra Chytilová in the 1960s have few equivalents in other countries and the surrealist films of Jan Švankmajer since that time remain unique. Many Slovak films of the late 1960s (those directed by Jakubisko, Dušan Hanák and Elo Havetta, for example) also hover on the fringes of the avant-garde. However, since there are separate chapters on both surrealism and on these particular Slovak directors, they will not be discussed here.

Czech avant-garde art in the 1920s was centred on the Devětsil group (1920–31) who took their name from that of a wild flower, the butterbur, with the literal meaning 'nine strengths'. Its activities extended across the whole artistic spectrum, including literature, the fine arts, design, music, architecture, theatre, cinema and criticism. Early publications featured articles on cinema by Jean Epstein, Louis Delluc and Karel Teige, later a prime mover in the development of the Poetist and Surrealist movements. Chaplin, Harold Lloyd and Douglas Fairbanks were made honorary members of the Devětsil.

The elevation of Hollywood stars was, of course, a reflection of the Devětsil's interest in popular and proletarian art (Teige viewed slapstick comedy as a precursor to proletarian art) and it is quite significant that the Devětsil failed to produce any films as such although, after the development of Poetism in the late 1920s, many artists began to produce screenplays. In some ways, the development of Poetist screenplays could be seen as an extension of the earlier Devětsil concept of the pictorial poem, which had taken its subjects from city life, the circus, variety shows, foreign travel, sport and other everyday subjects. Teige described the Poetist screenplay as 'a synthesis of picture and poem, set in motion by film'.[2] Among those to write Poetist screenplays were Voskovec, Nezval, E. F. Burian, Vančura and the poets, František Halas and Jaroslav Seifert. In did not matter that none of these screenplays were ever produced because, as Michal Bregant has suggested, the text itself was regarded as a complete creative act.[3]

The real founder of Czech experimental cinema was Alexandr Hackenschmied with his film *Aimless Walk* (*Bezúčelná procházka*, 1930). Hackenschmied emigrated to the United States in 1939 and, in 1946, adopted the name of Alexander Hammid. He had previously co-directed the pioneer film of the American avant-garde, *Meshes of the Afternoon* (1943) with his wife, Maya Deren. Although he continued to work with Deren as cinematographer and editor on three further films, he largely abandoned experimental work after their divorce in 1947.

Hackenschmied is a significant figure whose contribution to cinema is only gradually becoming recognised. One reason for this is undoubtedly the fact that he seems to have been quite content to accept the supporting role of cinematographer, editor or artistic consultant and to work on a wide variety of films, all of which would meet his criteria of being 'independent' without necessarily being experimental. In an article in *Studio* in 1930, he defined independent film as being broader than the avant-garde and, as such, a more genuine avant-garde that might result in 'the social and ideological reform of the film industry'.[4] He also argued that the independent film was not opposed to the film industry but sought to work in those fields that would otherwise be neglected. Particularly in his American films, this was to involve various kinds of documentary work. His work as a still photographer is also of considerable significance.

Hackenschmied's commitment to avant-garde work was made apparent when, together with Ladislav Kolda, he organised the First Week of Avant-Garde Film in Prague in November 1930. Alongside *Aimless Walk*, there were screenings of René Clair's *Entr'acte* (1924) and Jean Vigo's *A Propos de Nice* (1930). Two further weeks were organised in 1931 and a further programme of Czech avant-garde films in May 1937.

His work in cinema began as 'scene designer' for Gustav Machatý on his feature, *Erotikon* (1929) and he had a major credit as 'artistic collaborator' on his *From Saturday to Sunday* (1931) in 1930. He also has a credit as assistant director on Machatý's *Ecstasy* (1932). Machatý certainly had ambitions to be associated with the avant-garde and is, perhaps, the first Czech auteur in the sense with which we are now familiar. It is worth noting, therefore, that Hackenschmied's work with Machatý, the promotion of the first three avant-garde film weeks and the production of *Aimless Walk* all occurred within the same time frame.

Aimless Walk is a short silent film that follows a man as he walks around Prague. However, this is not a tourist's-eye view. Shots of the river emphasise barges, factory buildings, scaffolding and scenes of dereliction. As Jaroslav Anděl points out, the film consists of three elements – views including the protagonist, views from the protagonist's perspective and images of reflections.[5] Hackenschmied said that the idea of separating one human being into two had always fascinated him and it is this concept that supports the film, providing three sequences of separation or splitting at its end. In one of these sequences, a panning technique is used allowing both selves to appear in the same shot.

In an extended discussion of the film, Anděl points to the concern with reflection, manifested in repeated shots of reflections on water. He demonstrates the influence of the French photographer Eugène Atget on Hackenschmied's work, pointing out a number of influences in his still photography and also looking forward to the photographic work of the Czech surrealist, Jindřich Štyrský.[6]

The theme of *Aimless Walk* again appears in *Meshes of the Afternoon*. As Anděl suggests, 'both contain the motif of the mirroring and splitting of the main character and both represent a shift to a subjective vision, evoking the inner world of the dream or imagination'.[7] A look at Hackenschmied's photographic work and its concern with reflected images and masks certainly reveals these continuities of theme and vision.

In *Prague Castle* (*Na Pražském hradě*, 1931), Hackenschmied worked without a script and attempted to present the castle through an emphasis on its Gothic and Romanesque shapes. In his article, 'Film and Music', he said:

> In collaboration with the composer, František Bartoš, I have tried . . . to find the relationship between architectonic form and music; between an image and a tone; between the movement of a picture and the movement of music; and between the space of a picture and the space of a tone.[8]

Here, Hackenschmied is concerned with formal and syntactic relationships and argued the case for films in which image and music would be composed at the same time.

In Karel Plicka's *The Earth Sings* (1932), which was produced by Ladislav Kolda, Hackenschmied took on the role of editor. Based on extensive footage of Slovak folklore filmed by Plicka, it was edited to a specially commissioned score by František Škvor. It went beyond ethnographic record to become a visual and aural symphony, winning an award at the Venice Film Festival in 1934. In 1934, Hackenschmied also worked as cameraman on Otakar Vávra's experimental film, *November* (*Listopad*) and, in the same year, joined Kolda at the advertising film studios set up by the industrialist, Jan Bat'a, at Zlín. Here, he worked on a number of films including, *The Highway Sings* (*Silnice spívá*, 1937), which won first prize at the Paris exhibition. An advertisement for car tyres, it uses a woman's voice to personify a tyre as it moves towards the customer, who also adopts its perspective as his own. In a way, films such as this paralleled the marriage of the avant-garde and advertising that also occurred in Britain, where directors such as Humphrey Jennings and Len Lye worked for the GPO Film Unit.

Hackenschmied's final Czech film was the documentary *Crisis* (1938), about the political situation in the Sudetenland preceding the Munich Agreement in September. Co-directed with the US independent director, Herbert Kline, the footage was smuggled out of the country to Paris, where Hackenschmied emigrated to in February 1939. After working with Kline on *Lights Out in Europe* (1939), a documentary on the pre-war atmosphere in Britain, he left for the United States and, in 1940, he and Kline co-directed John Steinbeck's screenplay *The Forgotten Village* in Mexico. Subsequently, there was his work with Maya Deren, his feature film of Gian Carlo Menotti's opera *The Medium* (1951), films for the United Nations and pioneering works using multi-screen techniques and IMAX. In 1966, he and co-director Francis Thompson won an Oscar for *To Be Alive!* (1963), first shown at the New York World's Fair of 1963. Between 1976 and 1986, he edited five films using IMAX technology.

The work of the Czech avant-garde in the 1930s clearly related to the concerns of the international avant-garde in that it derived principally from inspirations in photography and the visual arts and was non-narrative in character. Svatopluk Innemann's *Prague Shining in Lights* (*Praha v záři světel*, 1928) recalled the city documentaries of Walter Ruttmann and Joris Ivens while Otakar Vávra's and František Pilát's *The Light Penetrates the Dark* (*Světlo proniká tmou*, 1930) and Frič's *Black and White Rhapsody* (*Černobílá rapsodie*, 1936) emphasised images of the city at night, the first of them focusing on the kinetic sculpture by Zdeněk Pešánek for the Edison Transformer Station.

Jan Kučera's *Burlesque* (*Burleska*, 1932) juxtaposed war footage, a card game and positive/negative images of a flower. Kučera, who was also an important theorist and critic, later worked in both documentary and newsreel. In 1938, Karel Dodal, one of the pioneers of Czech animation, made *The Bubble Game* (*Hra bublinek*), his abstract fantasy designed to advertise Sapona soap while, in the late thirties, Jiří Lehovec experimented with unusual and abstract images in *The Magic Eye* (*Divotvorné oko*, 1939) and *Rhythm* (*Rytmus*, 1941), the latter escaping censure during the Nazi protectorate by placing itself in an 'instructional' framework.

Vladislav Vančura, the first chairman of the Devětsil and a leading experimental novelist, was the main protagonist of experimental film-making in the field of feature film. His novels included *The Baker Jan Marhoul* (*Pekař Jan Marhoul*, 1924), *Marketa Lazarová* (1931) and *The End of Old Times* (*Konec starých časů*, 1934) and a number of them were filmed in the 1960s. Recognised for his linguistic inventiveness and virtuoso storytelling, he was one of the main advocates of a cinematic art free from commercial demands. Although his cinematic ambitions are generally considered to have been frustrated, he nonetheless directed or co-directed five features. He also brought many leading avant-garde artists together to work on his projects, including the novelists Ivan Olbracht and Karel Nový, the poet Vitězslav Nezval and the composers Bohuslav Martinů, E. F. Burian and Eman Fiala.

Vančura's best film was probably his first, *Before the Finals* aka *Before Matriculation* (*Před maturitou*, 1932), which was co-directed with Svatopluk Innemann. The story concerns the relationships between a narrow-minded mathematics teacher and his pupils at a boys' school. One of the pupils tries to shoot himself after failing his examinations but the teacher himself is accidentally shot and wounded. Basically a story of injustice and of the teacher's eventual humanisation, the film has a delicate and lyrical touch and strongly evokes the school community.

Much of its professionalism is no doubt due to the experienced hand of Innemann and the film is only really avant-garde in some of its effects. The music is exaggerated and satirical and the camera circles and tilts in a manner unusual for early sound cinema. In one scene, the sound of a fly is magnified on the soundtrack while, in another, we witness a staff meeting through a glass window, with the figures standing and gesticulating like puppets. Pavel Taussig suggests, however, that it was Innemann who was influenced by Vančura rather than the reverse.

> Vančura's influence . . . is also evident in the way interiors are modelled by means of illumination that frequently breaks through various objects and creates fantastic shadows on the walls. These images of the environment correspond to the moods and psychological states of the characters.[9]

The films solely directed by Vančura, *On the Sunnyside* (*Na sluneční straně*, 1933) and *Faithless Marijka* (1934), were both avant-garde and more abstract in their appeal and neither of them was based on his own screenplays. The first explored the ideas of the Soviet educationist A. S. Makarenko on the fates of children raised in different social classes. Set in a children's home, it explores the divisions caused by the injustices and inequities of the outside world. The screenplay was written by Nezval, the Russian linguistic theorist Roman Jakobson and Miloslav Disman. Vančura intended to employ the methods and insights of structuralism.

Unlike the more orthodox *Before the Finals*, the film does little to attract or involve the audience and constantly emphasises the disjunctive. Acting and costume are symbolic and stylised, the dialogue unrealistic, figures deliberately posed and montage is used aggressively to indicate class division. There is even a rather Brechtian puppet show commenting on the role of money that exposes the family itself as part of an unjust system. Although Vančura here seems to be using film form to expose the nature of bourgeois society, it is less successful than Russian montage cinema or the more polemical approach of the Slatan Dudow/Bertolt Brecht *Kuhle Wampe* (1932). The use of a constantly circling or overhead camera often serves merely to draw attention to its own technique than to underline the social drama.

Faithless Marijka is much more successful although this probably owes a good deal to its impressive locations and more orthodox drama. Filmed entirely on location in sub-Carpathian Ruthenia, it was scripted by the novelists Karel Nový and Ivan Olbracht, with music by Martinů (his only feature film score) and was produced by Ladislav Kolda. The interesting story centres on a young man whose wife has an affair while he is away doing seasonal work and ends with the death of her lover. Underpinning all of this is an analysis of the economic realities faced in one of the poorest areas of the country. The film is greatly influenced by Soviet montage, with images turned on their sides and an inventive use of split screen. Although it was a critical and commercial failure at the time, it is much more impressive with hindsight, not least because of its effective use of non-actors and its record of a lost world.

Vančura's last two films, *Our Swells* (*Naši furianti*) and *Love and People*

(*Láska a lidé*), both co-directed with Václav Kubásek in 1937, can more properly be regarded as mainstream productions with little of the imagination apparent in his earlier work. While Vančura's film work has its supporters and detractors, it is true to say that he is preoccupied with techniques of storytelling and formal innovation. During the Second World War, Vančura was one of those involved in planning for the future nationalisation of the film industry. He was one of the intellectuals executed by the Nazis in response to the assassination of the German Reichsprotektor, Reinhard Heydrich.

Given the Nazi occupation in the 1940s and the establishment of a Communist government in 1948, there was little evidence of experimental cinema in the 1940s and the 1950s save for Radok's *Distant Journey*. There was some scope within the permitted field of animation, but it was not until the 1960s that repressed avant-garde traditions began to re-express themselves. Of course, this move towards experiment was also motivated by a new generation of film-makers and the exposure to 'Western' film-makers such as Antonioni, Godard, Fellini and Lindsay Anderson, among others. The Czech New Wave certainly approached narrative from new perspectives and adopted a variety of approaches, ranging from realism to absurdism and resurrecting the traditions of surrealism and the avant-garde. Given their good Communist credentials, it was not surprising that the literary works of Vančura and Nezval were among those to be adapted for the screen.

The most radical of the directors to emerge in the 1960s was Věra Chytilová and, with films such as *Something Different* (1963), *Daisies* (1966) and *The Fruit of Paradise* (1969), she not only produced a remarkable sequence of work but also placed herself among the foremost feminist directors of the time. Chytilová's desire to 'break the rules' has, of course, been reflected in her subsequent work but rarely to such significant effect.

Chytilová's graduation films, *A Bagful of Fleas* and *Ceiling*, both 1962, revealed the then fashionable concern for cinéma-vérité. Although it was a 'staged' film, *A Bagful of Fleas* used non-professional actors and improvisation to create an illusion of reality. Set in the cotton mills of Náchod, it presented a situation similar to that in Forman's *Loves of a Blonde*, where the women outnumbered the eligible men by five to one. The film was criticised for its unflattering portrait of factory officials.

In the impressive *Ceiling*, she recreates the life of a fashion model. There is very little story, although the boring and amoral life of Marta is contrasted with the more innocent student life that she has forsaken. When it was first shown, it was its merits as a 'documentary' that impressed. However, it is, in fact, very artfully constructed, with an effective use of (mainly 'Western') popular music. At the beginning of the film, there is a sequence in which Marta is shown posing for a range of fashion photographs – against a tennis court, an airliner and a dredging machine – as a narrator expresses her subjective thoughts. The film's final sequence, as she walks through the city streets at night and eventually leaves the city, recalls the final abstract sequence of Antonioni's *L'Eclisse*, which appeared the same year.

The city streets at night, of course, recall a particular tradition in avant-garde film. There are typical images of the night – a couple, a cat, workmen mending tramlines and a man who tries to pick up Marta. Mannequins in a shop window, lampshades and a neon sign in the form of a rocket suggest a critique of consumerism but also seem strange and alien. The whole is accompanied by a modernist score by Jan Klusák, ending with images in which Marta is framed by a stone wall and passes through ranks of trees in what one takes to be a symbolic rebirth.

Something Different, Chytilová's first feature, is a logical development from both these early films. It consists of two separate stories that are intercut and combined with each other. As noted earlier, the first is a cinéma-vérité record of the life of the champion gymnast Eva Bosáková and follows through her preparation to her ultimate success in the world championships, while the second is a fictional account of the life of a housewife, recording her boredom and love affair. The two lifestyles and the two differing film structures provide a parallel commentary but are sometimes cut together for purely formal effect. Both lives are shown to be inadequate and incomplete but, in the end, both women choose their existing lives. Chytilová combines approaches that both point up a critical, feminist perspective while engaging in abstract and formal poetry (particularly in the gymnastic championships that form its conclusion). In one scene, where Bosáková is interviewed on camera, we become aware of camera and recorder as the means of creating her public image. The film, in fact, contrasts public and private lives but with the more authentic, cinéma-vérité style preserved for the public figure. In his interview with Chytilová in *Cahiers du Cinéma*, Jacques Rivette described his fascination with the two stories and how he found their alternation progressively more mysterious.[10]

Chytilová's next two features took her directly toward the avant-garde – indeed, it was difficult to find anything remotely similar within the feature film anywhere else. Although, they were not, of course, popular successes either with audiences or the authorities and therefore not promoted, they have remained a focus of critical attention until the present. *Daisies*, in particular, has been the subject of a number of extended studies.

Daisies is based on the story of two teenage girls who decide that, since the world has been spoiled, they will be spoiled too. A series of scenes or 'happenings' develop, based on the principle of the game 'Does it matter? No it doesn't'. Chytilová described the film as 'a philosophical documentary in the form of a farce' and usually sticks to the argument that it is principally a criticism of the girls' behaviour. At the same time, the script, which she wrote with Ester Krumbachová, was only the starting point for the film. The dialogue was the means by which she hoped to 'safeguard' the meaning of the film but with the film otherwise open to free thinking and improvisation. Inevitably, it supports many interpretations and, as cinematographer Jaroslav Kučera put it, many of the colour effects that were meant to provide critical commentary produced quite different results from those intended.

The girls seem to live in a kind of vacuum without past or future (or names) and, in one scene, they even discuss whether they exist (since they have no jobs or fixed address). Throughout the film, their cheating and provocation leads to the apparent destruction of both themselves and everything about them. The urge to consume is constantly linked to its other face – that of destruction – something that clearly connects with Chytilová's moral intent. Their journey reaches a climax when they sample and destroy a huge banquet, trample on the food in their stiletto heels and swing from the chandelier. This minor apocalypse is associated through newsreel footage with the world of real wars and a nuclear explosion.

In place of a progressive narrative, the film is comprised of five major sections, which is more analogous to musical construction. Repetitive variations frame them variously in a garden, a nightclub, with a lover, in the country and engaging in their final orgy. The film also becomes a sequence of audio-visual combinations – a creative and experimental interaction between sets, costume, cinematography and sound.

For instance, in a scene apparently centred on death, the girls' room is decorated with grass and wax-green leaves and, in the scene concerned with collection (of men), the walls and ceilings are covered in typographic decoration. In this latter scene, the musical accompaniment is that of a typewriter and there are equally unusual musical accompaniments for other scenes.

The cinematography often uses sets of colour and filter effects. In scenes where they pick up and exploit older men, who take them for meals, different filter effects are combined with a fragmented editing rhythm. In the nightclub scene, where the girls get drunk, their 'show' is in colour and the real floor show in sepia. As they become progressively inebriated, various colour effects are used – for example, one of them goes cross-eyed in red and the screen changes to yellow.

Another characteristic of the film is its use of accelerated montage and collage. In the scene in which the girls resort to cutting each other up with scissors, the screen itself becomes a combination of multiple jigsaw-like fragments.

Unlike most experimental films, *Daisies* does not take itself seriously, its experimentation is enthusiastic and its effects reflect an extraordinary joie de vivre. It is closer to the anarchist exuberance of Louis Malle's adaptation of Raymond Queneau's *Zazie dans le métro* (1960). It is this that has encouraged many writers to see Chytilová as identifying with her heroines rather than criticising them. After all, their targets are primarily men and the establishment

(Communism) and conforming to their expected roles as in the final scenes, where they appear wrapped in newspapers, only appears to trigger the final apocalypse.

Herbert Eagle makes a strong case for the film's direct links with Dadaism via its 'radical collision of signs from disparate cultural and artistic orders', with the principle of anarchy balanced by one of structure. Since women have been excluded from productive behaviour, they have turned to art and play. He argues for a link between the spoiled but creative characters and 'the spoiled (in terms of violating norms) and creative female artists (Chytilová and Krumbachová)'.[11]

While Chytilová defends her 'freedom' as a creator, she also respects the 'freedom' of the audience to interpret her films as they see fit and, in the case of *Daisies*, there is plenty of scope. The principal split in interpretation lies in the apparent criticism of the girls' mindless behaviour on the one hand and the film-makers' enjoyment of the process on the other – in other words, there is a conflict between the film's script and its overall aesthetics.

Zdena Škapová argues that this does not destroy the film's morality and, in this sense, supports Chytilová's own stated intentions. 'They [the girls] assert themselves with voracious energy and, in a reversal of the norms, take great pleasure in manipulating others, especially men . . . They are less an example of emancipation than a warning of the direction that emancipation might take.'[12] She argues for a deliberate ambiguity in which the girls' negative and selfish behaviour is superficially attractive and the viewer is invited 'to participate in an irresponsible game'.[13] Apart from their exploitation of men and attacks on Communist patriarchy, they also steal money from a cleaning woman, they 'destroy' each other and they consume and attack everything. These empty, bored and amoral creatures, bent on pleasure and destruction, find their ultimate reflection in the horrors of war – the images with which the film is framed.

As one of the most innovative film-makers of the 1960s, Chytilová's work is of particular interest in the context of feminist counter-cinema but it is worth noting that her key films preceded the development of feminist film writing in the 1970s. If she travelled the same route, it was in a different context. Writing of *Daisies* and of Krumbachová's *The Murder of Engineer Devil* (*Vražda ing. Čerta*, 1970), Petra Hanáková points out that they do not work with the conscious intention of subverting phallocentric meaning: 'Their subversiveness appears more as a by-product of female creativity itself, as a projection of the biting wit of the authors unpredictably criticizing the workings of patriarchy.'[14]

Drawing on the writings of Hélène Cixous and Luce Irigaray, Hanáková argues that *Daisies* allows the inscription of female desire and gratification and corrupts patriarchal language through nonsense and irony. Linguistic disintegration 'supports and mirrors narrative fragmentation and rupturing'.[15] She suggests that the 'moral message of the framing fails to impose itself on the impulsively "naughty" film core'.[16] However, the film's ending supports both comments on the girls and the society that produced them and against which they appear to revolt. It is possible to identify with the film-makers' breaking of norms and identify with the girls without approving of them. One factor, on which most could probably agree, is that the film is undoubtedly ambiguous.

In *Ceiling*, Chytilová focuses on a fashion model (she had been a model herself), someone who is dressed and made up to be looked at. In exposing the boredom and physical discomfort of existing for one's appearance, she also reveals the fashion world as one controlled by men and, in one scene, Marta's subjective thoughts are spoken by a man. In *Something Different*, Eva Bosáková exists for the media and for the public and, in some ways, similarly suffers as a public spectacle. In *Daisies*, the two girls repeatedly confront the camera and act out their happenings and, according to Škapová, they 'love to show off the most superficial attributes of femininity'.[17] They describe themselves as dolls and, in fact, act out a puppet-like spectacle.

In both *Ceiling* and *Something Different*, the films feature women as central characters, show the limitations of their roles and expose the ways in which they are constructed. In *Daisies*, what appears to have started as a similar exposé becomes, through its form, a mischievous identification in which the pleasure of transgressing norms leads to a beautiful and abstract object. There is little doubt that the film's aesthetic impact dominates its intended meaning – the play over the philosophy. However, while Chytilová is certainly a feminist (although she has denied this – no doubt mischievously), there is also little doubt that she was also attracted by the visual arts. Like the mostly male members of the New Wave, she was interested in new forms and new experiments – as was Kučera, to whom she was then married. Thus, while the form of *Daisies* can certainly be accommodated by feminist theory, there is little doubt that it is not solely the work of Chytilová and Krumbachová (but also of Kučera) or that its 'message' does not entirely support the total liberation of its protagonists.

With *The Fruit of Paradise*, Chytilová again worked with Krumbachová and Kučera, and produced a work of great formal beauty. Just as *Daisies* began in the Garden of Eden (where the girls pick a peach rather than an apple), so too does *The Fruit of Paradise*. A stylised introduction symbolises the expulsion of Adam and Eve from Paradise. Eva (Eve) and Josef (Adam) are then shown under a tree and an apple falls. A strange character called Robert also lurks in the garden. Dressed in scarlet, he is clearly meant to represent the devil but is also an assassin who has killed six women. He pursues Eva, his intended victim, but, in the end, the tables are turned and it is she who kills him. But, as Jan Žalman has noted, this is a film where the search for meaning and a logical storyline will not work[18] and the film is more of a kinaesthetic experience in which the cinematography of Kučera and the music of Zdeněk Liška play key roles.

After the film's credits, which consist of paintings of trees and fruit, the naked bodies of Adam and Eve are presented in slow motion. The bodies become a screen for the veins and textures of vegetation and are literally 'lost' in nature. Initially, the images are dominated by orange and blue, giving way to the rhythmic repetition of selected images – of leaves, daisies, a rose and white flowers.

In the central section of this prologue, a couple pose in various stylised positions to the chanting of God's words. If they were to pick golden apples from the tree, the result would be death. In the final section, a beautiful girl folds her hands over her breasts and is merged with the images of autumn leaves. A naked couple kiss in a stream and the leaves, rose and white flower reappear.

Inspired by biblical myth, the images and music here take flight, refusing their customary anchorage in the meanings created by classical narrative. The 'story' that follows is highly allusive. As Žalman argues, it is influenced by the *commedia dell'arte*, the actors adjust their roles to the level of naive art and the dialogue virtually functions as an artificial language.[19]

As with *Daisies*, the film's interest lies less in the 'what' and more in the 'how'. While there is some interest in the evolution of the story and its byways, the film operates primarily on the level of its stunning imagery. Also, as in *Daisies*, the function of the game (that is the creative freedom of the film-makers) remains much to the fore. Perhaps more than in *Daisies*, Kučera's photography seems to enjoy something of an independent role. His fascination with the textures of landscape (already apparent in Jasný's *All My Good Countrymen*), is here given full rein. The qualities of leaves, grass and tree bark are clearly defined and create an unusual impact. Examples of two purely 'aesthetic' scenes are those in which people play with an orange balloon on a lakeshore. Carefully selected colour points become blurred in images that recall the paintings of Seurat. In another scene, Eva's red-clad running figure is blurred, frozen and turned sideways to create a sequence of visual attraction and abstract fluidity.

After *The Fruit of Paradise*, which was one of the last filmic manifestations of the Prague Spring, Chytilová found herself unable to work again until 1976, when she made *The Apple Game* (*Hra o jablko*, 1976). However, the kinds of experiment represented by *Daisies* and *The Fruit of Paradise* were not permitted under the newly 'normalised' regime, for which such works were perceived as degenerate and subversive.

But, if Chytilová's subsequent films did not follow similar patterns and were superficially 'comprehensible', she continued to experiment with theme, narrative and cinematography, criticising both Communist and, subsequently, capitalist moralities. Of course, she never worked again with Kučera and only once more with Krumbachová on *The Very Late Afternoon of a Faun* (*Faunovo velmi pozdní odpoledne*, 1983). Kučera, despite a last fling with Juraj Herz's *Morgiana* (1972), found himself assigned to more conventional products and Krumbachová's career was virtually at an end. Although, Chytilová has continued to use disorienting camerawork, this has often been in the context of more conventional storylines where the emphasis has been on her collaboration with actors – notably her adaptation of the mime play *The Jester and the Queen* (*Šašek a královna*, 1987) in collaboration with Boleslav Polívka and her work with the theatrical group Sklep (The Cellar) on *Tainted Horseplay* (*Kopytem sem, kopytem tam*, 1988). Her summary of the geography, architecture and history of Prague, *Prague: The Restless Heart of Europe* (*Praha – neklidné srdce Evropy*, 1984), does, however, provide an interesting and effective use of her predilection for the constantly moving camera.

Apart from Chytilová, the 'New Wave' director most nearly associated with the avant-garde was Jan Němec. From the beginning, he made it clear that he had no desire to make 'realist' or what we would now call 'classical narrative' films. While at FAMU, Němec studied under Václav Krška, whose *Moon over the River* (1953) was described by Němec as the first Czech 'auteur' film. In the 1960s, he made two films almost without dialogue – *Diamonds of the Night* (1964) and *Martyrs of Love* (1966) – and another in which the dialogue never stops – *The Party and the Guests* (1966). All three rejected any classical construction.

Diamonds of the Night was based on the novella *Darkness Casts No Shadow* by Arnošt Lustig. As indicated earlier, it tells the story of two Jewish boys who escape from a Nazi transport train, stagger through the woods, ask for food at a farmhouse, are betrayed and then captured by the local Sudeten German volunteers. They are put on trial and condemned to death but they may or may not be executed. This is not, however, a conventional open ending since both endings are supplied.

Němec is not interested in telling a story or explaining the actions of his characters but attempts a close identification with their mental condition. Recognising their debilitated and exhausted state, he places great emphasis on the interaction between physical sensation and mental states. Flashbacks and fantasy are used to create a continuum in which past, present and future comprise a single reality. The hand-held camera is placed so close to the action that it becomes virtually a third participant in the flight. As the boys push on through the woods, memories and fantasies continually break into consciousness.

Although rarely attempted in cinema, this is an entirely logical approach to its subject. As noted earlier, Lustig described the film as the best to be based on his work and most nearly approximating his own experiences.[20] The focus on physical sensation is conveyed through texture, lighting and sound – harsh sunlight on jagged rocks, ants filling the socket of an eye (a nod towards Buñuel and Dalí), bruised feet painfully unwrapped and prodded, the sound of rain soaking into the earth, a bubble of blood in a dry mouth, a fantasy scene of childish laughter on crisp winter air.

The flashbacks (and sometimes flash-forwards – the status is not clear) include images of a tram moving along a street, a clock on a lamppost, women looking from windows, a montage of doors, door handles and steps, actions and incidents half perceived, that may or may not have taken place. While criticised by Luc Moullet for its 'false aesthetics,'[21] this can only be a view that fails to take account of the film's objectives, which are not to create a 'film school' exercise in virtuosity but to convey the reality of a particular set of experiences. Němec drew on the photographic talents of both Jaroslav Kučera and Miroslav Ondříček (who photographed a third of the film). Kučera's flair for photographic texture has already been mentioned while Ondříček was responsible for the film's remarkable use of hand-held camera.

Like many adaptations of Lustig's work, Němec's film expands from its historical context to emphasise an application to other situations and times. Here, there is a sense that the struggle against persecution and injustice is permanent and the film seems to be more concerned with the fact and experience of persecution rather than with providing any kind of historical analysis. The final image in which the heroes appear to march on into the woods suggests a situation without resolution.

Němec's work hovers on the fringes of both surrealism and the avant-garde and *The Party and the Guests* and *Martyrs of Love* are discussed, respectively, in the chapters on the absurd and on surrealism. He was forced into exile in the early 1970s, finally ending up in the United States, where he made wedding videos and was a special advisor on Philip Kaufman's adaptation of Milan Kundera's *The Unbearable Lightness of Being* (1987) which he had, at one stage, hoped to direct. When he returned to Czechoslovakia immediately after the fall of Communism, he made a feature film that had been long planned – *The Flames of Royal Love* (*V žáru královské lásky*, 1990), adapted from Ladislav Klíma's proto-Surrealist novel *The Sufferings of Prince Sternenhoch* (*Utrpení knížete Sternenhocha*), which had been first published in 1928. The film tells the story of the relationship between a prince and his sexually voracious wife. After locking her in a dungeon and killing her, he is haunted by her reincarnation and ghost. Němec updated the story to 1992 where Prague has become a small kingdom ruled over by a rock musician. A film designed to shock – and a mixture of horror, love story and comedy – it was undoubtedly ambitious but, for a variety of reasons, it failed to please critics and was also a box office failure. After failing also with his *Code Name Ruby* (*Jméno kódu Rubín*, 1997), he abandoned his brief flirtation with the post-Communist feature and opted for low-budget creative work that falls very much in the tradition of the avant-garde and marks a progression from much of his earlier work. One could almost say that the days of the 'caméra stylo' had arrived.

Late Night Talks with Mother (*Noční hovory s matkou*, 2001) was effectively the work of one man and a camera. A counterpart to Kafka's *Letter to the Father* (*Brief an den Vater*), the film is constructed as a dialogue with Němec's dead mother. As he walks to her graveside, he carries his camera before him (with a specially adapted wide-angle lens), photographing the streets and his own shadow on the wall. In this sense, it also recalls the city documentaries of the early avant-garde, its split and bent images echoing Vertov's *Man with a Movie Camera* (*Chelovek s kinoapparatom*, 1929). Němec is literally the writer, director, cameraman, composer and actor in his own film.

The film is, in effect, an autobiography but one that consists of personal recollection and politics, home movies and evocative and subjective images of present-day Prague. Film material recycled from other sources includes a record of his wedding, documentary footage he shot of the Soviet invasion in 1968, images of his period 'on the beach' in California (when twenty years passed almost without noticing), what appears to be an early film in which he enacts a scene from *The Trial* (*Der Prozess*, 1925) and interview footage he shot of his first wife, Ester Krumbachová, in which she advises him extensively on his alcoholism.

Krumbachová accuses him of narcissism and Němec indulges in both self-criticism and justification. He notes that there wasn't much love at home and that he regarded life as one big party. When his mother was in a coma, he was at a party. When his father was terminally ill, he had to take his only opportunity to leave the country (when he was offered a choice of exile or prison). In this context of funerals, he quotes the example of Meursault, the hero of Albert Camus' *The Outsider*, who was arrested not for committing a motiveless murder but for failing to cry at his mother's funeral.

While Němec appears on screen himself, he is also 'acted' by Karel Roden, with whom he also engages in conversation. He also denies some of his mother's imagined accusations (or she denies them). Did she describe his second wife, the singer Marta Kubišová as a 'cross-eyed goose'? Did she 'give birth to a monster'?

In many ways, the film is a significant achievement, revealing an instinctive ability to impose overall form on remarkably diverse material as well as providing a complex and contradictory self-portrait. Here Němec has achieved a film equivalent of poetry in which experience resonates through its provisional categories and is far removed from the certainties of the feature film.

Late Night Talks with Mother was one of the first films to be premiered on the internet, won the Grand Prix for best video film at Locarno in 2001 and was later converted to 35mm. In 2004, he followed it with *Landscape of my*

Heart (*Krajina mého srdce*) which has attracted less attention but is essentially a continuation of similar techniques.

When Němec left the country in 1974, he was taken off the plane and the screenplay he had written with his second cousin, Václav Havel, was confiscated by the police. *Heart-Beat* told the story of a group of 'the powerful' who ensured their own survival from heart disease by having healthy people murdered to provide donors. Pre-dating Michael Crichton's *Coma* (1978) as well as contemporary realities, Němec had planned to revisit the theme.

While he refers to this in *Landscape of my Heart*, the film is more closely linked to his own brush with death and a serious heart operation. In fact, the film begins and ends with references to his operation, ending with the putative quotation from the French nobleman executed during the Revolution, 'Is that all?' Němec seems to have been particularly struck by a film by the Hungarian documentary director, Tamás Almási, *A Matter of the Heart* (*Szivügyem*, 1996). Dealing with heart transplants, shots of the hands of surgeons feeling and manipulating a human heart permeate the film. Also, perhaps, predictably, Havel's trademark accompaniment to his signature, the drawing of a heart, also features. Towards the end of his presidency, it appeared somewhat incongruously, as a neon-lit heart against the outlines of Prague Castle.

Early views of ceiling lights seen from a hospital trolley suggest that the film is an approximation to the mental images conjured up under anaesthetic or in a state of semi-consciousness. Thus there are constant floods of images – mainly images of Prague but also of the arrival of George W. Bush by plane which was actually a real occurrence. Anyone who has undergone such experiences can testify that the real and the imaginary really do become unified.

Among the sequences appearing are: the night time arrival of Bush; unearthly images of a procession of cars in the night streets; lights in corridors; abstract shots of trees; documentary images of Dr Christian Barnard; an actor who personifies death; turning hands in white gloves; officials in a corridor; the sculptures of David Černý (large babies installed as if crawling up buildings); hands in front of the image; shots of people's legs walking; a red sunset over Prague, images of girls (with bare midriffs); and his newborn baby daughter – all contained by the repetition of images of the heart and of Bush's visit.

In the final analysis, if the film works less successfully than *Late Night Talks with Mother*, it is due less to a lack of authenticity than to the absence of the multilevel themes and materials that provided the 'attractions' of the earlier film.

In 2005, he made *Toyen*, a film about the relationship between the leading surrealist painter Toyen (real name Marie Čermínová) and the poet and photographer, Jindřich Heisler. Basically, it examines their life in Nazi-occupied

Prague when Toyen hid the Jewish-born Heisler in her flat and then follows them to Paris, where they went following the Communist takeover of 1948. The whole is framed by Toyen's painting *The Myth of Light* (*Le mythe de la lumière/Mýtus světla*, 1946), which now hangs in the Museum of Modern Art in Stockholm, where the film's third location is set.

Němec makes it clear in the subtitle for the film – *Splinters of Dreams* (a quotation from Toyen) – that this will be no ordinary work. The film includes documentary footage, actors playing Toyen and Heisler (Zuzana Stivínová and Jan Budař) and some striking reproductions of Toyen's paintings. It is also accompanied by a commentary made up of words by Toyen, Heisler, sometimes by Jindřich Štyrský, who was co-founder of the Czech Surrealist Group, and sometimes by Němec. But it really fits neither the category of documentary nor feature and is much more of an 'essay-film' in the tradition of *Late Night Talks with Mother* and *Landscape of my Heart*.

The film is primarily a visual and aesthetic exercise with a firm but, at the same time, an elusive and evocative structure. It begins with close-ups of small areas of Toyen's paintings, emphasising the textures of canvas and paint. It then moves to the Stockholm Museum and a close shot of *The Myth of Light*, in which we see the shadow of a hand curved like a bird and of a human head. Karel Srp suggests that the painting provides 'a meditation on the sense and scope of depiction itself',[22] noting also that it reflects the real situation under the Nazi Protectorate 'in which the surprising and prosaic were a common part of life'.[23]

During the film, Heisler sits for the painting, discovering when it is over

Figure 8.1   Jan Němec: *Toyen* (2005)

that Toyen has used only his shadow. Toyen explains that she painted it for Heisler because he loved light and the painting was to be hung in a place where there was full light. He loved light because, during the war, they were forced to live in semi-darkness. But the painting does not merely perform a framing function. It is also recalled during the film when we frequently see shadows of Toyen and Heisler. Flashes of the painting are also cut into the newsreels of the Communist show trial of their surrealist colleague, Žaviš Kalandra.

The enactment of their wartime existence is also achieved in an unusual way. There is no narrative development and no dialogue exchange, simply a series of situations. Stivínová does not look like the real Toyen and the actors simply signify or stand for the characters rather than representing them. Here it is worth recalling Němec's interest in Robert Bresson's use of actors, the distance between the actor and the role, the fact that even the best theatrical actors 'lie'.

The images of Toyen and Heisler alone in her flat (both in Prague and Paris) are claustrophobic and convey a sense of intimate detachment. Heisler sleeps in the bathtub, he appears with watch springs stuck up his nose and, together, they create a death mask for Štyrský. Their inner world is enhanced by fragments of their art and by specially shot home movies. The iconography of pre-war surrealism is also present – the face of the shop window manne-quin, the detached eye that is like a woman's breast, images from Štyrský's *Dreambook* (*Sny*, 1940).

While the film's most powerful images are those of Toyen herself, this is also very much a film by Němec. It recalls not only the use of subjective camera in *Late Night Talks with Mother* and *Landscape of My Heart* but also *Diamonds of the Night*. Just as in that film Němec evoked the characters' interior lives and subliminal thoughts through flashbacks to urban incidents and textures, *Toyen* includes a whole range of images of the city – cobblestones, the peeling plasters of walls, steps, shutters, grates, gutter outlets and keyholes.

The film also includes 'conventional' documentary footage of the political background. Here we see familiar images of Goebbels, the Nazi occupation, the assassination of Reichsprotektor Reinhard Heydrich, the liquidation of the village of Lidice in revenge, the Soviet liberation, the Communist show trials and the sentencing of Kalandra. The no doubt intentional mundanity of these images is contrasted with the heightened reality of Toyen's black-and-white images of war in *The Shooting Party* (*Střelnice*, 1939–40) and *Hide, War!* (*Schovez se, válko!*, 1944) as well as her illustrations for a book on Lidice. In *The Shooting Party*, she uses children's toys to confront the reality of war while *Hide, War!* sets the skeletons of strange creatures against devastated landscapes.

The film is notable for a complex and evocative use of sound. Throughout

Toyen, Němec uses 'natural' sounds in counterpoint to the images – a tram and a bell, a ship's siren, railway tracks, children playing, the sound of a typewriter, church bells, the wartime call sign, a film projector, a ticking clock and car horns. While many of these sounds are suggested by the subjects of individual scenes, others enjoy a free play across scenes.

In *Toyen*, Němec seems to work by association, forging links between the real world and a world of imagination which, it can be argued, emerges as a higher form of reality. While the film reminds us of its artificiality by using images of the optical track, it also evokes the spirit of the pre-war avant-garde in its use of superimposition and its mixture of genres. As Ždena Škapová observes, 'At no time does the film evoke an impression of connection; the image continually disintegrates, its shapes merge and spill over.'[24] If the visual track is a composition of disparate but evolving elements – in effect, a poem – the soundtrack presents a complementary symphonic reality in its juxtaposition of silence, sound, poetry and fragments of reminiscence. *Toyen* provides a unique approach to the life of an artist. In its avoidance of the art historian's categorisations, it searches instead for creative sources and inner meaning.

During the twenty years of normalisation (1969–89) that followed the Prague Spring, there was no opportunity for formal innovation within the feature film and Chytilová's works within that period must be seen as attempts to break with increasingly restrictive norms. Innovation, of course, certainly continued within the area of the short film, with Jan Švankmajer (discussed elsewhere) its foremost exponent. But he was banned from film-making for seven years and most of his films ended up proscribed for one reason or another.

However, it would not be true to say that work in the visual avant-garde entirely ceased during the years of normalisation – but it could certainly not be seen and acknowledged. The work of Petr Skala is a clear, and probably the only, example. Skala, who sees his work as a continuation of Pešánek's interest in kineticism and of the work of his teacher, Jiři Lehovec, issued a DVD of his work from 1969 to 1993 in 2005.

Skala graduated from FAMU in 1975 and pursued a career in documentary and promotional film while producing his experimental work privately. Although in no sense political, he kept his activities secret, even from his own children. Not only were his resources acquired 'semi-legally' but it was inevitably work that was uncontrolled and unauthorised and, hence, subversive. He explains in an interview that it was never intended for public presentation and that the groupings and themes outlined on his DVD were arrived at in retrospect. Nonetheless, he always regarded his work in documentary as a way of making a living – his real creativity was expressed in his private films.

Skala's original work was based on painting, scratching, engraving and drawing directly on raw or exposed film. This work was clearly an extension from earlier work by Len Lye and Norman McLaren and various members of the US underground (Stan Brakhage, Harry Smith, Carolee Schneeman and others). His use of gestural and abstract expressionist techniques was, however, not so much a following of international trends as a continuation of the art movement known as Czech Informal Art (Český Informel). Skala refers to the work of Vladimír Boudník and the fact that such techniques were 'in the air' when he began to develop his film work. He marks his development through the 1970s under the headings 'Informel Studies', 'Colour as Emanation of Light', 'From Abstraction to Figuration' and 'Spiritual Expression'. His film loops are no more than four minutes in length but, nonetheless, they represent a fundamentally continuing process. As Bohdana Kerbachová puts it, Skala viewed the motion picture as 'the most adequate medium for presenting his own specific interpretation of the world, for visualising the idea of interconnectedness of material and spiritual elements in the universe, as well as for expressing the complexity of time and space'.[25] In time, his work was precisely structured in a manner analogous to a music score, in an attempt to bring the structure of abstract film closer to musical composition. His work – particularly in the 1980s – reveals a use of silhouettes of female figures and eventually that of a pregnant woman, concentrating on the 'self-sustaining capacity of the universe and the metaphor of birth'. From 1982 onward, he began to work with video technology and, in the late 1980s, was able to organise some public screenings and, in 1987, together with Radek Pilař, he established the video section of the Union of Czech Visual Arts.

If we move to the post-Communist period, it is clear that the avant-garde has remained at the margins and that, with the possible exception of Švankmajer (who depends very much on his international reputation), avant-garde ideas have been almost absent from films shown in mainstream cinemas. Even the work of established names such as Jan Němec and Karel Vachek seems to have been restricted to the small worlds of enthusiasts within the film clubs.

But independent cinema has continued, albeit rarely interacting with the world of major film festivals. Among a number of films to reach international audiences have been: *Adam Quadmon* (*Adam Kadmon*, 1993–94) by Martin Čihák and Jan Daňhel; *Before* (*Dříve než . . .*, 1996) by Petr Marek; *The Last Heroes* (*Poslední hrdinové*, 1997) by Martina Kudláček ; *In the Wind* (*Ve větru*, 1997) by Vít Pancíř; and *Voice on the Telephone* (*Hlas v telefonu*, 2000) by Martin Blažíček. *Adam Quadmon* focuses on black-and-white images of the human body while investigating its archetypal subject, an individual who encompasses all ideas. Other work by the expanded cinema Ultra group (Blažíček, František Wirth, Alice Růzičková) – for example, *Units* (2000–02) – has combined film with live music improvisation and multi-screen projection. Petr Marek has subsequently made the feature films *Love from Above* (*Láska shora*, 2002) and *Not of Today* (*Nebýt dešní*, 2005) while Jan Daňhel, a member of the Surrealist Group, has worked as editor on the films of Bohdan Slama. Pancíř and Čihák have recently collaborated on a feature adaptation of Jáchym Topol's novel *Sister* (*Sestra*, 2008). Martina Kudláček has made important documentary films on both the Czech and international avant-garde with her *L'Amour fou: Ludvík Šváb* (1995) about the psychiatrist, film critic and leading member of the Surrealist Group, *Aimless Walk: Alexander Hammid* (*Bezúčelná procházka: Alexander Hammid*, 1996) and *In the Mirror of Maya Deren* (2001).

In Slovakia, the avant-garde has followed a less continuous course, although *The Earth Sings* was made as early as 1934. Svatopluk Ježek commented at the time that the film could, without a doubt, be attributed to the avant-garde since it was completely different from anything else then produced.[26] With its Slovak subject and production and its Czech contributors, it could also be regarded as a genuine Czech–Slovak collaboration. Its director and photographer, Karel Plicka, of course, produced many other films, some in collaboration with Hackenschmied and Kolda, and is widely regarded as the founder of Slovak cinematography. In general, though, his work tends to be categorised more as creative documentary, analogous to the work of Robert Flaherty.

Václav Macek suggests that Slovak experimental film really begins in the 1960s with the work of Martin Slivka and Dušan Hanák,[27] both of whom had their roles in established film-making. Slivka, like Plicka, was a key figure in the creation of Slovak cinematography and in the area of ethnographic film. His film *Water and Work* (*Voda a práca*, 1963) was nominally a film about old wooden water constructions that moved in the direction of abstraction through its imagery and editing, combined with absence of commentary and an electronically based soundtrack. He was the subject of Martin Šulík's feature documentary *Martin Slivka – 'The Man Who Planted Trees'* (*Martin Slivka – 'Muž, ktory sadil stromy'*, 2007).

Prior to his feature debut, Hanák made the key experimental films *Old Shatterhand Has Come to See Us* (*Prišiel k nám Old Shatterhand*, 1965) and *Impressions* (*Impresia*, 1966). The subject of the first is the influx of foreign tourists following the Cold War and is based on the initial problems of mutual linguistic comprehension. 'Old Shatterhand' is the popular hero from the western novels and German westerns based on the novels of Karl May. The film is a collage of documentary images, arranged situations, newspaper headlines, songs and sounds which together create a satirical portrait of an ambiguous relationship with the West. In *Impressions*, inspired by the music of Debussy, he cuts together images of musical instruments and playing hands with images of impressionist paintings and shots of dancing and ballet, with the whole affected by the play of light and association.

In what many regard as his best experimental film, *Day of Joy* (*Deň radosti*, 1971), he again focuses on montage and collage. It is centred on the popular festival 'If All the Trains in the World', organised by the artist Alex Mlynárčik, in which large numbers of artists and non-artists participated. It combined shots of a journey on the old Orava railway in northern Slovakia together with performances by visiting artists and archival material. In Andrew James Horton's words:

> Still photography, live action, interviews, old etchings and archive footage of old train journeys are skilfully blended to create a sympathetic and humorous portrait of the romance of an old steam train and the joy of artists and the general public in participating in this children's game for adults.[28]

In the 1970s, Macek notes that the avant-garde shifted to more 'unofficial' areas – that is the visual arts – where the re-imposed dogmas of Socialist Realism were less stringent. In the sculptor Vladimír Havrilla's film *Lift* (1974), he suggests an impression of levitation based on shots of people at the peak of successive jumps.[29] It is actually an animation and, as Jozef Macko notes, 'The film expresses Havrilla's desire to be raised out of the material world into the spiritual world. It can be done through the play-game, the play-game of contradictions.'[30] Havrilla went on to make other films including *Woman on Fire* (*Horiaca žena*, 1974), *No Limit* (*Nelimitované*, 1976) and *Yellow Danger* (*Žlté nebezpečenstvo*, 1977) in the mid 1970s.

The films of Vladimír Kordoš and Ľubomír Ďurček seem to have been very much based in the tradition of performance art. In Ďurček's *Information About Hands and People* (*Informácia a rukách a ľud'och*, 1982), a group of blindfolded young people meet around a table against a devastated landscape. The only means of communication is through touch. The film, notes Macek, 'is a picture of the state of a society in which the natural means of communication are lost and people have to seek other ways of contact which, however, need not be emotionally less intensive'.[31]

One film-maker whose work has extended from the pre- to post-Communist worlds is Samo Ivaška – *Subject* (*Subjekt*, 1984) and *The Run at the End of Summer* (*Beh na konci leta*, 1993). Of course, as in the Czech Republic, the shift towards video art – even more of a separate field than the old avant-garde – has been inevitable and here one should mention the prolific work of Peter Rónai.

If the work of the avant-garde has been discontinuous and often has gone unrecognised, there is undoubtedly a continuing line of development, extending from the work of Hackenschmied, Vančura and Machatý through to the New Wave of the 1960s and beyond.

NOTES

1. Constance Penley and Janet Bergstrom, 'The Avant-Garde: History and Theories', in Bill Nichols (ed.), *Movies and Methods*, Vol. II (Berkeley: University of California Press, 1985), p. 293.
2. Karel Teige, quoted in Michal Bregant, 'The Devětsil Film Dream', in Rostislav Švácha (ed.), *Devětsil: The Czech Avant-Garde of the 1920s and 30s* (Oxford: Museum of Modern Art; London: Design Museum, 1990), p. 72.
3. Ibid.
4. Alexandr Hackenschmied, quoted in Thomas E. Valášek 'Alexander Hammid: A Survey of his Filmmaking Career', *Film Culture*, 67–9, 1979, p. 251.
5. Jaroslav Anděl, *Alexandr Hackenschmied* (Prague: Torst, 2000), p. 8.
6. Ibid.
7. Ibid., p. 17.
8. Alexandr Hackenschmied, 'Film and Music', translated by Karel Santar, *Cinema Quarterly* (Edinburgh), 1, Spring 1933, quoted in Valásek, p. 257.
9. Pavel Taussig, 'On the Sunny Side of Film', in Jaroslav Anděl, Anne Wilkes Tucker, Alison De Lima Greene, Ralph McKay, Willis Hartshorn (curators), *Czech Modernism, 1900–1945* (Houston: Museum of Fine Arts; Boston: Bulfinch Press, 1990), p. 205.
10. Michel Delahaye and Jacques Rivette, 'Le champ libre: entretien avec Věra Chytilová', *Cahiers du Cinéma*, 198, February 1968, p. 53.
11. Herbert Eagle, 'Dadaism and Structuralism in Věra Chytilová's *Daisies*', *Cross Currents 10: A Yearbook of Central European Culture* (New Haven: Yale University Press, 1991), p. 229.
12. Zdena Škapová, *Sedmikrásky (Daisies)*, in Peter Hames (ed.), *The Cinema of Central Europe* (London: Wallflower Press, 2004), p. 133.
13. Ibid., p. 135.
14. Petra Hanáková, 'Voices from Another World: Feminine Space and Masculine Intrusion in *Sedmikrásky* and *Vražda ing. Čerta*', in Anikó Imre (ed.), *East European Cinemas* (New York: Routledge, 2005), p. 64.
15. Ibid., p. 74.
16. Ibid., p. 67.
17. Škapová, p. 133.
18. Jan Žalman, '*Le Fruit de Paradis (Ovoce stromů rajskych jíme)*', in Peter Cowie (ed.), *International Film Guide 1971* (London: The Tantivy Press, 1970), p. 107.
19. Ibid., pp. 106–7.
20. Arnošt Lustig, 'A Small Stone in a Big Mosaic', interviewed by Pavlina Kostková, *Central Europe Review*, 3, 28, 22 October 2001. http://www.ce-review.org/01/28/kostkova28.html [Accessed 02/03/02].
21. Luc Moullet, 'Contingent 65 1 A', *Cahiers du Cinéma*, 166–7, May–June 1965, p. 62.
22. Karel Srp, *Toyen*, translated by Karolina Vočadlo (Prague: Argo/City Gallery, Prague, 2000), p. 180.
23. Ibid.
24. Zdena Škapová, '*Toyen*', in Marie Grofová (ed.), *41st Karlovy Vary International Film Festival Catalogue 2006*, p. 89.
25. Bohdana Kerbachová, 'Petr Skala – A Hidden Experimenter', DVD leaflet (Prague: Narodní filmový archiv, 2005), p. 30.
26. Svatopluk Ježek, '*La terre chante (Zem spieva)*', in Ivan J. Kovačevič (ed.), *Le cinéma en Tchécoslovaquie*), Vol. 1, July 1936 (Prague: Le studio cinématographique de l'association pour la production cinématographique en Tchécoslovaquie), p. 103.

27. Václav Macek, 'Slovakia', in Peter Tscherkassky (ed.), *Avant-garde Films and Video from Central Europe* (Vienna: Sixpack Film, 1998), p. 24.
28. Andrew James Horton, 'Avant-garde Film and Video in Slovakia', *Central Europe Review*, 0, 3, 12 October 1998. http://www.ce-review.org/kinoeye/kinoeye3old. html [Accessed 22/04/08].
29. Macek, 'Slovakia', p. 24.
30. Jozef Macko, 'Slovak Alternative and Experimental Film', *Moveast*, 2, 1992, p. 29.
31. Macek, 'Slovakia', p. 24.

9. SURREALISM

It is often argued that surrealism has played a key role in Czech culture and also in its cinema. As evidence, one could cite the work of Jan Švankmajer, which Michael Richardson has described as 'one of the major achievements of surrealism'.[1] Švankmajer has been making films from the 1960s to the present and has made all his films since 1970 as a member of the Surrealist Group. However, it would also be true to say that he is a somewhat isolated figure, set apart from other film-makers, with his work deriving much more from the collective investigations of the Surrealist Group itself.

As a strong centre for surrealism in the 1930s, Czechoslovakia has seen a great deal of work in the visual arts and literature produced in a surrealist ambience or influenced by it. Despite the suppression of the group under the Nazi occupation and in the Stalinist years, these traditions re-emerged as an influence in the 1960s. In the 1930s, the founders of the Surrealist Group included the poet Vítězslav Nezval, who had collaborated with Gustav Machatý on three features between 1929 and 1932, and the theatre and film director Jindřich Honzl, who directed Voskovec's and Werich's debut films in the early 1930s. Among the directors of the 1960s whose work has been described as 'surrealist' in one context or another have been Jan Němec, Pavel Juráček, Antonín Máša, Věra Chytilová, Štefan Uher, Juraj Jakubisko, Elo Havetta and Jaromil Jireš among others. However, none of them was ever a member of the Surrealist Group or has claimed themselves to be a surrealist.[2] It is at best a connection linked to historical and stylistic influences and a 'loose' and, in some cases, rather wild critical categorisation.

As Jan Švankmajer has argued, there is a great deal of misunderstanding surrounding surrealism. 'Art historians consider it an art movement of the interwar avant-garde, others describe it as something beyond logic and reality. Politicians have even begun using the word as a synonym for nonsense. Others confuse surrealism with absurdity.' Above all, he insists, surrealism is not art.[3]

Aside from the work of Švankmajer, which can be considered a product of surrealist practice, three other films were, in various ways, inspired by earlier surrealist work – Jan Němec's *Martyrs of Love* (1966), which has been linked with some justification to the precursor of the surrealist movement, Poetism; Štefan Uher's *The Miraculous Virgin* (*Panna zázračnica*, 1966), an adaptation of a novel by the Slovak surrealist, Dominík Tatarka; and Jaromil Jireš's *Valerie and her Week of Wonders* (1969), adapted from a novel by one of the founders of the Czech Surrealist Group, Vítězslav Nezval. All of these were completed or prepared prior to the re-emergence of the Surrealist Group during the Prague Spring. However, it would be useful, first of all, to outline briefly the development of the Surrealist Group in Czechoslovakia.

I have earlier mentioned the development of Poetism and the phenomenon of Poetist screenplays. In his first Poetist manifesto, published in 1924, Karel Teige argued that, while the noblest expression of modern art would be reflected in the products of technological civilisation (that is constructivism), there was also a side of man that needed the bizarre, the fantastic and the absurd. This was the function of Poetism – to offer a way of life and art that was 'playful, unheroic, unphilosophical, mischievous, and fantastic'. It should give rise to 'a magnificent entertainment, a harlequinade of feeling and imagination . . . a marvellous kaleidoscope'.[4] In the 'Second Manifesto of Poetism' (1927–28), he linked Poetism to psychoanalysis and subconscious inspiration, paving the way for its later development into surrealism in 1934.

The *Poesie 1932* (*Poetry 1932*) exhibition was the first exhibition of surrealist work in Czechoslovakia and, besides exhibits by most of the Paris group, included work by many Czech sympathisers. The Czech Surrealist Group was founded in 1934 under Nezval, with founder members including the painters Toyen and Jindřich Štyrský, the composer Jaroslav Ježek and the theatre and film director Honzl. Karel Teige, who joined later, was to become its main theoretician. Apart from the visual arts and poetry, Czech surrealism was also closely linked to the theatre and to the Prague Linguistic Circle and it can be argued that there were strong connections within the avant-garde in general at this time. Since the formation of the *Left Front* (*Léva fronta*) of the Devětsil in 1929 by Teige, Nezval, Toyen and others, there had been a commitment to dialectical materialism and the cause of revolution and this was carried over into the Surrealist Group.

At the 1934 Congress of Soviet Writers, Nezval argued for the compatibility of surrealism with Socialist Realism. Poetry was the 'adaptation of reality by fantasy', using the tools of dramatisation, condensation and substitution. He also told the Czechoslovak Communist Party that the Surrealist Group reserved the right to independence in its experimental methods. Nonetheless, when the Left Front separated into pro- and anti-Socialist Realist factions, Nezval sided with the former and in 1938 attempted to dissolve the group.

During the Nazi occupation (1939–45), surrealist publications were outlawed and the group was disbanded after the death of Štyrský in 1942. Despite this, a number of clandestine groups were formed, including the Ra Group (Skupina Ra) in 1942 and the Surrealists of Spořilov in 1943. After the war, Teige re-founded the group around the journal *Signs of the Zodiac* (*Znamení zvěrokruhu*). Under the Communists, Teige was hounded by the secret police and, following his death in 1951, leadership of the group passed to the poet, Vratislav Effenberger. Toyen and Jindřich Heisler emigrated to France in 1947 where they became members of André Breton's group. Švankmajer recounts that, when he was a student in the 1950s, it was impossible to see or discuss modern art of any description and that he saw his first reproduction of Dalí in a book condemning 'bourgeois' art. It was only during the limited 'thaw' that followed Khrushchev's speech to the Soviet Communist Party's 20th Congress (1956) that he became acquainted with the work of Ernst, Dalí, Toyen and Štyrský. During 1967 to 1968, the period leading up to the Prague Spring, the group was again allowed a public space. After the Soviet invasion, in 1969, the Czech and French surrealists issued 'The Prague Platform' ('Pražská platforma') as a joint manifesto and, in the same year, the first issue of the surrealist magazine *Analogon* appeared. Edited by Effenberger, it was banned after only one issue. It reappeared after 1989 and has now reached over fifty issues.

While many directors of the Czech New Wave demonstrated an interest in experiment, it is Jan Němec who has proved the most consistently committed and whose films come most close to surrealist concerns. An interest in surrealism is readily apparent in his first film *Diamonds of the Night* (1964), which merges dream, hallucination and reality and includes an explicit homage to Buñuel's and Dalí's *Un chien andalou* (1928). While an admirer of Buñuel, his best-known film, *The Party and the Guests* (1966), was made before Němec had seen the film it most resembles, *The Exterminating Angel* (*El angel exterminador*, 1962), and the later *The Discreet Charm of the Bourgeoisie* (*Le charme discret de la bourgeoisie*, 1972). Further affiliations can be seen in his adaptation of Ladislav Klíma's proto-surrealist novel *The Sufferings of Prince Sternenhoch* (1928) as *The Flames of Royal Love* (1990) and his recent film *Toyen* (2005), which was based on the relationship between the surrealist artists, Toyen and Heisler, during the Second World War.

Martyrs of Love was made by Němec in 1966, the same year as *The Party and the Guests*, and was again a collaboration with Ester Krumbachová. While it was described at the time as providing a rest from 'significant' film-making, it seems very much an exercise in the kind of play reminiscent of Teige's comments on Poetism. Josef Škvorecký wrote that it was a predominantly lyrical film 'affecting the innermost centres of the viewer, his feeling and emotions, and not his reason'. He went on to argue that the film's lyricism placed it within the great traditions of Czech art – '[I]f it was necessary to determine the Czech contribution to world art, its major offerings would be found in the realm of [the] poetic and lyrical presentation of reality.'[5] Largely forgotten today, the film survives remarkably well despite its stylistic location in a pre-war Never-Never Land and its references to the pop and jazz worlds of the 1960s.

Referring to the film as comprising 'three gloomy farces', Němec described its three stories as 'an evocation of the atmosphere of various films – classical silent comedies, sentimental stories and social comedies . . . It could, perhaps, bear the subtitle 'From the Reminiscences of a Filmgoer''.[6] Inspired initially by Chaplin – the influence is particularly evident in the bowler hat and cane of the hero in the film's first episode – the film also recalls scenes from the work of Voskovec and Werich. The film's sense of nostalgia constantly summons up images that seem familiar without providing any sense of obvious recognition. It seems entirely within the spirit of that admiration for slapstick comedy associated with the Devětsil and the early years of Poetism. Alongside the tall buildings of Prague, we are taken into a dream world deriving from the inspiration of Kafka, Chaplin and Magritte.

The film consists of three separate stories, 'Temptations of a White-Collar Worker' ('Pokušení manipulanta'), 'Nastěnka's Reveries' ('Nastěnčiny sny') and 'Orphan Rudolf's Adventure' ('Dobrodružství sirotka Rudolfa'). In the first episode, an office worker dreams of a romantic (and mildly erotic) nightlife and ends up back at his desk. In the second, Nastěnka, a waitress, dreams of finding a rich or respectable mate but escapes a bourgeois fate by catching a passing train. In the third, Rudolf, an orphan, discovers a house by accident, where he is welcomed as a long lost member of the family. At the end of the film, he tries to rediscover the house but is unable to find it. Němec's 'sensitive, mostly unsuccessful people'[7] are searching for love and fulfilment. No doubt a film about desire, one of surrealism's fundamental concerns, all of the characters are incomplete, longing for lost identity and belonging.

The sentimental dreams of these ordinary, unsophisticated protagonists recall works of romantic fiction but were also intended to evoke the world of the 'chanson'. In fact, music is a key constituent of the film, with contributions from both the popular composer Karel Mareš and avant-garde composer Jan Klusák. Alongside the singers Marta Kubišová and Karel Gott and jazz singer Eva Olmerová are featured the band of Ferdinand Havlík and the now well-known jazz musicians Miroslav Vitouš and Jan Hammer. If Vladimír Svitáček's tribute to the Semafor Theatre, *If a Thousand Clarinets* (*Kdyby tisíc klarinetů*,

1964) is the most inclusive tribute to the role of popular music in the culture of the 1960s, *Martyrs of Love* is surely the most creative.

The unnamed white-collar worker, Nastěnka and Rudolf all have their associated song of longing which embodies disappointment and the impermanence of dreams and desire. The lyrics were written by Krumbachová and the film, made almost back to back with *Daisies*, also shows some of that film's joie de vivre (with Chytilová's two heroines making a guest appearance in a nightclub, giggling and blowing up paper bags). Other guest appearances include the novelist and screenwriter Jiří Mucha (son of Alfons Mucha) and British film director Lindsay Anderson

An important contribution to the film's mood is provided by Miroslav Ondříček's cinematography. Ondříček, who is normally associated with the more realist and transparent approaches of Forman's Czech films, had been assistant to Kučera on Němec's *Diamonds of the Night*, where he had been responsible for much of the disorienting, hand-held camerawork. Here, together with Němec, he creates an authentic poetic atmosphere from the streets of Prague. The scenes of the white-collar worker's life are particularly striking. For instance, as he looks from his window at life in other apartments, he sees a variety of everyday scenes in adjoining flats, shining out from the darkness of the night. The images – the silhouette of a girl, a baby, a woman washing her hair and an old couple gazing through net curtains – are on one level banal but are also given a sense of sadness by the night. Interestingly, Ondříček carried over some of this mood into his British debut on Lindsay Anderson's *The White Bus* in the following year.

If one were to focus on a year that re-established links with the avant-garde and surrealist traditions, it would be 1966 with *The Party and the Guests*, *Daisies*, *Martyrs of Love*, *Closely Observed Trains* and, in Slovakia, *The Miraculous Virgin*. Also in the pipeline was Vláčil's adaptation of Vančura's *Marketa Lazarová*. But, if Němec's film established a spiritual link with Poetism, Štefan Uher's *The Miraculous Virgin* was the first to forge a direct link with surrealism.

Slovak surrealism, although influenced by Poetism and Nezval, had followed a separate course and, rather perversely, achieved its greatest influence during the Second World War. Peter Petro has argued that, in Slovakia, it was the most important movement of the century and, more predictably, that it challenged both the cultural and political establishment.[8] Tatarka's novel, first published in 1944, is set during the period of the wartime state and focuses on a group of artists who were unable to practise their work. Tatarka spoke of the need for indirect expression and to oppose what he described as 'realistic verbalism'.

The film centres on the dream figure of Annabella, the 'miraculous virgin', played by Polish actress Jolanta Umecká, the star of Polański's *Knife in the Water* (*Nóz w wodzie*, 1962). She is a central focus of the artists' desires.

According to the film's story, they are unable to feel her sorrow and only Havran, the sculptor, understands her fate. A film full of fantasy, in which Giorgio di Chirico paintings come to life, a raven perches on a stuffed dress and horses undergo metamorphosis, it is dominated by a concern for landscape. Through its promotion of fantasy and imagination, Uher saw it as a provocation to those only concerned with the material world. As a director who had already, in *Sunshine in a Net*, created a multiple world of half-understood images, this was surely a logical progression.

Jaromil Jireš's adaptation of Nezval's *Valerie and her Week of Wonders* (1969) was, together with Juraj Herz's *Oil Lamps* (*Petrolejové lampy*, 1971) and *Morgiana* (1972), one of the last films to reflect the cinematic freedoms of the 1960s. As noted earlier, he filmed his controversial adaptation of Kundera's *The Joke* during the Soviet invasion, following up very rapidly with this long-planned exercise in fantasy, which he described as his own favourite from among his films. It ended up with the name of Ludvík Toman, one of the arch-normalisers, on the credits as executive producer.

But Nezval, of course, despite his surrealist commitments, had been one of the first to abandon the group, dutifully contributing a hymn to Stalin in 1949. Key avant-garde artists such as himself and Vančura, safely dead, were high in the Communist pantheon even if their creative work would hardly have found favour in the present. One can see why Jireš may have got the green light on this project, even if the authorities subsequently disapproved of the result.

Originally written in 1935, Nezval's novel wasn't published until ten years later, when it received little attention. Clearly inspired by fairy stories and the Gothic novel, it was intended to appeal to those who 'gladly pause at times over the secrets of certain old courtyards, vaults, summer houses and those mental loops which gyrate around the mysterious'.[9]

The novel reflects many surrealist preoccupations. Giuseppe Dierna points to the importance and influence of Souvestre's and Allain's *Fantômas* novels, published in Czech in the early 1930s, and Max Ernst's collage novel *A Little Girl Dreams of Taking the Veil* (*Rêve d'une petite fille qui voulut entrer au Carmel*, 1930). One might also mention Nezval's admiration for Matthew Lewis's novel *The Monk* (1796), for which he commissioned a Czech translation and F. W. Murnau's film *Nosferatu* (*Nosferatu, eine Symphonie des Grauens*, 1922). In a review of the latter, Nezval wrote, 'In art horror is delightful . . . In art, horror must be more than horror, it must be poetry.'[10] Nezval described *Valerie* as a 'free, concretely irrational psychic collage of everything from the genre of so-called pulp literature that belongs to the nethermost regions of our unconscious'.[11]

In his film adaptation, Jireš softens the impact of the original novel by presenting the film's Gothic effects with a lush and intentionally reassuring colour cinematography. Valerie's relations with her grandmother, father and brother run through a whole spectrum of threat and temptation without destroying her innocence. The central character in her fantasies is Tchoř (variously translated as Polecat, Skunk or Weasel), a vampire, who doubles as her father, as well as a 'bishop' and a 'constable'. Grandmother may also be her second cousin or her mother. Her brother Orlík (Eagle), a poet and a singer, may also be her lover. It is in the nature of these figures that their identity can never be fixed. Throughout the film, Valerie escapes from the threats of death or rape through the use of her magic earrings.

In setting the film within the family and during Valerie's 'week of wonders' – that is the week in which she begins to menstruate and move towards sexual maturity – both novel and film draw on Freudian analyses and also, of course, on documented fantasies and fears. Valerie is concerned with imagining the possible secret lives of her relatives and the threats that might be directed towards her.

In the original work, Nezval drew deliberately on the serial novel, constructing short chapters that are full of action and unexpected reversals. This is similarly maintained in the film and underlined by a constant change of shot and angle, often reminiscent of comic book narrative. The images as stills exert a considerable power and, as in many of his other films, Jireš demonstrates his interest in narrative virtuosity and lyrical camerawork.

The film quite openly declares the permanence of fantasy by pretending several conclusions to its complex story and choosing none. The concluding scenes, in which all the characters seem to be reconciled, almost like a theatrical curtain call, recalls the parade of characters at the end of Fellini's *8½* (1963).

Undoubtedly, one has the sense that Valerie's horrors are not to be taken too seriously, that she has not been too profoundly affected – that they may just be daydreams. However, audiences have different reactions and many find the film both horrific and unnerving. On the other hand, the rich colours of the countryside and Orlík's reassuring lullaby ensure that Valerie will remain safe. As the final words of the film elaborate, as the characters dance around her childish cot:

> Goodnight, my dear
> Goodnight, sweet dreams
> When you awake
> Keep safe your secret.

It is this sense of reassurance and 'innocence' that seems to suggest, as Michael Richardson points out, that *Valerie* is not a 'real' surrealist film, that it does not shock us with the truth of a newly revealed reality.[12] And yet, it is a film that has deeply affected many and is subject to continual rediscovery.

If one accepts Švankmajer's arguably partial view that surrealism is not art, then *Valerie* does not meet the strictest of criteria. It is a beautifully structured art object, the compositions are striking, the colours and textures of summer landscape predominate and it boasts a sensitive and original music score by one of Czechoslovakia's leading contemporary composers, Luboš Fišer. It is designed to provide aesthetic pleasure. But so also, one might argue, are the films of Feuillade, the paintings of Toyen and the poems and film projects of the Poetists. It is, to recall Teige, 'a harlequinade of feeling and imagination, an intoxicating film track, a marvellous kaleidoscope'.[13] The film is all of these and its play with narrative was, for its time, stimulating and inventive and without the portentousness of Resnais and Robbe-Grillet.

Within the context of Czechoslovakia in the 1960s – and certainly the 1970s – the film is clearly subversive. From an official perspective, it was not only incomprehensible and decadent – concerning itself with vampires, the church and sexuality – but it failed to address its audience with the naive platitudes that were to become staple requirements in the early 1970s. It also, of course, presented a challenge to authority.

Nezval's attack on the Catholic Church was evident but, if one takes the film's attacks on church authority, morality and double standards as representing the Communist Party, the film's targets can be seen as being closer to home. Explicit parallels are drawn between the arrival of the missionaries and that of the actors. Grandmother suggests that Valerie should be interested in the former rather than the latter. Here, Jireš draws attention to the film's opposition between repressive morality (or ideology) versus art, fantasy and play. Orlík, the artist and dreamer, is young whereas the representatives of morality are old, vicious and/or hypocritical. Here, a suppressed cultural tradition emerges to join forces with youthful revolt.

Of course, it could be argued that not everything should be politicised, that to do this is to go beyond the film's conscious intent, but, to recall my earlier comments, in the 1960s, everything was politicised and, in the 1970s and 1980s, this specifically Czechoslovak reality became even more exaggerated.

While the international reputation of Jan Švankmajer really dates from the 1980s, he actually made his first film in 1958 when he worked as an assistant on Emil Radok's puppet film *Faust* (*Johannes doktor Faust*), a film to which he made a significant contribution. With the exception of a seven-year period in the 1970s, when he was unable to work in film, he has worked regularly since his debut film *The Last Trick* (1964) through to the present, working in the field of short film until the production of his first feature *Alice* aka *Something From Alice* (*Něco z Alenky*, 1987), which was made as a Swiss-British co-production.

Švankmajer's early short films were dominated by his background in puppetry and his interest in the secret life of objects. While the films impressed audiences and won many awards, they were not initially perceived as surrealist and Švankmajer does not recognise any of his films as surrealist prior to his

The Garden (*Zahrada*, 1968). At the same time, he also recognises the influence of surrealism on his early work and it would not be appropriate to regard them separately. Surrealist influences were readily apparent in such mid- to late-sixties work as *J. S. Bach: Fantasia in G Minor* (*J. S. Bach: Fantasia g-moll*, 1965), *The Flat* (1968) and *A Quiet Week in a House* (*Tichý týden v domě*, 1969). In *J. S. Bach: Fantasia in G Minor*, a tribute to the surrealist photographer Emila Medková, Bach's music accompanies the visual expression of stone surfaces, chipped plaster, old doors and locks – an independent world of development and decay.

It is not surprising that many writers have focused on Švankmajer's use of objects. In one of the most perceptive essays, Roger Cardinal points to Švankmajer's interest in collage, which he also describes as a paradigm of all modes of surrealist activity. Collage can initially be characterised in terms of 'plurality, discomposure, and incongruity'. The successful surrealist collage, suggests Cardinal, 'frequently allows the rational viewer to grasp its meaning while still preserving its irrational heterogeneity'.[14]

Švankmajer's work can usefully be compared with that of the Habsburg court painter, Giuseppe Arcimboldo (1527–93). Celebrated for his famous 'trick portraits' made of everyday objects, he was also overseer of the Habsburg cabinet of curiosities. Švankmajer's fascination with Arcimboldo is, indeed, explicit, with Arcimboldo-like portraits appearing not only in his ceramic heads and other 'fine art' forms but also in a wide range of films. Cardinal suggests an affinity in such early works as *Game with Stones* (*Spiel mit steinen*, 1965), *Historia Naturae, Suite* (*Historia naturae, suita*, 1967) and *The Ossuary* (*Kostnice*, 1970).

Game with Stones is divided into five sections, each with contrasting games made up entirely of stones. Stones emerge from a tap and fall into a bucket from which the games develop. They progress via humanoid shapes and Arcimboldo-like figures finally ending in a game in which the stones are split and destroy the bucket itself. In *Historia Naturae, Suite*, Švankmajer provides a classic example of his attempts to categorise the heterogeneous. It is a kind of filmic *Bilderlexikon* comprised of eight natural history categories. Between each section, a human mouth chews and swallows a piece of meat and, in the last image, converts to a skull. The film suggests man's attempts to assert primacy over the natural world and the desire to collect specimens and fix categories. The film implies, argues Cardinal, that, 'for all our human methodicality, the world remains alien, irreducible, absurd, fundamentally *unquotable*'.[15]

The Ossuary was originally begun as a straightforward documentary about the Sedlec ossuary near Kutná Hora. Here a Cistercian chapel houses the bones of around 50,000 victims of the Hussite wars and a later plague. Švankmajer's film progresses through mountains of bones and skulls that, over many years, have been turned into decorative and artistic combinations ranging from armorial bearings to an ornate chandelier. Here, suggests Michael Richardson, the past resonates in the very textures of the objects.[16]

Švankmajer's concern with the 'life' of objects is well known. While he collects and portrays them for their associations, he also believes that they have an interior life.

> I believe in the 'conservation' of certain contents in objects that have been touched by beings in a state of 'heightened' sensitivity . . . I don't actually animate objects. I coerce their inner life out of them – and for that animation is a great aid which I consider to be a sort of magic rite or ritual.[17]

In fact, during the 1970s, when he was unable to work in film, his experiments with the Surrealist Group included an investigation of touch and the eventual publication of his samizdat *Touch and Imagination* (*Hmat a imaginace*, 1983).

In his adaptation of Edgar Allan Poe's *The Fall of the House of Usher* (*Zánik domu Usherů*, 1980), he tells the story entirely in terms of objects – stone, furniture, trees, mud – drawing on Poe's own psychological studies. He notes that Poe's stories are full of tactile descriptions and argues that the sense of touch becomes highly sensitive at moments of psychic tension. It is more fundamental than sight, he suggests, and less contaminated by the aesthetic.

Dimensions of Dialogue (*Možnosti dialogu*, 1982), perhaps his best-known short film, encompasses not only this concern with objects but also the serial progression that is a virtually uniform aspect of his work. The film consists of three sections. In the first section, in an explicit homage to Arcimboldo, a human head consisting of crockery and kitchen implements devours another made of fruit and vegetables. The two heads then merge in chaotic synthesis, re-form and undergo further transformations. To close the first section, a perfectly modelled human head emerges and begins to vomit replicas of itself.

In the second section, a male and female figure touch and embrace in gestures of love but finally enter into conflict and tear each other to pieces. In the final section, as I have described elsewhere:

> two heads are formed from the same matter and take part in complementary activities. From the mouth of one emerges a toothbrush and from the other a tube of toothpaste to be squeezed onto the brush, a knife spreads butter on a piece of bread, a shoe is laced, and a pencil sharpened. But the process then goes wrong and each head produces the wrong object and chaos and destruction follow.[18]

Aside from its subject, an examination of dialectics and the (im)possibilities of human dialogue, the film emphasises the qualities of materials – 'of bristle and plastic when they are sharpened, of bread when it is tied with shoelaces, of pencil lead when it penetrates toothpaste'.[19]

The film could be interpreted as an illustration of the surrealist view of life as a dialectic and great force derives from the tactile resonance of his objects. If viewed as a commentary on human 'possibilities' of dialogue, the conclusions are resoundingly negative. In the first episode 'Eternal Dialogue', various assemblies of alternatives finally combine to provide a single uniform truth. 'Passionate Dialogue', the dialogue of lovers, ends in destructive conflict and, in 'Exhausting Dialogue', attempts at complementary activity are doomed to failure. Historically, it was probably the film that made the greatest single impact on foreign critics and audiences.

Švankmajer's origins in puppetry and masked theatre are readily apparent in early films such as *The Last Trick* (1964), *Punch and Judy* aka *The Coffin Shop* (*Rackvičkárna*, 1966) and *Don Juan* (*Don Šajn*, 1970). In the first and last of these, he uses puppet actors – that is actors inside puppets. His first film to use 'real' actors was *The Garden* (1968) which, at nineteen minutes, was not only his longest to date but, as mentioned earlier, the first that he acknowledges as surrealist.

Filmed in black and white and based on a short story by Ivan Kraus called *Living Fence* (*Živý plot*, the Czech for 'hedge'), *The Garden* was, in its use of narrative and actors, Švankmajer's most 'conventional' film. František is invited for a weekend at the house of his friend, Josef. There are premonitions that all may not be as expected as they pass a hearse going in the opposite direction. Upon arrival, František discovers that the house is surrounded by a 'living fence' of people with their hands linked. Josef even unlocks a 'gate' in the line of linked people to gain access.

The people who make up the fence are ignored as individuals and merely function as elements in a structure supporting Josef's life in the country. František has been selected to take his place in this structure. The film, as Švankmajer acknowledges, has some superficial similarities with Němec's *The Party and the Guests*. Both films can be interpreted as attacks on Stalinism and both demonstrate a situation in which people acquiesce in their own oppression and manipulation. But *The Garden* operates on quite a different level.

František Dryje notes similarities between the screenplays of the leader of the Surrealist Group, Vratislav Effenberger, none of which were ever filmed, and Švankmajer's work on *The Garden*. He refers here to Effenberger's notion of 'parapoetry', which Effenberger identifies with the critical function of absurdity. If parapoetry is the attempt to transplant 'the realistic absurdity of modern life' into an artistic composition or dramatic expression, 'the most authentic parapoetry is found in the real situations themselves, and the reworking may have the character of a mere analogon'.[20] In *The Garden*, notes Dryje, the 'fashionable' aesthetic categories of the grotesque and the absurd, or the symbols and allegories of a Resnais or Buñuel are irrelevant. The concrete and realistic content of an absurd situation 'provides a clear denunciation of everyday, contemporary reality . . . The force of imagination clashes with the "barbarity of life".'[21]

It is worth considering Effenberger's ideas on the role of the imagination. In one of his articles, he argues that '[i]magination exists only when it has not been tamed and taught to produce an aesthetic and moral deodorant for a rotting social hierarchy'. Stressing the role of humour, analogy and negation, he supports the Bretonian view of surrealism as placed at a point where destruction and construction meet. Imagination is not a turning away from reality but a reaching through to its 'dynamic core' – it is not irrational but 'liberates reason from the bonds of servitude to the status quo'.[22]

One can see here why Effenberger and Švankmajer both respect the early 'realist' work of Miloš Forman and also that of Karel Vachek. Both expose the irrationality in the real world. Effenberger praised Forman's *The Firemen's Ball* for its 'active understanding of reality' and 'feeling for contemporary forms of aggressive humour, and for the critical functions of absurdity'.[23] In the first issue of the surrealist magazine *Analogon*, published in 1969, he praised Vachek's discovery of 'a new type of cinematic expression' which violated both old and new conventions and explored an 'irrational reality'.[24] By contrast, he condemned Chytilová's *Daisies* as mere decorative cynicism.

The influence of Effenberger's ideas can clearly be seen in Švankmajer's subsequent work as well as in the wider activities and preoccupations of the group. As Dryje suggests, collective projects not only influenced Švankmajer's work but 'he works and modifies himself within the network of coordinates (which he is at the same time creating) of permanent surrealist research'.[25]

Alice is probably the best-known as well as the most accessible of his feature films for a general audience. It was not Švankmajer's first encounter with the work of Lewis Carroll since he had already explored the child's world of play in his *Jabberwocky* aka *Jabberwocky or Straw Hubert's Clothes* (*Žvahlav aneb šatičky Slaměného Huberta*, 1971), which had been inspired by both Carroll and Nezval. *Alice's Adventures in Wonderland* is, of course, a text much admired by the surrealists and Carroll is a surrealist precursor, according to Švankmajer, because of 'his perfect understanding of the 'logic of dreams".[26] The original title of the film, *Something from Alice*, indicates that the film was never intended as an 'adaptation' of the novel but is an interpretation 'fermented' by his own childhood 'with all its particular obsessions and anxieties'.[27]

The differences are, in fact, less radical than this suggests. However, as Philip Strick has observed, where Carroll attributes the origins of Alice's dreams to the reassuring sounds of the countryside, Švankmajer 'anticipates the images of her fantasy in the brooding preliminary shots of her room, with its shelves of relics and mysteries from other, previous lives – the furniture she has not yet earned the right to use'.[28] Alice's quest, suggests Strick, is a hunt for her own context.

Švankmajer has rendered her dream encounters more explicitly threatening – here, no doubt influenced by his own childhood but also his earlier film *Down to the Cellar* (*Do pivnice/Do sklepa*, 1982), with its origins in the Surrealist Group's *Inquiry on Fear* (*Anketa o stracha*, 1978). The White Rabbit plays a key role throughout, also taking on the role of the Duchess in the 'Pig and Pepper' sequence and that of the Executioner in the film's conclusion. This is a far from reassuring creature – one who is frequently perceived as a personal threat – and, suggests Brigid Cherry, in his constant need to resurrect himself by eating sawdust, he represents the Undead.[29]

Alice is played by a real little girl (Krystýna Kohoutová) while the world of her imagination is represented by puppets and animated figures. Her constant transformations in size are represented by a change from human to doll – where the eyes do not move and the movements are anything but realistic. Švankmajer thereby suggests a definite and tangible problem of identity in the film's central character and a positioning between dream and reality.

The puppet world she enters is peopled almost entirely by old and discarded toys, as if left over from another era. Thus, the White Rabbit's stuffing repeatedly falls out and he has to be secured with a safety pin; the March Hare's eye has to be pulled back into place and he has to be wound up. Other figures take on more disturbing or comical shapes. For instance, the caterpillar constructs himself out of an old sock, a pair of false teeth and false eyeballs. However, 'the animals', who attack her from outside the White Rabbit's house, are entirely based on the skeletal monsters and combinations that Švankmajer first constructed in the early 1970s for his Natural Science Cabinet. They include:

> a coach pulled by chickens with skull heads, driven by a Punch figure wearing a red hat over a skull with two different coloured eyes; a fish-like object-skeleton with legs; a skull dragging a bone body with arms but no legs; a skull head that comes out of a jam pot; and a flying cot with arms, legs, and claws.[30]

The scene, Tina-Louise Reid suggests, recalls Max Ernst's painting *The Temptation of St Anthony* (*Die Versuchung des hl. Antonius*, 1945): 'Švankmajer's menacing hybrids . . . resemble the bird-like, aquatic, and crustacean creatures made of talons, fangs and eyes from Ernst's paintings'.[31]

Švankmajer's dialectic between human and artificial figures was to continue through his following three features, *Faust* (1994), *Conspirators of Pleasure* (*Spiklenci slasti*, 1997) and *Little Otik* (*Otesánek*, 2000).

Faust was originally intended as a production for the *Laterna magika* theatre. Švankmajer describes it as a 'variety collage' in which elements from Marlowe, Goethe, Christian Dietrich Grabbe, Gounod and the Czech folk puppet play (Kopecký) are all framed by the reality of contemporary Prague. In his last performance, the stage and screen actor Petr Čepek takes on the role of Faust in a performance of some subtlety, shifting between different realities and aesthetic contexts.

The film's hero, an ordinary man in a dirty raincoat, lives in a rundown flat in Prague. Here (as in *Conspirators of Pleasure*), it is noticeable that Švankmajer avoids any exotic images of 'tourist Prague', preferring nondescript streets and down-at-heel cafes serving nauseous food. One day, the man finds a leaflet showing the path to a house. He follows the instructions and, despite himself, is drawn into the world of the Faust legend. Like Alice, Faust moves from scene to scene and from one world to another but, this time, also from text to text, with time out for the occasional cigarette or glass of beer. While Faust only becomes a puppet for the scenes involving puppet theatre, he remains throughout under the control of an unseen manipulator.

In both *Alice* and *Faust*, we encounter narratives in which the identity of the central character is unstable and an episodic and serial construction recalling Švankmajer's short films. In fact, on its first release, some critics suggested that *Alice* was like a compendium of short films and it was difficult to watch because of the intensity of its content and expression. Švankmajer recognises that, in the short film, communication is more direct and that films with actors are inevitably longer because the use of dialogue implies a more 'roundabout' expression. Despite this, he once remarked that he saw little essential difference between making a short film and a long film.

However, Švankmajer's ignoring certain aspects of classical narrative construction is no different from what Antonioni, Godard, Miklós Jancsó, Chytilová and others have done – in each case the audience is, in some way, challenged and required to make an adjustment. In *Faust*, the narrative is constantly fragmented by the shift from text to text, from opera to folk puppetry, from the 'high' to the 'low'. As Švankmajer himself puts it, 'high and low together create a certain magic'.[32]

Conspirators of Pleasure was Švankmajer's first film with a multiple cast and was originally planned as a short film based on his script *Pale Bluebeard* (*Bledomodrovouš*), which now forms one of the film's overlapping stories. Its story is that of two neighbours, Mr Pivoňka and Mrs Loubalová. Each devotes time to making effigies of the other which they then take to different locations, subject to various kinds of sadistic abuse and then 'murder'. One night, Švankmajer wrote an additional four stories dedicated to the principle of desire, under the original title of *The Pleasure Principle* (after Freud).

The conspirators' desires take various forms. The post-woman snorts balls of bread, the newsagent creates a masturbation machine that enables him to

Figure 9.1   Jan Švankmajer: *Conspirators of Pleasure* (*Spiklenci slasti*, 1996)

achieve climax while watching his favourite newsreader on television, the police chief collects kitchen implements which he then rolls over himself in acts of auto-eroticism and the real newsreader (the police chief's wife) has her feet sucked by a bowl of carp while she is reading the news.

Providing it is not taken too seriously, the film is very funny but also disturbing. Many of the ideas come from Švankmajer's non-film work – the tactile objects in the police chief's workshop and the mystificatory masturbation machine (Švankmajer once suggested that they be supplied at the entrance to hospitals, hotels and waiting rooms as a public service). On the other hand, the violence done to the pathetic effigies of Loubalová and Pivoňka is genuinely disturbing. Again referring to it as his most surrealist film to date, he lists his 'technical advisors' at the end as Buñuel, Freud, Ernst, Sade, Sacher-Masoch and the Czech psychoanalyst and surrealist Bohuslav Brouk.

With *Little Otík* (*Otesánek*, 2000), Švankmajer returned to a slightly more conventional area – the Czech folk tale. A version of the tale familiar from K. J. Erben's collection, it tells the story of a childless couple who adopt a human-looking tree root as a baby. The wish is father to reality and the piece of wood develops into a real creature with an enormous and ultimately cannibalistic appetite. The idea for the film developed from a project of his wife, the surrealist painter, ceramicist and writer, Eva Švankmajerová to adapt the traditional story as an animated film. This idea was maintained and becomes, in effect, a film within a film.

The principal story of Mr Horák and Mrs Horáková is treated quite realistically. It is an extension of real-life problems involving issues such as phantom pregnancies and the theft of babies, all involving contacts with social services and, in the final analysis, the police. As the strange story of Otesánek or Little Otík develops, the neighbour's daughter, Alžbětka, suspects that something odd is afoot. She also desperately wants the Horáks to have a child since she wants a friend. When she begins to read Erben's *Fairy Tales*, the key to the development of the animated 'film within a film', she tries to protect Otík from the inevitable fate predicted by the tale.

In a way, the character of Otík is a kind of puppet but is experienced as a total entity in very few scenes. The various models for the body are not animated, this being reserved for his mouth which, in effect, substitutes for a face. This orifice also at various times incorporates teeth, a tongue and an eye. Otík is a representation of primal forces. Like *Conspirators of Pleasure* and *Lunacy* (*Šílení*, 2005), it is a film about desire.

Švankmajer has completed around thirty films and it has been possible to discuss only a few in the context of a brief summary. However, I would like to conclude with a more detailed consideration of *Lunacy* partly because it is, in some ways, his most controversial film but also because it is yet another in which he comes close to fulfilling his surrealist objectives.

It is the first of his features in which there are no artificial figures – no puppets, no dolls (other than the carving of Christ which the Marquis treats as a ritual fetish), no masks and no Otík. Švankmajer uses more actors than usual, many of whom can be regarded, in a Czech context, as stars – Pavel Liška, Jan Tříska, Jaroslav Dušek and Anna Geislerová. However, he has drawn attention to the fact that, although there are no puppets, he treats his actors *as* puppets. He also notes that he habitually selects his actors on the basis of their eyes and mouths. He also emphasises a frontal address to the camera. He avoids the self-contained realist scenes to which we are accustomed, arguing that the characters' exchanges pass through the viewer.

In *Lunacy*, which he describes as his 'most surrealist' film, he tells the story of Jean Berlot, a young man who is returning from his mother's funeral at the asylum of Charenton. While staying at an inn, he suffers a nightmare from which he is rescued by a fellow guest known as the Marquis. The Marquis invites him to stay at his chateau, where Jean witnesses an orgy and, subsequently, the apparent death of his host. After the Marquis's recovery following his 'premature burial', he invites Jean to visit the local asylum to work through his feelings about his mother's death. Here, he meets Dr Murloppe and his 'daughter', Charlota, both of whom had participated in the previous day's orgy. Jean agrees to become a patient in order to help Charlota, who explains that the real staff of the asylum are locked up in the cellars and that Murloppe and the Marquis are mad. Despite the Marquis's warning that Charlota is a nymphomaniac and a hysteric, Jean helps her to free the staff, including Dr Coulmiere, the head of the asylum. The Marquis and Murloppe are subjected to extreme (unspecified) physical punishment. Jean himself is declared insane and prepared for the first of Coulmiere's graded system of corporal punishment.

Before the story begins, Švankmajer appears on screen and notes that the film is a 'philosophical horror story' and a debate on how to run a lunatic asylum, presenting the two extremes of treatment, freedom or punishment. There is a third way, he suggests, that combines the worst aspects of the other two '[a]nd that is the madhouse we are living in today'. He acknowledges his debts to the Marquis de Sade and Edgar Allan Poe, stressing that his film is not a work of art and that, today, art is all but dead anyway.

On one level, the film's narrative is straightforward and, given Švankmajer's introduction, we are given instructions on how to read it. However, with the exception of the trusting and naive Jean, with whom we identify, the status of the other characters remains ambiguous. Nonetheless, even if the Marquis and Murloppe are mad, their system based on freedom seems infinitely preferable to that of Coulmiere – and the beautiful Charlota does seem to embody the Marquis' warnings.

The motifs derived from Poe are simply that. The Marquis' earlier death and resurrection are based on *The Premature Burial* while the basic premise of the alternative therapies and the lunatics taking over the asylum are derived from Poe's *The System of Dr Tarr and Prof. Fether*. In Poe, the 'system' referred to is the tarring and feathering of the real staff of the asylum.

The film has a strong sense of being set in late-eighteenth- or early-nineteenth-century France not only because of its historical costumes and the Marquis and his carriage but also in its references to Delacroix – the patients re-enact *Liberty Guiding the People* (*La Liberté guidant le peuple*) as a tableau – and 'La Marseillaise' which is played backwards during the credits. But we are not in the eighteenth or nineteenth century. When the 'cast' from the opening scenes at the inn depart, they are transported by motor coach and, as Jean and the Marquis travel towards his chateau, they pass over a modern motorway. Unlike Němec's *Martyrs of Love*, another film that mixes artefacts from different historical periods, there is no attempt to create a single 'reality' and the references to the present retain their dissonance.

In evoking the era of the French Revolution and its aftermath, Švankmajer returns to the world of the real Marquis de Sade, his real madness and his involvement in both sexual and political revolution. Here, it is worth recalling that Sade was an aristocrat who supported the revolution, declared his own rebellion against God, opposed the death penalty and was sacked from his revolutionary duties for undue lenience. During his own incarceration at Charenton, Sade also, of course, staged plays using the inmates.

The surrealist interest in Sade can be taken as read, not least among the Czech surrealists. Štyrský published a biographical sketch on Sade in 1931 and the following year undertook a photographic pilgrimage to the ruins of Sade's castle. In 1932, Toyen illustrated a Czech translation of Sade's *Justine*. The influence of Sade is also apparent in some of Švankmajer and Eva Švankmajerová's non-film work of the mid 1990s. *Lunacy* quotes directly from both Sade and from Joris-Karl Huysmans' *Là-bas*, making the film, one might say, a genuine compendium of surrealist concerns and issues.

The film is not without animation since, like *Little Otík*, it is permeated by a parallel text, based around the subject of meat. The credit sequence is preceded by the bloodless evisceration of a pig and the film ends with the image of meat 'breathing' under cellophane wrappers in a supermarket. In between, and inter-cut with the narrative, are scenes of tongues and other meat products which undergo various processes, are animated and foreshadow elements of the plot. 'They go mad,' writes František Dryje, 'die, brawl, eat each other and copulate, they are minced; and it is not by chance that they appear in one scene as mari-onettes on the stage of a puppet theatre.'[33] For Švankmajer, this 'metaphorical and analogical action introduces into the film a certain drastic but at the same time also ironic poetry'.[34]

Švankmajer has travelled some way since the attraction and novelty of his early films and the 'aesthetic' appeal that he has progressively attempted to outgrow. In *Lunacy*, he brings us face to face with the brute reality of his themes and an essentially pessimistic view of human destiny. He has himself commented on the relevance of his attack on religion in an age of increased religious fundamentalism (although he is referring principally to Christian fun-damentalism). And, of course, the tortures inflicted on his inmates have become an everyday staple of international political reality.

His portrait of woman via Charlota is not, of course, 'progressive' – she is a sex object, nymphomaniac, untrustworthy and duplicitous but also, like the other characters, he alleges, she is a victim. But his portrait of 'man' is even less complementary and, in this respect, he is merely being even handed. One is also here reminded of Angela Carter's comments on Sade – 'He was unusual in his period for claiming rights of free sexuality for women, and in installing women as beings of power in his imaginary worlds.'[35]

Despite the undoubted power of Švankmajer's work, it is clear that he has consistently drawn on the experimentation of the Surrealist Group and its mutual interaction. Since surrealist perspectives are not limited by time or place, there is no reason to believe that they will cease although, in the future, they may well acquire different forms. With the progressive ageing of the Czech and Slovak group, much will depend on the work of younger members, who currently include Švankmajer's son, Václav, who has made some promising works of animation, and the theatre director David Jařab.

Jařab has collaborated with František Dryje on a number of *Analogon* evenings for both theatre and television, while his stage productions have included Charles Maturin's *Melmoth the Wanderer* and Ladislav Klíma's *The Sufferings of Prince Sternenhoch*. His feature film debut, *Vaterland – Pages from a Hunting Notebook* (*Vaterland – lovecký deník*, 2004), a fantasy thriller about an aristocratic family that returns home from exile and finds instructions on how to hunt the mysterious creatures inhabiting the local hills, might best be described as surrealist science fiction. The question is whether economics will allow them to pursue an independent course or whether, like their predecessors in the 1930s avant-garde, they become absorbed by the commercial world.

Notes

1. Michael Richardson, *Surrealism and Cinema* (Oxford: Berg, 2006), p. 121.
2. The Slovak artist and screenwriter, Albert Marenčin, who *is* a member of the Surrealist group was, together with Karol Bakoš, head of a Slovak production group in the 1960s, that was responsible for the major films by Uher, Jakubisko, and Havetta, as well as Alain Robbe-Grillet's *The Man Who Lies* (*L'Homme qui ment/Muž, ktorý luže*, 1968) and *Eden and After* (*L'Eden et après/Eden a potom*, 1970).
3. Jan Švankmajer, interviewed by Peter Hames, in Peter Hames (ed.), *The Cinema of Jan Švankmajer: Dark Alchemy* (London: Wallflower Press, 2008), p. 112.
4. Karel Teige, 'Poetism', *Host*, May 1924, quoted in Alfred French, *The Poets of Prague: Czech Poetry Between the Wars* (London: Oxford University Press, 1969), p. 39.
5. Josef Škvorecký, *All the Bright Young Men and Women: A Personal History of the Czech Cinema* (Toronto: Peter Martin Associates, 1971), p. 130.
6. Jan Němec, interviewed by Oldřich Adamec, *Continental Film Review*, 13, October 1966, pp. 18–19.
7. Ibid.
8. Peter Petro, 'Dominik Tatarka – An Introduction to a Rebel', *Cross Currents*, 6, 1987, p. 281.
9. Vítězslav Nezval, Foreword to *Valerie and Her Week of Wonders*, translated by David Short (Prague: Twisted Spoon Press, 2005), p. 11.
10. Nezval, 'Upír Nosferatu', *Dílo*, XXV (Prague: Československý spisovatel, 1974), pp. 465–6, quoted in Giuseppe Dierna, 'On Valerie, Nezval, Max Ernst, and Collages: Variations on a Theme', in ibid., p. 204.
11. Vítězslav Nezval, 'Předmluva k dosavadnímu dílu', in *Most* (Prague: Borový, 1937), quoted in Dierna, p. 212.
12. *Surrealism in the Cinema*, pp. 121–2.
13. Teige, op. cit., p. 39.
14. Roger Cardinal, 'Thinking through things: the presence of objects in the early films of Jan Švankmajer', in Peter Hames (ed.), *The Cinema of Jan Švankmajer: Dark Alchemy* (London: Wallflower Press, 2008), pp. 67–8.
15. Ibid, p. 70.
16. *Surrealism in the Cinema*, p. 127.
17. Švankmajer , in Wendy Jackson, 'The Surrealist Conspirator: An Interview with Jan

Švankmajer', *Animation World Magazine*, 2–3 June, 1997. http://www.awn.com/mag/issue2.3/issue2.3pages/2.3jacksonsvankmajer.html [Accessed 14/01/07].

18. Peter Hames, 'Czechoslovakia: After the Spring', in Daniel J. Goulding (ed.), *Post New Wave Cinema in the Soviet Union and Eastern Europe* (Bloomington: Indiana University Press, 1989), pp. 132–3.

19. Ibid., p. 134.

20. Vratislav Effenberger, quoted in František Dryje, 'The Force of Imagination', in Hames (ed.), *The Cinema of Jan Švankmajer*, p. 178, translated by Valerie Mason from *Realita a poesie* (Prague: Mladá fronta, 1969), p. 337.

21. Ibid., p. 180.

22. Vratislav Effenberger, 'The Raw Cruelty of Life', *Cross Currents*, 6, 1987, p. 439.

23. Effenberger, quoted in Antonín J. Liehm, *The Miloš Forman Stories* (New York: International Arts and Sciences Press, 1975), p. 86.

24. Effenberger, 'Nová vlna v českém filmu a Karel Vachek', *Analogon*, 1, June 1969, pp. 93–4.

25. Dryje, p. 183.

26. Švankmajer, 'Švankmajer on *Alice*', *Afterimage*, 13, Autumn 1987, pp. 51–3.

27. Ibid.

28. Philip Strick, '*Alice*', *Monthly Film Bulletin*, 55, 658, 1988, pp. 319–20.

29. Brigid Cherry, 'Dark Wonders and the Gothic Sensibility: Jan Švankmajer's *Něco z Alenky* (*Alice*, 1987)', *Kinoeye*, 2, 1, 7 January 2002. http://www.kinoeye.org/02/01cherry01.html [Accessed 08/01/02].

30. Peter Hames, 'The Core of Reality: Puppets in the Feature Films of Jan Švankmajer', in Hames (ed.), *The Cinema of Jan Švankmajer: Dark Alchemy*, pp. 89–90.

31. Tina-Louise Reid, 'Něco z Alenky/Alice', in Peter Hames (ed.), *The Cinema of Central Europe* (London: Wallflower Press, 2004), p. 222.

32. Švankmajer, quoted in Michael O'Pray, 'Between Slapstick and Horror', *Sight and Sound*, 4, 9, 1994, p. 23.

33. Dryje, p. 200.

34. Švankmajer, interviewed by Peter Hames, in Hames (ed.), *The Cinema of Jan Švankmajer: Dark Alchemy*, p. 137

35. Angela Carter, *The Sadeian Woman: An Exercise in Cultural History* (London: Virago, 1979), p. 36.

10. ANIMATION

Czechoslovak animation dates back to the 1920s but first attracted attention when Karel Dodal's work was shown at the 1937 Exposition in Paris. His best-known film, as already mentioned, was *The Bubble Game* (1936), an advertising film for Sapona soap. His assistant, Hermina Týrlová, made her debut as a puppet film-maker with *Ferda the Ant* (*Ferda mravenec*, 1942), thus beginning a long career in which she worked exclusively on children's films. However, it was the nationalisation of the industry in 1945 that provided the foundation for consistent development and the production of feature-length animation films that offered a genuine alternative – if not opposition – to the domination of the Disney studios.

The leading figures in the animated film industry were Jiří Trnka, who specialised in puppet films, and Karel Zeman, well known for his fantasy films in which he mixed animation and live action. Trnka and Zeman both made their debuts in 1945 and both won prizes at the first Cannes Festival in 1946. Trnka completed five feature-length films and Zeman eleven and both can be regarded as genuine auteurs. Many of their features were brought into Western distribution in the 1950s and 1960s and it is a tragedy that so many are now unknown. In the age of DVD, the time is ripe for their reappearance, although many of the films seem to be mired in disputes over copyright.

Animated production was based both in Prague, at the Bratři v triku (Trick Brothers) studio and at Zlín (renamed Gottwaldov during the Communist period after the first Communist President, Klement Gottwald). Established in 1935, the Prague studio was originally concerned with the production of special effects or 'tricks' for mainstream films and was expanded during the Second World War under German direction. It was Trnka's idea to name the studio Bratři v triku and it was re-named the Jiří Trnka studio after his death in 1969. Trnka directed his first film *Grandfather Planted a Beet* (*Zasadil dědek řepu*) in 1945, the year that marked the end of the war. It was, he said, 'a time for experiments'.

Trnka was regarded as a master and still enjoys a cultural status in the Czech Republic beyond that of other animators. He was, of course, not only an animator and puppet master. He is also renowned as an illustrator (particularly of children's books and folk tales), a theatre designer and painter. Thus his puppet films were very much part of an integrated vision. According to the writer and animator Jiří Brdečka, 'the quality of his work was such that all of us tried to equal or surpass it . . . He made art films, and this was somewhat revolutionary at the time'.[1]

Trnka's interest in puppets dated from his childhood and he was already making his own figures at the age of four. He was born in Plzeň and his art teacher from the age of eleven was the legendary puppeteer, Josef Škupa. After leaving school at fourteen, he became Škupa's assistant, learning to make marionettes and receiving a full technical grounding. His own marionettes first attracted attention when they were exhibited in Prague in 1929. In 1934, he produced a play at Škupa's theatre in Plzeň.

Plzeň is quite possibly the only city in the world boasting a statue of puppet characters – Škupa's extremely popular figures, Spejbl and Hurvinek. Here it is worth recalling the special role of puppets in the Czech lands. Puppet theatre went far beyond the marginalised existence which, in many countries, is now the norm. In the 1840s there were no less than seventy-nine travelling puppet families in Bohemia alone and, as late as 1958, there were ten professional theatres and an estimated 2000 amateur ones. Besides substituting for conventional theatre, puppet theatre also played a role in upholding the Czech language. As František Daniel put it, in the seventeenth and eighteenth centuries:

> there were no Czech schools, there were no Czech theatres, no Czech university, no books published in Czech . . . [I]t was the puppet theatre that carried on the tradition of the language and the national art, because the puppet theatres performed not just for children but for grown-up audiences as well.[2]

It was also credited with performing a resistant political function during the Nazi occupation. It was not uncommon for major writers, artists and musicians to work with puppet theatre and the styles and conventions developed by the various puppet families have been maintained until the present.

According to Giannalberti Bendazzi, the interwar period saw an increase in the number of specialised theatres. 'There was no theatrical genre in which puppets were not employed . . . In Czechoslovakia more than anywhere else, this tradition entered cinema with the greatest spontaneity. There is no visible hiatus between puppet theatre and animated puppet cinema'.[3]

In the 1930s and 1940s, Trnka established his reputation as an illustrator and theatrical scene designer. Working mainly with the stage producer Jiří Frejka, he worked on eleven productions, including plays by Goldoni and Shakespeare. His illustrations featured in over fifty books, including work by K. J. Erben, the Brothers Grimm and the poet and former surrealist Vítězslav Nezval. Writing of Trnka's illustrations for Helena Chvojková's children's book *Zuzana Discovers the World* (*Zuzana objevuje svět*, 1940), Nezval commented, 'Jiří Trnka's interpretation . . . is a poetic universe where originality and mystery consist in the presentation of an excessively pure style and an inimitable dream. It's a world that the poet of the plastic arts shares with the child'.[4]

Trnka's early work in animation was in the more conventional form of two-dimensional animation. His interest in experimentation was already evident and in his third film *The Gift* (*Dárek*, 1946), a parody on the corruption of artistic taste by commerce, the design moved beyond illustration toward abstraction. The French critic J-P. Coursodon described it as the *Citizen Kane* of animation and its modernism as 'explosive'.[5] John Halas and Joy Batchelor described his 'pure sense of graphic design' and noted that, in all his films, he reached a higher pictorial level than that achieved in American cartoons.[6] Stephen Bosustow, head of UPA (United Productions of America), creators of *Mister Magoo* and *Rooty Toot Toot*, recognised *The Gift* as having a decisive influence on their own work.[7]

However, for Trnka, the production of two-dimensional animation was too industrialised and he decided to work with puppets. He began by animating a short film 'Bethlehem' ('Betlém'), a portrait of the celebration of Christmas in the Czech countryside. It was drawn from the book *The Czech Year* (*Špaliček*), which had originally been illustrated by the nineteenth-century artist Mikuláš Aleš. The book was an account of the Czech year through the customs, rituals, work, superstitions and legends of country life. Eventually, Trnka produced a feature cycle of six episodes (*The Czech Year*, 1947), which also included 'Carnival' ('Masopust'), 'Spring' ('Jaro'), 'The Legend of St Prokop' ('Legenda o svatem Prokopu'), 'Fair' ('Pout") and 'Feast' ('Posvícení'). The film has no central narrative and the six stories function more like a musical suite – and indeed, the music of Václav Trojan remains central.

Many were struck by Trnka's evocation of a traditional world in which man and nature co-exist within the realities of the seasons. The puppets themselves are like the products of a child's imagination – short fat bodies, little legs, hands without fingers and simple doll-like faces. The music uses children's voices, moving from classical to jazz, and employs bagpipes. It was not surprising the French critics should evoke Le Douanier Rousseau. It was simple, charming and naive in the best sense. To portray such a world required sensitivity and sophistication.

After *The Czech Year*, Trnka moved on to adapt two fairy stories – Hans Christian Andersen's *The Emperor's Nightingale* (*Císařův slavík*, 1948) and *Prince Bajaja* (*Bajaja*, 1950) – from the collection originally assembled by the nineteenth-century writer Božena Němcová.

Trnka has recorded how Andersen's tales had stayed with him since childhood and, in 1939, he exhibited five illustrations based on Andersen. In *The Emperor's Nightingale*, he tells the parallel and stories of a sick boy and the Chinese emperor who is imprisoned in his palace and longs to hear the song of a real nightingale. The story of the boy, filmed in reality, interacts with the world of the fairy story, with the different objects in his room transferred to the world of puppets. Jean-Marc Boillat points out that the puppets remain childlike and are types and symbols rather than individuals.[8] Trnka's elegant but simple vision works without language (although Jean Cocteau added a commentary to the French version and Boris Karloff spoke a persuasive commentary for the American one). It was one of a number of films to meet with official Czech criticism the following year.

Prince Bajaja is based on the traditional tale of a young villager who saves three beautiful princesses from the clutches of three dragons. All the while, he has to remain unknown in order to ensure his future happiness. Here Trnka combines the poetry of Nezval and the music of Trojan to great effect, drawing his visual inspiration from pre-renaissance and Gothic art. His movement of puppets also achieves greater sophistication in its depiction of the interior world of his characters and he creates major crowd scenes for the first time – the tournament, the ball, and the marriage.

Old Czech Legends (*Staré pověsti české*, 1953) in some ways marked a return to the inspiration of *The Czech Year*. Again, there are six separate stories and again Trnka turned to the folk tradition. This time, his work was adapted from the book by Alois Jirásek who, in 1894, published *Old Czech Legends*, a collection of legends based on old chronicles and records about the earliest periods of Czech history. Here history is mixed in with mythology. However, Trnka did not solely restrict himself to legend and also took recent archaeological research into account in an attempt to provide a social and cultural context for his stories.

The film was the first in which Trnka's puppets spoke. Apart from dialogue, the film also has a commentary, using words both to underline the action, and in an almost musical fashion. Blažena Urgošiková argues that the film marks a fundamental metamorphosis in his work. In comparison with the previous works, where the puppets manifested fragility and charm, the puppets in *Old*

Czech Legends 'are monumentally dramatic and tragic, more individualized; their countenance expresses their character, the inner essence of the represented person'.[9]

The six stories selected by Trnka comprise: the story of the arrival of Father Čech in the lands of Bohemia; the legend of Bivoj and the story of his struggle with the wild boar; the legend of Přemysl the Ploughman, founder of the Přemyslid dynasty that ruled until the fifteenth century; the story of the Young Women's War; the story of Horymír, the defender of the farmers; and the story of the Lucanian War, in which the cowardly Duke Neklan is replaced by the people's hero Čestmír. The crowd scenes are impressive and extend here to battle scenes employing close to a hundred puppets, ranging from mass scenes to individual conflict and symbolic images. Trnka wanted to remain close to popular visualisation of the stories and, in particular, drew upon the paintings of Mikuláš Aleš. The musical conventions of the times were largely unknown but Trojan felt that Janáček was best suited and drew his inspiration from this source.

Trnka had plans to make a puppet opera based on Mozart but moved next to Shakespeare with *A Midsummer Night's Dream* (*Sen noci svatojánské*, 1959). The story represented three worlds – that of the Athenian court, the forest world of Oberon and the world of the Athenian workers – each represented in their own style. Here the puppets dance, change form and tell their stories. The fairy world naturally comes into its own with Titania's train a mass of flowers and glittering insect-like fairies and elves. Puck frequently metamorphoses into a bird or an animal.

It is a film of enormous charm and humanity, in which puppetry, set design and music achieve a virtually flawless balance. Trnka uses the full repertoire of 'normal' film techniques – long shots, close shots, a variety of angles, tracking shots and zooms. The film also lends itself to stage-like settings and the use of lighting and shadows, with the puppet performances supplemented by two-dimensional animation and superimposition. There are complex sequences in which they perform in groups and react to each other as in a stage performance.

The graceful design and movements of the puppets do not merely imitate human movements but move like figures in a ballet, with a subtlety often exceeding 'real' bodily expression. It is as if one of Trnka's pictures or illustrations had simply come to life. One could almost describe it as a film that, like Martin Frič's two-part film *The Emperor's Baker* and *The Baker's Emperor* (1952), defies the political realities of the fifties. Filmed in Scope, it was Trnka's most ambitious project and his last full-length film. Although he said at the time that he felt he had experimented with all dimensions of puppet film, he continued to work until 1965 and made a further five films.

I have so far focussed on Trnka's features but short animation films are frequently more ambitious than larger projects. Here Trnka was also to achieve some remarkable work. Among his most notable films were: *Novel with a Contrebass* (*Román s basou*, 1949), adapted from Chekhov; *Song of the Prairie* (1949), a parody of the Western; *The Devil's Mill* (*Čertův mlýn*, 1950), a folk tale; *The Merry Circus* (*Veselý Cirkus*, 1951), a remarkable use of paper cut-outs in which he employed the more modernist talents of noted artists such as František Tichý and Kamil Lhoták; *Cybernetic Grandmother* (*Kybernetická babička*, 1962), based on Ivan Klíma's vision of a technological future in which man has become redundant; *The Archangel Gabriel and Mother Goose* (*Archanděl Gabriel a paní Husa*, 1964), a fantastic story from Boccaccio's *Decameron*; and, of course, *The Hand* (*Ruka*, 1965), one of his best-known films today and one that courted political controversy.

Song of the Prairie was based on Jiří Brdečka's parodic stories about the cowboy hero, Lemonade Joe, which had first been published in the early 1940s. As mentioned earlier, they were subsequently adapted as a successful stage play in 1946. Trnka's film rigorously adheres to the characters and stereotypes of the conventional western. The film was, in many ways, a breakthrough – not merely in the detail of its characterisation but also in its use of drama and parodic humour. Its famous theme, sung by its yodelling hero, was composed by Jan Rychlík as a parody of the theme from John Ford's *Stagecoach* (1939) – interestingly enough, itself derived from folk music. Trnka's film seems to be in direct descent from the early silent *Arizona Bill* and perhaps the comic strip *Arizona Jim* referred to in Renoir's *Le Crime de Monsieur Lange* (1936). It had an influence on other animated films from East-Central Europe and, of course, *Lemonade Joe*, directed by its original stage director, Oldřich Lipský, became an enormously successful feature film in 1964 – which, in turn, quite likely influenced the production of Hollywood's comedy western *Cat Ballou* the following year.

The Hand, which appeared just after the first films of the New Wave but before the more politically conscious works, tells the story of a happy potter whose simple creative life is ruined by the demands of the state. An enormous hand commissions him to make official works but the potter refuses. Initially the hand tries to persuade him, offering money and women, but ultimately resorts to force. After being locked in a golden cage, the potter manages to escape and return to his humble craft. His attempts to resist sculpting the monumental hand lead to terrifying hammerings at his door and his eventual death from a heart attack. The state nonetheless places a medal on his coffin before ending with a Fascist salute. It was, in many ways, the most explicit attack on Stalinism made in the 1960s and marked the end of his career – although it was his own poor health rather than censorship that was the cause.

The fact that Trnka's work was often achieved within the folk tradition and reached such a high artistic level suggests that there must have been some accommodation with the regime or that he was, at least, working within an approved programme. There is an inevitable tightrope walked when the state harnesses national traditions to its own ideological purposes. Of course, his scripts were approved but, as Mira Liehm and Antonín J. Liehm have pointed out:

> [S]cripts for animated, and particularly for puppet films, are difficult for the layman to understand, and the world of dreamlike fairy-tale fantasy in which they move is on the periphery of consciousness, difficult to measure by criteria that authorities at all levels are accustomed to using. So these authorities were presented with the finished work, which frequently received disapprobation – most of Trnka's films did – but which were defended from the consequences of disapproval both by their artistic quality and by the immediate international response that they evoked, both of which were more than rare at the time.[10]

They also suggest that the workshop-style organisation necessary for the production of animated work provided a model for the production group system that later allowed the flowering of the feature film in Czechoslovakia, Poland, Hungary and other East-Central European countries.

But how should one summarise Trnka's art? Most detailed accounts of his work tend to concentrate on the evolving designs of his puppets and the technical and logistical challenges he surmounted and, of course, what one remembers above all is its enormous charm. There is little doubt that his contribution to the puppet film was unique and that his work was experimental in both its avant-garde and pioneering senses. Some of his inspiration undoubtedly derives from the 'less is more' approach advocated by his mentor, Josef Škupa. In particular, Trnka avoided the constantly changing mouths, eyes and eyebrows of the conventional puppet film. Bendazzi writes:

> Trnka discovered that these faces had the same role as theatrical masks, and therefore were to be as fixed and sacred as masks. His puppets, characterised by contained expressions and almost stately movements, artistically surpassed those artists who had tried to loosen their puppets' joints or give them the same contortions as animated drawings.[11]

The characters received their expression through framing and lighting, while psychological elements and the internal world were also expressed. As his assistant, Břetislav Pojar noted, when Trnka painted his puppets, he always gave their eyes an undefined look.

> By merely turning their heads, or by a change in lighting, they gained smiling or unhappy or dreamy expressions. This gave one the impression

that the puppet hid more than it showed, and that its wooden heart harboured even more.[12]

However, Trnka's significance extended well beyond the area of puppet cinema. Aside from his international sources – Andersen, Shakespeare, Boccaccio and Chekhov – he will be most remembered for his specific evocations of Czech traditions in films such as *The Czech Year*, *Old Czech Legends*, the Czech fairy tale *Prince Bajaja* and, of course, the more recent folk hero, *The Good Soldier Švejk*, I–III (*Osudy dobrého vojáka Švejka*, I–III, 1954–1955). It has been suggested that he was a 'peasant-poet', that he 'brought to cinema a deep love for nature and a lyric faith in a people's traditions and their eternal spirit, which inspired his full-blooded sense of humour and his faith in life'.[13] Indeed, it is the interpenetration of his puppet world with nature, enhanced by the music, in particular, of Václav Trojan, that is perhaps the defining characteristic of his major films. As Jaroslav Boček points out, this lyricism had its reflection in the feature film, notably the work of Vojtěch Jasný.[14] Ronald Holloway suggests that Jasný's *All My Good Countrymen* 'can be interpreted as a hymn to the seasonal pastoral landscape in a land both he and Trnka loved with passion'.[15]

Trnka himself observed that '[p]uppet film is unique and original only when it oversteps the limits of the acted film, wherever stylisation, pathos or lyricism as presented by live actors would appear improbable, ludicrous, and uncomfortable'.[16]

In a discussion on Trnka held in Seattle in 1980, in which the participants included Antonín J. Liehm, František Daniel and Ronald Holloway, the following conclusion was reached:

> Trnka was a connecting link among different art forms therefore. His activities aided the cross-fertilisation of ideas within the Prague artistic community. One of his most important accomplishments was to bring modernist art forms into film when 'formalism' was officially frowned upon in his country. Drawing from surrealism and the pre-Second World War theatre of Jiří Voskovec and Jan Werich, Trnka showed the way to cinematic innovation in the midst of the Stalin era. Thus his contribution to the Czech cinema was significant indeed.[17]

Boček wrote that, at a time when 'Czechoslovak art was answerable to temporary needs of propaganda, Trnka polarised the entire development of cinematography with his orientation toward permanent values and ideas that for years comprised both the development of national history and the essence of Czech culture'.[18]

Karel Zeman's career in some respects shadows that of Trnka. After completing studies in commercial art, he worked in Paris in the 1930s (1930–36) as a poster designer and window dresser. He joined the Zlín studios as an animator in 1943, then worked as an assistant director to Hermina Týrlová and, in 1945, became director of the production group for puppet films.

His first film, *A Christmas Dream* (*Vánoční sen*) was made in 1945 and, from 1950 onwards, he specialised principally in feature-length films. Technically, he worked on puppet film before Trnka and had followed *A Christmas Dream* with his five comic films based around the character of Mr Prokouk. In 1949, he made *Inspiration* (*Inspirace*), a remarkable animation using blown-glass figures, and this was followed by the puppet film *King Lávra* (*Král Lávra*, 1950), a short feature based on the satire by Karel Havlíček Borovský. His move to features began with *The Treasure of Bird Island* (*Poklad Ptačího ostrova*, 1952), *A Journey to Primeval Times* (*Cesta do pravěku*, 1955) and *An Invention for Destruction* (*Vynález zkázy*, 1958), the last of which was based on Jules Verne's *Face au drapeau*.

The Treasure of Bird Island is adapted from a Persian fairy tale and based on the style of Persian paintings. Using semi-relief puppets and a drawn background, the figures form part of an overall stylisation. The story is set on an island whose inhabitants, on discovering treasure, divide it between themselves and stop working. However, they have nothing to eat and it is only when the treasure is stolen by a pirate that they return to work and life reassumes a balanced existence. The commentary consists of children's verses by the poet František Hrubín, spoken by children, with the music composed by Zdeněk Liška.

A combination of animation and live action, *A Journey to Primeval Times* was designed as an educational project with schools as a target audience. An exposition of natural history therefore takes precedence over dramatic conflict and adventure. A boy finds a footprint with a trilobite imprint on it in front of a cave and wants to see the creature in reality. Together with three other boys, he decides to sail through the cave on a river of time – a journey through prehistoric times. Thus they journey through an ice age and the Mezoic, Cretaceous and Carboniferous periods, ending up on the coast of the Silurian Sea, where life on earth was created. Zeman deliberately avoids any naturalistic integration and the boys' encounter with prehistory remains on the level of children at play. Nonetheless, the film was a remarkable achievement in which Zeman recreated and animated over thirty species of prehistoric animal. It was one of Czech cinema's most notable international successes.

An Invention for Destruction was based on a number of Jules Verne's novels in addition to its source material and was co-scripted with František Hrubín. Professor Roch, the inventor of a strong explosive substance, is kidnapped by Count Artigas and taken to an apparently abandoned island. He does not appreciate that his discovery will be used by a gang of criminals planning to take

Figure 10.1   Karel Zeman: *An Invention for Destruction* (*Vynález zkázy*, 1958)

over the world. Roch's assistant, Hart, sees through the scheme and escapes in a balloon. Finally realising the intended use for his invention, Roch blows up the island. Here, Zeman's visual style is inspired by the steel engravings for the original novel by Edouard Riou and Leon Benett. Zeman's extraordinary juxtapositions also recall the magic of Georges Méliès – the various flying machines and ships, the bicycle-cum-Zeppelin, camels on roller skates and so forth. Perhaps most impressive are the underwater scenes involving strange fish – looking forward to *Baron Münchhausen* (*Baron Prášil*, 1961) – the fight with a giant octopus, the procession of underwater divers and underwater transport that precedes the later worlds of James Bond. As an admirer of both Méliès and Verne, Zeman emphasises the poetic wonder of Verne's world over the more mundane elements of plot.

In 1961, Zeman made what was perhaps his finest film with *Baron Münchhausen*. Adapted from Gottfried Bürger's tales about the legendary Münchhausen, the film begins on the moon when a cosmonaut, Toník, meets some of his predecessors – Cyrano de Bergerac, Münchhausen and Verne's astronauts, Nicholl, Barbican and Arden. The Baron assumes Toník to be a native of the moon and invites him to visit Earth. A series of adventures ensue: at Constantinople, they rescue the beautiful Princess Bianca and fight with the Dutch against the Turkish fleet; they enter the belly of a whale; and Münchhausen flies on the proverbial cannon ball. Finally, they acquire enough gunpowder to blow themselves back to the moon.

This time, Zeman uses the engravings of Gustave Doré as his inspiration but he also, importantly, uses a number of star performers – Miloš Kopecký as the Baron, Jana Brejchová as the Princess, along with Karel Höger, Jan Werich and Rudolf Hrušínský among others. The dialogue and the music (Liška again) combine to establish a beautiful, dreamlike atmosphere – a film that, despite its bold action, achieves a lulling and reflective mood.

Zeman noted that, in a world of unlimited technical possibility, man was following in the footsteps of what the poets had already imagined. He argued that he drew on images of the past because, from our perspective, they have already become fantastic. As the world of the film is so stylised, he also aimed for an acting approach somewhere between pantomime and ballet. The stylisation becomes apparent on the levels of both acting and design.

The film relies primarily on different colour tinting, with individual objects or points of colour used to establish particular points. The characters move through the drawn sets and designs with perfect feasibility, with imaginary monsters and sea serpents becoming natural constituents of a fantastic world. The Baron sits comfortably smoking his pipe as he lands in the Sultan's palace, rides in the claws of a giant bird or is blown back to the moon in his armchair. Perhaps most striking are the ride from the moon in a sailing ship, carried by flying horses, and an underwater journey on a kind of elaborate seahorse, passing various imaginary creatures and going through a 'push-me-pull-you' fish with a head at both ends. One cannot imagine a film made in such a witty, almost throwaway style being attempted in contemporary cinema.

After *Baron Münchhausen*, Zeman completed three more features combining actors with animation. *The Jester's Tale* (*Bláznova kronika*, 1964), set during the Thirty Years War, a comic allegory co-scripted by Pavel Juráček, was narrated primarily as an orthodox feature, with obviously artificial sets and animation used to highlight and comment on his central story. He returned to the inspiration of Verne with his *The Stolen Airship* (*Ukradená vzducholod'*, 1966) and *On the Comet* (*Na kometě*, 1970). In his final films, he abandoned the use of live actors with *A Thousand and One Nights* (*Pohádky tisíce a jedné noci*, 1974), using paper cut-outs and inspired by Persian miniatures, the compelling but little seen *The Sorcerer's Apprentice* aka *The Magician's Apprentice* (*Čarodějův učeň*, 1977) and *The Tale of Honzík and Mařenka* (*Pohádka o Honzíkovi a Mařence*, 1980).

Among other full-length animated films to emerge from the Czech studios, one should also mention Eduard Hoffman's enchanting *The Creation of the World* (*Stvoření světa*, 1957), based on Jean Effel's drawings, with a commentary by Jan Werich and music by Jan Rychlík. Trnka's former assistants, Břetislav Pojar and Stanislav Latal, also went on to make major contributions to the development of puppet film. Among many other outstanding film-makers to emerge from the Czech studios were Jiří Brdečka, Václav Bedřich, Zdeněk Miler – internationally known for his delightful *Mole* (*Krtek*) series – and

Jaroslav Doubrava, who formed a compelling partnership with writer Miloš Macourek and the graphic artist Adolf Born. In Slovakia, the leading figure was Viktor Kubal who made two feature films, *Jurko the Outlaw* (1976), about Jánošík, and *The Bloody Lady* (*Krvavá pani*, 1980), in which he returned to the legend of Erzsébet Bathory. The most significant figure to emerge in the mid 1960s was Jan Švankmajer, whose work is considered in the chapter on surrealism. Although trained in puppetry and despite its fundamental role in his imaginative development, he shared little in common with Trnka and the school of puppetry that had subsequently developed.

In the 1980s, the most distinctive work in the field of puppet animation was that of Jiří Barta, which could certainly be said to be hovering on the verges of surrealism. He first attracted attention with his *The Extinct World of Gloves* (*Zaniklý svět rukavic*, 1982), where he takes an array of gloves in different styles and from different historical periods and animates them as a short history of the cinema. The film moves from silent cinema via pastiches of Buñuel and Fellini through to political propaganda (presumably Leni Riefenstahl, although the targets could be closer to home), ending in a junkyard where tin cans become police cars and a film can converts into a spacecraft. The gloves are initially found on a landfill site along with the rolls of film recording the stories and the films are linked by an unknown figure lacing up the films on a projector while drinking beer and smoking cigarettes.

Barta, who is an admirer of Švankmajer's work, shows a similar interest in contrast, texture and juxtaposition. Here the brute reality of everyday life (the earth, the dredger, the beer, the cigarettes) is contrasted with the fantasy world of gloves in a manner similar to Švankmajer's later *Virile Games* (*Mužné hry*, 1988). In *The Last Theft* (*Poslední lup*, 1987), Barta created a bizarre fantasy world in which a thief breaks into a crypt and finds several vampires sitting at a table. He joins them in a game of dice and, blinded by wealth, is oblivious to his final fate. His sole feature was the remarkable *The Pied Piper* (*Krysař*, 1986). It was adapted from a 1915 novella by the Czech poet Viktor Dyk, which Arne Novák describes as a symbolic work with an archaic theme and ballad-like presentation that was 'not only significant for the author, who had thus found a stylistic equivalent for his bitter wisdom about *hubris*, but also for the Czech novel as an autonomous literary genre'.[19]

In the story, rats gradually take over in a medieval town totally given over to the pursuit of greed – the hording of money, jewels and clothes and the excessive and gratuitous consumption of food. The piper (or the rat-catcher, to give the correct Czech translation) is employed to lure the rats to the city walls, from where they fall and drown. The town reverts to its previous ways and offers him a button for his services. The following day, he plays from the church tower and the people themselves are converted into rats and ultimately drowned.

Alongside this is the story of a beautiful maiden, Agnes, who the piper twice rescues from the attentions of a grotesque suitor who plies her with jewels. On the night before the piper's revenge, her house is broken into by drunken men and she is raped and murdered. At the end of the film, a boatman, who had resided outside the town, enters its deserted streets and rescues a baby, the sole survivor. The piper has dissolved into nothingness, with only his cloak remaining.

The film is unique in its style. The Expressionist sets are carved from wood and even overhead shots are similarly carved, with many figures and carts seen going about their daily business. The puppet figures are made principally from walnut and complement the sets to provide a single stylistic impact. The swirls and shapes, which are reminiscent of Robert Wiene's *The Cabinet of Dr Caligari* (*Das Cabinet des Dr Caligari*, 1920) and Paul Wegener's *The Golem* (*Der Golem*, 1915, also 1920), are followed, in turn, by the film's camera movements.

The puppets, as Ivana Košuličová has demonstrated, are contrasted. Whereas the townspeople are constructed with square cubist shapes, the piper and Agnes are constructed of different materials. The piper is fashioned from dark wood with deep set eyes that remain unseen 'until the moment of imminent apocalypse'.[20] As Barta himself notes, 'the person of the Pied Piper . . . belongs to the world of time, of Saturn. He is a symbol of nobody, of death, of time, destiny'.[21] The purity of Agnes contrasts with the evil of the city and her figure is made of light wood in a form reminiscent of Trnka.

The film's music, composed by Michal Kocáb, principally using electric guitar and flute, is disturbing and chilling throughout and the speech of the townspeople is conveyed in artificial language. There are striking images of the piper, with his cloak blowing in the wind, or returning to the city, the gargoyles lit up as he passes and of the banging doors in deserted houses. Like Švankmajer in *The Last Trick*, Barta uses contrast between wood and live creatures – in this case the rats, which are a combination of both real creatures and animation. Real food is thrust into wooden mouths.

Košuličová suggests that, just as E. F. Burian's stage production of *The Pied Piper* in 1940 had provided a metaphor for the Nazi occupation, so Barta's film comments on the declining years of 'socialism'. Barta's last major film, released in 1989, was *The Club of Discarded Ones* (*Klub odložených*), a story in which a group of abandoned mannequins interact in abandoned rooms.

> Of course, this is a metaphor for the Prague society we were living in. It was a society before the [Velvet] Revolution; it was a conformist system, and everything was very boring, everything was very empty, everything was very average and closed in boxes. So we decided to use manikins because they represented the world of robots. They are like something between puppets and actors. They are bizarre objects.[22]

If Barta finished the 1980s with two powerful moral fables that were clearly seen as commentaries on the last years of the Communist era, it is surely ironic that this also seemed to mark the end of his career. After 1989, one of the country's leading film-making talents was to remain idle save for one or two commercial exercises.

Of course, his was not a unique situation. The failure of the Czech government to ensure regular and stable financing for the film industry has been at the heart of the problem. As President Václav Klaus famously said when rejecting proposals for a new film law in 2006, the film industry was 'a business like any other'. In other words, film art had to cut its cloth to the dimensions of the market place. Animation, in particular, was hard hit. According to the Ministry of Culture's report in 1997, animation production fell from 140 films a year to fifty in the year 1996. Alongside this, it has to be remembered that the country's best-known director, Jiří Menzel, retreated to theatre, Jan Němec virtually became an 'underground' film-maker and even the relentless Věra Chytilová found difficulty in mounting new projects.

Barta's new project, an adaptation of Gustav Meyrinck's novel *The Golem*, was not appropriate for the times. Significantly, no major feature animation proved possible after the denationalisation of the film industry but a number of films based on independent stories have been released. The first of these was *The Magnificent Six* (*Šest statečných*, 2000), featuring three Czech stories (by Tereza Kučerová, Martin Repka and Aurel Klimt) and three Slovak ones (by Vlado Král, Vojtěch Mašek, and Jaro Vojtek). Essentially a device for getting their films to audiences, it was followed by two puppet feature compilations based on the stories of Jan Werich – *Jan Werich's Fimfárum* (*Fimfárum Jana Wericha*, 2002) and *Fimfárum 2* (2006).

The first of these was a collaboration between the veteran puppet animator Vlasta Pospíšilová who had collaborated with Trnka and Švankmajer as well as producing her own work. In fact, the three episodes she contributed to the film were all made earlier – in 1987, 1991 and 2000. They were re-released together with two new episodes by Aurel Klimt. On the back of the film's success, *Fimfárum 2* resulted in four additional stories, two from the older generation (Břetislav Pojar and Pospíšilová) and two from the younger (Aurel Klimt and Jan Balej).

Using Werich's recorded readings (he died in 1980), the films simply illustrate the stories – moral tales mainly set in a kind of traditional idea of a Czech village peopled by farmers, innkeepers, teachers and blacksmiths. While, in some respects, the films recall the pre-war drawings of Josef Lada (famous for his illustrations of *The Good Soldier Švejk*), it is clear from the presence of spirits, the devil and the aristocracy, that we are also in the pre-socialist world of the fairy tale.

While Pojar and Pospíšilová not unsurprisingly stay with a sophisticated take on tradition, Klimt and Balej show a pronounced predilection for the grotesque. Klimt's early films such as *Maschkin Killed Koschkin* (*Maškin zabil Koškina*, 1996), *The Enchanted Bell* (*O kouzelném zvonu*, 1998), which was released as part of *The Magnificent Six*, and *The Fall* (*Pád*, 1999) signalled the arrival of an important talent.

Klimt's two contributions to *Fimfárum* are *Fearless Franta* (*Franta Nebojsa*) and the title episode. In the first, a boy who doesn't understand fear is exposed to a night in the local pub where spirits from the graveyard take over. This provides plenty of opportunity for grotesque effects – frightening visions of split heads, body parts and misshapen skulls of considerable variety in a vision reminiscent of George Grosz. In the title episode, *Fimfárum*, a blacksmith is required to perform a range of impossible tasks by the local nobleman on pain of death. In fact the nobleman is encouraged in these demands by his footman who is having an affair with the blacksmith's sexy wife and wants to be rid of him. In his defence, the blacksmith enlists help from the devil and a water spirit. One can be sure that the wife, with her torpedo like breasts and the frequently incontinent one-eyed nobleman, would have found no place in the world of Jiří Trnka. In *Fimfárum 2*, Klimt tells the story of *The Hunchbacks of Damascus* (*Hobáči z damašku*), an Arabian Nights-style story about three swordsmen, all hunchbacks, who are blind in the left eye, lame in the right leg and indistinguishable from one another.

But Klimt's major achievement remains *The Fall* which, like *Maschkin Killed Koschkin*, was adapted from the work of the Russian 'absurdist' writer, Daniil Kharms, who died in a Stalinist prison in 1942. Even for the world of animated film, Kharms's 'incidences', as he called them, remain thumbnail sketches and Klimt's films are much more elaborate.

In *The Fall*, Klimt turns Kharms's story of 'The Plummeting Old Women' ('Vyvalivayushchie starukhi), about an old woman who fell from a window out of curiosity, to be followed by several others, into an elaborate portrait of a Russian city in the 1940s. Kharms wrote specifically about Leningrad but Klimt's story feels much more like Moscow. The film begins with a man and a cat on a rooftop. The cat (a female) falls to the ground after being sexually assaulted from behind by a tomcat. In the meantime, the man slowly slides down the roof until he falls off and clings to the guttering. There he remains throughout the film.

The first of the old women struggles to open her window and falls, to be followed by a succession of others as in Kharms's original. A hearse arrives in anticipation of the man falling from above, a coffin is deposited in the street and the two attendants proceed to drink vodka. Other services – an ambulance and a fire engine arrive – but are soon dispatched. In the meantime, old women continue to throw themselves unremarked from windows. Eventually a lorry arrives and their bodies are pitchforked into it. When night falls, the hearse leaves with the man still clinging to the guttering.

On to this absurdist tale is added a downbeat Russian street scene with identical women queuing, identical women falling and drunkenness as endemic – all presided over by Lenin (in one intercut scene) and the Red Star over the city at its conclusion. The bedraggled, stylised puppets provide a bleak and inspired extension of the absurdity of Kharms's world.

Jan Balej has had considerable success with his work for children's animation for television and, in 2000, had an international success with his *One Night in One City* (*Jedné noci v jednom městě*). He subsequently added two more stories to create the feature length *One Night in One City* (2007) which, apart from Švankmajer's work, was the first feature length 'auteur' animation to appear since 1989.

Balej's rather Kafkaesque but, at the same time, mundane visions were apparently inspired by life in the Žižkov district of Prague. In the first episode, 'Ulity', various inhabitants of a decrepit apartment block pursue their secret hobbies. In one flat, a man conducts a toy circus using dead insects. In another, a man dresses as a forester and sits in an artificial tree amongst wooden and plastic animals. His fantasy of being a bear hunter is enacted through dressing his pet dog in a bearskin.

When the dog is called out by a mean-faced woman (probably his wife), she begins to take it for a walk. However, the dog is enticed into a nearby room where the woman soon follows. It appears that the occupant's vocation and business is the cremation of dogs and it is his clear intention to photograph the dog for his gallery, cremate it and add its ashes to the urns stored in his backroom. He takes the woman there, where they make love, but the dog manages to get away. The final stages of this central story are intercut with another two vignettes – the poor woman who serves soup to her family while preparing special treats for a donkey she keeps in the next room and the final scene of a man snuffing up a line of cocaine complete with the ants that have became embedded in it.

The film's second story, 'Větvička and Ploutvička', is rather less bleak. Throughout the four seasons of the year, we follow the lives of an animated tree and a fish who live together in a flat. In spring, birds nest in the tree's branches (that is its hair); in summer, it has a nightmare about being sawn up and dreams of becoming a guitar; in autumn, it takes the sole apple it has produced to its wife's grave; and, at Christmas, it receives a nesting box as a present.

The final episode, 'One Night in One City', consisting of three sections, returns to the bleak night world of the first episode – but with an additional helping of humour. It begins with a lamplighter and his dog and a man playing an accordion (against the background of a peeling poster advertising a Karel Gott concert). A red-haired violinist leaves him a tip (something wrapped in newspaper) and displays how his music should sound to someone with a true ear for music. Interspersed with this, a mechanical, flat, tin policeman gesticulates ineffectually. When the accordionist returns to his flat, he notices the package vibrating to the sound of music and opens it to reveal a severed ear. He cuts off his own ear and sews on the new one – but his music does not improve and he begins to paint like Van Gogh.

In the second section, 'Frozen Time' ('Zastavený čas'), the lamplighter's dog finds the accordionist's ear and eats it. Here we are told the story of a disappointed romantic, complete with a bouquet, who ends up in a bar at closing time. The far from helpful waiter is encouraged to operate the player piano and, as a result, the bar gradually begins to fill with people, including ladies of ill repute. When the piano stops, they disappear. These spirits (or fantasies) seem to be embodied in the piano and, at the end of the story, we see them mirrored in a painting on the wall of the bar.

In the final section, 'Djinn' ('Džin'), an elephant spirit grants two men their wishes, starting with alcohol, then moving to food with meat, fish, mustard, cigarettes and so forth appearing in a revolting Švankmajeresque mush. They sail off in a couple of cups on a fairground fantasy ride dedicated to erotic females, ending up outside a junkyard. Although, on one level, this is the most entertaining, it is also perhaps the least successful of the stories.

Balej's puppets are distorted but are also recognisably 'real' portraits of characters that might exist. Only the tin dogs and cats of the final episode are really grotesque but, given that Balej was responsible for both the design and the direction, his vision is remarkably sustained. There are certainly echoes of other films – *The Cremator* and *Conspirators of Pleasure* (episode one), *Little Otík* (episode two) and *The Shining* (episode three) – but Balej, together with co-writer Ivan Arsenjev, has produced an authentically inspired world. The film's producer, Martin Vandas, who had been co-producer of both *Fimfárum* films, notes that *One Night in One City* was one of only two features produced since 1989 not to use traditional funding sources.

To end on an optimistic note, the increase in money allocated to the film industry in 2007, while still lacking a firm legislative backing, saw a significant investment in animation. Both Barta and Švankmajer began new features – respectively, *In the Attic – Who Has a Birthday Today?* (*Na půdě aneb Kdo má dneska narozeniny?*) and *Surviving Life (Theory and Practice)* (*Přežít svůj život (teorie a praxe)*. Alongside these were *Car Fairy Tales* (*Autopohádky*) and a third *Fimfárum*, with Pojar, Klimt and Pospíšilová all active. Given the fact that Czech and Slovak animation together averaged some forty films per year over many years, it deserves a history that would go way beyond any account given here.

NOTES

1. Jiří Brdečka, 1977, quoted in Giannalberto Bendazzi, *Cartoons: One Hundred Years of Cinema Animation* (London: John Libbey, 1994), p. 167.

2. František Daniel, in David Paul (ed.), *Politics, Art and Commitment in the East European Cinema* (London: Macmillan, 1983), p. 255.
3. Gianalberto Bendazzi, *Cartoons*, p. 168.
4. Nezval, quoted in Jean-Marc Boillat, *Jiří Trnka 1912–1969* (Anthologie du Cinéma), supplement to *L'Avant-Scène du Cinéma*, 149–50, July–September, 1974.
5. J-P. Coursodon, 'Jiří Trnka cinéaste par excellence', *Cinéma*, 40, 1960, quoted in Boillat, *Jiří Trnka 1912–1969*, p. 489.
6. John Halas and Joy Batchelor, 'European Cartoon: A Survey of the Animated Film', *Penguin Film Review*, 8 (London: Penguin Books, 1949), p. 14.
7. Stephen Bosustow, in Coursodon, p. 489.
8. Jean-Marc Boillat, *Jiří Trnka 1912–1969*, p. 499.
9. Blažena Urgošiková, 'Staré pověsti české (Old Czech Legends)', in Christopher Lyon (ed.), *The International Dictionary of Films and Filmmakers: Volume 1: Films* (London: Firethorn Press, 1986), p. 450.
10. Mira Liehm and Antonín J. Liehm, *The Most Important Art: East European Film After 1945* (Berkeley: University of California Press, 1977), pp. 110–11.
11. Bendazzi, p. 170.
12. Břetislav Pojar, quoted in Bendazzi, p. 170.
13. Bendazzi, p. 170.
14. Jaroslav Boček, *Modern Czechoslovak Film 1945–1965* (Prague: Artia, 1966), pp. 21–2.
15. Ronald Holloway, 'The Short Film in Eastern Europe: Art and Politics of Cartoons and Puppets', in David W. Paul (ed.), *Politics, Art and Commitment in the East European Cinema* (London: Macmillan, 1983), p. 235.
16. Jiří Trnka, 'Interview with the Film Puppeteer Jiří Trnka', by Jaroslav Brož, *The Czechoslovak Film*, VIII, 6, 1955, p. 8., quoted in *The Most Important Art*, p. 108.
17. David W. Paul (ed.), *Politics, Art and Commitment in the East European Cinema*, p. 254.
18. Jaroslav Boček, *Film a doba*, 5, 1965, quoted in *The Most Important Art*, p. 108.
19. Arne Novák, *Czech Literature*, translated by Peter Kussi (Ann Arbor: Michigan Slavic Publications, 1986), p. 278.
20. Ivana Košuličová, 'The Morality of Horror: Jiří Barta's *Krysař* (*The Pied Piper*, 1986), *Kinoeye*, 2, 1, 7 January 2002. http://www.kinoeye.org/02/01_no2.html [Accessed 08/01/02].
21. Jiří Barta, in Phil Ballard, 'Magic against materialism: Czech animator Jiří Barta interviewed', *Kinoeye*, 3, 9, 15 September 2003. http://www.kinoeye.org/03/09/ballard09.php [Accessed 28/09/03].
22. Ibid.

11. SLOVAK DIRECTIONS

During the Communist period, Slovak films frequently emphasised folk culture and the Slovak countryside and this was often perceived as supporting the regime or performing an escapist function. However, there is little doubt that many of the best Slovak films have also reflected a deep attachment to roots in folk culture and rural life. Directors such as Juraj Jakubisko and Elo Havetta have both drawn on folk culture, not out of conformity but as a focus for liberation and opposition.

In this chapter, I shall consider a number of key Slovak directors – Uher, Jakubisko, Havetta, Hanák and Šulík – each of which has played a key role in Slovak cinema since the 1960s. They have all drawn closely on Slovak culture – it is unlikely that many of their films could be mistaken for Czech ones – and they have also been united by a common inventive attitude to narrative form and a significant emphasis on the visual.

If we consider Czech and Slovak cinema as interactive, it can also be argued that many of these directors played a crucial role in the development of the Czechoslovak New Wave. At the end of the 1960s, Mira Liehm and Antonín J. Liehm noted that, with the debuts of Jakubisko, Havetta and Hanák, the focus of innovation was shifting to Slovakia.[1] But, although the development of the Czech wave is normally dated from the debuts of Forman, Jireš and Chytilová in 1963, it should be remembered that an important Slovak film – Uher's *Sunshine in a Net* (1962) – had preceded this.

ŠTEFAN UHER

While there had been significant Czech antecedents to the New Wave – notably Jasný's *Desire* and Vláčil's *The White Dove* – they had primarily dissented from the status quo through their use of visual poetry. Uher's *Sunshine in a Net*, on the contrary, was innovative on many levels, and remains one of the key films of the decade, albeit relatively unknown outside of the country.

Adapted in collaboration with the novelist, Alfonz Bednár, the film centres on a young teenager, nicknamed Fajolo, and his relationship with the fair-haired Bela. When their relationship undergoes a temporary crisis, Fajolo joins a work brigade on a collective farm where he also undergoes his sexual initiation. He begins to write letters to Bela, which she reads out aloud to her new boyfriend. Their relationship recommences on his return but, after he learns that she has shown his letters to the other boy, they break up again. Against this story of young love, we are also introduced to their parents' world. Fajolo's mother is always at work, her presence only indicated by the meals she leaves in the fridge for Fajolo and his father. Bela's mother is blind and is seen as a burden on her husband. Her blindness is the result of an interrupted suicide attempt in response to her husband's infidelity. To construct her view of the world, she is consistently dependent on the descriptions of others but, in the main, these are deliberately misleading. The two generations never interact.

Martin Votruba points out that a number of these themes – teenagers changing partners, remote parents, a philandering husband and attempted suicide – would hitherto have been unacceptable. He also suggests that Fajolo's attendance at a 'voluntary work camp' is a result of his parents' membership of the intelligentsia.[2] The reality of a badly run collective farm was also an unusual appearance on screen, although this theme had already been touched on in Helge's *Great Seclusion*.

The film's main strength, however, lies in its poetic approach. The title *Sunshine in a Net* suggests the impossible and is reflected by the image of a bottle in a fisherman's net, apparently capturing the rays of the sun. An eclipse had been experienced in Bratislava the previous year and the film centres its vision on this. A commentary stresses the role of the sun together with the fact that it can blind – during an eclipse, it must be viewed through smoked glass.

A whole sequence of poetic images is introduced in the film's opening scenes, looking forward to the film's major themes. A bird's nest with eggs floats beside a stone causeway; a youth is outlined on a roof in a forest of television aerials; and children stand on dustbins reaching out towards the sun. The film's story seems to emerge from its poetic context and, in particular, the streets and rooftops of Bratislava. The sun and the eclipse suggest a range of associations – life, death, light, dark, love and blindness.

Fajolo is an obsessive photographer and, like the film's makers, searches for the revealing image. He is mainly interested in the expressive power of hands. Later in the film, he photographs the hands of a peasant, with the camera moving in and out of focus, exposing the visual process of photography. In this way, he mirrors the film-makers' own investigation.

Fajolo's period at the collective farm seems to reflect the city–country polarity of many Slovak films but also the constructive role of the work camp, an entirely acceptable Communist theme. Uher, however, examines the problems objectively, without any emphasis on simplified ideology. The problems of relationships between the work brigades and the peasants and the failures and problems of the collective farms are dealt with in a mature fashion.

The film's mosaic of impressionist effects and short evocative scenes, the cross-cutting of parallel themes, its use of ambiguous symbolism, its sense of time and place, its use of unknown and non-actors and its realism and lyricism all helped to create a film that was unique for its time and undoubtedly set the standard for the Czech and Slovak films of the 1960s that were soon to follow.

Uher's subsequent work has been little charted but, as Václav Macek suggests, with:

> every new work and each new type of material, Uher tried to cover new ground, to give a new slant to diverse themes. This effort, which precluded a return to tried-and-true-methods, was the basis of Uher's artistic vision, but to a certain extent, it reflected a period that dreamed of the removal of all barriers: physical, spiritual, moral, ideological, etc.[3]

With *The Organ* (*Organ*, 1964), Uher and Bednár made a striking and rather oppressive film set during the wartime state. A Polish organist escapes from the Nazis and takes refuge in a Franciscan monastery, where he assumes the name of Father Felix. Felix has the capacity, in the words of the monastery's superior, to 'convey the beauty of holiness through music'. The treatment of the Church was, in itself, an unusual theme but one assumes that its story of institutional intolerance was justified as an attack on the 'clerico-Fascist state'. However, Peter Konečný suggests that it is also a parable on the totalitarian nature of the Communist regime.[4] The music of J. S. Bach dominates throughout, symbolising nobility and humanity, while juxtaposed with the superficial pseudo-moral facade of many of the characters (the monastery's superior reports Felix to the authorities). The music becomes part of the drama in which philosophy and art are as significant as narrative development. As Macek puts it, Uher opens the door:

> to a different kind of stylisation – metaphysical realism, in which a conversation with God is as important as a drunkard's weakness in the local

tavern. Almost every shot is a reference to the hidden or obvious metaphor of things, faces, and sounds.[5]

In 1966, Uher made the overtly surrealist *The Miraculous Virgin*, adapted from the novel by Dominík Tatarka, the first Czech or Slovak film of the 1960s to explore the common inheritance of Surrealism, which is briefly discussed in the chapter on Surrealism. The religious theme again appears in *Three Daughters* (*Tri dcéry*, 1967), a story of nuns expelled from their convents during the Communist campaign against Catholicism in the early 1950s. Against this background, Uher tells the story of a peasant who put his daughters in a convent and, after their dissolution, tries to help them. Macek described it as the first introspective film about the most difficult years of Communism and said that it owed its success to Uher's complex mix of emotion, metaphysics and surrealism.[6]

Uher, like Vláčil, Menzel and Chytilová, continued to make important films during the normalisation years, many in collaboration with Bednár. In 1982, he also made *Concrete Pastures* aka *She Grazed Horses on Concrete* (*Pásla kone na betóne*), which he adapted along with Milka Zimková, the film's leading actress, from her own short stories. Set in a remote village in eastern Slovakia and filmed in an East Slovak dialect, it dramatises the problems of an unmarried mother across two generations. His last film, *Down to Earth* (*Správca skanzenu*, 1988), told the story of a scientist who becomes the curator of an open-air museum in his native village in protest against the misuse of his scientific work. Scripted by Ondrej Šulaj, it was one of the most profound attacks on the distortions of normalisation.

Juraj Jakubisko

Uher's continuing innovation suggests that the sudden creative impact of Jakubisko, Havetta and Hanák in the late 1960s was not without a Slovak foundation. Yet Mira Liehm and Antonín J. Liehm wrote that Jakubisko's *Crucial Years* (*Kristove roky*, 1967) sounded an entirely new note. 'This film signalled not only the birth of an exceptional talent, but also the birth of a Slovak style, with roots in different, more natural, and wilder soil than the style of the Czech young wave.'[7]

Jakubisko, of course, grew up with the Czech New Wave and, while he was at FAMU, worked on both Chytilová's *Ceiling* and Jireš's *Hall of Lost Footsteps* (*Sál ztracených kroků*, 1960). At the end of his first year at FAMU, he made the short film *The Last Air Raid* (*Posledný nálet*, 1960), about a little girl disturbed by an air raid siren during World War Two. Everything depended on the use of camera. In his highly sophisticated graduation work *Waiting for Godot* (*Čekají na Godota*, 1966), he examined the lives of young people on the night that several of them are due to join up for national service in the army. Basically the story of a party in which they drink, talk, dance and play games, it is the evocation of an era. The influence of Godard is fairly evident – as Jakubisko observes, Godard broke all the rules they were being taught 'in terms of editing, themes, the use of non-professional actors, location shooting, lighting, the handheld camera'.[8]

Crucial Years is, in many ways, a continuation of his student work. It focuses on the life of a Slovak painter living in Prague who, having reached his thirties ('Christ's years'), realises that he has been living a superficial life. Together with his brother (a pilot), he decides to change for the better. Macek summarises *Crucial Years* as 'a rejection of socially relevant themes, simple causality in the storyline, psychological realism, and a preference for the individual over the masses'.[9]

Jakubisko's work as a painter clearly forms the basis of his visual style and he continues to produce work on a regular basis. At art school, he studied graphic design but was really interested in photography and originally applied to FAMU to study cinematography. In fact, he was turned down but accepted for direction and studied photography 'on the side'. He was initially very interested in the work of the Russian cinematographer Sergei Urusevski who worked with Mikhail Kalatozov on *The Cranes Are Flying* (*Letyat zhuravli*, 1957) and *I Am Cuba* (*Ja-Kuba/Soy Cuba*, 1964). He was also encouraged by his FAMU supervisor, Václav Wasserman, who had made a Slovak feature himself – *The Devil's Wall* (*Čertova stěna*, 1948) – to draw inspiration from his Eastern Slovak roots.

All of these influences were to come together in *The Deserter and the Nomads* aka *Deserters and Pilgrims* (*Zbehovia a pútnici*, 1968). The film consists of three parts, the first of which was initially shown as 'The Deserter' or 'Deserters' ('Zbehovia'), in 1967. This first story, which was adapted from a novel by Ladislav Ťažký, tells of a gypsy, Kalmán, who deserts from the Austro-Hungarian army during the First World War. He becomes associated with another deserter, Martin, a Bolshevik, who attempts to promote revolution, and the two are hunted down by soldiers. Jakubisko once argued that the script was primarily 'a set of instructions for getting things started' and the narrative remains subservient to his improvisation and visual poetics.[10]

The film's inspiration in folklore is made apparent from the first through the personification of Death. When Kalmán is first introduced, he is associated with images of a violet flower, a stag caught in rays of sunlight and two dwarfs with scarlet uniforms and hunting horns. He discovers his hands covered in blood and remembers an old folk story that advises he should thrust his hands into a fire. His hands are burned but he is nursed and sheltered by a young girl. Lila, Kalmán's wife, happens to pass with a gypsy band on their way to a wedding and they are soon reunited. It is to save Lila that

Kalmán finally dies. At the wedding feast, she is approached by Death and Kalmán has to throw off his disguise as a woman. An absurd and farcical chase ensues.

From the beginning, the film emphasises the indiscriminate killing of war as the figure of Death stalks the battlefield. The violence of the Austro-Hungarian soldiers is indiscriminate but so also is that of Martin the Bolshevik. When the soldiers try to find Martin, the attempt turns into a bloody farce, with blood unexpectedly spurting from a soldier's mouth as the camera pulls away from him sitting at a table. Martin's revolt begins with the accidental shooting of a child and the treatment meted out to landowners is grotesque and degrading.

At the conclusion of the film, the bodies of Kalmán and Martin are placed side by side on a marriage bed, as the party goes on around them. A peasant cracks a whip, the celebration becomes more frantic and their bodies topple over. Martin falls between the legs of Kalmán in a grotesque parody of intercourse as the bells on the wedding bed jingle.

The Deserter is a deliberately cruel film but, to quote Jakubisko, the cruelty is stylised so that 'it is almost beautiful'.[11] Celebration when faced with death and the peasant's laughter at the search for happiness show a healthy disdain for civilised expectations. When Jakubisko found that he was unable to use cinematographer Igor Luther, who had worked with him on *Crucial Years*, he decided to do the camerawork himself, thus fulfilling his original ambitions. He decided to use a hand-held camera. Many of the colour effects arose from problems with film stock and he often had to use positive stock, resulting in unusual colour changes and stimulating some of the film's 'oneiric' or 'surrealist' passages. The result of all this, when compared with conventional film, is a unique and disorienting vision.

The second story, 'Dominika', presents a highly unorthodox portrait of the liberation of Slovakia by the Soviet army at the end of the Second World War. The Russians take over a farm and get systematically drunk and eat until they make themselves sick. One of the soldiers attempts to pursue the farmer's older daughters into the hayloft but is too drunk to climb the ladder while the captain fires off rounds from his pistol into the air. The farmyard latrine plays a central role throughout. Two outsiders – a wandering egg-seller who is suspected of being a spy and is shot and a neighbour who has his son's body hidden in a wagon-load of branches and is locked up – penetrate the continuing orgy. Finally the Germans arrive and scenes of carnage follow. The figure of Death emerges from beneath the branches in the wagon.

Throughout the story, the mixture of farce and violence is continued, with the whole ending on a sequence of disturbing dream images – Kalmán on the lap of a girl, blood streaming down a girl's legs, a German and a saxophone and the dead body of a naked boy next to a swan. There is plenty of scope for wider interpretation of the subject – particularly in the year of the Prague Spring and not least the fact that the original version of the film contained footage of the invading armies.

The third story, 'Nomads' ('Pútnici'), is set in the aftermath of a nuclear war. Its opening scenes must rank among some of the most nightmarish yet filmed. It begins in an underground shelter full of naked old people – a kind of underground mental home. One could definitely say that the senile bodies and exposed genitals are exploited, with the shock effects completed when a terrified man vomits pus at the camera – the pus discolours and eventually turns red. Death is one of the inmates. Together with a girl called Nevěsta, he escapes through a tunnel leading to the upper world.

But the world of light offers no reassurance – the earth has turned to ashes and people are no more than piles of green dust. Death prays that people should again be rebellious, then dresses as a Nazi and pursues Nevěsta across a barren landscape. The quest for Man is fruitless. Death and Nevěsta decide to invent an imaginary Eden, casting themselves as Adam and Eve. Death plays the violin and Nevěsta puts on make-up recalling Gelsomina (Giulietta Masina) in Fellini's *La strada* (1954).

The film's conclusion brings together elements from the previous two stories, joining in harvest festivities. Nevěsta searches for God at the top of a haystack but only encounters a lascivious old peasant who kills her. Death encounters a little girl with a pipe. 'Have you come to tell me anything?' he asks. Her response is to reveal black stockings and suspenders and to beat him with a stick. Death is destroyed by a plane which shoots him, drops a bomb and leaves only a crater. Thus Jakubisko completes a triptych on the nature of war and violence, uniting all three stories with a hallucinatory style and the exaggerations and freedoms of peasant art.

With his next film, *Birds, Orphans and Fools* aka *Birdies, Orphans and Fools* (*Vtáčkovia, siroty a blázni*,1969), he produced a film that many Slovak critics consider one of the best. 'Life is beautiful!' announces Yorick (Jiří Sýkora), who has been raised in an institution for mentally handicapped children. He envies the children's ignorance of the true nature of the world and, in order to reject its cruelty himself, decides to take on the role of a Fool. A triangle relationship develops involving his best friend Andrzej (Phillippe Avron), a Pole, and Marta (Magda Vášáryová), a young Jewish woman. The situation is reminiscent of Truffaut's *Jules et Jim* (1962) but Jakubisko's heroes are all orphans – their parents killed each other and they are the product of the absurdity of our world.

The three of them live together in a flat and a variety of scenes are shot in beds, wardrobes and baths. They address each other (and the camera) with philosophical statements or comments about the meaning of life. After rescuing Marta, Yorick offers her to Andrzej since he has never had a woman. When

Figure 11.1   Juraj Jakubisko: *Birds, Orphans and Fools* (*Vtáčkovia, siroty a blázni,* 1969)

Yorick returns from prison at the end of the film, he finds that Marta is pregnant by Andrzej. He murders her and the unborn child and commits suicide.

Jakubisko originally drafted the story in 1967 in an attempt to answer a question he thought characterised his generation – 'Why are we all fools and why do we find craziness the only acceptable form of existence?' The script was developed with Karol Sidon who had co-scripted the final episode of *The Deserter and the Nomads.* Its mixture of tragedy, comedy and farce is disturbing and rests on a highly complex web of game-playing.

Martin Kaňuch suggests that Jakubisko's concern to adopt the vision of a child is rooted in anxieties about old age, to which only death can provide the answer.[12] Their landlord, who appears at intervals, embodies such fears and is symbolised in the scene where they name the disgusting symptoms of age – saliva, the smell of urine and so forth. Significantly, Jakubisko allowed the children in the institute to handle the camera.

Besides the orphans and the fools, their flat is also inhabited by the 'birdies' (little birds). As Kaňuch points out, their dwelling place has a variety of entrances apart from doors and windows. There are holes in the walls, the floor and the roof and a tree grows through the middle of it. Another entrance is via the wooden beams that lean against the adjoining institute for mentally handicapped children. Birds ranging from parakeets to sparrows share the lives of the three protagonists and the flat becomes a nest in itself.

The film is also full of post-modernist borrowings and references. The link to Shakespeare's *Hamlet* is not only made apparent through the hero's name but also by quotations from the play. Kaňuch points out that the theme of 'foolishness' continues on a number of levels – via décor, costume and behaviour – and with references to *Ship of Fools*, Erasmus's *In Praise of Folly*, Cervantes and Rabelais.[13]

The theme of history is also addressed through specifically Slovak illusions and obsessions. This is focused, in particular, on the figure of Milan R. Štefánik who, together with Masaryk and Beneš, had helped create the state of Czechoslovakia after the First World War but was killed in a plane crash in 1919 within sight of the Slovak capital of Bratislava. His statue occupies Yorick's room. 'All he left me was a statue and madness,' he remarks. At the end of the film, he drags the statue to the bridge over the Danube, where he sets fire to himself and also uses its weight to both hang and drown himself.

In another scene, the trio play games around the monument to the Slovak National Uprising of 1944, calling for the partisans and the Germans to come out. There are also references to the political radicalism of the 1960s, with fighting in the streets, a guerrilla band of old women and references to 'Uncle Mao'.

Finally, the film would not be of its time without filmic in-references and self-consciousness. At the beginning of the film, Jakubisko introduces himself as the director, presents his theme through voiceover and shows the film crew shooting in the asylum. Later in the film, the characters emerge from a bog festooned in strips of celluloid like Laocoön. They refer to MGM, Columbia and Mosfilm before setting the heap of film on fire. They then urinate on it, announcing, 'Watch out! The New Wave.'

The film is an exercise in constant and unremitting invention – Jakubisko even uses the dynamic frame, with the film's enthusiasm and striking visual beauty acting as an antidote to its grim and ultimately negative story. The film's ending – the murder of the future (the death of Marta and her unborn child) and Yorick's suicide attached to the statue of Štefánik – has a specific resonance in the year following the invasion of the country. In fact, Yorick's suicide was seen by some as a reference to the suicide of Jan Palach in protest against the Soviet invasion in January 1969. The film was suppressed and Jakubisko was investigated by the secret police. But the film also testifies to a visionary freedom that has moved well beyond the more tentative formal and thematic innovations with which the decade began.

Jakubisko collaborated with Sidon again on *See You in Hell, Fellows!* (*Dovidenia ve pekle, priatelia!*), which was started in 1970 and only officially completed in 1990. Like *Birds, Orphans and Fools*, it is centred on a ménage à trois – this time between Rita, Petras and an ageing colonel in whose house they take refuge. 'Rita smokes a cigar, the colonel sleeps in a fly net, a wooden rabbit on a wire slides across the room . . . and Petras sits in a bath wearing a hat and goggles. Rita may give birth to twins, one for each husband.'[14]

The story, which is arguably more complex than the previous films, centres on the forthcoming deluge and the mission of two nuns to rescue souls for the Ark, which is somehow equated with Communism. Donkeys figure prominently in the film. In the final scenes, they appear with portraits of Brezhnev pinned to them. When he saw the unedited version of the film in 1977, Josef Škvorecký found it almost incomprehensible, yet his observations are still apposite. Describing it as a pure cinematographic spectacle, he noted that the characters misbehaved with a total freedom, ignoring the laws of dramaturgy, aesthetics and society. 'Above all . . . it is about the hypnotic power of freedom, which binds you to your seat in the theatre so that you can't tear your eyes away from the screen.'[15]

All four of Jakubisko's films were banned during the next twenty years and he was unable to resume work in features until 1979, when he made *Build a House, Plant a Tree* (*Postav dom, zasad' strom*) but, even then, it was not made available for international audiences for a further ten years. The hero was a thief who Jakubisko turned into a hero and, as a result, he was banned from making films on contemporary subjects (except in comedies) and was confined to historical subjects and children's films. Naturally the style he had adopted in the late 1960s, which also implied a thematic freedom, was not allowed. Nonetheless, from an auteurist perspective, one can see marked continuities, particularly in the area of continuing folk interests and the visual and thematic elements that saw him dubbed 'the Slovak Fellini'. In fact, the link was also a tangible one – the two directors knew and admired each other's work and, in 1985, Fellini's wife, Giulietta Masina, starred in Jakubisko's *Perinbaba*, adapted from 'Lady Winter' by the Brothers Grimm.

Jakubisko's most acclaimed film from this period was his *The Millennial Bee* (*Tisícročná včela*, 1983), adapted from the novel by Peter Jaroš. Scripted in collaboration with the novelist, it was a film that, for its time, gained a rare international attention. Divided into two halves, it charts the history of a Slovak village from 1887 to 1917, telling the story of Martin Pichanda (Jozef Kroner) in its first half and that of his son, Samo (Štefan Kvietik), in the second. Jaroš's story, a mixture of folklore, reality and fantasy, certainly deserves the description of 'magic realism', an approach close to that of Jakubisko himself. Some of the novel's more extraordinary sequences are missing but Jakubisko maintains the image of the beehive and the presence of the 'millennial' or 'thousand-year-old' bee that intermittently perceives and comments on the action. The millennial bee represents the Slovaks, who have worked like bees for a thousand years.

It is one of the films where Jakubisko made both a cinema version and a longer version intended for television serialisation. Here one has the sense that the film is less a narrative than a summary of key events and high points, with many of them conveyed off-screen or through the voice of a narrator. Particularly in the early stages, the numbers of characters are multiple and the film consists of significant scenes and incidents. But the force of Jakubisko's visual imagination and his use of landscape and tradition provide a powerful and condensed effect within almost every episode, with the film becoming a succession of almost iconic images. One remembers, in particular, Martin Pichanda's funeral procession with a brass band which ends in a toboggan (coffin) ride through the snow, with the coffin, band and whole procession cascading like a stream down a snowy hillside.

As the end of the Communist era approached, Jakubisko returned to his earlier style with *I'm Sitting on a Branch and I Feel Well* aka *Flying High* (*Sedím na konári a je mi dobre*, 1989), in which his two male heroes escape from the Germans and set up house with a red-haired girl called Ester. Ester is killed and, during the 1950s, they end up in jail. In the late fifties, they are released and reclaim Ester's child. As they climb a tree, she grows into the woman they had previously loved. It was a clear variation on the theme of *Birds, Orphans and Fools* and similarly a mix of farce and tragedy. Although, in Czechoslovakia, the image of a carnival Stalin marching arm in arm with a carnival Hitler was still daring, in the era of glasnost, the film won an award at the Moscow Film Festival.

In the post-Communist era, Jakubisko's expansive vision has inevitably had difficulty attracting finance. His first film, *It's Better to Be Healthy and Wealthy than Poor and Ill* (*Lepšie byť bohatý a zdravý, ako chudobný a chorý*, 1992), told the story of two women and their lover returned from abroad and was one of the few post-1989 films to satirise the new changes. After the country split in 1993, Jakubisko moved to Prague and set up a production company with his wife, the actress Deana Horváthová, who has subsequently acted as his producer. However, the links with Slovakia remain strong and the company also has a base in Bratislava. His two principal films *An Ambiguous Report on the End of the World* (*Nejasná zpráva o konci světa*, 1997) and *Báthory* (2008) are among the most expensive produced in the post-invasion period. The first is technically Czech and the second Slovak but both draw on his Slovak roots.

An Ambiguous Report on the End of the World was, in many ways, a summation of his previous folk-inspired work. Taking Nostradamus as his starting point, he tells an allegorical story about a village on the edge of the world. He explicitly draws on the village where he was born, where there were no cars and people still wore traditional costume. 'Many of the customs in my films are specific to this village and many elements in *An Ambiguous Report on the End of the World* are autobiographical: the giant woman, the dwarf, the dress.'[16]

The film is a powerful ballad, laced with atmospheric photography and with an impressive musical score. It was well received critically and even hailed as 'a work of genius' by Jiří Kříž but somehow failed to attract the international interest that might have been expected.[17]

ELO HAVETTA

The films of Elo Havetta, who died in 1975, show a marked affinity with those of Jakubisko. He studied alongside Jakubisko at the School of Applied Arts in Bratislava and again at FAMU, where they also collaborated. Macek remarks that, for Havetta, film became a circus tent in which the viewer could experience 'a marvellous world of conjuring tricks, acrobatics, and beauty'.[18] In this respect, his two completed films, *The Party in the Botanical Garden* (*Slávnosť v botanickej záhrade*, 1969) and *Lilies of the Field* (*Ľalie poľné*, 1972) both share recognisable links with those of Jakubisko. Havetta described the links between the Slovak directors as follows, 'Maybe the common bond is folklore, a mood, a mentality . . . a living tradition.'[19] He also noted that it was a sensibility still alive among the Yugoslavs. Here, it is perhaps worth remembering that many film-makers from the former Yugoslavia studied at FAMU, including Emir Kusturica. Kusturica also noted that *The Deserter and the Nomads* had been an influence on his approach in *Underground* (1994) which was, of course, a co-production with the Czech Republic among others.

The Party in the Botanical Garden is an astonishingly 'free' film, set in the wine-growing region of the Little Carpathians. Mária the innkeeper has eight daughters all of them by the same father, Pišta, who lives in a hermit's hut outside the vineyards. Their lives are disturbed by the arrival of a wanderer, Pierre, who wants to work a miracle and then settle down. He brings new life to the village of Bábindol and its individual characters, who also include the priest, the postman, the carpenter, the crazy Veronez and the botanist Gašpar. Gašpar, besides his botany, is responsible for the local marionette theatre. In a sense the two are rivals – Gašpar (or Caspar) is the name for the character of the jester in puppet theatre and Pierre is Pierrot from the commedia dell'arte. Pierre's miracle is achieved during the celebration of the vintage when local legends about a spring of red wine merge with Jesus's transformation of water into wine. Havetta describes the film as oscillating between comedy and tragicomedy and as particularly influenced by French films of the 'golden era', especially René Clair's *An Italian Straw Hat* (*Un chapeau de paille d'Italie*, 1928).

Narrative is not Havetta's primary concern and, for Jana Dudková, it is 'one of the most disjointed, episodic, and seemingly incoherent Slovak films ever made'.[20] Although it has elements in common with the work of Jakubisko, it is a film that is arguably unique in the history of cinema. Dominated by visual imagination above all, Dudková characterises its approach as the 'associative sequencing of scenes' and its result as 'the expression of joy and freedom'. Combined with its origins in carnival is an emphasis on visual impressionism and lyricism.

One can point to an almost post-modernist combination of elements, with reference to folk culture, drama, literature, painting and film. Dudková draws parallels with the grotesque realism associated with the Bratislava theatre, the Theatre on the Promenade (Divadlo na korze), while the film's intertitles were inspired by the picaresque narratives of Henry Fielding. As far as painting is concerned, Havetta himself mentions Le Douanier Rousseau, Monet and Renoir, just as Jakubisko evokes Chagall and Dalí in *Birds, Orphans and Fools*. Apart from the evocation of French cinema's golden era, there is direct reference to the Lumière brothers and, towards the end of the film, Havetta and his camera also begin to appear in the film. As Dudková suggests, film is treated both as an entertainment on a par with the attractions at the village fair but also as a miracle of artistic creation. Havetta is not slow to use a range of effects from the blank screen to reverse action.

And, of course, there are the 'attractions' themselves – an elephant, tight-rope walkers and masks – and the actors can even fly with the aid of ropes. As Macek puts it, 'The carnival-like inversion of the elevated and the earthbound, the high and the low, renews the primeval joy of living that every person experiences in childhood, but prodigally wastes in his adulthood.'[21] Like Jakubisko, Havetta returned to his roots and shot the film in his native village – the party, the miracle and the film coincide and the film itself becomes a collective celebration. The part of Gašpar is played by Jiří Sýkora, who played the lead roles in *Crucial Years* and *Birds, Orphans and Fools*.

In his next film, *Lilies of the Field*, Havetta turned his attention to the period following the end of the First World War. Two veterans, a clarinet player, Matej Hegyeš, and an undergraduate theologian, Krujbel, wander round their homeland trying to find a home and put down roots. It was scripted by the novelist, Vincent Šikula, based on motifs from his *Isn't There Usually a Pub on Every Hill* (*Nebýva na každom vŕšku hostinec*, 1966). The characters 'bear in themselves the inner consequences, inner injuries, which seem to us to be more complicated and more important for this story than physical consequences'.[22] The lives of these wanderers and outcasts are contrasted with traditional farming work, which is seen as natural and normal. But what of the 'lilies of the field' who toil not?

Havetta wrote that, if dedications were written for film, *Lilies of the Field* would be dedicated 'to our grandfathers, who lost the best years of their lives in the senseless First World War'. Because the film is based on the stories and memories of grandfathers, its visual inspiration came from 'old photographs which, in our childhood, we had seen being taken by the grandfathers from soldiers' old wooden suitcases . . . this story was shown in the nostalgic tone of old brownish photographs with their corners broken off'.[23]

Lilies of the Field depends much more on narrative than *The Party in the Botanical Garden*. Matej, who makes his living as a wandering musician, 'serving the seeds of truth', has his clarinet stolen by two vagabonds with whom he shares the same barn. He then visits Paula whose husband has died, leaving her with a dumb servant, with whom she manages to scrape a living. When Matej makes sexual advances Paula rejects him but he returns at night and they sleep together.

The following morning, he is about to leave when the widow Paula stops him. She takes him, 'dressed like a minister', to church and the prospects for a stable life seem to be on offer. Before she makes love to him in a field, she confesses that she cannot marry him because she 'couldn't live with [him] for long'. When they reach the village fair, Matej meets up with Krujbel again and they drive off in the widow's cart. She believes that they have robbed her.

After a hallucinatory journey during which they discuss many things, the screen changes colour and they acquire various other passengers who sing and play music, including an old woman who repairs prayer books. Matej returns to the widow's house, where she is already entertaining another male visitor (a hen seller). In the meantime, Krujbel speaks his particular line in religious nonsense and profundity from the tower of the church and accidentally falls. Although we assume that he dies, the film actually ends with aerial shots of the village over which he seems to be flying as much as falling

Again, the film is infected with the spirit of festival and carnival and features no less than three festive gatherings. Although the two wanderers do not manage to integrate, this is nonetheless a vibrant portrait of a collective world in which even beggars and cripples seem to be a part and are able to retain a strong sense of their worth and identity.

Among the film's iconic images are those of the hen seller on his bike (together with two hens) – a motif with its own musical theme – and the fat monk who travels with his donkey while playing the flute. Other characters to make their mark include the old woman selling prayer books, a legless man with a hand-driven tricycle, a little girl in a tree and a crippled accordion player. A priest chases a gander and a horse eats apples from a window shelf. When a solitary bus arrives (the only means of mechanical transport), it becomes the focus of chaos and attention from the village children.

Jan Jaroš emphasises the film's concern with close-ups of faces marked by adversity.[24] And yet the characters who have suffered so much express an exuberance and a life-affirming energy. The film continues to reveal the influences of folk culture and naive painting. Shot mainly in monochrome, with full colour for the final sequence, its tinted images do create the sense of old photographs. There are occasional flourishes – red for scenes of passion, with

dramatic colourisation recalling *The Deserter and the Nomads* for the hallucinatory cart ride – but the photographic imagery principally works to recall
a past life. The film is also constructed on the model of music composition
with a range of motifs and leitmotifs repeated and combined in different ways.
Perhaps most important is Zdeněk Liška's music, with its rhythms, themes and
relentless energy driving the film forward. Of course, apart from the crippled
and itinerant musicians, the firemen's bands, folk songs and military fanfares
suggest a tendency for life to become music and music to become life.

Havetta followed *Lilies of the Field* with work in television while his script
on the Slovak National Uprising formed the basis (uncredited) for Štefan
Uher's *If I Had a Gun* (*Keby som mal pušku*, 1971), a remarkably authentic
portrait of children growing up in wartime and one of the few films from that
era to show any kind of conviction.

Dušan Hanák

The third major director to emerge in the late 1960s was Dušan Hanák, whose
work was to range across a number of genres but always presented a dramatic
challenge to the status quo. In *322* (1969), adapted from a short story by Ján
Johanides, he examined the situation of a man thought to be dying of cancer.
Initially, he is not told of his diagnosis (322 is the code for cancer) but he is registered disabled and begins to re-examine his life. The real subject, of course, is
the society that surrounds him and which he has helped to build. The film is full
of alienation, lack of belief and violence while the shadow of the police state
predominates. As the doctor comments, 'Everything changes. Only human
hatred expands, and there is no medicine that can cure it.' Macek writes:

> [T]he young filmmaker connected historical trauma – his main character
> suffers pangs of guilt for his role in the forced collectivization of private
> farms in the 1950s – with the central theme of his generation, that is,
> what lies beneath the concept of 'an authentic life'. It is no accident that
> the embodiment of this ideal is a teenager who ignores all the rules and
> then becomes the person who is able to teach the main character . . . the
> meaning of the simple things of life.[25]

Following on from his experimental short films, Hanák adopts a complex
and multilevel approach to his subject. The film's combination of short scenes
are each introduced by titles, quotations, and lines of dialogue, and the whole
is accompanied by a fluid jazz score by Ladislav Gerhardt. Its bleak images of
urban landscapes, scenes in a slaughterhouse, the dream of a frozen lake and a
dance of naked bodies have a disturbing and evocative effect.

With *Pictures of the Old World* (*Obrazy starého sveta*, 1972), Hanák directed an outstanding documentary inspired by the photographs of the Slovak photographer, Martin Martinček, who principally documented the landscape and people of the Liptov region. In an introduction to a book on his work, Hanák observed how Martinček, from early morning, would search:

> for patterns, lights and the right moments in the countryside and in people's faces. We should acknowledge . . . the moral archetype of Slovak (and even universal) Man who he has discovered. The people shown in his photographs are full of life, spiritual and ascetic.[26]

Hanák documents old people living in the Liptov, Orava and Kysuce regions. He provides extended records of nine old people living in relative poverty, five of whom had been recorded in Martinček's photographs. His approach is to interweave still images with moving sequences, using forty of Martinček's photographs and others by himself and the photographer Vlado Vavrek.

Among the characters recorded are: a man who uses himself as a draught animal to pull his plough; a man crippled from the knees down who nonetheless looks after his sheep, chops wood and has built a house; another with an obsessive interest in space; an old woman who cleans the church and spends much of her time tending the graves of her relatives in the cemetery; a man who served in the Austro-Hungarian army and now digs potatoes; one who plays the bagpipes to his sheep; and a bedridden man who still plays the double bass in a trio with a couple of friends.

There are several montage sequences where old people respond to simple questions about death, and the meaning and value of life. The responses range from 'I don't know', 'I'm deaf' and 'I forgot' to 'I never went to school'. Their values include health, peace, man, happiness, sadness, work, children, kindness and love, respect for God and life itself.

The film moves beyond the lyrical style of folk photography characteristic of Karel Plicka's *The Earth Sings* to provide a more textured and sombre world. In fact, Hanák is content to examine his subjects on film in the same way that Martinček did in still photography. The textures of faces, of hands and of landscape predominate – as do his characters' obstinate vitality and desire to live. Hanák's sensitive and careful handling constitutes one of the great works of documentary film-making. Of course, it was condemned for its 'aesthetics of ugliness' and banned until 1988 before winning several international awards the following year. In 2000, the Slovak critics voted it the best Slovak film of all time.

In 1976 Hanák made the much more obviously entertaining *Rose-Tinted Dreams* aka *Rosy Dreams* aka *Pink Dreams* (*Ružové sny*), a lyrical and romantic story about the love affair between a Slovak, Jakub (Juraj Nvota), and a young gypsy girl, Jolanka (Iva Bittová). The first of his films with the writer Dušan Dušek, it was one of the few films from the mid 1970s to recall the creative freedom, humanity and lyricism of the Czechoslovak New Wave. Superficially, its teenage boy-meets-girl theme is reminiscent of elements in *Loves of a Blonde* and *Closely Observed Trains*. The young hero, Jakub, with his postman's cap, even recalls Miloš, the hero of *Closely Observed Trains*.

Besides its central romance, the film was one of the first to address the problems of relations between the Roma and Slovak communities, which are shown in the film to live in a state of mutual suspicion. Jolanka is not encouraged to go out with a 'paleface', is instantly rejected by Jakub's parents and is automatically suspected of stealing in a supermarket.

The scenes in the Roma community were filmed on location, and there is no attempt to gloss over the poor living conditions. The film incidentally touches on a range of problems including the psychological trauma attached to resettlement and marriage and children used as a means of increasing government allowances. Two years later, Charter 77 published a document arguing that the government's policy entirely ignored the rights of the Roma and exploited the attitude of the public 'which vacillates between indifference and racism'.[27] The film was initially held up. In Dušek's words, 'It wasn't state policy to consider the assimilation of Roma communities at that time.'[28] Even so, it was only allowed a limited release.

The film's grounding in the realities of life in the two communities provides it with the strength to support the delicate fantasy of its superstructure. Jakub impresses Jolanka by performing acrobatic tricks on his bike and produces birds from under his hat on demand. She puts a spell on him by slipping a hair from her armpit into his coat pocket. Their elopement is accompanied by the kind of lyricism that can be traced back to Jasný's *Desire*, although here it is a result of a collaboration with the Slovak cinematographer, Dodo Šimončič, who had previously worked on Havetta's two features. Romantic love scenes in the countryside and a cycle ride accompanied by sunlight flashing through the trees are handled with delicacy and there is a nice touch during a Roma dance when the music fades and Jolanka and Jakub dance to the cooing of doves.

The idyll is broken when Jakub is arrested by the police for stealing money for them to live on and the Roma make their own efforts to ensure Jolanka's return. She goes back to her arranged marriage as Jakub prepares for military service where, his parents hope, he will learn to control his daydreaming. She appears happily adjusted to life within the community while Jakub dreams of a universal reconciliation. Jolanka tells him that she also loved him. A Roma girl marries a Slovak repairman – suggesting that such relationships may be possible.

The film's flair for fantasy and the absurd recalls elements of both Slovak and Czech films and is given great emotional force through the use of Roma music and its respect for Roma culture (the Roma expert Milena Hübschmannová was an advisor on the film). Apart from its foregrounding of the central romance, it also allows the Roma culture to predominate over the Slovak. The film features Iva Bittová, now an internationally known singer, musician and composer, in her first film role as Jolanka as well as Věra Bílá, now an internationally known Roma singer, in a subsidiary role.

I Love, You Love (*Ja milujem, ty miluješ*, 1980), also with a rural setting, was rather more pessimistic, did not meet with official approval and was banned until 1989, when it won the prize for best direction at the Berlin Film Festival. Also written in association with Dušan Dušek, it tells a number of tragicomic stories centred on a railway post office. The film focuses on the central character of a bachelor, Pišta, played by Polish actor Roman Klosowski, who is physically unattractive and unwanted by women. He almost achieves success but, at the end of the film, is rejected by the girl he loves because of his inability to give up drink. While the deglamorised characters are sometimes reminiscent of Miloš Forman, the background of the film, with its emphasis on drunkenness and sexual infidelity – even suicide – encouraged an official response that condemned it for defeatism and an 'aesthetics of loathing'.

In his next two films, *Silent Joy* (*Tichá radosť*, 1985) and *Private Lives* (*Súkromné životy*, 1990), Hanák turned to more orthodox dramatic subjects but they were made with precision and deal with important subjects. In *Silent Joy*, he told the story of a nurse who decides to leave her husband and ends by successfully creating a career of her own. But while she leaves a selfish husband, she also rejects the romantic alternatives. At the end of the film, she confronts her own reflection – a recognition of her own identity, the 'silent joy' of the film's title. *Private Lives* examines the lives of two stepsisters, an actress and a psychologist, each unable to speak and communicate with each other and, as Eva Zaoralová puts it, affected by 'the syndrome of totality'.[29] His last film, *Paper Heads* (*Papierové hlavy*, 1995), is a powerful compilation film that examines the history of Czechoslovakia from the 1950s to the 1990s, using previously suppressed archive material and interviews to provide an understanding of a submerged history.

While Hanák's work differed from that of Jakubisko and Havetta, it is recognisably Slovak in its frequent rural locations and in its examination of problems of identity and history. He is probably the director who has varied his work the most, ranging from the avant-garde to the art film, from fantasy to documentary, and, in each case, producing exemplary examples of the genre.

Martin Šulík

Martin Šulík, who made his feature debut with *Tenderness* (*Neha*, 1991), has become one of the most distinctive directors to have emerged in either the Czech or Slovak Republics since 1989. Despite the fact that he did not study at FAMU, he has made significant contributions to Czech as well as Slovak cinema. His most famous film, *The Garden* (1995) also attracted a good deal of European attention. Significantly, he has also worked with screenwriters such as Ondrej Šulaj and Dušan Dušek, who had worked with Hanák and Uher. In this sense, it can be argued that there is a continuity with previous generations although it has to be admitted that, apart from Šulík's work, there have been no major developments in Slovak cinema post-1989.

Here perhaps it is worth considering the strong role of writers in Slovak cinema. Ondrej Šulaj points out that, in the late 1950s and early 1960s, there was a lack of original screenwriters and many leading Slovak novelists became involved in cinema. They included Rudolf Sloboda, Peter Jaroš, Vladimír Mináč, Dominík Tatarka and Juraj Spitzer.[30] This close association has continued. Šulaj himself is perhaps one of the few 'specialists' in the genre of screenwriting and has played a key role in Slovak cinema since the late 1970s.

With *Tenderness*, Šulaj's script analysed the nature of human relations in a post-Communist society affected by the moral corruption of the years of normalisation. It examined the relationship of a young man, Šimon, to a married couple, Viktor and Mária, whose relations are based on a strange mixture of tenderness and self-torture. Šimon is drawn into their relationship, becoming an intermediary between the two. Apparently with Viktor's support, Šimon tries to seduce Mária but his attempt to live a life outside of morality is doomed to failure. He discovers the roots of the relationship in their past – how intolerance can be combined with a curious solidarity. An intense and dramatic film focusing on psychological exploitation, its theme recalls the Polański of *Knife in the Water* (1962) but with a style closer to Bergman's *Scenes from a Marriage* (*Scener ur ett äktenskap*, 1974). Šulík deliberately seeks a more universal relevance through his casting of the Hungarian star György Cserhalmi as Viktor and Polish actress Maria Pakulnis as Maria. *Tenderness* was considered one of the most profound Slovak films since the late 1960s.

Zuzana Gindl-Tatarová has commented on how the film moved beyond the ideological restraints of the 1970s and 1980s and the unwritten laws of classic dramatic composition, ignoring the psychosocial classification of characters and the precise identification of place and time. In attempting to 'truthfully reflect reality', Šulík created a stylised and abstract film that 'did not directly reflect social reality but rather a certain feeling of the period – connected loosely with the political and economic changes determining the development of society'.[31]

Everything I Like (*Všetko čo mám rád*, 1992), also scripted by Šulaj, is a complex existential 'art movie' that analyses the situation of a young Slovak, Tomáš (Juraj Nvota) and his relationship with Ann (Gina Bellman), a teacher of English. The disruptions of the post-Communist world are reflected in his relationship with his ex-wife, his desertion of his son and his relations with his father. His wife constantly refers to his English girlfriend as American and his thoughts of going to England in those pre-EU days could not go beyond daydreaming. The film, like the work of Havetta and Hanák in the 1960s, employs a range of evocative sub-headings: 'Sunrise'; 'Landscape with a Balloon'; 'Something from Joyce'; 'Picture from an Old World'; 'Thoreau, Goethe, Kant and Others'. The film's title apparently derives from the film team's desire to escape the melancholy of *Tenderness* and to make a film based on a list of everything they liked. Comic, poetic, evocative and still bleak, it is a film in which one has the sense that life has passed by, that real decisions and developments are taking place elsewhere. Šulík cast his own father in the role of Tomáš's father and the film also features the Slovak writer, Rudolf Sloboda, and Jiří Menzel. In the end, despite all his doubts about the country, Tomáš decides to remain.

In *The Garden* (1995), scripted by Marek Leščák, Šulík adopts a similar fragmentary style. Jakub (Roman Luknár) is another man in 'Christ's years'. He is having an affair with Tereza, a married woman, and is thrown out by his father so he takes over his grandfather's deserted house and garden in the countryside. Here he meets a number of strange characters with the names of philosophers – St Benedict, Rousseau and Wittgenstein – and Helena, a 'miraculous virgin' (echoing Tatarka's novel), and learns to understand what is normally not understandable.

Helena has no education but was taught to write by Jakub's grandfather and now writes backwards (something that Jakub tries to learn). She teaches him the wisdom of the irrational, standing with him in an ants' nest and painting his legs white to stop rabbits nibbling at him in winter. He accidentally finds his grandfather's diary and learns to decode it. The film is again about characters in crisis but, this time, Šulík takes on an imaginative world in which cats, dogs, the absurd and the surreal all have a role to play. Jakub rejects town life and his previous affair and accommodates himself to a new reality. When Helena levitates, even Jakub's father concludes that everything is as it should be. It is an intimate chamber film with a slow pace and a sensitive music score by Vladimír Godár.

Like the heroes of Šulík's previous films, Jakub is unknowingly searching for a kind of knowledge. As Gindl-Tatarová observes, Jakub's invasion of the garden 'changes his 'urban life of debauchery' into the initiatory silence of Robinson Crusoe's solitude, into the mystical space of genuine knowledge'.[32] He begins to see the world as 'a mystery in which the intuitive merges with the rational and the female principle interpenetrates the male. Helena is the personification of this mystery'.[33]

Yet again, the film is divided into 'chapters' – this time there are fourteen. Each is introduced by the narrator and shows how the hero will gain new knowledge but, while the film reflects the traditional Slovak emphasis on the restorative powers of nature, Šulík mixes his observations with wit and humour, notably in his portrayal of the three 'spiritual' visitors. *The Garden* is, in fact, extraordinarily complex, 'an unrepeatable mosaic . . . a polyphonic dialogue without hierarchy: a dialogue between the traditional and the modern, popular wisdom and philosophy, the empirical and the intellectual'.[34]

Landscape (*Krajinka*, 2000), was co-scripted with Dušek, who had written Hanák's *Rose-Tinted Dreams* and *I Love, You Love*. Here Šulík deals with the Slovak experience through ten episodes, the last of which is located after the Prague Spring. A film that emphasises the personal and the imaginative, the unforgettable characters combine with the beauty of Martin Štrba's photography and Iva Bittová's singing to create a multilayered and deeply felt film.

While Šulík's earlier films had concerned themselves with the quest for identity, this one is much more obviously directed at 'the nation'. Šulík and Dušek had reached the conclusion that, in Slovakia, something like a cultural memory scarcely existed, that the events of the twentieth century had triggered successive crises in identity.

> We wanted to talk about what remains in people's memories not from the 'big' history but from normal, everyday experience, in which real occurrences are intertwined with fairytales and adventures that never really happened but are passed down from one generation to the next. We wanted to tell a story about what remains in that normal, everyday memory, not in the historical memory, which is constantly changing, twisting and actually seems to be on the margins of that other kind of history.[35]

They took *The Decameron* as their model, a work that told 'happy stories' in a time of suffering. 'But the more we wrote, and the closer we got to the present, the sadder the stories became. In the end, we just left it like that.'[36]

Many of the stories came from their parents, brothers and friends and there is a two-part television version with an additional three stories. But the format is certainly unusual. Superficially, it recalls Jasný's *All My Good Countrymen*. However, unlike Jasný's film, the characters rarely continue between episodes, and the role of the voiceover narration acquires an enhanced significance. While the television company that co-produced the film wanted to have a production based on a more orthodox narrative, Šulík was able to maintain his structure based on vignettes. The beauty of the photography and the music imposes unity on a diverse structure that includes a wide range of themes and genres.

The stories include those of: the cartographer in the Austro-Hungarian army who wins a watch from a watchmaker's widow in reward for his amorous activities, only to discover that the rest of his regiment has preceded him; the deaf-mute shepherd who swallows a snake in the field while asleep; the tramp who escapes punishment for stealing food by falling into a cesspit; the drunk who is an expert at nose wrestling; the middle-aged woman who emigrated to Prague but returns to find that she might have been better off at home; and the poacher and his son who lead a bleak life in rural Slovakia. Short archive clips serve to situate the stories in the First World War, the Second World War, the Holocaust, the 1950s and the suppression of the Prague Spring.

The overwhelming sense of the film is one of regret for a past that was never so perfect in the first place. It was, of course, not liked by the nationalists who saw it as focusing on dysfunctional families and an attack on traditional Slovak values (one imagines that similar criticisms would have been made in the Communist era). It remains a decidedly ambiguous, if multilayered, tribute to Slovak popular memory. One senses that, when the narrator observes, 'This country never was, and never will be', national identity may be the least of his concerns.

I have discussed the problems of post-Communist cinema in Slovakia in the introduction. Generally speaking, there has been a failure in terms of both quantity and consistency of production, with many of the best films remaining dependent on screenwriters such as Šulaj and Dušek. At the same time, established directors such as Hanák, Balco and Dušan Trančík have made very few films. However, it is worth noting the debut of the actor and stage producer, Juraj Nvota, familiar for his roles in films by Hanák, Šulík and others, with his films *Cruel Joys* (2002) and *Music* (*Muzika*, 2007).

Based on a screenplay by Scarlett Čanakyová, *Cruel Joys* is set in a small and idyllic Slovak village in 1933 and tells of the impact of the arrival of sixteen-year-old Valentina following the death of her mother. Focusing on issues of love, affection and responsibility, its evocation of small-town life and a society centred on the church is captured with a Chekhovian elegance. In the rather different *Music*, he filmed a Šulaj script adapted from a short story by Peter Pišt'anek, author of *Rivers of Babylon*.

NOTES

1. Mira Liehm and Antonín J. Liehm, *The Most Important Art: East European Film After 1945* (Berkeley: University of California Press, 1977), p. 300.
2. Martin Votruba, 'Historical and National Background of Slovak Filmmaking', in Martin Votruba (ed.), *Slovak Cinema*, special issue of *KinoKultura*, December 2005. http://www.kinokultura.com/specials/3/votruba,shtml [Accessed 07/01/06].
3. Václav Macek, 'From Czechoslovak to Slovak and Czech Film', in Martin Votruba (ed.), *Slovak Cinema*, special issue of *KinoKultura*, December 2005. http://www.kinokultura.com/specials/3/macek.shtml [Accessed 17/11/06].
4. Peter Konečný, 'The Organ (*Organ*)', in Martin Votruba (ed.), *Slovak Film Making*, *KinoKultura*. http://www.kinokultura.com/specials/3/organ.shtml [Accessed 18/11/06].
5. Macek, op. cit.
6. Macek, op. cit.

227

7. *The Most Important Art*, p. 298.
8. Juraj Jakubisko, 'Down from the Mountain', interviewed by Peter Hames, *Sight and Sound*, 14, 3, March 2004, p. 8.
9. Macek, op. cit.
10. Juraj Jakubisko, interviewed in Antonín J. Liehm *Closely Watched Films: The Czechoslovak Experience* (New York: International Arts and Sciences Press, 1974), p. 358.
11. Jakubisko, in Liehm, p. 359.
12. Martin Kaňuch, '*Vtáčkovia, siroty a blázni/Birds, Orphans and Fools*', in Peter Hames (ed.), *The Cinema of Central Europe* (London: Wallflower Press, 2004), p. 168.
13. Ibid., p. 167.
14. Peter Hames, *The Czechoslovak New Wave* (London: Wallflower Press, second edition, 2005) pp. 219–20.
15. Josef Škvorecký, 'Venice Biennale', in Škvorecký, *Talkin' Moscow Blues*, ed. Sam Solecki (London: Faber, 1989) p. 303.
16. Jakubisko, 'Down from the Mountain', p. 9.
17. Jiří P. Kříž, 'O konci světa, lidskosti a konci lásky', *Film a doba* (reproduced in *An Ambiguous Report about the End of the World*, press pack).
18. Macek, op. cit.
19. Elo Havetta, interviewed by Antonín J. Liehm, p. 370.
20. Jana Dudková, '*The Gala in the Botanical Garden (Slávnosť v botanickej záhrade)*', in Martin Votruba (ed.), *Slovak Cinema*, special issue of *KinoKultura*, http://www.kinokultura.com/specials/3/slavnost.shtml [Accessed 19/03/06].
21. Macek, op. cit.
22. Elo Havetta, *Pravda*, 7 October, 1972, quoted in *Wild Lilies*, in *The Best of Slovak Film*, leaflet package (Bratislava: Slovak Film Institute, 1993).
23. Havetta, quoted in '*Ľalie poľnie (Lilies of the Field)*', in Táňa Bretyšová and Marie Grofová (eds), *Spřízněni volbou/Elective Affinities*. 27th International Film Festival Karlovy Vary 1990 (Prague: Czechoslovak Film, 1990), p. 16.
24. Jan Jaroš, quoted in ibid.
25. Macek, op. cit.
26. Dušan Hanák, in Marián Pauer, *Martin Martinček* (Martin: Matica Slovenská; Wauconda, Il: Bolchazy-Carducci, 2003), p. 16.
27. See 'Czechs 'Harass Gypsies'', *The Observer* (London), 17 December 1978.
28. 'Demanding work, but always creative: Ondrej Šulaj and Dušan Dušek Interviewed', interview by Peter Hames. *Kinoeye*, 2, 2, 21 January 2002 http://www.kinoeye.org/02/02/hames02.html [Accessed 20/03/02].
29. Eva Zaoralová, '*Súkromné životy (Private Lives)*', in Peter Cowie (ed.), *Variety International Film Guide 1992* (London: Andre Deutsch; Hollywood: Samuel French, 1991), p. 135.
30. Šulaj, op. cit.
31. Zuzana Gindl-Tatarová, '*Záhrada/The Garden*', in Peter Hames (ed.), *The Cinema of Central Europe*, p. 245.
32. Gindl-Tatarová, ibid., p. 247.
33. Ibid, p. 249.
34. Ibid, p. 249.
35. Martin Šulík, 'Our cultural identity isn't holding up . . .', interviewed by Christina Manetti, *Central Europe Review*, 3, 7, 19 February 2001. http://ce-review.org/01///kinoeye/_interview.html [Accessed 11/03/01].
36. Ibid.

BIBLIOGRAPHY

Adams, Bradley F. (2005) *The Struggle for the Soul of the Nation: Czech Culture and the Rise of Communism*. Lanham: Rowman and Littlefield.

Agnew, Hugh LeCaine (1993) *Origins of the Czech National Renascence*. Pittsburgh: University of Pittsburgh Press.

Anděl, Jaroslav, et al. (curators) (1989) *Czech Modernism 1900–1945*. Houston: Museum of Modern Art; Boston: Bulfinch Press.

Anděl, Jaroslav (1989) 'Artists as Filmmakers', in Jaroslav Anděl, et al. (curators), *Czech Modernism 1900–1945*. Houston: Museum of Modern Art; Boston: Bulfinch Press, 165–81.

—— (2000) *Alexandr Hackenschmied*, translated by Derek Paton. Prague: Torst.

Augustin, L. H. (2002) *Jiří Trnka*. Prague: Academia.

Ballard, Phil (2003) 'Magic against materialism: Czech animator Jiří Barta interviewed', *Kinoeye*, 3, 9, 15 September, http://www.kinoeye.org/03/09/ballard09.php [Accessed 28 September 2003].

Balski, Grzegorz (1992) *Directory of Eastern European Film-Makers and Films 1945–1991*. Trowbridge: Flicks Books.

Bendazzi, Giannalberto (1994) *Cartoons: One Hundred Years of Cinema Animation*, translated by Anna Taraboletti-Segre. London: John Libbey.

Benešová, Marie and Zdeněk Stabla (1968) 'Entretien avec Otakar Vávra', *Image et Son*, 193, April, 24–31.

Bernard, Jan (1994) *Evald Schorm a jeho filmy: Odvahu pro všední den*. Prague: Primus.

Bicât, Zoë (2003a) 'Jan Stallich: *Extase* 1933', in Roger Sears (ed.), *Making Pictures; A Century of European Cinematography*. New York: Abrams, 206–7.

—— (2003b) 'Jan Čuřík: *The White Dove* 1960', in Roger Sears (ed.), *Making Pictures: A Century of European Cinematography*. New York: Abrams, 260–1.

—— (2003c) 'Jaroslav Kučera: *Diamonds of the Night* 1964', in Roger Sears (ed.), *Making Pictures: A Century of European Cinematography*. New York: Abrams, 276–7.

—— (2003d) 'Miroslav Ondříček: *Loves of a Blonde* 1965', in Roger Sears (ed.), *Making Pictures: A Century of European Cinematography*. New York: Abrams, 282–3.

—— (2003e) 'Jaromir Šofr: *Closely Observed Trains* 1966', in Roger Sears (ed.), *Making Pictures: A Century of European Cinematography*. New York: Abrams, 286–7.

Bird, Daniel (2001) 'Can We Live with the Truth? Věra Chytilová's 'Ovoce stromů rajských jíme', *Central Europe Review*, 3, 17, 14 May, http://www.ce-review.org/01/17/kinoeye17_bird.html [Accessed 14 May 2001].

—— (2002) 'To excess; the grotesque in Juraj Herz's Czech films', *Kinoeye*, 2, 1, 7 January, http://www.kinoeye.org/02/01/bird01.html [Accessed 8 January 2002].

Biro, Yvette (1983) 'Pathos and Irony in East European Films', in David W. Paul (ed.), *Politics, Art and Commitment in the East European Cinema*. London: Macmillan, 28–48.

Boček, Jaroslav (1965) *Modern Czechoslovak Film*, translated by Alice Denešová, Brno: Artia.

—— (1967a) 'Na okraj Markety Lazarové', *Film a doba*, 591–4.

—— (1967b) *Looking Back on the New Wave*. Prague: Československý Filmexport.

—— (1968a) *Kapitoly o filmu*. Prague: Československý Filmexport.

—— (1968b) 'En marge de *Marketa Lazarová*', *Image et Son*, no. 221, November, 70–81.

Boillat, Jean-Marc (1974) *Jiří Trnka 1912–69*, Anthologie du Cinéma, Supplement to *L'Avant-Scène du Cinéma*, 149–50, July–September.

Bond, Kirk (1968) 'The New Czech Film', *Film Comment*, 5, 1, Fall, 70–9.

Brázda, Marián, Martin Kaňuch and Peter Michalovič (eds) (2000) *Svet pohyblivých obrazoch Martina Šulika*. Bratislava: Slovenský filmový ústav.

Bregant, Michal (1989) 'Několik poznámek na téma Jiří Voskovec a film', *Iluminace*, 1, 95–125.

—— (1990) 'The Devětsil Film Dream', in Rostislav Švácha (ed.), *The Czech Avant-Garde of the 1920s and 30s*. Oxford: Museum of Modern Art; London: Design Museum, 70–3.

—— (1992) 'Avantgardni tendence v českem filmu'. In *Filmový sborník historický*, 3. Prague: Československý filmový ústav, 137–74.

—— (1997) '*Extase*', *Iluminace*, 9, 3, 153–6.

—— (1998) 'Czech Republic', in Peter Tcherkassky (ed.), *Avant Garde Films and Videos from Central Europe*. Vienna: Sixpack Film, 19.

—— (2001) '*Little Otik*', *Film Comment*, 37, 6, November–December, 74.

Brooke, Michael (2006) 'The Film and the Flesh' (*The Cremator*), *Sight and Sound*, 16, 6, June, 88.

—— (2007a) 'Free Radical' (Jan Švankmajer), *Vertigo*, 3, 5, 38–41.

—— (2007b) 'Taking over the Asylum' (*Lunacy*), *Sight and Sound*, 17, 7 (July), 44–5.

Brož, Jaroslav (1967) *The Path of Fame of the Czechoslovak Film*. Prague: Československý Filmexport.

Brož, Jaroslav and Myrtil Frída (1959) *Historie Československého filmu v obrazech, 1898–1930*. Prague: Orbis.

—— (1964) *Historie Československého filmu v obrazech 1930–1945*. Prague: Orbis.

Brumagne, Marie-Magdeleine (1969) *Jeune cinéma tchécoslovaque*. Lyon: SERDOC.

Buchar, Robert (2004) *Czech New Wave Film Makers in Interviews*. Jefferson and London: McFarland.

Burian, Jarka M. (1982) 'The Liberated Theatre of Voskovec and Werich', in Ladislav Matejka and Benjamin Stolz (eds), *Cross Currents 1: A Yearbook of Central European Culture*. Ann Arbor: University of Michigan Press, 315–38.

—— (2000) *Modern Czech Theatre: Reflector and Conscience of a Nation*. Iowa City: University of Iowa Press.

Cardinal, Roger (2008 [1995]) 'Thinking Through Things: The Presence of Objects in the Early Films of Jan Švankmajer', in Peter Hames (ed.), *The Cinema of Jan Švankmajer: Dark Alchemy*. London: Wallflower Press.

Černý, Oldřich and Gerald O'Grady (eds) (1990) *The Banned and the Beautiful: A Survey of Czech Filmmaking 1963–90*. New York: The Public Theater.

Cieslar, Jiří (2004) '*Daleká cesta (Distant Journey)*', in Peter Hames (ed.), *The Cinema of Central Europe*. London: Wallflower Press, 45–52.

Cherry, Brigid (2002) 'Dark Wonders and the Gothic Sensibility: Jan Švankmajer's *Něco z Alenky (Alice)*', *Kinoeye*, 2, 1, 7 January, http://www.kinoeye.org/02/01cherry01,html [Accessed 8 January 2002].

Chitnis, Rajendra A. (2005) *Literature in Post-Communist Russia and Eastern Europe: The Russian, Czech and Slovak Fiction of the Changes, 1988–1998*. London and New York: RoutledgeCurzon.

—— (2007) Vladislav Vančura, the Heart of the Czech Avant-Garde, Prague: Charles University Karolinum Press.

Clouzot, Claire (1966) 'Sons of Kafka', *Sight and Sound*, 36, 1, Winter, 35–7.

—— (1967) '*Intimate Lighting*', *Film Quarterly*, 20, 3, Spring, 39–41.

—— (1968) '*Daisies*', *Film Quarterly*, 21, 3, Spring, 35–7.

Cockrell, Eddie (2003) 'Jan Hřebejk', in Daniel Rosenthal (ed.), *Variety International Film Guide 2004*. London: Button Publishing, 19–24.

—— (2004) 'Petr Zelenka', in Daniel Rosenthal (ed.), *Variety International Film Guide 2005*. London: Button Publishing, 38–42.

Cornwall, Mark and R. J. W. Evans (eds) (2007) *Czechoslovakia in a Nationalist and Fascist Europe*. Oxford: Oxford University Press for the British Academy.

Čulík, Jan (2007) *Jací jsme: Česká společnost v hraném filmu devadesátých a nultých let*. Brno: Host.

Daniel, František (Frank) (1983) 'The Czech Difference', in David W. Paul (ed.), *Politics, Art and Commitment in the East European Cinema*. London: Macmillan, 49–56.

Dawisha, Karen (1984) *The Kremlin and the Prague Spring*. Berkeley: University of California Press.

Delahaye, Michel and Jacques Rivette (1968) 'Le champ libre: entretien avec Věra Chytilová', *Cahiers du Cinéma*, 198, February, 46–73.

Demetz, Peter (2008) *Prague in Danger: The Years of German Occupation: Memories and History, Terror and Resistance, Theater and Jazz, Film and Poetry, Politics and War*. New York: Farrar, Straus and Giroux.

Dewey, Langdon (1968) *Věra Chytilová's 'Daisies'*. London: Federation of Film Societies.

—— (1971) *Outline of Czechoslovakian Cinema*. London: Informatics.

Diski, Jenny (1994) 'Nouvelle Prague', *Sight and Sound*, 4, 2, February, 69.

Dominková, Petra (2008) '"We Have Democracy, Don't We?" Czech Society as Reflected in Contemporary Czech Cinema', in Oksana Sarkisova and Péter Apor (eds), *Past for the Eyes: East European Representations of Communism in Cinema and Museums after 1989*. Budapest and New York: Central European University Press.

Dubček, Alexander (1993) *Hope Dies Last: The Autobiography of Alexander Dubček*, edited and translated by Jiří Hochman. London: HarperCollins.

Dudková, Jana (2005) '*The Gala in the Botanical Garden (Slávnost' v botanickej záhrade)*', in Martin Votruba (ed.), *Slovak Cinema*, special issue of *KinoKultura*, December 2005, http://www.kinokultura.com/specials/3/slavnost.shtml [Accessed 19 March 2006].

Durgnat, Raymond (1968) 'Martyrs of Love', Films and Filming, 14, 6, March, 24–5.

Dryje, František (2008) 'The Force of Imagination', translated by Valerie Mason, Roman Dergam and Daniel Bird, in Peter Hames (ed.), The Cinema of Jan Švankmajer: Dark Alchemy. London: Wallflower Press.

Dyer, Peter John (1965) 'Star Crossed in Prague' (Forman), Sight and Sound, 35, 1, Winter, 34–5.

Eagle, Herbert (1977) 'The Syntagmatic and Paradigmatic Axes in Closely Watched Trains', in Ben Lawton and Janet Staiger (eds), Film Studies Annual, part one. New York: Redgrave, 45–57.

—— (1991) 'Dadaism and Structuralism in Věra Chytilová's Daisies', in Ladislav Matejka (ed.), Cross Currents 10: A Yearbook of Central European Culture. New Haven: Yale University Press, 223–34.

Effenberger, Vratislav (1969) 'Nová vlna v českém filmu a Karel Vachek', Analogon, 1, June, 93–4.

—— (1987a) 'Between Idea and Reality: Švankmajer's Castle of Otranto, translated by Gaby Dowdell, Afterimage 13, 44–6.

—— (1987b) 'The Raw Cruelty of Life and the Cynicism of Fantasy', in Ladislav Matejka (ed.), Cross Currents 6: A Yearbook of Central European Culture. Ann Arbor: University of Michigan Press, 435–44.

Eidsvik, Charles (1991) 'Mock Realism: The Comedy of Futility in Eastern Europe', in Andrew S. Horton (ed.), Comedy/Cinema/Theory. Berkeley: University of California Press, 91–105.

Elley, Derek (1974) 'Ripples from a Dying Wave', Films and Filming, 20, 10, July, 32–6.

Ello, Paul (ed.) (1969) Dubček's Blueprint for Freedom. London: Kimber.

Esslin, Martin (1962) The Theatre of the Absurd. London: Eyre and Spottiswoode.

Felperin, Leslie (1997) 'Conspirators of Pleasure', Sight and Sound, 7, 2, February, 39.

—— (2001) 'Little Otik', Sight and Sound, 11, 11, November, 49–50.

Field, Simon (1986) 'Jabberwocky', Monthly Film Bulletin, 53, 630, July, 222.

—— (1988) 'A Quiet Week in a House', Monthly Film Bulletin, 55, 659, December, 378–9.

Forman, Miloš (1967) 'Chill Wind on the New Wave', Saturday Review, 23 December, 10–41.

Forman, Miloš and Jan Novák (1994) Turnaround: A Memoir. London: Faber.

French, Alfred (1969) The Poets of Prague: Czech Poetry Between the Wars. London: Oxford University Press.

—— (1982) Czech Writers and Politics 1945–1969. Boulder, CO: East European Monographs.

Gindl-Tatárová, Zuzana (2004) 'Záhrada (The Garden)', in Peter Hames (ed.), The Cinema of Central Europe. London: Wallflower Press, 245–53.

Goetz-Stankiewicz, Marketa (1979) The Silenced Theatre: Czech Playwrights without a Stage. Toronto: University of Toronto Press.

—— (ed.) (1992) Good-bye, Samizdat: Twenty Years of Czech Underground Writing. Evanston: Northwestern University Press.

Golan, Galia (1971) The Czechoslovak Reform Movement: Communism in Crisis 1962–1968. Cambridge: Cambridge University Press.

—— (1973) Reform Rule in Czechoslovakia: The Dubček Era. Cambridge: Cambridge University Press.

Greene, Graham (1972 [1936]) 'Jánošík', in Graham Greene, The Pleasure Dome: The Collected Film Criticism 1935–40, edited by John Russell Taylor. London: Secker and Warburg, 86–7.

Greenhalgh, Cathy (2003) 'Shooting from the Heart – Cinematographers and their Medium', in Roger Sears (ed.), *Making Pictures: A Century of European Cinematography*. New York: Abrams.

Grenier, Cynthia (1960) 'East-West Meeting Ground', *Sight and Sound*, 29, 4, Autumn, 182–3.

Halada, Andrej (1997) *Český film devatesátych let: Od Tankového praporu ke Koljovi*. Prague: Lidové noviny.

Halas, John and Joy Batchelor (1949) 'European Cartoon: A Survey of the Animated Film', *Penguin Film Review*, 8. London: Penguin, 9–15.

Hames, Peter (1974) 'Czech Mates', *Films and Filming*, 20, 7, April, 54–7.

—— (1979) 'The Return of Věra Chytilová', *Sight and Sound*, 48, 3, Summer, 168–73.

—— (1989) 'Czechoslovakia: After the Spring', in Daniel J. Goulding (ed.), *Post New Wave Cinema in the Soviet Union and Eastern Europe*. Bloomington: Indiana University Press, 102–42.

—— (1994) 'Forman', in Daniel J. Goulding (ed.), *Five Filmmakers: Tarkovsky, Forman, Polański, Szabó, Makavejev*. Bloomington: Indiana University Press, 50–91.

—— (2000a) '*The Good Soldier Švejk* and After: The Comic Tradition in Czech Film', in Diana Holmes and Alison Smith (eds), *100 Years of European Cinema; Entertainment or Ideology?* Manchester: Manchester University Press, 64–76.

—— (2000b) 'Czech Cinema: From State Industry to Competition', in Janina Falkowska (ed.), *National Cinemas in Postwar East-central Europe*, special issue of *Canadian Slavonic Papers*, 42, 1–2, 63–85.

—— (2000c) 'Czechs on the Rebound', *Sight and Sound*, 10, 7, July, 32–4.

—— (2002) 'Demanding Work, But Always Creative: Ondrej Šulaj and Dušan Dušek interviewed', *Kinoeye*, 2, 2, 21 January, http://www.kinoeye.org/03/09/hames09.php [Accessed 20 March 2002].

—— (2004a) 'Down from the Mountain' (Juraj Jakubisko), *Sight and Sound*, 14, 3, March, 8–9.

—— (ed.) (2004b) *The Cinema of Central Europe*. London: Wallflower Press.

—— (2004c) '*Ostře sledované vlaky* (*Closely Observed Trains*)', in Peter Hames (ed.), *The Cinema of Central Europe*. London: Wallflower Press, 117–27.

—— (2004d) '*O slavnosti a hostech* (*The Party and the Guests*)', in Peter Hames (ed.), *The Cinema of Central Europe*. London: Wallflower Press, 139–48.

—— (2004e) '*Marketa Lazarová*', in Peter Hames (ed.), *The Cinema of Central Europe*. London: Wallflower Press, 151–61.

—— (2005a) *The Czechoslovak New Wave*, second edition. London: Wallflower Press.

—— (2005b) 'The Ironies of History: The Czech Experience', in Anikó Imre (ed.), *East European Cinemas*. New York and London: Routledge, 135–49.

—— (2006a) 'The Czechoslovak New Wave: A Revolution Denied', in Linda Badley, R. Barton Palmer and Steven Jay Schneider (eds), *Traditions in World Cinema*. Edinburgh: Edinburgh University Press, 67–79.

—— (2006b) 'A Business Like Any Other: Czech Cinema since the Velvet Revolution', in Peter Hames (ed.), *Czech Cinema*, special issue of *KinoKultura*, http://www.kinokultura.com/specials/4/hames.shtml [Accessed 14 November 2006].

—— (2006c) 'Jan Němec: *Toyen*', in Peter Hames (ed.), *Czech Cinema*, special issue of *KinoKultura*, http://www.kinokultura.com/specials/4/toyen,shtml [Accessed 16 November 2006].

—— (ed.) (2008a) *The Cinema of Jan Švankmajer: Dark Alchemy*, second edition. London: Wallflower Press.

—— (2008b [1995]) 'The Film Experiment', in Peter Hames (ed.), *The Cinema of Jan Švankmajer*, second edition. London: Wallflower Press, 8–39.

—— (2008c) 'Interview with Jan Švankmajer', translated by Karolina Vočadlo, František Fröhlich and Roman Dergam, in Peter Hames (ed.), *The Cinema of Jan Švankmajer*, second edition. London: Wallflower Press, 104–39.

—— (2008d) 'The Core of Reality: Puppets and Objects in the Feature Films of Jan Švankmajer', in Peter Hames (ed.), *The Cinema of Jan Švankmajer*, second edition, London: Wallflower Press, 83–103.

Hanáková, Petra (2005) 'Voices from Another World: Feminine Space and Masculine Intrusion in *Sedmikrásky* and *Vražda ing. Čerta*', in Anikó Imre (ed.) *East European, Cinemas*. New York and London: Routledge, 63–77.

Havel, Václav, et al. (1985) *The Power of the Powerless: Citizens Against the State in East-Central Europe*, edited by John Keane, translated by Paul Wilson and A. G. Brain. London: Hutchinson.

Havel, Václav (1990) *Disturbing the Peace: A Conversation with Karel Hvížd'ala*, translated by Paul Wilson. New York: Knopf.

—— (2007) *To the Castle and Back*, translated by Paul Wilson. New York: Knopf.

Heiss, Gernot and Ivan Klimeš (eds) (2000) *Obrazy času: Český a rakouský film 30. let/ Bilder der Zeit: Tschechischer und österreicher Film der 30er Jahre*. Prague: Národní filmový archiv; Brno: Österreichisches Ost- und Südosteuropa-Institut.

Hibbin, Nina (1969) *Eastern Europe* (*Screen* series). London: Zwemmer.

Holloway, Ronald (1983) 'The Short Film in Eastern Europe', in David W. Paul (ed.), *Politics, Art and Commitment in the East European Cinema*. London: Macmillan, 225–51.

Holy, Ladislav (1996) *The Little Czech and the Great Czech Nation: National Identity and the Post-Communist Transformation of Society*. Cambridge: Cambridge University Press.

Horton, Andrew James (1998a) 'Avant-garde Film and Video in the Czech Republic', *Central Europe Review*, 0, 2, 5 October, http://www.ce-review.org/kinoeye/kino-eye2old.html [Accessed 10 May 2000].

—— (1998b) 'Slovakia Rediscovered (Part 1): Martin Šulík's *Záhrada*', *Central Europe Review*, 0, 9, 23 November, http://www.ce-review.org/kinoeye/kinoeye9old.html [Accessed 12 May 2000].

—— (1998c) 'Slovakia Rediscovered (Part 2); Vlado Balco's *Rivers of Babylon*', *Central Europe Review*, 0, 10, 30 November, http://www.ce-review.org/kinoeye/kinoeye-10old.html [Accessed 12 May 2000].

—— (1999) 'The Discreet Charm of the Czech Bourgeoisie: Petr Zelenka's *Knoflíkáři*', *Central Europe Review*, 0, 15, 4 January, http://www.ce-review.org/kinoeye/kino-eye15old/html [Accessed 12 May 2000].

Hrabal, Bohumil (1989) *I Served the King of England*, translated by Paul Wilson, London: Chatto and Windus.

—— (1990) *Closely Observed Trains*, translated by Edith Pargeter. London: Abacus.

Image et Son: La Revue du Cinéma (1968) *Cinéma tchécoslovaque*, Special issue, November.

Iordanova, Dina (2003) *Cinema of the Other Europe: The Industry and Artistry of East Central European Film*. London: Wallflower Press.

Jachnin, Boris (1995) 'Karel Kachyňa: Four Decades of a Great Czech Director', *Kinema*, Fall, http://arts.waterloo.ca/FINE/juhde/jachnin952.htm [Accessed 21 January 2003].

Jackson, Wendy (1997) 'The Surrealist Conspirator: An Interview with Jan Švankmajer', *Animation World Magazine*, 2–3 June, http://www.awn.commag/issue2.3pages/2.3ja cksonsvankmajer.html [Accessed 14 January 2007].

Jasný, Vojtěch (1999) *Život a film*. Prague: Národní filmový archiv.

Ježek, Svatopluk (1936) '*La terre chante (Zem spieva)*', in Ivan J. Kovačevič (ed.), *Le cinéma en Tcéchoslovaquie*, Volume 1, July. Prague: Le studio cinématographique de l'association pour la production cinématographique en Tchéchoslovaquie, 103.

Juráček, Pavel (2001) *Postava k podpírání*, edited by Miloš Fikejz. Prague: Havran.

—— (2003) *Deník (1959–1974)*, edited by Jan Lukeš. Prague: Národní filmový archiv.

Juráček, Pavel and Jan Schmidt (1966) *Josef Kilián* (screenplay), in *L'Avant-Scène du Cinéma*, 60, June, 38–46.

Kaňuch, Martin (2004) '*Vtáčkovia, siroty a blázni (Birds, Orphans and Fools)*, translated by Zuzana Dudašová, in Peter Hames (ed.), *The Cinema of Central Europe*. London: Wallflower Press.

Kerbachová, Bohdana (2005) 'Petr Skala – A Hidden Experimenter', DVD leaflet. Prague: Národní filmový archiv.

Klevan, Andrew (2000) 'Delays Around Events: Miloš Forman's *Loves of a Blonde*', in Andrew Klevan, *Disclosure of the Everyday: Undramatic Achievement in Narrative Film*. Trowbridge: Flicks Books, 103–26.

Kofroň, Václav (2004) '*Hej-rup! (Heave-Ho!)*', in Peter Hames (ed.), *The Cinema of Central Europe*. London: Wallflower Press.

Konečný, Peter (2005) '*The Organ (Organ)*', in Martin Votruba (ed.), *Slovak Cinema*, special issue of *KinoKultura*, December 2005, http://www.kinokultura.com/specials/3/slavnost.shtml [Accessed 19 March 2006].

Kopaněva, Galina (2000) 'The Czech Film; Searching for New Ways of Survival', in *East of Eden: Countries in Transition, Cinema in Experiment*, special issue of *Kino* (Bulgaria), 45–50.

Kosík, Karel (1975 [1963]) 'Hašek and Kafka', *Telos 23*, Spring, 84–8.

—— (1976) *Dialectics of the Concrete: A Study of Problems of Man and World*, translated by Karel Kovanda and James Schmidt. Dordrecht and Boston: Reidel.

—— (1995) *The Crisis of Modernity: Essays and Observations from the 1968 Era*, edited by James H. Satterwhite. Lanham: Rowman and Littlefield.

Kostková, Pavlina (2001) 'Arnošt Lustig: A Small Stone in a Big Mosaic' (interview), *Central Europe Review*, 3, 28, 22 October, http://www.ce-review.org/01/28/kostkova28.html [Accessed 2 March 2002].

Kosuličová, Ivana (2001a) 'The Ceremony of the Everyday: Jiří Menzel's film adaptations of Bohumil Hrabal's prose', *Central Europe Review*, 3, 9, 5 March, http://ce-review.org/01/9kinoeye9_kosulicova.html [Accessed 11 March 2001].

—— (2001c) 'The Free Expression of Spirit: Jan Němec's conception of "pure film" in his post-1989 works', *Central Europe Review*, 3, 17, 14 May, http://www.ce-review.org/01/17/kinoeye17_kosulicova.html [Accessed 14 May 2001].

—— (2002a) 'The Morality of Horror: Jiří Barta's *Krysař (The Pied Piper)*', *Kinoeye*, 2, 1, 7. January 2002, http://www.kinoeye.org/02/01_no2.html [Accessed 8 January 2002].

—— (2002b) 'The void behind the mask: Game-playing in the films of Věra Chytilová', *Kinoeye*, 2, 8. http://www.kinoeye.org/02/08/kosulicova1.html [Accessed 5 September 2002].

—— (2003) 'After the Black Wave: poetry and tragedy in the post-1960s films of Karel Kachyňa, *Kinoeye*, 3, 1, 20 January, http://www.kinoeye.org/03/09/kosulicova09.php [Accessed 23 September 2003].

Král, Petr (1993) *Voskovec a Werich čili Hvezdy klobouky*. Prague: Gryf.

Kratochvil, Miloš (1955) 'Jan Hus', *The Czechoslovak Film*, VIII, 6, 1955, 4–5.

Kroupa, Vladimír and Milan Šmid (1998) 'The Limitations of a Free Market: Czech Republic', in *The Development of the Audiovisual Landscape in Central Europe Since 1989* (European Commission in association with Eureka Audiovisuel). Luton: University of Luton Press/John Libbey Media, 61–109.

Krzywinska, Tanya (2003) 'Transgression, transformation, and titillation: Jaromil Jireš's *Valerie a týden divů (Valerie and her Week of Wonders)*', *Kinoeye*, 3, 9, 15 September, http://www.kinoeye.org/03/09/krzywinska09.php [Accessed 28 September 2003].

Kundera, Milan (1984) 'A Kidnapped West – or Culture Bows Out', translated by Edmund White, *Granta 11*, 93–118.

—— (1987) 'Candide Had to be Destroyed', in Jan Vladislav (ed.), *Václav Havel or Living in Truth*. London: Faber, 258–60.

Kusin, Vladimír (1971) *The Intellectual Origins of the Prague Spring: The Development of Reformist Ideas in Czechoslovakia 1956–67*. Cambridge: Cambridge University Press.

—— (1978) *From Dubček to Charter 77: A Study of 'Normalisation' in Czechoslovakia 1968–1978*. Edinburgh: Q Press.

Lane, Anthony (2002 [1994]) 'Švankmajer', in *Nobody's Perfect: Writings from The New Yorker*. London: Picador, 540–8.

Liebmann, Stuart and Leonard Quart (1996) 'Czech Films of the Holocaust', *Cinéaste*, 22, 1, 49–51.

Liehm, Antonín J. (1968) 'The Reckoning of a Miracle: An Analysis of Czechoslovak Cinematography', *Film Comment*, 5, 1, Fall, 64–9.

—— (1973) *The Politics of Culture*, translated by Peter Kussi. New York: Grove Press.

—— (1974) *Closely Watched Films: The Czechoslovak Experience*. New York: International Arts and Sciences Press.

—— (1975) *The Miloš Forman Stories*, translated by Jeanne Němcová. New York: International Arts and Sciences Press.

—— (1983) 'Miloš Forman – The Style and the Man', in David W. Paul (ed.), *Politics, Art, and Commitment in the East European Cinema*. London: Macmillan, 211–24.

—— (1993) *Příběhy Miloše Formana*. Prague: Mladá fronta.

—— (2001) *Ostře sledované filmy: Československá zkušenost*. Prague: Národní filmový archiv.

Liehm, Mira and Antonín J. Liehm (1977) *The Most Important Art: East European Film After 1945*, translated by Káča Poláčková-Henley. Berkeley: University of California Press.

Lim, Bliss Cua (2001) 'Dolls in Fragments: *Daisies* as Feminist Allegory', *Camera Obscura*, 47, 16, 2, Fall, 37–77

Lipták, Ľubomír (2000), 'Slovakia in the 20th Century', in Elena Mannová (ed.), *A Concise History of Slovakia*. Bratislava: Historický ústav SAV, 241–305.

Lovejoy, Alice (2006) 'Center and Periphery, or How Karel Vachek Formed a New Government', in Peter Hames (ed.), *Czech Cinema*, special issue of *Kino Kultura*, November, http://www.kinokultura.com/specials/4/lovejoy.shtml [Accessed 16 November 2006].

Lukeš, Jan (1993) *Orgia střídmosti aneb Konec československé státní kinematografie*. Prague: Národní filmový archiv.

Macek, Václav (1990) *Elo Havetta (1938–1975)*. Bratislava: Slovenský filmový ústav.

—— et al. (1992) *Slovenský film 1946–69*. Bratislava: Slovenský filmový ústav-Narodné kinematografické centrum.

—— (1992) *Slovenský film 1970–1990*. Bratislava: Slovenský filmový ústav-Narodné kinematografické centrum.

—— (1996) *Dušan Hanák*. Bratislava: FOTOFO/Slovenský filmový ústav.

—— (1998) 'Slovakia', in Peter Tscherkassky (ed.), *Avant-Garde Films and Videos from Central Europe*. Vienna: Sixpack Film.

—— (2002) *Štefan Uher 1930–1993*. Bratislava: Slovenský filmový ústav.

—— (2005) 'From Czechoslovak to Slovak and Czech Film' in Martin Votruba (ed.),

Slovak Cinema, special issue of *KinoKultura*, December, http://www.kinokultura. com/specials/3/macek.shtml [Accessed 18 November 2006].

Macek, Václav and Jelena Paštěková (1997) *Dejiny slovenskej kinematografie*. Martin: Osveta.

Macko, Jozef (1992) 'Slovak Alternative and Experimental Film', *Moveast*, 2, 25–37.

Mamber, Stephen (1974) *Cinéma Vérité in America: Studies in Uncontrolled Documentary*. Cambridge, MA: The MIT Press.

Manetti, Christina (2001a) 'The country behind the landscape: Martin Šulík's *Krajinka*', *Central Europe Review*, 3, 7, 19 February, http://www.ce-review.org/01/7kinoeye/-manetti.html [Accessed 11 March 2001].

—— (2001b) 'Our cultural identity isn't holding up . . . An interview with Slovak filmmaker Martin Šulík', *Central Europe Review*, 3, 7, 19 February, http://www.ce-review.org/01/7/kinoeye/_interview.html [Accessed 11 March 2001].

Manley, Sebastian (2007) 'Life Sentence: Dreams of Captivity and Freedom in Jan Švankmajer's *Šílení*', *Senses of Cinema*, 44, July–September, http://www.sensesofcin-ema.com/contents/07/44/svankmajer-sileni.html [Accessed 2 September 2007].

Mannová, Elena (ed.) (2000) *A Concise History of Slovakia*. Bratislava: Historický ústav SAV.

Masaryk, Tomáš G. (1974) *The Meaning of Czech History*, introduced and edited by René Wellek, translated by Peter Kussi. Chapel Hill: University of North Carolina Press.

Menefee, Emory and Ernest Callenbach (1969) '*Marketa Lazarová*', *Film Quarterly*, 22, 4, Summer, 35–7.

Menzel, Jiří and Bohumil Hrabal (1971) *Closely Observed Trains* (script), translated by Josef Holzbecher. London: Lorrimer.

Měřínský, Zdeněk and Jaroslav Mezník (1998) 'The making of the Czech state: Bohemia and Moravia from the tenth to the fourteenth centuries', in Mikuláš Teich (ed.), *Bohemia in History*. Cambridge: Cambridge University Press, 39–58.

Michalovič, Peter and Vlastimil Zuska (2005) *Juraj Jakubisko*. Bratislava: Slovenský filmový ústav.

Mistríková, Ľubica (2004) '*Obchod na korze (A Shop on the High Street)*', in Peter Hames (ed.), *The Cinema of Central Europe*. London: Wallflower Press.

Montmarte, Danièle (1991) *Le Théâtre Libéré de Prague: Voskovec et Werich*. Paris: Institut d'études slaves.

Moullet, Luc (1965) 'Contingent 65 1 A', *Cahiers du Cinéma*, 166–7, May–June 1965, 62.

Musil, Jiří (ed.) (1995) *The End of Czechoslovakia*. Budapest: Central European University Press.

Nahodilová, Jana (2006) '*Bored in Brno (Nuda v Brně)*', in Peter Hames (ed.), *Czech Cinema*, special issue of *KinoKultura*, November 2006 http://www.kinokultura.com/ specials/4/boredbrno.shtml [Accessed 16/11/06].

Národní filmový archiv (1995) *Český hraný film I: 1898–1930/Czech Feature Film I: 1898–1930*. Prague: Národní filmový archiv.

—— (1998) *Český hraný film II: 1930–1945/Czech Feature Film II: 1930–1945*. Prague: Národní filmový archiv.

—— (2001) *Český hraný film III: 1945–1960/Czech Feature Film III: 1945–1960*. Prague: Národní filmový archiv.

—— (2004) *Český hraný film IV: 1961–1970/Czech Feature Film IV: 1961–1970*. Prague: Národní filmový archiv.

—— (2007) *Český hraný film V: 1971–1980/Czech Feature Film V: 1971–1980*. Prague: Národní filmový archiv.

Navrátil, Jaromír (ed.) (1998) *The Prague Spring 1968*, translated by Mark Kramer, Joy Moss and Ruth Tosek. Budapest: Central European University Press.

Nezval, Vitězslav (2005 [1945]) *Valerie and her Week of Wonders*, translated by David Short. Prague: Twisted Spoon Press.

Novák, Arne (1986) *Czech Literature*, translated by Peter Kussi. Ann Arbor: Michigan Slavic Publications.

O'Pray, Michael (1986) 'In the Capital of Magic', *Monthly Film Bulletin*, 53, 630, July, 218–19.

—— (1987) 'A Švankmajer Inventory', *Afterimage*, 13, 10–21.

—— (1994) 'Between Slapstick and Horror', *Sight and Sound*, 4, 9, September, 20–3.

—— (2008 [1995]) 'Jan Švankmajer: A Mannerist Surrealist', in Peter Hames (ed.), *The Cinema of Jan Švankmajer*. London: Wallflower Press.

Parrott, Cecil (1982) *Jaroslav Hašek: A Study of Švejk and the Short Stories*. Cambridge: Cambridge University Press.

—— (1989) 'The Liberated Theatre: Voskovec and Werich', in Alan Ross (ed.), *The London Magazine 1961–1985*. London: Paladin/Grafton, 242–60.

Pauer, Marián (2003), *Martin Martinček*. Martin: Matica Slovenská; Wauconda, Il: Bolchazy-Carducci.

Paul, David W. (ed.) (1983) *Politics, Art and Commitment in the East European Cinema*. London: Macmillan.

Pavlíček, František and František Vláčil (1998) *Marketa Lazarová* (screenplay). Prague: Film a doba.

Penley, Constance and Janet Bergstrom (1985) 'The Avant-Garde: History and Theories', in Bill Nicholls (ed.), *Movies and Methods*, vol. II. Berkeley: University of California Press, 287–300.

Petley, Julian (1986a) '*Historia Naturae, Suita*', *Monthly Film Bulletin*, 53, 630, July, 221–2.

—— (1986b) '*Dimensions of Dialogue*', *Monthly Film Bulletin*, 53, 630, July, 222–3.

—— (1988) '*The Ossuary*', *Monthly Film Bulletin*, 55, 658, November, 346.

Petráň, Josef and Lydia Petránová (1998) 'The White Mountain as a symbol in modern Czech history', in Mikuláš Teich (ed.), *Bohemia in History*. Cambridge: Cambridge University Press, 143–63.

Petro, Peter (1987) 'Dominik Tatarka-An Introduction to a Rebel', in Ladislav Matejka (ed.), *Cross Currents 6: A Yearbook of Central European Culture*. Ann Arbor: University of Michigan Press, 281–97.

—— (1995) *A History of Slovak Literature*. Montreal and Kingston: McGill-Queens University Press.

Petro, Peter and Donald Rayfield (2007) 'Introduction', in Peter Pišt'anek, *Rivers of Babylon*, translated by Peter Petro, London: Garnett Press.

Pišt'anek, Peter (2007) *Rivers of Babylon*, translated by Peter Petro. London: Garnett Press.

Pithart, Petr (1986) 'Recognising a Prophet in the Czech Lands: T. G. Masaryk and Our Society', translated by Erazim Kohák, *Kosmas: Journal of Czechoslovak and Central European Studies*, 5, 2, 1986, 33–56.

Polt, Harriet R, (1964) 'The Czechoslovak Animated Film', *Film Quarterly*, 17, 3, 31–40.

Přádna, Stanislava (2007) 'The Czech Cinema', available at www.artmargins.com/content/cineview/pradna20020130.html [Accessed 20 February 2007].

Přádna, Stanislava, Zdena Škapová and Jiří Cieslar (2002) *Démanty všednosti: Český a Slovenský film 60. let*. Prague: Pražská scéna.

Preskett, Mark (2001) 'A Little Bit of Money and a Lot of Love: Alice Nellis's *Ene bene*', *Central Europe Review*, 3, 21, 11 June 2001 http://www.ce-review.org/01/21/kinoeye21_preskett.html [Accessed 15 May 2007].

Pryl, Karel (pseud) (1971) 'Swan Song', *Sight and Sound*, 40, 3, Summer, 125–6.

Pynsent, Robert B. (ed.) (1990) *Modern Slovak Prose: Fiction Since 1954*. London: Macmillan.
—— (1994) *Questions of Identity: Czech and Slovak Ideas of Nationality and Personality*. London and Budapest: Central European University Press.
Pytlík, Radko (2000) *The Sad King of Czech Literature: Bohumil Hrabal, his Life and Work*, translated by Katheleen Hayes, Prague: Emporius.
Reid, Tina-Louise (2004) '*Něco z Alenky (Alice)*', in Peter Hames (ed.), *The Cinema of Central Europe*. London: Wallflower Press.
Richardson, Michael (2006) *Surrealism and Cinema*. Oxford and New York: Berg.
Rocamora, Carol (2004) *Acts of Courage: Václav Havel's Life in the Theater*. Hanover, NH: Smith and Kraus.
Rotha, Paul and Richard Griffith (1967) *The Film Till Now*, fourth edition. London: Spring Books.
Rychlík, Jan (2007) 'Czech-Slovak Relations in Czechoslovakia', in Mark Cornwall and R.J.W. Evans (eds), *Czechoslovakia in a Nationalist and Fascist Europe 1918–1948*. Oxford: Oxford University Press for the British Academy, 13–25.
Salt, Barry (2003) 'Dodo Šimončič: *Fête in the Botanical Garden* 1969', in Roger Sears (ed.), *Making Pictures: A Century of European Cinematography*. New York: Abrams, 310–11.
Sayer, Derek (1998) *The Coasts of Bohemia: A Czech History*. Princeton: Princeton University Press.
Schofield, Adam (2007) 'A Black Pearl of the Deep: Juraj Herz's *The Cremator*', *Senses of Cinema*, http://www.sensesofcinema.com/contents/07/43/cremator-juraj-herz.html [Accessed 10 October 2007].
Schonberg, Michal (1989) 'The Theatre and Films of Jiří Voskovec and Jan Werich', in Jaroslav Anděl, et al. (curators) *Czech Modernism 1900–1945*. Houston: Museum of Modern Art; Boston: Bulfinch Press, 183–91.
Schöpflin, George and Nancy Wood (eds) (1989) *In Search of Central Europe*. Cambridge: Polity Press.
Shawcross, William (1990) *Dubček: Dubček and Czechoslovakia 1918–1990*, second edition. London: The Hogarth Press.
Short, David (ed.) *Bohumil Hrabal (1914–97) Papers from a Symposium*. London: School of Slavonic and East European Studies, University College.
Šimečka, Milan (1984) *The Restoration of Order: The Normalization of Czechoslovakia*, translated by A. G. Brain. London: Verso.
Škapová, Zdena (2004) '*Sedmikrásky (Daisies)*', in Peter Hames (ed.), *The Cinema of Central Europe*. London: Wallflower Press, 129–36.
—— (2006a) '*Marriage Stories (Manželské etudy*, 1987–2005)', in Peter Hames (ed.), *Czech Cinema*, special issue of *KinoKultura*, November, http://www.kinokultura. com/specials/4/marriagestories.shtml [Accessed 16 November 2006].
—— (2006b) '*Toyen*', in Marie Grofová (ed.), *41ˢᵗ Karlovy Vary International Film Festival 2006*, catalogue, 89.
Skilling, H. Gordon (1976) *Czechoslovakia's Interrupted Revolution*. Princeton: Princeton University Press.
—— (1981) *Charter 77 and Human Rights in Czechoslovakia*. London: Allen and Unwin.
—— (1994) *T. G. Masaryk: Against the Current, 1882–1914*. Basingstoke: Macmillan.
Škvorecký, Josef (1971) *All the Bright Young Men and Women: A Personal History of the Czech Cinema*, translated by Michael Schonberg. Toronto: Peter Martin Associates.
—— (1982) *Jiří Menzel and the History of the Closely Watched Trains*. Boulder, CO: East European Monographs.

—— (1986) 'What Was Saved from the Wreckage', *Sight and Sound*, 55, 4, Autumn, 278–81.

—— (1989) *Talkin' Moscow Blues*, edited by Sam Solecki. London: Faber.

—— (1991) *Všichni ti bystří mladi muži a ženy: osobní historie českého filmu*. Prague: Horizont.

Slivka, Martin (1999) *Karol Plicka – básnik obrazu*. Martin: Vydavateľstvo Osveta; Bratislava: Národné centrum pre audiovizuálne umenie; Vydavateľstvo Fénix.

Smatlák, Martin and André Zmecek (1998) 'Market Intentions Restrained: Slovak Republic', in *The Development of the Audiovisual Landscape in Central Europe since 1989* (European Commission in association with Eureka Audiovisuel). Luton: University of Luton Press/John Libbey Media.

Smatláková, Renata (1999) *Katalog slovenských celovečerných filmov 1921–1999 (The Catalogue of Full-Length Feature Films)*. Bratislava: Slovenský filmový ústav.

Smatláková, Renata and Martin Smatlák (2005) *Fimové profily: Slovenskí režiséri hraných filmov / Film Profiles: Slovak Feature Film Directors*. Bratislava: Slovenský filmový ústav.

Sorfa, David (2003) 'Architorture: Jan Švankmajer and Surrealist Film', in Mark Shiel and Tony Fitzmaurice (eds), *Screening the City*. London: Verso, 100–12.

—— (2006) 'The Object of Film in Jan Švankmajer', in Peter Hames (ed.), *Czech Cinema*, Special issue 4, *KinoKultura*, November, http://www.kinokultura.com/specials/4/sorfa.shtml [Accessed 16 November 2006].

Srp, Karel (2000) *Toyen*, translated by Karolina Vočadlo. Prague: Argo.

Steiner, Peter (2000) *The Deserts of Bohemia: Czech Fiction and Its Social Context*. Ithaca and London: Cornell University Press.

Stojanova, Christina (2005) 'Fragmented Discourses: Young Cinema from Central and Eastern Europe', in Anikó Imre (ed.), *East European Cinemas*. New York and London: Routledge, 213–27.

—— (2006a) '*Czech Dream*: Capitalism with a Human Face?', in Peter Hames (ed.), *Czech Cinema*, special issue of *KinoKultura*, http://www.kinokultura.com/specials/4/stojanova.shtml [Accessed 16 November 2006].

—— (2006b) '*Czech Dream* and the Mission of Documentary Cinema: A Conversation with Helena Třeštíková', in Peter Hames (ed.), *Czech Cinema*, special issue of *Kino Kultura*, http://www.kinokultura.com/specials/4/stojanova-trestikova,shtml [Accessed 16 November 2006].

—— (2006c) 'Petr Zelenka: *Buttoners (Knoflíkáři)*', in Peter Hames (ed.), *Czech Cinema*, special issue of *KinoKultura*, http://www.kinokultura.com?specials/4/buttoners,shtml [Accessed 16 November 2006].

Strick, Philip (1988a) '*Alice*', *Monthly Film Bulletin*, 55, 658, November, 319–30.

—— (1988b) '*The Garden*', *Monthly Film Bulletin*, 55, 659, December, 379.

—— (1994) '*Faust*', *Sight and Sound*, 4, 10, October, 40–1.

Švankmajer, Jan (1987) 'Švankmajer on *Alice*', *Afterimage*, 13, Autumn, 51–3.

—— (1996) *Faust: The Script*, translated by Valerie Mason. Trowbridge: Flicks Books.

Švankmajer, Jan and Eva Švankmajerová (1998) *Anima Animus Animation: Between Film and Free Expression*. Prague: Slovart, Arbor Vitae Foundation.

Sviták, Ivan (1969) 'Les héros de l'aliénation', *Image et Son*, 221, November, 51–69.

Taussig, Pavel (1989) 'On the Sunnyside of Film', in Jaroslav Anděl, et al. (curators), *Czech Modernism*. Houston: Museum of Modern Art/Boston: Bulfinch Press, 193–207.

Taylor, Richard, Nancy Wood, Julian Graffy and Dina Iordanova (eds) (2000) *The BFI Companion to Eastern European and Russian Cinema*. London: British Film Institute.

Teich, Mikuláš (ed.) (1998) *Bohemia in History*. Cambridge: Cambridge University Press.

Theiner, George (ed.) (1971) *New Writing in Czechoslovakia*. Harmondsworth: Penguin.

Toman, Ludvík (1972) 'Czech Feature Films: Variety of Genres and Subjects', *Czechoslovak Film*, 1–2, 6–13.

Tucker, Aviezer (2000) *The Philosophy and Politics of Czech Dissidence from Patočka to Havel*. Pittsburgh: University of Pittsburgh Press.

Tyler, Parker (1962) *Classics of the Foreign Film*. London: Spring Books.

Uhde, Jan (1989) 'The Film World of Jan Švankmajer', in *Cross Currents 8: A Yearbook of Central European Culture*. Ann Arbor: University of Michigan Press, 195–208.

—— (1994) 'Jan Švankmajer: the Prodigious Animator from Prague', *Kinema*, 2, 30–41.

Ulver, Stanislav (ed.) (1996) *Film a doba: Antologie textu z let 1962–70*. Prague: Film a doba.

—— (ed.) (2004) *Animace a doba: Sborník textů z časopisu Film a Doba 1955–2000*. Prague: Film a doba.

Urgošiková, B. (Blažena) (1986) '*Staré pověsti české (Old Czech Legends)*', in Christopher Lyon (ed.), *The International Dictionary of Films and Filmmakers: Volume 1: Films*. London: Firethorn Press, 450.

Valášek, Thomas E. (1979) 'Alexander Hammid: A Survey of His Filmmaking Career', *Film Culture*, 67–9, 250–322.

Vincendeau, Ginette (ed.) (1995) *Encyclopedia of European Cinema*. London: Cassell/British Film Institute.

Vladislav, Jan (ed.) (1987) *Václav Havel or Living in Truth*, translated by A. G. Brain, Paul Wilson, Erazim Kohák, Roger Scruton, J. R. Littleboy, D. Armour, Deryck Viney, M. Pomichalek, A. Mozga, K. Seigneurie and George Theiner. London: Faber.

Voráč, Jiří (1997) 'Czech Film After 1989 : The Wave of Young Newcomers', *Kinema*, Spring, http://arts.uwaterloo.ca/FINE/juhde/vorac97/htm [Accessed 10 May 2000].

Votruba, Martin (ed.) (2005a) *Slovak Cinema*, special issue of *KinoKultura*, December.

—— (2005b) 'Historical and National Background of Slovak Filmmaking', in Martin Votruba (ed.), *Slovak Cinema*, special issue of *KinoKultura*, December, http://www.kinokultura.com/specials/3/votruba.shtml [Accessed 7 January 2006].

Warner, Marina (2007) 'Dream Works' (Švankmajer), *Guardian Review*, 16 June, 12–13.

Wells, Paul (1997) 'Body consciousness in the films of Jan Švankmajer', in Jayne Pilling (ed.), *A Reader in Animation Studies*. London: John Libbey, 177–94.

—— (2002) 'Animated Anxiety: Jan Švankmajer, Surrealism, and the 'agit-scare', *Kinoeye*, 2, 16, 21 October, http://www.kinoeye.org/02/16/wells16.html [Accessed 14 March 2003].

Williams, Kieran (1997) *The Prague Spring and Its Aftermath: Czechoslovak Politics, 1968–1970*. Cambridge: Cambridge University Press.

—— (ed.) (2000) *Slovakia after Communism and Mečiarism*. London: School of Slavonic and East European Studies, University College.

Wolff, Larry (1994) *Inventing Eastern Europe: The Map of Civilization on the Mind of the Enlightenment*. Stanford: Stanford University Press.

Wood, James (2004) *The Irresponsible Self: On Laughter and the Novel*. London: Cape.

Young, Jeffrey (1993) 'A Conversation with Arnošt Lustig and Miroslav Holub', *Trafika*, 1, Autumn, 155–69.

Žalman, Jan (1967) 'Question Marks on the New Czechoslovak Cinema', *Film Quarterly*, 21, 2, Winter, 18–27.

—— (1968) *Films and Filmmakers in Czechoslovakia*. Prague: Orbis.

—— (1969) '*Everyone a Good Fellow Countryman*', in Peter Cowie (ed.), *International Film Guide 1970*. London: Tantivy Press, 83–4.

—— (1970) '*Le Fruit du Paradis (Ovoce stromů rajských jíme)*', in Peter Cowie (ed.), *International Film Guide 1971*. London: Tantivy Press, 106–7.

—— (1993) *Umlčený film: Kapitoly z bojů o lidskou tvář československého filmu*. Prague: Národní filmový archiv.

Zaoralová, Eva (1991) '*Súkromné životy (Private Lives)*', in Peter Cowie (ed.), *Variety International Film Guide 1992*. London: Andre Deutsch; Hollywood: Samuel French, 135.

Zaoralová, Eva and Jean-Loup Passek (eds) *Le Cinéma Tchèque et Slovaque*. Paris: Centre Georges Pompidou.

FILMOGRAPHY

Adamík, Kasia, and Agnieszka Holland, 2009: *The True Story of Juraj Jánošík and Tomáš Uhorčík* (*Pravdivá história o Jurajovi Jánošíkovi a Tomáš Uhorčíkovi*) (in production).

Almási, Tamás, 1996: *A Matter of the Heart* (*Szivügyem*).

Anderson, Lindsay, 1967: *The White Bus*.

Anton, Karel, 1930: *Tonka of the Gallows* (*Tonka Šibenice*).

Antonioni, Michelangelo, 1960: *L'Avventura*.

—— 1961: *La Notte*.

—— 1962: *L'Eclisse*.

Babinská, Karin, 2007: *Dolls* (*Pusinky*).

Balco, Vladimír (Vlado), 1998: *Rivers of Babylon*.

Balej, Jan, 2006: *Fimfárum 2* (co-directed by Aurel Klimt, Břetislav Pojar and Vlasta Pospíšilová).

—— 2007: *One Night in One City* (*Jedné noci v jednom městě*).

Barta, Jiří, 1982: *The Extinct World of Gloves* (*Zaniklý svět rukavic*).

—— 1986: *The Pied Piper* (*Krysař*).

—— 1987: *The Last Theft* (*Poslední lup*).

—— 1989: *The Club of Discarded Ones* (*Klub odložených*).

—— 2009: *In the Attic – Who Has a Birthday Today?* (*Na půdě aneb Kdo má dneska narozeniny?*).

Baxter, John, 1941: *Love on the Dole*.

Bergman, Ingmar, 1957: *The Seventh Seal* (*Det sjunde inseglet*).

—— 1960: *The Virgin Spring* (*Jungfrukällan*).

—— 1974: *Scenes from a Marriage* (*Scener ur ett äktenskap*).

Bielik, Pal'o, 1948: *Wolves' Lairs* (*Vlčie diery*).

—— 1962–63: *Jánošík* (two-part film).

Blažíček, Martin, 2000: *Voice on the Telephone* (*Hlas v telefonu*).

Bočan, Hynek, 1968: *Honour and Glory* (*Čest a sláva*).

—— 1997: *Boomerang* (*Bumerang*).
Borský, Vladimír, 1947: *Jan Roháč of Duba* (*Jan Roháč z Dubé*).
Brabec, F. A., 2000: *Wild Flowers* (*Kytice*).
Brynych, Zbyněk, 1960: *Skid* (*Smyk*).
—— 1962: *Transport from Paradise* (*Transport z ráje*).
—— 1964: *The Fifth Horseman is Fear* (*. . .a pátý jezdec je Strach*).
Buñuel, Luis, 1928: *Un chien andalou* (co-directed by Salvador Dalí).
—— 1962: *The Exterminating Angel* (*El angel exterminador*).
—— 1972: *The Discreet Charm of the Bourgeoisie* (*Le charme discret de la bourgeoisie*).
Čáp, František, 1939: *Fiery Summer* (*Ohnive léto*) (co-directed by Václav Krška).
Chaplin, Charles, 1931: *City Lights*.
Chytilová, Věra, 1962: *Ceiling* (*Strop*).
—— 1962: *A Bagful of Fleas* (*Pytel blech*).
—— 1963: *Something Different* (*O něčem jiném*).
—— 1965: 'At the World Cafeteria' ('Automat svět'), episode in *Pearls of the Deep* (*Perličky na dně*).
—— 1966: *Daisies* (*Sedmikrásky*).
—— 1969: *The Fruit of Paradise* (*Ovoce stromů rajských jíme*).
—— 1976: *The Apple Game* (*Hra o jablko*).
—— 1979: *Prefab Story* (*Panelstory*).
—— 1983: *The Very Late Afternoon of a Faun* (*Faunovo velmi pozdní odpoledne*).
—— 1984: *Prague: the Restless Heart of Europe* (*Praha – neklidné srdce Evropy*).
—— 1987: *The Jester and the Queen* (*Šašek a královna*).
—— 1988: *Tainted Horseplay* (*Kopytem sem, kopytem tam*).
—— 1992: *Inheritance or Fuck-Boys-Gutntag* (*Dědictví aneb Kurvahošigutntag*).
—— 1998: *Traps* (*Pasti, pasti, pastičky*).
Cieslar, Milan, 2000: *The Spring of Life* (*Pramen života*).
Čihák, Martin, and Jan Daňhel, 1994: *Adam Quadmon* (*Adam Kadmon*).
Clair, René, 1924: *Entr'acte*.
—— 1928: *An Italian Straw Hat* (*Un chapeau de paille d'Italie*).
—— 1931: *A nous la liberté*.
Costa-Gavras, 1970: *The Confession* (*L'Aveu*).
Crichton, Michael, 1978: *Coma*.
Dalí, Salvador, 1928: *Un chien andalou* (co-directed by Luis Buñuel).
Daněk, Oldřich, 1963: *The Nuremburg Campaign* (*Spanilá jízda*).
—— 1968: *The King's Blunder* (*Královský omyl*).
Deren, Maya, 1943: *Meshes of the Afternoon* (co-directed by Alexandr Hackenschmied (Alexander Hammid)).
De Sica, Vittorio, 1948: *Bicycle Thieves* (*Ladri di bicyclette*).
—— 1952: *Umberto D.*
Dobeš, Marek, 2004: *Choking Hazard*.
Dodal, Karel, 1938: *The Bubble Game* (*Hra bublinek*).
Dostal, Zeno, 1995: *Golet in the Valley* (*Golet v údolí*).
Dovzhenko, Alexander, 1930: *Earth* (*Zemlya*).
Dudow, Slatan, 1932: *Kuhle Wampe*.
Ďurček, Ľubomír, 1982: *Information about Hands and People* (*Informácia a rukách a l'ud'och*).
Duvivier, Julien, 1936: *The Golem* (*Le Golem/Golem*).
Eisenstein, Sergei, 1929: *The General Line* (*General'niya Linya*).
Fellini, Federico, 1954: *La Strada*.
—— 1963: 8½.

Flaherty, Robert, 1948: *Louisiana Story*.
Ford, John, 1939: *Stagecoach*.
—— 1946: *My Darling Clementine*.
Forman, Miloš, 1963: *Talent Competition (Konkurs)*.
—— 1963: *Black Peter (Černý Petr)*.
—— 1965: *Loves of a Blonde (Lásky jedné plavovlásky)*.
—— 1967: *The Firemen's Ball (Hoří, má panenko)*.
—— 1971: *Taking Off*.
—— 1975: *One Flew Over the Cuckoo's Nest*.
—— 1984: *Amadeus*.
Frič, Martin, 1933: *The Inspector General (Revizor)*.
—— 1933: *The Twelve Chairs (Dvanáct křesel)* (co-directed by Michał Waszyński).
—— 1934: *Heave-Ho! (Hej-rup!)*.
—— 1935: *Jánošík*.
—— 1936: *Black and White Rhapsody (Černobílá rapsodie)*.
—— 1937: *The World Belongs to Us (Svět patří nám)*.
—— 1939: *Kristian*.
—— 1942: *Valentin the Kind (Valentin Dobrotivý)*.
—— 1949: *The Poacher's Ward (Pytlákova schovanka)*.
—— 1951: *The Emperor's Baker (Císařův pekař)* and *The Baker's Emperor (Pekařův císař)* (two-part film).
—— 1961: *The Bear (Medvěd)* (TV film).
Furie, Sidney J., 1965: *The Ipcress File*.
Gedeon, Saša, 1995: *Indian Summer (Indiánské léto)*.
—— 1999: *Return of the Idiot (Návrat idiota)*.
Gerron, Kurt, 1945: *Theresienstadt: a Documentary from the Jewish Settlement Area (Theresienstadt: ein Dokumentarfilm aus dem Jüdischen Siedlungsgebiet)*.
Godard, Jean-Luc, 1968: *Weekend*.
Haas, Hugo, 1937: *The White Disease (Bílá nemoc)*.
Hackenschmied, Alexandr (Alexander Hammid), 1930: *Aimless Walk (Bezúčelná procházka)*.
—— 1931: *Prague Castle (Na Pražském hradě)*.
—— 1938: *Crisis* (co-directed by Herbert Kline).
—— 1939: *Lights Out in Europe* (co-directed by Herbert Kline).
—— 1940: *The Forgotten Village* (co-directed by Herbert Kline).
—— 1943: *Meshes of the Afternoon* (co-directed by Maya Deren).
—— 1951: *The Medium* (co-directed by Gian Carlo Menotti).
—— 1963: *To Be Alive!* (co-directed by Francis Thompson).
Hammid, Alexander, see Alexandr Hackenschmied.
Hanák, Dušan, 1965: *Old Shatterhand Has Come to See Us (Prišiel k nám Old Shatterhand)*.
—— 1966: *Impressions (Impresia)*.
—— 1969: *322*.
—— 1971: *Day of Joy (Deň radosti)*.
—— 1972: *Pictures of the Old World (Obrazy starého sveta)*.
—— 1976: *Rose-Tinted Dreams (Ružové sny)*.
—— 1980 (released 1988): *I Love, You Love (Ja milujem, ty miluješ)*.
—— 1985: *Silent Joy (Tichá radost')*.
—— 1990: *Private Lives (Súkromné životy)*.
—— 1995: *Paper Heads (Papierové hlavy)*.
Havetta, Elo, 1969: *The Party in the Botanical Garden (Slávnosť v botanickej záhrade)*.

—— 1972: *Lilies of the Field* (*Ľalie poľné*).
Havrilla, Vladimír, 1974: *Lift*.
—— 1974: *Woman on Fire* (*Horiaca žena*).
—— 1976: *No Limit* (*Nelimitované*).
—— 1977: *Yellow Danger* (*Žlté nebezpečenstvo*).
Hejtmánek, Tomáš, 2003: *Sentiment*.
Helge, Ladislav, 1957: *School for Fathers* (*Škola otců*).
—— 1959: *Great Seclusion* (*Velká samota*).
—— 1961: *Spring Breeze* (*Jarní povětří*).
—— 1967: *Shame* (*Stud*).
Herz, Juraj, 1968: *The Cremator* (*Spalovač mrtvol*).
—— 1971: *Oil Lamps* (*Petrolejové lampy*).
—— 1972: *Morgiana*.
—— 1985: *I Was Caught by the Night* (*Zastihla mě noc*).
Hofman, Eduard, 1957: *The Creation of the World* (*Stvoření světa*).
Honzl, Jindřich, 1931: *Powder and Petrol* (*Pudr a benzin*).
—— 1932: *Your Money or Your Life* (*Peníze nebo život*).
Hřebejk, Jan, 1993: *Big Beat* (*Šakalí léta*).
—— 1999: *Cosy Dens* (*Pelíšky*).
—— 2000: *Divided We Fall* (*Musíme si pomáhat*).
—— 2003: *Pupendo*.
—— 2004: *Up and Down* (*Horem pádem*).
Innemann, Svatopluk, 1928: *Prague Shining in Lights* (*Praha v záři světel*).
—— 1932: *Before the Finals* (*Před maturitou*) (co-directed by Vladislav Vančura).
Ivaška, Samo, 1984: *Subject* (*Subjekt*).
—— 1993: *The Run at the End of Summer* (*Beh na konci leta*).
Jakubisko, Juraj, 1960: *The Last Air Raid* (*Posledný nálet*).
—— 1966: *Waiting for Godot* (*Čekají na Godota*).
—— 1967: *Crucial Years* (*Kristove roky*).
—— 1968: *The Deserter and the Nomads* (*Zbehovia a pútnici*).
—— 1969: *Birds, Orphans and Fools* (*Vtáčkovia, siroty a blázni*).
—— 1970 (completed and released 1990): *See You in Hell, Fellows!* (*Dovidenia v pekle, priatelia!*).
—— 1979: *Build a House, Plant a Tree* (*Postav dom, zasad' strom*).
—— 1983: *The Millennial Bee* (*Tisícročná včela*).
—— 1985: *Perinbaba*.
—— 1989: *I'm Sitting on a Branch and I Feel Well* (*Sedím na konári a je mi dobre*).
—— 1992: *It's Better to Be Wealthy and Healthy than Poor and Ill* (*Lepšie byt' bohatý a zdravý ako chudobný a chorý*).
—— 1997: *An Ambiguous Report on the End of the World* (*Nejasná zpráva o konci světa*).
—— 2008: *Báthory*.
Jakubowska, Wanda, 1948: *The Last Stage* (*Ostatni etap*).
Jařab, David, 2004: *Vaterland – Pages from a Hunting Notebook* (*Vaterland – lovecký deník*).
Jasný, Vojtěch, 1954: *It Will All Be Over Tonight* (*Dnes večer všechno skončí*) (co-directed by Karel Kachyňa).
—— 1958: *Desire* (*Touha*).
—— 1968: *All My Good Countrymen* (*Všichni dobří rodáci*).
—— 1999: *Return to the Lost Paradise* (*Návrat ztraceného ráje*).
Jireš, Jaromil, 1960: *Hall of Lost Footsteps* (*Sál ztracených kroků*).
—— 1963: *The Cry* (*Křik*).

—— 1965: 'Romance', episode in *Pearls of the Deep* (*Perličky na dně*).
—— 1968: *The Joke* (*Žert*).
—— 1969: *Valerie and her Week of Wonders* (*Valerie a týden divů*).
—— 1972: *And Give My Love to the Swallows* (. . . *a pozdravuji vlaštovky*).
—— 1974: *People of the Metro* (*Lidé z metra*).
—— 1982: *Incomplete Eclipse* (*Neúplné zatmění*).
—— 1986: *Lion with a White Mane* (*Lev s bílou hřívou*).
Junghans, Carl, 1929: *Such Is Life* (*Takový je život/Si ist das Leben*).
Juráček, Pavel, 1963: *Josef Kilián* (*Postava k podpírání*) (co-directed by Jan Schmidt).
—— 1965: *Every Young Man* (*Každý mladý muž*).
—— 1969: *A Case for the Young Hangman* (*Případ pro začínajícího kata*).
Jutzi, Piel, 1929: *Mother Krausens Journey to Happiness* (*Mutter Krausens Fahrt ins Glück*).
—— 1931: *Berlin – Alexanderplatz*.
Kachyňa, Karel, 1954: *It Will All Be Over Tonight* (*Dnes večer všechno skončí*) (co-directed by Vojtěch Jasný).
—— 1961: *Stress of Youth* (*Trápení*).
—— 1961: *Fetters* (*Pouta*).
—— 1964: *The High Wall* (*Vysoká zed'*).
—— 1965: *Long Live the Republic* (*At' žije republika*).
—— 1966: *Coach to Vienna* (*Kočár do Vídně*).
—— 1967: *Night of the Bride* (*Noc nevěsty*).
—— 1969: *Funny Old Man* (*Směšný pán*).
—— 1970 (released 1990): *The Ear* (*Ucho*).
—— 1979: *The Golden Eels* (*Zlatí úhoři*) (TV film).
—— 1986: *Death of the Beautiful Roebucks* (*Smrt krásných srnců*).
—— 1990: *The Last Butterfly* (*Poslední motýl*).
—— 1999: *Hanele*.
Kadár, Ján, and Elmar Klos, 1963: *Death is Called Engelchen* (*Smrt si říká Engelchen*).
—— 1965: *A Shop on the High Street* (*Obchod na korze*).
Kalatozov, Mikhail, 1957: *The Cranes Are Flying* (*Letyat zhuravli*).
—— 1964: *I Am Cuba* (*Ja-Kuba/Soy Cuba*).
Kaufman, Philip, 1987: *The Unbearable Lightness of Being*.
Klimt, Aurel, 1996: *Maschkin Killed Koschkin* (*Maškin zabil Koškina*).
—— 1998: *The Enchanted Bell* (*O kouzelném zvonu*) (also an episode in *The Magnificent Six* (*Šest statecných*, 2000).
—— 1999: *The Fall* (*Pád*).
—— 2002: *Jan Werich's Fimfárum* (*Fimfárum Jana Wericha*) (co-directed by Vlasta Pospíšilová).
—— 2006: *Fimfárum 2* (co-directed by Jan Balej, Břetislav Pojar and Vlasta Pospíšilová).
Kline, Herbert, 1938: *Crisis* (co-directed by Alexandr Hackenschmied).
—— 1939: *Lights Out in Europe* (co-directed by Alexandr Hackenschmied).
—— 1940: *The Forgotten Village* (co-directed by Alexandr Hackenschmied).
Klusák, Vít, and Filip Remunda, 2004: *Czech Dream* (*Český sen*).
Kolar, Jan S., 1929: *St Václav* (*Sváty Václav*).
Král, Vlado, 2000: *The Magnificent Six* (*Šest statecných*) (co-directed by Aurel Klimt, Tereza Kučerová, Vojtěch Mašek, Martin Repka and Jaro Vojtek).
Krejčík, Jiří, 1979: *The Divine Emma* (*Božská Ema*).
Krška, Václav, 1939: *Fiery Summer* (*Ohnivé léto*) (co-directed by František Čáp).
—— 1945: *Magic of the River* (*Řeka čaruje*).

—— 1953: *Moon over the River* (*Měsíc nad řekou*).
—— 1954: *The Silver Wind* (*Stříbrný vítr*).
—— 1955: *From My Life* (*Z mého života*).
—— 1956: *Dalibor*.
Krumbachová, Ester, 1970: *The Murder of Engineer Devil* (*Vražda ing. Čerta*).
Kubal, Viktor, 1976: *Jurko the Outlaw* (*Zbojník Jurko*).
—— 1980: *The Bloody Lady* (*Krvavá paní*).
Kubásek, Václav, 1937: *Our Swells* (*Naši furianti*) (co-directed by Vladislav Vančura).
—— 1937: *Love and People* (*Láska a lidé*) (co-directed by Vladislav Vančura).
Kubrick, Stanley, 1980: *The Shining*.
Kučera, Jan, 1932: *Burlesque* (*Burleska*).
Kučerová, Tereza, 2000: *The Magnificent Six* (*Šest statecných*) (co-directed by Aurel Klimt, Vlado Král, Vojtěch Mašek, Martin Repka and Jaro Vojtek.
Kudláček, Martina, 1995: *L'Amour fou: Ludvík Šváb*.
—— 1996: *Aimless Walk: Alexander Hammid* (*Bezúčelná procházka: Alexander Hammid*).
—— 1997: *The Last Heroes* (*Poslední hrdinové*).
—— 2001: *In the Mirror of Maya Deren*.
Kusturica, Emir, 1994: *Underground*.
Lamač, Karel, 1926: *The Good Soldier Švejk* (*Dobrý voják Švejk*).
—— 1944: *It Started at Midnight*.
Lehovec, Jiří, 1939: *The Magic Eye* (*Divotvorné oko*).
—— 1941: *Rhythm* (*Rytmus*).
Lipský, Oldřich, 1964: *Lemonade Joe* (*Limonádový Joe*).
—— 1974: *Joachim, Put it in the Machine* (*Jáchyme, hod' ho do stroje!*).
—— 1976: *Mareček, Pass Me a Pen* ('*Marečku, podejte mi pero!*').
—— 1977: *Nick Carter in Prague* (*Adéla ještě nevečeřela*).
Machatý, Gustav, 1926: *The Kreutzer Sonata* (*Kreutzerova sonata*).
—— 1929: *Erotikon*.
—— 1931: *From Saturday to Sunday* (*Ze soboty na něděli*).
—— 1932: *Ecstasy* (*Extase*).
Mackendrick, Alexander, 1955: *The Ladykillers*.
Malle, Louis, 1960: *Zazie dans le métro*.
Marek, Petr, 1996: *Before* (*Dříve než . . .*).
—— 2002: *Love from Above* (*Láska shora*).
—— 2005: *Not of Today* (*Nebýt dešní*).
Marhoul, Václav, 2003: *Smart Philip* (*Mazaný Filip*).
Marshall, George, 1939: *Destry Rides Again*.
Máša, Antonín, 1966: *Hotel for Foreigners* (*Hotel pro cizince*).
Mašek, Vojtěch, 2000: *The Magnificent Six* (*Šest statecných*) (co-directed by Aurel Klimt, Vlado Král, Tereza Kučerová, Martin Repka and Jaro Vojtek.
Menzel, Jiří, 1965: 'The Death of Mr Balthazar' ('Smrt pana Baltazara'), episode in *Pearls of the Deep* (*Perličky na dně*).
—— 1966: *Closely Observed Trains* (*Ostře sledované vlaky*).
—— 1967: *Capricious Summer* (*Rozmarné léto*).
—— 1969 (released 1990): *Skylarks on a String* (*Skřivánci na niti*).
—— 1974: *Who Looks for Gold* (*Kdo hledá zlaté dno*).
—— 1976: *Seclusion Near a Forest* (*Na samotě u lesa*).
—— 1980: *Cutting it Short* (*Postřižiny*).
—— 1983: *The Snowdrop Festival* (*Slavnosti sněženek*).
—— 1985: *My Sweet Little Village* (*Vesničko má středisková*).
—— 1989: *The End of Old Times* (*Konec starých časů*).

—— 1991: *The Beggar's Opera* (*Žebrácká opera*).

—— 1993: *The Life and Extraordinary Adventures of Private Ivan Chonkin* (*Život a neobyčejná dobrodružství vojáka Ivana Čonkina*).

—— 2006: *I Served the King of England* (*Obsluhoval jsem anglického krále*).

Miler, Zdeněk, 1957–2002: *The Mole (Krtek)* (film series).

Mináč, Matej, 1999: *All My Loved Ones* (*Všichni moji blízcí*).

—— 2001: *Nicholas Winton – The Power of Good* (*Sila ľudkosti Nicholas Winton*).

Morávek, Vladimír, 2003: *Bored in Brno* (*Nuda v Brně*).

Moskalyk, Antonín, 1965: *A Prayer for Kateřina Horovitzová* (*Modlitba pro Kateřinu Horovitzovou*) (TV film).

—— 1967: *Dita Saxová*.

—— 1984: *Cuckoo in the Dark Forest* (*Kukačka ve temném lese*).

Mungiu, Cristian, 2007: *4 Months, 3 Weeks, 2 Days* (*4 luni, 3 saptamini si 2 zile*).

Murnau, F. W., 1922: *Nosferatu* (*Nosferatu, eine Symphonie des Grauens*).

Najbrt, Marek, 2004: *Champions* (*Mistři*).

Nellis, Alice, 2000: *Eeny Meeny* (*Ene bene*).

—— 2002: *Some Secrets* (*Výlet*).

Němec, Jan, 1964: *Diamonds of the Night* (*Démanty noci*).

—— 1965: 'Imposters' ('Podvodníci'), episode in *Pearls of the Deep* (*Perličky na dně*).

—— 1966: *The Party and the Guests* (*O slavnosti a hostech*).

—— 1966: *Martyrs of Love* (*Mučedníci lásky*).

—— 1990: *The Flames of Royal Love* (*V žáru královské lásky*).

—— 1997: *Code Name Ruby* (*Jméno kódu Rubín*).

—— 2001: *Late Night Talks with Mother* (*Noční hovory s matkou*).

—— 2004: *Landscape of My Heart* (*Krajina mého srdce*).

—— 2005: *Toyen*.

Nikolaev, Petr, 2005: *A Little Piece of Heaven* (*Kousek nebe*).

—— 2007: *It's Gonna Get Worse* (. . . *a bude hůř*).

Novák, Ivo, 1962: *Green Horizons* (*Zelené obzory*).

Nvota, Juraj, 2002: *Cruel Joys* (*Kruté radosti*).

—— 2007: *Music* (*Muzika*).

Olivier, Laurence, 1955: *Richard III*.

Olmer, Vít, 1991: *The Tank Battalion* (*Tankový prapor*).

Ondříček, David, 2000: *Loners* (*Samotáři*).

Pancíř, Vít, 1997: *In the Wind* (*Ve větru*).

—— 2008: *Sister* (*Sestra*).

Papoušek, Jaroslav, 1968: *The Best Age* (*Nejkrásnější věk*).

—— 1969: *Ecce Homo Homolka*.

Passer, Ivan, 1964: *A Boring Afternoon* (*Fádní odpoledne*).

—— 1965: *Intimate Lighting* (*Intimní osvětlení*).

Pilát, František, 1930: *The Light Penetrates the Dark* (*Světlo proniká tmou*) (co-directed by Otakar Vávra).

Plicka, Karel, 1933: *The Earth Sings* (*Zem spieva*).

Podskalský, Zdeněk, 1978: *Ball Lightning* (*Kulový blesk*) (co-directed by Ladislav Smoljak).

Pojar, Břetislav, 2006: *Fimfárum 2* (co-directed by Jan Balej, Aurel Klimt and Vlasta Pospíšilová).

Polák, Jindřich, 1968: *Riders in the Sky* (*Nebeští jezdci*).

Polański, Roman, 1962: *Knife in the Water* (*Nóz w wodzie*).

Pospíšilová, Vlasta, 2002: *Jan Werich's Fimfárum* (*Fimfárum Jana Wericha*) (co-directed by Aurel Klimt).

—— 2006: *Fimfárum 2* (co-directed by Jan Balej, Aurel Klimt and Břetislav Pojar).

Powell, Michael, 1960: *Peeping Tom*.
Pražský, Přemysl, 1927: *Battalion* (*Batalion*).
Pudovkin, Vsevolod, 1926: *Mother* (*Mat'*).
Radok, Alfréd, 1949: *Distant Journey* (*Daleká cesta*).
Radok, Emil, 1958: *Faust* (*Johannes doktor Faust*).
Reiner, Rob, 1984: *This Is Spinal Tap*.
Reisz, Karel, 1959: *We Are the Lambeth Boys*.
Renoir, Jean, 1936: *Partie de campagne*.
—— 1936: *Le Crime de Monsieur Lange*.
—— 1951: *The River*.
Repka, Martin, 2000: *The Magnificent Six* (*Šest statecných*) (co-directed by Aurel Klimt, Vlado Král, Tereza Kučerová, Vojtěch Mašek and Jaro Vojtek.
Resnais, Alain, 1961: *Last Year at Marienbad* (*L'Année dernière á Marienbad*).
Robbe-Grillet, Alain, 1968: *The Man Who Lies* (*L'Homme qui ment*/*Muž, ktorý luže*).
—— 1970: *Eden and After* (*L'Eden et après*/*Eden a potom*).
Rovenský, Josef, 1933: *The River* (*Řeka*).
Rychlík, Břetislav, 2005: *God's Stone Quarry* (*Kamenolom Boží*).
Schmidt, Jan, 1963: *Josef Kilián* (*Postava k podpírání*) (co-directed by Pavel Juráček).
—— 1990: *Rebounds* (*Vracenky*).
Schorm, Evald, 1964: *Everyday Courage* (*Každý den odvahu*).
—— 1965: 'House of Joy' ('Dům radosti'), episode in *Pearls of the Deep* (*Perličky na dně*).
—— 1966: *Return of the Prodigal Son* (*Návrat ztraceného syna*).
—— 1967: *Saddled with Five Girls* (*Pět holek na krku*).
—— 1968: *End of a Priest* (*Farářův konec*).
—— 1968 (released 1990): *Confusion* (*Zmatek*).
—— 1969 (released 1990): *Seventh Day, Eighth Night* (*Den sedmý, osmá noc*).
Ševčíková, Jana, 2001: *Old Believers* (*Starověrci*).
Siakel', Jaroslav, 1921: *Jánošík*.
Silverstein, Elliott, 1965: *Cat Ballou*.
Sirový, Zdenek, 1992: *The Black Barons* (*Černí baroni*).
Sláma, Bohdan, 2001: *Wild Bees* (*Divoké včely*).
—— 2005: *Something Like Happiness* (*Štěstí*).
Slivka, Martin, 1963: *Water and Work* (*Voda a práca*).
Smoljak, Ladislav, 1978: *Ball Lightning* (*Kulový blesk*), (co-directed by Zdeněk Podskalský).
—— 1980: *Run, Waiter, Run!* (*Vrchní, prchni!*).
—— 1983: *Jára Cimrman, Lying, Asleep* (*Jára Cimrman, ležící, spící*).
—— 1984: *Dissolved and Let Out* (*Rozpuštěný a vypuštěný*).
—— 1987: *Uncertain Season* (*Nejistá sezóna*).
Steklý, Karel, 1947: *The Strike* (*Siréna*).
Šulík, Martin, 1991: *Tenderness* (*Neha*).
—— 1992: *Everything I Like* (*Všetko čo mám rád*).
—— 1995: *The Garden* (*Záhrada*).
—— 1997: *Orbis Pictus*.
—— 2000: *Landscape* (*Krajinka*).
—— 2005: *City of the Sun* or *Working Class Heroes* (*Sluneční stat aneb hrdinové dělnické třídy*).
Švankmajer, Jan, 1964: *The Last Trick* (*Poslední trik pana Schwarcewalldea a pana Edgara*).
—— 1965: *J. S. Bach: Fantasia in G Minor* (*J. S. Bach: Fantasia g-moll*).

—— 1965: *Game with Stones* (*Spiel mit steinen*).
—— 1966: *Punch and Judy* (*Rackvičkárna*).
—— 1967: *Historia naturae (suite)* (*Historia naturae (suita)*).
—— 1968: *The Flat* (*Byt*).
—— 1968: *The Garden* (*Zahrada*).
—— 1969: *A Quiet Week in a House* (*Tichý týden v domě*).
—— 1970: *The Ossuary* (*Kostnice*).
—— 1970: *Don Juan* (*Don Šajn*).
—— 1971: *Jabberwocky* (*Žvahlav aneb šatičky Slaměného Huberta*).
—— 1980: *The Fall of the House of Usher* (*Zánik domu Usherů*).
—— 1982: *Dimensions of Dialogue* (*Možnosti dialogu*).
—— 1982: *Down to the Cellar* (*Do pivnice/Do sklepa*).
—— 1987: *Alice* (*Něco z Alenky*).
—— 1994: *Faust* (*Lekce Faust*).
—— 1997: *Conspirators of Pleasure* (*Spiklenci slasti*).
—— 2000: *Little Otík* (*Otesánek*).
—— 2005: *Lunacy* (*Šílení*).
—— 2009: *Surviving Life (Theory and Practice)* (*Přežít svůj život (teorie a praxe)*) (in production).
Svěrák, Jan, 1991: *The Elementary School* (*Obecná škola*).
—— 1996: *Kolya* (*Kolja*).
—— 2001: *Dark Blue World* (*Tmavomodrý svět*).
—— 2007: *Empties* (*Vratné lahve*).
Svitáček, Vladimír, 1964: *If a Thousand Clarinets* (*Kdyby tisíc klarinetů*).
Svoboda, Jiří, 1990: *Family Matters* (*Jen o rodinných záležitostech*).
Thompson, Francis, 1963: *To Be Alive!* (co-directed by Alexander Hammid (Alexandr Hackenschmied).
Thorpe, Richard, 1952: *Ivanhoe*.
—— 1955: *The Adventures of Quentin Durward*.
Třestíková, Helena, 1975: *The Miracle* (*Zázrak*).
—— 1987–2005: *Marriage Stories* (*Manželské etudy*).
—— 2007: *Marcela*.
Trnka, Jiří, 1945: *Grandfather Planted a Beet* (*Zasadil dědek řepu*).
—— 1946: *The Gift* (*Dárek*).
—— 1947: *The Czech Year* (*Špalíček*).
—— 1948: *The Emperor's Nightingale* (*Císařův slavík*).
—— 1949: *Novel with a Contrebass* (*Román s basou*).
—— 1949: *Song of the Prairie* (*Árie prérie*).
—— 1950: *The Devil's Mill* (*Čertův mlýn*).
—— 1950: *Prince Bajaja* (*Bajaja*).
—— 1951: *The Merry Circus* (*Veselý Cirkus*).
—— 1953: *Old Czech Legends* (*Staré pověsti české*).
—— 1954–55: *The Good Soldier Švejk, I–III*, (*Osudy dobrého vojáka Švejka, I–III*).
—— 1959: *A Midsummer Night's Dream* (*Sen noci svatojánské*).
—— 1962: *Cybernetic Grandmother* (*Kybernetická babička*).
—— 1964: *The Archangel Gabriel and Mother Goose* (*Archanděl Gabriel a paní Husa*).
—— 1965: *The Hand* (*Ruka*).
Trnka, Tomáš, 1932: *Storm Over the Tatras* (*Bouře nad Tatrami*).
Truffaut, François, 1962: *Jules et Jim*.
Tuček, Benjamin, 2002: *Girlie* (*Děvčátko*).
Tyc, Zdeněk, 2002: *Brats* (*Smradi*).
Týrlová, Helena, 1942: *Ferda the Ant* (*Ferda mravenec*).

Uher, Štefan, 1962: *Sunshine in a Net* (*Slnko v sieti*).
—— 1964: *The Organ* (*Organ*).
—— 1966: *The Miraculous Virgin* (*Panna zázračnica*).
—— 1967: *Three Daughters* (*Tri dcéry*).
—— 1971: *If I Had a Gun* (*Keby som mal pušku*).
—— 1982: *Concrete Pastures* (*Pásla kone na betóne*).
—— 1988: *Down to Earth* (*Správca skanzenu*).
Ultra Group, 2000–02: *Units*.
Vachek, Karel, 1963: *Moravian Hellas* (*Moravská Hellas*).
—— 1968: *Elective Affinities* (*Spřízněni volbou*).
—— 1992: *New Hyperion or Liberty, Equality, Fraternity* (*Nový Hyperion aneb Volnost, rovnost, bratrství*).
—— 1996: *What is to be Done? Or How I Journeyed from Prague to Česky Krumlov and Formed My Own Government* (*Co dělat? Cesta z Prahy do Českého Krumlova aneb Jak jsem sestavoval novou vládu*).
—— 2001: *Bohemia docta or the Labyrinth of the Soul and the Paradise of the Heart (A Divine Comedy)* (*Bohemia docta aneb Labyrint světa a lusthauz srdce (Božská komedie)*).
—— 2003: *Who Will Guard the Guard? Dalibor or the Key to Uncle Tom's Cabin* (*Kdo bude hlídat hlidače? Dalibor aneb Klíč k Chaloupce strýčka Toma*).
—— 2006: *Záviš, the Prince of Pornofolk Under the Influence of Griffith's 'Intolerance' and Tati's 'Monsieur Hulot's Holiday' or the Foundation and Doom of Czechoslovakia (1918–1992)* (*Záviš, kníže pornofolku pod vlivem Griffithovy Intolerance a Tatiho Prázdnin pana Hulota aneb vznik a zánik Československá, 1918–1992*).
Václav, Petr, 1996: *Marian*.
—— 2001: *Parallel Worlds* (*Paralelní světy*).
Vančura, Vladislav, 1932: *Before the Finals* (*Před maturitou*) (co-directed by Svatopluk Innemann.
—— 1933: *On the Sunnyside* (*Na sluneční straně*).
—— 1934: *Faithless Marijka* (*Marijka nevěrnice*).
—— 1937: *Our Swells* (*Naši furianti*) (co-directed by Václav Kubásek).
—— 1937: *Love and People* (*Láska a lidé*) (co-directed by Václav Kubásek).
Vávra, Otakar, 1930: *The Light Penetrates the Dark* (*Světlo proniká tmou*) (co-directed by František Pilát).
—— 1935: *November* (*Listopad*).
—— 1937: *A Philosophical Story* (*Filosofská historie*).
—— 1938: *The Guild of Kutná Hora Maidens* (*Cech panen kutnohorských*).
—— 1945: *Rosina the Foundling* (*Rozina sebranec*).
—— 1946: *The Mischievous Tutor* (*Nezbedný bakalář*).
—— 1948: *Krakatit*.
—— 1954: *Jan Hus*.
—— 1955: *Jan Žižka*.
—— 1956: *Against All* (*Proti všem*).
—— 1958: *Citizen Brych* (*Občan Brych*).
—— 1969: *Witchhammer* (*Kladivo na čarodějnice*).
—— 1977: *A Meeting with Love and Honour* (*Příběh lásky a cti*).
—— 1983: *The Wanderings of Jan Amos* (*Putování Jana Amose*).
—— 1984: *Oldřich and Božena* (*Oldřich a Božena*).
—— 1986: *Veronika*.
Vertov, Dziga, 1929: *Man with a Movie Camera* (*Chelovek s kinoapparatom*).
Vigo, Jean, 1930: *A Propos de Nice*.
Vláčil, František, 1960: *The White Dove* (*Holubice*).

—— 1961: *The Devil's Trap* (*Ďáblova past*).
—— 1967: *Marketa Lazarová*.
—— 1967: *Valley of the Bees* (*Údolí včel*).
—— 1969: *Adelheid*.
—— 1973: *The Legend of the Silver Fir* (*Pověst o stříbrné jedli*).
—— 1974: *Sirius*.
—— 1976: *Smoke on the Potato Fields* (*Dým bramborové natě*).
—— 1979: *Concert at the End of Summer* (*Koncert na konci léta*).
—— 1984: *The Shades of Ferns* (*Stín kapradiny*).
—— 1987: *The Magus* (*Mág*).
Vojnar, Ivan, 1997: *The Way Through the Bleak Woods* (*Cesta pustým lesem*).
Vojtek, Jaro, 2000: *The Magnificent Six* (*Šest statecných*) (co-directed by Aurel Klimt, Vlado Král, Tereza Kučerová, Vojtěch Mašek and Martin Repka.
Vorlíček, Václav, 1966: *Who Would Kill Jessie?* (*Kdo chce zabít Jessii?*).
—— 1967: *End of an Agent* (*Konec agenta W4C prostřednictvím psa pana Foustky*).
—— 1971: *Girl on a Broom* (*Dívka na koštěti*).
—— 1977: *What Do You Say to a Plate of Spinach?* (*Což takhle dát si špenát?*).
Votoček, Otokar, 1990: *Wings of Fame*.
Wasserman, Václav, 1948: *The Devil's Wall* (*Čertova stena*).
Waszyński, Michał, 1933: *The Twelve Chairs* (*Dvanáct křesel*) (co-directed by Martin Frič).
Wegener, Paul, and Henrik Galeen, 1915: *The Golem* (*Der Golem*).
Wegener, Paul, and Carl Boese, 1920: *The Golem* (*Der Golem: Wie er in die Welt kam*).
Weiss, Jiří, 1935: *People in the Sun* (*Lidé na slunci*).
—— 1947: *The Stolen Frontier* (*Uloupená hranice*).
—— 1957: *The Wolf Trap* (*Vlčí jáma*).
—— 1959: *Romeo, Juliet and Darkness* (*Romeo, Julie a tma*).
—— 1990: *Martha and I* (*Martha und Ich/Marta a já*).
Welles, Orson, 1941: *Citizen Kane*.
—— 1948: *Lady from Shanghai*.
Wiene, Robert, 1920: *The Cabinet of Dr Caligari* (*Das Cabinet des Dr Caligari*).
Yutkevich, Sergei, 1943: *New Adventures of Švejk* (*Noviye pokhozdeniya Shveika*).
Žbanić, Jasmila, 2006: *Esma's Secret* (*Grbavica*).
Zelenka, Petr, 1996: *Mňága – Happy End*.
—— 1997: *Buttoners* (*Knoflíkáři*).
—— 2002: *Year of the Devil* (*Rok d'ábla*).
—— 2005: *Wrong Side Up* (*Příběhy obyčejného šílenství*).
—— 2008: *The Karamazovs* (*Karamazovi*).
Zeman, Karel, 1945: *A Christmas Dream* (*Vánoční sen*).
—— 1949: *Inspiration* (*Inspirace*).
—— 1950: *King Lávra* (*Král Lávra*).
—— 1952: *The Treasure of Bird Island* (*Poklad Ptáčího ostrova*).
—— 1955: *A Journey to Primeval Times* (*Cesta do pravěku*).
—— 1958: *An Invention for Destruction* (*Vynález zkázy*).
—— 1961: *Baron Münchhausen* (*Baron Prášil*).
—— 1964: *The Jester's Tale* (*Bláznova kronika*).
—— 1966: *The Stolen Airship* (*Ukradená vzducholod'*).
—— 1970: *On the Comet* (*Na kometě*).
—— 1974: *A Thousand and One Nights* (*Pohádky tisíce a jedné noci*).
—— 1977: *The Sorcerer's Apprentice* (*Čarodějův učeň*).
—— 1980: *The Tale of Honzík and Mařenka* (*Pohádka o Honzíkovi a Mařence*).

INDEX